PROVERBS

ABINGDON OLD TESTAMENT COMMENTARIES

PROVERBS

CHRISTINE ROY YODER

Abingdon Press
Nashville

ABINGDON OLD TESTAMENT COMMENTARIES
PROVERBS

Copyright © 2009 by Abingdon Press

Library of Congress Cataloging-in-Publication Data

Yoder, Christine Elizabeth, 1968-
    Proverbs : Abingdon Old Testament commentaries / Christine Roy Yoder.
        p. cm.
    Includes bibliographical references and index.
    ISBN 978-1-4267-0001-9 (binding: pbk.,trade pbk. : alk. paper)
    1. Bible. O.T. Proverbs—Commentaries. I. Title.
    BS1465.53.Y63 2008
    223'.7077--dc22

                                                                            2008011882

Continued on page 315

09 10 11 12 13 14 15 16 17 18—10 9 8 7 6 5 4 3 2 1
MANUFACTURED IN THE UNITED STATES OF AMERICA

For Arthur P. and Sara Hinrichsen Roy

"The glory of children is their parents." (Prov 17:6b)

Contents

Foreword xiii

Acknowledgments xvii

Abbreviations xix

Introduction xxi
    Occasion and Context xxi
    Reading Proverbs and the Book of Proverbs xxvi
    Theology and Ethics xxix
    Using This Commentary xxxiii

Commentary 1

*Proverbs 1–9: "The proverbs of Solomon, the son of
David, king of Israel"* 1

    Proverbs 1:1-7: The Prologue 1
        Literary Analysis 1
        Exegetical Analysis 2
            Excursus on "Fear of the LORD" (1:7) 6
        Theological and Ethical Analysis 8

    Introduction to Proverbs 1:8–9:18 10

    Proverbs 1:8-33 13
        Literary Analysis 13

CONTENTS

Exegetical Analysis 13

Theological and Ethical Analysis 20

Proverbs 2 23

Literary Analysis 23

Exegetical Analysis 24

  Excursus on "the Heart" 25

  Excursus on "the Path(s)" 28

Theological and Ethical Analysis 34

Proverbs 3 36

Literary Analysis 36

Exegetical Analysis 37

  Excursus on "Abomination of the LORD" 48

Theological and Ethical Analysis 48

Proverbs 4 51

Literary Analysis 51

Exegetical Analysis 52

Theological and Ethical Analysis 59

Proverbs 5 60

Literary Analysis 60

Exegetical Analysis 61

Theological and Ethical Analysis 68

Proverbs 6 70

Literary Analysis 70

Exegetical Analysis 71

Theological and Ethical Analysis 80

Proverbs 7–8 81

Literary Analysis 81

Exegetical Analysis 84

Theological and Ethical Analysis 99

Proverbs 9 103

Literary Analysis 103

Exegetical Analysis 104

Theological and Ethical Analysis 108

CONTENTS

Proverbs 10:1–22:16: "The proverbs of Solomon" 110

Introduction to Proverbs 10:1–22:16 110

Proverbs 10:1–15:33 114
Theological and Ethical Overview 114

Proverbs 10 117
Literary Analysis 117
Exegetical Analysis 118

Proverbs 11 130
Literary Analysis 130
Exegetical Analysis 130

Proverbs 12 141
Literary Analysis 141
Exegetical Analysis 141

Proverbs 13 149
Literary Analysis 149
Exegetical Analysis 150

Proverbs 14 157
Literary Analysis 157
Exegetical Analysis 158

Proverbs 15 167
Literary Analysis 167
Exegetical Analysis 167

Proverbs 16:1–22:16 175
Theological and Ethical Overview 175

Proverbs 16 180
Literary Analysis 180
Exegetical Analysis 181

Proverbs 17 190
Literary Analysis 190
Exegetical Analysis 190

Proverbs 18 196
   Literary Analysis 196
   Exegetical Analysis 197

Proverbs 19 202
   Literary Analysis 202
   Exegetical Analysis 202

Proverbs 20 208
   Literary Analysis 208
   Exegetical Analysis 208

Proverbs 21 215
   Literary Analysis 215
   Exegetical Analysis 216

Proverbs 22:1-16 222
   Literary Analysis 222
   Exegetical Analysis 222

Proverbs 22:17–24:22: "Words of the wise" 227
   Introduction and Literary Analysis 227
   Theological and Ethical Overview 229
   Exegetical Analysis 231

Appendix: Proverbs 24:23-34: "These also are of the wise" 242
   Literary Analysis 242
   Exegetical Analysis 242

Proverbs 25–29: "These also are proverbs of Solomon, which the officials of King Hezekiah of Judah transmitted" . 244

Introduction to Proverbs 25–29 244

Proverbs 25–27 245
   Literary Analysis 245
   Theological and Ethical Overview 246
   Exegetical Analysis 248

Proverbs 28–29 263
   Literary Analysis 263

CONTENTS

Theological and Ethical Overview 264
Exegetical Analysis 266

Proverbs 30: "The words of Agur" 278
Literary Analysis 278
Exegetical Analysis 279
Theological and Ethical Analysis 287

Proverbs 31: "The words of Lemuel, king of Massa,
which his mother taught him," and The woman of
substance 288
Literary Analysis 288
Exegetical Analysis 290
Theological and Ethical Analysis 297

Select Bibliography 301

Index 311

FOREWORD

The *Abingdon Old Testament Commentaries* are offered to the reader in hopes that they will aid in the study of Scripture and provoke a deeper understanding of the Bible in all its many facets. The texts of the Old Testament come out of a time, a language, and sociohistorical and religious circumstances far different from the present. Yet Jewish and Christian communities have held to them as a sacred canon, significant for faith and life in each new time. Only as one engages these books in depth and with all the critical and intellectual faculties available to us can the contemporary communities of faith and other interested readers continue to find them meaningful and instructive.

These volumes are designed and written to provide compact, critical commentaries on the books of the Old Testament for the use of theological students and pastors. It is hoped that they may be of service also to upper-level college or university students and to those responsible for teaching in congregational settings. In addition to providing basic information and insights into the Old Testament writings, these commentaries exemplify the tasks and procedures of careful interpretation.

The writers of the commentaries in this series come from a broad range of ecclesiastical affiliations, confessional stances, and educational backgrounds. They have experience as teachers and, in some instances, as pastors and preachers. In most cases, the authors are persons who have done significant research on the book that is their assignment. They take full account of the most important current scholarship and secondary literature, while not attempting to summarize that literature or to engage in technical academic debate. The fundamental concern of each volume is analysis and discussion of the literary, sociohistorical, theological, and ethical dimensions of the biblical texts themselves.

The *New Revised Standard Version of the Bible* is the principal translation of reference for the series, though authors may draw upon other interpretations in their discussion. Each writer is attentive to the original Hebrew text in preparing the commentary. But the authors do not presuppose any knowledge of the biblical languages on the part of the reader. When some awareness of a grammatical, syntactical, or philological issue is necessary for an adequate understanding of a particular text, the issue is explained simply and concisely.

Each volume consists of four parts. An *introduction* looks at the book as a whole to identify *key issues* in the book, its *literary genre* and *structure*, the *occasion and situational context* of the book (including both social and historical contexts), and the *theological and ethical* significance of the book.

The *commentary* proper organizes the text by literary units and, insofar as is possible, divides the comment into three parts. The *literary analysis* serves to introduce the passage with particular attention to identification of the genre of speech or literature and the structure or outline of the literary unit under discussion. Here also, the author takes up significant stylistic features to help the reader understand the mode of communication and its impact on comprehension and reception of the text. The largest part of the comment is usually found in the *exegetical analysis*, which considers the leading concepts of the unit, the language of expression, and problematical words, phrases, and ideas in order to get at the aim or intent of the literary unit, as far as that can be uncovered. Attention is given here to particular historical and social situations of the writer(s) and reader(s) where that is discernible and relevant as well as to wider cultural (including religious) contexts. The analysis does not proceed phrase by phrase or verse by verse but deals with the various particulars in a way that keeps in view the overall structure and central focus of the passage and its relationship to the general line of thought or rhetorical argument of the book as a whole. The final section, *theological and ethical analysis*, seeks to identify and clarify the theological and ethical matters with which the unit deals or to which it points. Though not aimed primarily at contemporary issues of faith and life, this section should provide readers a basis for reflection on them.

Each volume also contains a select bibliography of works cited in the commentary as well as major commentaries and other important works available in English.

The fundamental aim of this series will have been attained if readers are assisted not only to understand more about the origins, character, and meaning of the Old Testament writings but also to enter into their own informed and critical engagement with the texts themselves.

Patrick D. Miller
General Editor

ACKNOWLEDGMENTS

I am grateful to *Abingdon Old Testament Commentaries* for the invitation to contribute this volume on Proverbs. I am indebted especially to Carol A. Newsom and Patrick D. Miller for their guidance and editorial insights, and to C. L. Seow for inspiring my interest in Proverbs years ago and continuing to share so generously of his time and wisdom.

I completed most of the research and writing of this commentary during two sabbaticals. I am grateful for the generous support of my institution, Columbia Theological Seminary in Decatur, Georgia, and for the additional resources afforded to me by a Lilly Theological Research Grant (2002–2003), a Catholic Biblical Association Fellowship (2006–2007), grants from the Griffith Foundation (2003, 2007), and a stipend from the Center of Theological Inquiry (CTI) in Princeton, New Jersey, where I was in residence from August 2006 to July 2007. I am indebted to my colleagues at CTI for their wisdom and friendship; in particular, I want to thank Jan-Olav Henriksen for his thoughtful engagement of this work, and William F. Storrar, Director of CTI, and the staff for the warm and gracious hospitality they extended to my husband, Reinald, and me.

I am thankful for the many opportunities I have had to present portions of this commentary to others, most notably my colleagues and students at Columbia, and congregations, pastors, and educators in various settings. As "iron sharpens iron" (Prov 27:17a), I am mindful how so many people have, in ways known and unknown to them, honed my thinking. I am grateful for my colleagues in Old Testament at Columbia—for Kathleen M. O'Connor and Walter Brueggemann, who read early drafts of this work, and for William P. Brown, whose contributions to the study of Proverbs guided me long before I knew the privilege of serving with him on the same faculty. I am indebted to Ulrike Guthrie, who edited the entire manuscript and held me to my deadlines, and to Sara Hayden, who devoted many hours to checking my citations. Any errors that remain are, of course, entirely my responsibility.

I find it difficult to put in words my profound gratitude for Reinald—for his loving and steadfast companionship, his encouragement and patience, and his quick humor that makes me laugh and not take it all so seriously.

Finally, I dedicate this work to my parents, Arthur P. and Sara Hinrichsen Roy, who inspired in my sisters and me a love for learning, provided tirelessly and generously for our formation and education, and care deeply for our well-being. Thank you for keeping the door open and the light on for us as we each find our way in the world.

ABBREVIATIONS

AB	Anchor Bible
ABRL	Anchor Bible Reference Library
AEL	*Ancient Egyptian Literature*. M. Lichtheim. 3 vols. Berkeley, 1973–1980
ALASP	Abhandlungen zur Literatur Alt-Syrien-Palästinas und Mesopotamiens
ANEP	*The Ancient Near East in Pictures Relating to the Old Testament*. Edited by J. B. Pritchard. 2d ed. with supplement. Princeton, 1969
ANET	*Ancient Near Eastern Texts Relating to the Old Testament*. Edited by J. B. Pritchard. 3d ed. with supplement. Princeton, 1969
AOAT	Alter Orient und Altes Orient
Bib	*Biblica*
BSac	*Bibliotheca sacra*
BTB	*Biblical Theology Bulletin*
BWL	*Babylonian Wisdom Literature*. W. G. Lambert. Oxford, 1960
BZAW	Beihefte zur Zeitschrift für die alttestamentliche Wissenschaft
CBQ	*Catholic Biblical Quarterly*
CBQMS	Catholic Biblical Quarterly Monograph Series
ConBOT	Coniectanea biblica: Old Testament Series
HS	*Hebrew Studies*
ICC	International Critical Commentary
ITC	International Theological Commentary
JANES	*Journal of the Ancient Near Eastern Society*
JBL	*Journal of Biblical Literature*

JETS	*Journal of the Evangelical Theological Society*
JSOT	*Journal for the Study of the Old Testament*
JSOTSup	Journal for the Study of the Old Testament: Supplement Series
KTU	*The Cuneiform Alphabetic Texts from Ugarit, Ras Ibn Hani, and Other Places*. Edited by M. Dietrich, O. Loretz, and J. Sanmartín. 2d ed. ALASP 8. Münster, 1995
LXX	Septuagint
m.	masculine
MT	Masoretic Text (BHS)
NAB	New American Bible
NASB	New American Standard Bible
NCB	New Century Bible
NEB	New English Bible
NICOT	New International Commentary on the Old Testament
NIV	New International Version
NRSV	New Revised Standard Version
OTE	*Old Testament Essays*
OTL	Old Testament Library
pl.	plural
PSB	*Princeton Seminary Bulletin*
RB	*Revue biblique*
REB	Revised English Bible
SBLDS	Society of Biblical Literature Dissertation Series
sg.	singular
TAD	*Textbook of Aramaic Documents from Ancient Egypt*. Edited by B. Porten and A. Yardeni. 4 vols. Winona Lake, Ind., 1986–1999
TANAKH	New Jewish Publication Society Version
VT	*Vetus Testamentum*
VTSup	Supplements to Vetus Testamentum
WBC	Word Biblical Commentary
ZAW	*Zeitschrift für die alttestamentliche Wissenschaft*
//	is parallel to

INTRODUCTION

The book of Proverbs is for the ordinary of days. Proverb after proverb, page after page, it invites us into an ancient and ongoing conversation about what is good and wise and true in life. How can we discern right from wrong in a world of fiercely competing claims? What values do we treasure and why? What makes for strong families and just communities? What characterizes a good neighbor, loving partner, or trusted friend? How do we understand money, the role of integrity, and the power of speech? And how do we teach it all to our children? The book of Proverbs, part of the Wisdom literature of the Old Testament that includes Ecclesiastes, Job, Sirach, and the Wisdom of Solomon takes up such questions as part and parcel of the reverent life. It acknowledges the ordinary as the arena in which we develop our moral character and work out our faithfulness step by step, day after day. And it commends for the journey wisdom born of the experiences and musings of generations who have gone before us—poetry wrought and recited time and again by the people of God. Not all of their assumptions will resonate as true for us across the gap of centuries and different worldviews. Not all of their insights will prove apt for our present-day circumstances. But proverb after proverb, page after page, Proverbs inspires and requires of us fresh theological and ethical reflection about our lives, our communities, and our world.

OCCASION AND CONTEXT

Situating the book of Proverbs in a particular sociohistorical context or setting is complicated. The superscriptions, or titles, to the book as a whole (1:1) and to two of its sections (10:1–22:16; 25:1–29:27) attribute authorship to Solomon, the second and last king of the united monarchy (ca. 966–926 BCE) and the quintessential sage of Israel. Tradition testifies that Solomon's wisdom was granted by God, surpassed that of all others ("vast as the sand on the seashore," 1 Kgs 4:29), and was celebrated and sought by the world leaders of his day (1 Kgs 3–11). Solomon's name lends authority and authenticity to Proverbs. At the same time, Solomon's larger-than-life status as a patron and author of wisdom cautions against interpreting the superscriptions as historically reliable. Like David with the psalms and Moses with the law, Solomon is identified conventionally with wisdom; other Israelite wisdom texts that date to the postexilic period are associated with him (Wisdom of Solomon, Ecclesiastes; see also Song of Songs, Psalms of Solomon, Odes of Solomon, and the Testament of Solomon). Furthermore, the proverbs never speak overtly from a king's perspective. Instead, they imply as background a variety of social groups and circumstances. And when the royal court does figure more prominently in the last half of the book, most of the advice is how to regard kings, be invited "up" (25:6-7; cf. 22:29), and behave in their presence (e.g., 16:14; 23:1-5)—guidance we do not imagine Solomon giving to his son, the heir apparent to the throne. The name Solomon thus commends Proverbs as important and trustworthy—it provides a certain imprimatur—but it is unlikely that Solomon wrote much if any of the book. (In ancient Egypt, similarly, we find pseudepigraphical wisdom texts attributed to kings, officials, or sages; e.g., *AEL* 1.58-59, 59-61, 61-80, 135-139.)

Proverbs gives few other clues as to its sociohistorical context. Reference to "the officials of King Hezekiah of Judah" (25:1) suggests that at least one section of the book was shaped during the late eighth to early seventh centuries BCE. But there is no explicit mention of Israel or of such significant figures or moments in its history as the matriarchs and patriarchs, Moses, Exodus and wilderness wanderings, settlement in the promised land, the prophets, the Babylonian exile, and the return. Only a few proverbs refer to religious practices (e.g., 3:9; 7:14; 15:8, 29). And personal names other than Solomon and Hezekiah are unfamiliar to us from other sources: Agur (30:1) and Lemuel (31:1). Superscriptions, or titles, further suggest the book is comprised of sections woven together over time:

1:1–9:18	"The proverbs of Solomon, the son of David, king of Israel"
10:1–22:16	"The proverbs of Solomon"
22:17–24:22	"Words of the wise"
24:23-34	"These also are of the wise"
25:1–29:27	"These also are proverbs of Solomon, which the officials of King Hezekiah of Judah transmitted"
30:1-33	"The words of Agur"
31:1-9	"The words of Lemuel, king of Massa, which his mother taught him"
31:10-31	(The woman of substance*)

*This section lacks a superscription but stands apart as an alphabetic acrostic, a poem in which each line begins with the next letter of the Hebrew alphabet.

Interpreters continue to date Proverbs or portions of it on the basis of themes, alleged biblical or extrabiblical parallels, and/or linguistic evidence, but such conclusions are tentative and disputed. Notably, the very factors that confound our efforts to pin the book down conclusively to a time and place contribute to a sense that Proverbs is timeless and universal. It reads as wisdom for everyone because it appears particular to no one.

Mindful of these challenges, many interpreters consider 10:1–29:27 to be the oldest portions of Proverbs, consisting primarily of originally oral folk proverbs that sages or scribes associated with the royal court (e.g., 25:1, 24:23) gathered together during the period of the monarchy—from the mid-tenth century BCE (Solomon) to the Babylonian exile in 587 BCE. The framing units of Proverbs 1–9 and 31:10-31 were added later in the postexilic period (late sixth to third centuries BCE), arguably in the Persian period (ca. 538–333 BCE). Compilation of the book thereby began early in Israel's history, continued over generations, and drew to a close when the community reclaimed and framed the book in the aftermath of exile. From external evidence, we know that the formation of Proverbs was complete before the mid-second century BCE. Ben Sira drew on Proverbs around 190 BCE, paraphrasing and adapting proverbs for his context. The Greek translation, or Septuagint (LXX), similarly dates to the first half of the second century BCE. And the two manuscript fragments of the book found at Qumran (4QProv^a = 4Q102 and 4Q Prov^b = 4Q103) are dated to the mid-first century BCE and mid-first century CE respectively.

This overview of the book's development calls attention to several matters. First, the bulk of Proverbs are originally oral proverbs, a fact that affects how we "hear" proverbs and think about them as part of a literary work. Second, the "authors" of Proverbs are, in essence, the community of Israel—countless unnamed and unknown persons who passed these proverbs from generation to generation (hereafter the "sages" to whom I refer). Although the book undoubtedly bears the handprints of court scribes or sages who gathered and edited the proverbs, its authority springs from its deep roots in the whole community. Third, as the wisdom of many, Proverbs manifests diverse and at times contradictory perspectives, some of which may be due to its origins in different social groups, and some of which may simply reflect the situational nature of wisdom; thoughtful people often hold views that are in conflict with one another and decide between them as circumstances warrant (e.g., "look before you leap" and "she who hesitates is lost"). Fourth, proverbs are building blocks of a culture. They convey well and rightly a community's values and convictions and, as such, can stabilize and/or challenge the status quo. This particular collection began during the period of monarchy and was consolidated finally when, in the aftermath of the monarchy's collapse, the community struggled to rebuild and reconstitute itself as a colony on the fringe of the Persian Empire. Not surprisingly, they turned to age-old wisdom. Proverbs orient and reorient people as to who they are.

It follows that Proverbs was likely compiled not as a first-time introduction to the community's proverbs, but as a permanent resource for readers largely familiar with them. By writing things down, the sages preserved the integrity of the proverbs, and created a tool that could be used to educate and enculturate the young—"to reinforce emergent writing and reading competencies," and "to socialize youths in the basic values and worldview of the given culture" (Carr 2005, 126). The book facilitated ongoing, accurate recitation and memorization of proverbs in what was primarily an oral process of education; note, for example, that Proverbs 1–9 is cast as nearly all speech, and the youth is told repeatedly to "listen" and "incline [the] ear" to gain knowledge (e.g., 1:8; 2:2; 4:1, 20; 5:1; 8:32-34). One imagines elders referring to Proverbs much as actors review scripts they have memorized, or musicians read scores that they know (Carr 2005, 4), while the young—particularly young men bound for positions of leadership—recite the proverbs again and again so as to "write" them on their hearts and minds (3:3; 7:3; cf. 4:4, 21; 6:21; excursus in Proverbs 2). Those who mastered the book (along with other texts significant to the community) and exemplified its values would be consummate cultural "insiders"—part of the minority of literate elite (Carr 2005, 131).

In what setting did this education occur? Was this wisdom taught mainly in households or in schools connected with the royal court or the temple? Portions of Proverbs suppose the household: father-to-son instruction marks chapters 1–9 and recurs elsewhere (NRSV: "my child" or "children" is in Hebrew "my son[s]"; cf. 19:27; 23:15-16, 19, 26; 24:13, 21; 27:11) and mothers teach (1:8; 6:20; cf. 31:1-9, 26). That many ancient Egyptian wisdom texts are also a father's words to his son—several apparently actually so—indicates that the setting was common, even standard (e.g., the *Instruction of Amenemope* [AEL 2:146-163]; the *Instruction Anii* [AEL 2:135-146]). Moreover, there is little compelling evidence for the existence of "schools" in Israel prior to the late period (Ben Sira's "house of study," 51:23). Thus, ional the education of children, especially sons, was uptions home by their biological parents, particular

Present-day readers engage the presur setting variously. Many rightly challe about gender and authority and ponder how those influence women who read the book. Some find value in its emphasis on the role and responsibility of parents, particularly fathers, in the moral formation of children, when our own time is marked increasingly by broken homes and the absence of fathers. The setting of the book is one of many aspects of the sages' worldview that invite us to vigorous moral and theological reflection.

READING PROVERBS AND THE BOOK OF PROVERBS

It is significant, I think, that a book devoted to teaching wisdom, which takes up such everyday matters as relationships, faith, business, money, sex, and alcohol, does so not with a series of recommended "to-do lists," innovative strategies, slogans, or clichés, but with *poetry*—exquisite, crafted speech that has been polished and pertinent for centuries. Perhaps the sages appreciate the power of poetry to illumine the crags and crevices of the human situation, to convey honestly and gracefully its ambiguities and wonder, and, as a result, to be remembered. Perhaps they recognize our instinct, time and again, to fashion beauty from disarray, to honor life's twists and turns by creative expression. Perhaps they know what most of us soon discover: that navigating life wisely and well is itself nothing less than an art form—and so the inspiration and cultivation of good, faithful lives requires speech up to the task. That conviction, I expect, in part motivates preachers and teachers today as it did Ecclesiastes, a sage and "preacher," long ago. Weighing, studying, and arranging proverbs, he sought to find for his community words that were "pleasing"—apt and aesthetically satisfying—and he wrote "words of truth plainly" (Eccl 12:9-10). He sought to bring old truths to bear in a new situation.

The term *mašal* ("proverb," e.g., 1:1; 10:1) encompasses a wide of speech, from one-line sayings to extended poems. In the most prevalent form is the two-line proverb: the first an observation or claim, which the second then develor motivates. The proverb's parallel structure cona balanced, orderly view of the world—while its details captivate and complicate. As Ecclesiastes' search for "pleasing words" suggests (Eccl 12:10), proverbs are artistic. The sages teach with vivid metaphors and similes, wordplay, rhythm, alliteration (repetition of the same or similar consonant[s] in a line or group of lines), assonance (repetition of the same vowel), ambiguity, irony, humor, and so on. The artistry invites us to linger—to read slowly—and, when we do, we discover what the sages knew well: proverbs provoke thought. We interpret a proverb's words, phrases, and syntax, the relationship between its lines, *and* imagine when it might be applicable. Proverbs are multivalent "slices of truth." A proverb may have several possible meanings, and it likely "means" differently depending on who says it and how, to whom, and in what circumstances. Proverbs thus inspire and teach moral imagination. Far from self-evident, weary "moralisms," G. von Rad observes: "The single line [proverb comprised of two parallel sections] often enough makes higher claims and demands a greater degree of intentional participation than a developed didactic poem" (1972, 27). Becoming wise is therefore not only about learning proverbs but about learning to read the world so that one might use proverbs rightly ("a word fitly spoken / is like apples of gold in a setting of silver," 25:11; cf. 15:23).

Proverbs gathered in a collection prompt additional reflection. The juxtaposition of individual proverbs one after the other generates a literary context that may inform our interpretation of a proverb. To borrow a metaphor from E. B. White, it is as though we are gazing at a literary mosaic (White 1984, 40). We focus initially on the small pieces of the variously colored proverbs, each a polished entity unto itself, and then on those immediately around it, noting ways the colors interact with or are distinct from one another. At times, we observe that features that animate an individual proverb extend to create units of two or more—so catchwords, wordplay, sound, and metaphors, for example, form proverb pairs or larger units (e.g., 11:10-11; 13:7-8; 15:8-9). Elsewhere, we find thematic threads or *inclusios*, the repetition of a word or phrase at the beginning and ending of a unit, which invite us to read a group of proverbs together (e.g., 3:13-18; 10:1-5).

These connections highlight how proverbs may comment on one another and, as such, usher us into a larger conversation across the book—one replete with agreement, nuance, and contradiction.

But to what extent are connections we see between proverbs intentional on the part of the book's editors? With particular regard to Proverbs 10–29, some interpreters argue there is deliberate, subtle, and extensive editorial arrangement (e.g., Meinhold 1991; Hildebrandt 1998; Heim 2001). Others, including myself, observe fewer associations between the individual proverbs and are reticent to construe all of them as purposeful. Lack of consensus as to the criteria by which to identify broader structures and what they are warrants caution. Moreover, even if such subtle connections exist, most readers miss them. Readers tend to experience Proverbs 10–29 as a loose collection of proverbs—one complete unit of meaning after another, each for the most part disconnected from the proverbs that precede and follow. Such a loose arrangement is typical of ancient Near Eastern wisdom literature. Compare, for example, the Egyptian *Instruction of Ptahhotep* (*AEL* 1:61-80) and *Instruction of Anii* (*AEL* 2:135-146), the Aramaic *Proverbs of Ahiqar* (*TAD* 3.1.1), and the Babylonian *Counsels of Wisdom* (*BWL* 96-107).

The relative lack of clear connections between individual proverbs in 10:1–29:27 does not mean Proverbs is without editorial arrangement, however. Each section of the book accents different themes and genres than the others. And portraits of two women, who lexical and thematic parallels suggest we should identify with each other, frame Proverbs: personified wisdom (Prov 1–9) and the "woman of substance" (31:10-31). The implied reader begins as a silent youth urged to pursue and love wisdom, to accept the invitation to her household (chs. 1–9), and ends as an esteemed adult who resides in wisdom's household (31:10-31). So, does each section of the book somehow contribute to this "growing up"? Asked differently, does the book of Proverbs form or "mature" readers by its content *and* arrangement? R. C. Van Leeuwen, for example, identifies Proverbs 1–9 as "threshold speeches" that prepare the youth to cross from adolescence to a more mature position (1990). W. P. Brown argues that the book's progression from Israelite to international wisdom, increasing variety and complexity of literary forms, and expanding breadth and complexity of moral purview, suggest an "overarching editorial arrangement and pedagogical movement of the book as a whole" (2002, 152). And I maintain that the reader's experiences of repetition and contradiction across Proverbs buttress vital claims that its proverbs make about the relativity and frailty of human knowledge—making it more likely that readers develop the humility characteristic of "fearers of the LORD" (Yoder 2005). These and related studies—and now this commentary—ponder how the pedagogy and arrangement of the book's sections and mosaic of proverbs may contribute to the book's goal to form wise readers.

Finally, the sages of Proverbs were part of a much larger ancient Near Eastern wisdom tradition. Available to us are wisdom texts from Egypt, Mesopotamia, and Syria—study of which alongside Proverbs contributes to our understanding (for a helpful introduction to these resources, see Fox 2000, 17-27). We find individual proverbs have parallels in the wisdom literatures of other cultures. The genre of father-to-son instruction is common. And most interpreters consider "Words of the wise" (22:17–24:34) to be an artful adaptation of the Egyptian *Instruction of Amenemope* (*AEL* 2:146-163). In short, Israelite sages created analogous wisdom and/or adopted and modified the wisdom of other cultures to teach their community about the ways of wisdom. Their search for knowledge is international and ecumenical in scope—so much so that they include in the book two sections that are arguably attributed to foreigners (Agur, 30:1-33; Lemuel, 31:1-9). Perhaps this esteem for the wisdom of others and the sages' strategies for adapting that wisdom for use in their context may encourage our efforts today to engage in cross-cultural and interfaith public moral discourse.

THEOLOGY AND ETHICS

Proverbs strikes many readers as commonplace. It does not appear particularly "revelatory," namely, received as a word from

God. Nor does God ever speak—as in the ancestral narratives or through Moses and the prophets. Rather, the book is a compilation of wisdom based on the experiences of ordinary, faithful people trying to live wisely every day, striving to discern what is good and right and true for themselves and their community. Their insights have proved resilient; their claims reaffirmed by generations. Proverbs is time-worn "common sense."

That is precisely what makes the book invaluable for our theological and ethical reflection. Proverbs prompts us to think about what it means to live as "fearers of the LORD" day after day "when water does not pour forth from rocks and angels do not come to lunch" (Davis 2000, 12). It urges us to examine our convictions about the human place in the world, the power and presence of God, the frame and fibers of moral character, the nature of knowledge, the contours of good and evil, the role of tradition, our assumptions about gender and "strangers," and the power and contingencies of speech. Sitting with the sages in the heart of the ordinary—"in the street; in the squares" (1:20; cf. 8:1-2)—we contemplate with them who we are and what it means to live our lives well.

The human portrait in Proverbs is outlined with certain brush-strokes. First, the self is *in relation*. The sages emphasize that we are formed by our relationships and, in turn, are accountable to the community, creation, and God. Second, the self is *embodied*. Prevalent are references to the human body, temperament, and organs of perception, motion, and expression: ears and eyes, the heart or mind (see excursus in Proverbs 2), hands and feet, and, most frequently, the mouth, lips, and tongue (e.g., 4:20-27; 6:12-19; 10:11). Learning engages the whole person, and character is indivisible from behavior and speech. Third, the self has *choice* and bears responsibility for the consequences. Our choices set us on one of two "ways" or paths—wisdom or folly, righteousness or wickedness (see excursus in Proverbs 2). Life is a journey and each step advances or hinders our progress. Finally, the self is *a creation of God*, gifted with capacities and bounded by God's sovereignty. There are limits to what we can know. Human determination and ingenuity only take us so far. Accordingly, the sages understand a wise person to be first and foremost a "fearer of the LORD"—reverent, ever learning, and humble (see excursus in Proverbs 1).

Throughout Proverbs, the sages identify God as YHWH, the God of Israel (eighty-seven times, compared to five references to "God" or *ĕlōhim*). The God of Proverbs is all-powerful and mysterious, one who gathers the winds in the hollow of the hand (30:4) and lingers, close as breath, between a person's thought and speech (16:1). God's knowledge is boundless; God's scrutiny is as deep as the underworld and as vast as the human heart (e.g., 15:3, 11; 16:2). Prominent in the sages' theology is God's ardent concern for justice in all things: relationships, business practices, judicial procedures, and so on. God reacts to us, delighting in righteousness and loathing wickedness (e.g., 12:22; 15:8-9; see excursus in Proverbs 3). And God acts to ensure justice, protecting and providing for the just while opposing and punishing the unjust (e.g., 10:3; 12:2). Of particular concern to God are the poor and defenseless in society, those whom, the sages stress, God created and safeguards (e.g., 14:31; 17:5; 22:2). God sets up the widow's boundaries (23:10-11; cf. 15:25). God pays the debt of the poor (19:17; cf. 28:8). God is the orphan's redeemer (23:10-11). The God of Proverbs is not neutral.

Nor is the world that God created. By wisdom, God knit together the fabric of creation, giving it shape, meaningful order, and coherence that God sustains (e.g., 3:19-20; 8:22-31). Therefore, dispositions and behaviors have predictable and appropriate consequences. Just conduct is rewarded; wrongs are eventually set right. At times, the sages identify God explicitly as the agent of justice; at times, their use of impersonal constructions and passive verbs leaves it ambiguous: *somehow* things work out rightly. To "find" wisdom—to seek after and receive it as a gift from God (2:6)—is to glimpse God's handiwork, align oneself with it, and, as a result, prosper. Conceived this way, the search for knowledge is a search for God; there is no distinction between "sacred" and "secular," "spiritual" and "practical" as ways of knowing. Everyday experiences and concerns are theological. Moreover, the natural world contributes to our theological and ethical understanding. The sages urge us to "Go to the ant!" and look to the eagle and snake, the badger and locusts, the lion and rooster, so that we too might be wise and dignified creatures (e.g., 6:6-8; 30:18-19, 24-28, 29-31). Although the sages may strike some as rather sanguine about the world as "self-righting," they are not naive. They know well that the righteous struggle, the vulnerable suffer, and the wicked may thrive (e.g., 13:23; 29:2). The sages simply insist that such moments are never the last word— because God, God's creation, and God's people work for justice, goodness, and joy.

The varied ways the sages speak about wisdom confounds an easy definition of the term. Like the quality gems to which wisdom is compared favorably (e.g., 3:15; cf. 31:10), wisdom has many facets. It is knowledge about how to live well—a sort of "street smarts." It is a capacity to discern what is good in particular circumstances and to act accordingly. It is a disposition that loves beauty and honesty and goodness, hates wickedness, and desires to do right. It is a worldview, a web of meaning that connects oneself to others, the world, and God. Wisdom is outside the self and must be pursued tenaciously every day of one's life; it is inside the mind and heart as a gift from God. "All that you may desire cannot compare" with it (8:11). The quest for wisdom is vital.

To persuade readers of this, the sages use evocative images and metaphors for wisdom and its rival, foolishness. Wisdom is a "tree of life" (3:18), a shield (2:7), fine jewelry (3:22), and one's most precious possession (4:7). Folly, in turn, is a trap (1:17)—bitter as wormwood, sharp as a two-edged sword (5:4). The most vivid metaphors for wisdom and folly are the personifications of them as women in Proverbs 1–9 and, in the case of wisdom, as a "woman of substance" in 31:10-31. As we will see, these women have long been the subject of much interpretation and debate, their presence variously compelling and dangerous to readers. But the sages' steady juxtaposition of wisdom and folly in Proverbs 1–9—the entwining of speeches by and about them, the similarities between them (e.g., seeking the youth's attention, persuading with speech, moving about in city streets and squares, offering wealth and luxuries, and issuing the same invitation, 9:4, 16)—

lends gravity and urgency to our choices. The difference between wisdom and folly is not always obvious; the way to life is often obscure. Hence our need for wisdom of the sort that Proverbs teaches us.

Using This Commentary

In accordance with the guidelines of this series, this volume is organized by literary units, each of which I interpret in three sections: through literary analysis, exegetical analysis, and theological and ethical analysis. The three sections in that order work well for Proverbs 1–9, 30, and 31—chapters that contain longer literary units. For the comparatively disparate collection of proverbs in 10:1–29:27, however, I offer a theological and ethical overview of each main unit (10:1–15:33; 16:1–22:16; 22:17–24:34; 25:1–27:27; 28:1–29:27) *prior* to commenting on the individual proverbs therein. My hope is that this arrangement will highlight the distinctive aspects of each unit and invite further reflection about theological and ethical continuities and discontinuities between them. Lastly, I provide cross-references as possible throughout the commentary so that readers may pursue wisdom readily across the book—following threads of conversation and debate, tracing themes and characters, and catching contradictions and nuance. The treasure hunt itself—to "search for [wisdom] as for hidden treasures" (2:4)—teaches us something about becoming wise: it requires persistence and proves well worth the effort.

COMMENTARY

PROVERBS 1–9: "THE PROVERBS OF SOLOMON, THE SON OF DAVID, KING OF ISRAEL"

PROVERBS 1:1-7: THE PROLOGUE

Literary Analysis

The book of Proverbs opens with a title or superscription (1:1, see Introduction to this book) and a prologue (1:2-7). The superscription provides the name, ancestry, and position of the teacher—"Solomon, the son of David, king of Israel"— as a means to commend the book to possible readers. Such titles are found in other ancient Near Eastern wisdom texts. For example, the Egyptian *Instruction of Ptahhotep* begins: "Instruction of the Mayor of the city, the Vizier Ptahhotep" (*AEL* 1:62). Similarly, the first line of the *Instruction of Anii* reads: "Beginning of the educational instruction made by the scribe Anii of the palace of Queen Nefertari" (*AEL* 2:136).

The prologue (1:2-7) promotes the book of Proverbs as instruction for a lifetime, as a primer for the young and an advanced textbook for the more experienced. It unfolds in a series of phrases that introduce the goals of the book (1:2-6). Each phrase, with the exception of verse 5, begins with an infinitive (e.g., "for learning," 1:2; "to teach," 1:4), a syntactical construction that connects the phrase back to the title (1:1). The result is an extended description, an advertisement replete with wisdom terminology, of what may be gained from studying "the proverbs of Solomon." The prologue culminates in what many interpreters call the "motto" of the book: "The fear of the LORD is the beginning [or epitome] of knowledge" (1:7; cf. 9:10).

1

Exegetical Analysis

The Title (1:1)

The superscription (1:1) identifies the content of chapters 1–9, and by extension of the book as a whole, as "proverbs" and ascribes this content to "Solomon, the son of David, king of Israel." A "proverb" is a statement of an apparent truth that is based on experience and that endures in the life of a community over time. The word is used of a wide range of utterances (e.g., one-line sayings, riddles, admonitions, maxims, extended poems). This particular collection of proverbs is attributed to Solomon, the second and last king of the united monarchy (ca. 966–926 BCE). Endowed with wisdom by God (1 Kgs 3:3-15), Solomon is the quintessential sage of Israel and purported author of three thousand proverbs and one thousand and five songs (1 Kgs 4:32; cf. 1 Kgs 3–11). Collections of Israelite wisdom are conventionally associated with him (cf. 10:1; 25:1; Wisdom of Solomon; and Eccl 1:1, 12 [implied]), in much the same way that the psalms are to David and the laws to Moses. The superscription of Proverbs thereby commends the book on two grounds: first, by the widespread use of its content by the community (proverbs) and, second, by the name, title, and ancestry of the one in whose name the book is issued (Solomon). Both lend authority to what follows.

The Prologue (1:2-7)

Like a blurb on a dust jacket, the prologue (1:2-7) announces the aim of the book—in this case, to impart wisdom, to shape persons and communities of moral character. The handful of terse lines nearly burst with vocabulary the sages consider essential to that endeavor: discipline, prudence, justice, and so on. The terms are, on the one hand, familiar and self-explanatory. On the other, they name concepts that are complex and deeply contested in the world. What is justice? What does equity look like? What constitutes knowledge? And who decides? Such questions are at the heart of the sages' work, and the thirty-one chapters of Proverbs reflect manifold attempts to address them, to speak about what is good for people amid the complexities and contingencies of the everyday.

That Proverbs begins with a "vocabulary list" of wisdom terms and so closely attends to speech throughout is arguably no mistake. To teach persons how to be moral, faithful beings is, after all, to teach a language—a language that envisions the world and guides people's practices so that such a world might be realized. Proverbs orients and opines, describes and prescribes, corrects and nurtures so that its readers might regard and enact the world in particular ways. And, as we expect from teachers of any language, Proverbs requires its students to pay close attention. Note that the prologue calls the wise to hear (1:5); the father repeatedly urges the youth to listen (1:8; 4:1; 5:7; 7:24; cf. "incline your ear" in 4:20; 5:1, 13); and personified wisdom promises safety and prosperity to those who hear her (1:33; 8:6, 32-34). Similarly, the youth is told to keep his father's instructions as the "apple of [his] eye" (7:2), never letting them out of his sight (3:21; 4:21). Such repeated summons are reminders that language is neither simple nor ever finally mastered. Even the wise must listen again and again.

The sages signal at the beginning that this book will demand much from readers. The phrase "wisdom and instruction" that frames the prologue (1:2, 7) is more appropriately translated "wisdom and *discipline*." The latter term is *mûsār*, which nearly always refers to correction made by one with authority, such as YHWH (3:11; cf. Job 5:17; Deut 11:2), personified wisdom (8:10, 33), teachers (5:13), and parents (1:8; 4:1; 13:1; 15:5). In Proverbs, *mûsār* is associated with rebuke (13:1) and reproof (e.g., 5:12; 6:23; 10:17), and with physical punishment (13:24; 22:15; 23:13-14). Elsewhere in the Old Testament, *mûsār* refers similarly to verbal warnings and reprimands (e.g., Ps 50:17; Jer 7:28; 17:23) and to physical chastisement (Isa 53:5; Jer 2:30; 5:3). The term thus connotes authoritative discipline, whether verbal or physical. It evokes the image of a stern teacher poised with a ruler to rap a student's knuckles or, as in the case of the Egyptian hieroglyph for "teachings," an instructor holding a rod above his head. The sages are clear: this book requires obedience to authority figures and their correction.

Throughout Proverbs, discipline is a celebrated virtue. Discipline is how one navigates through life successfully (6:23; 10:17). By discipline, a teacher demonstrates devotion to a student (3:11-12; 13:24). By loving discipline, a student embraces knowledge (12:1; cf. 19:27; 23:12), acquires insight (4:1), and becomes wise (8:33). The sages therefore urge that one acquire discipline and never sell it (23:23), value it more than silver (8:10), and keep hold of it always (4:13). Only a fool would despise discipline (15:5; cf. 5:23; 12:1) because hatred of discipline is a form of self-hatred (15:32) that results in public disgrace and, ultimately, death (5:14, 23).

Proverbs 1:3a specifies that the book teaches *mûsar haśkēl* (NRSV: "instruction in wise dealing"), discipline that imparts "insight" or "cleverness" (cf. Job 34:35; Dan 1:17). This "discipline of insight" is about "righteousness, justice, and equity" (1:3b; cf. 2:9), terms that together refer comprehensively to ethical, honest, and neighborly conduct in personal and communal relationships. The terms occur fairly often in Proverbs— righteousness (9x), justice (20x), and equity (5x)—and all three are associated with personified wisdom (8:6, 8, 15-16, 20). The lessons of insight, therefore, are not abstract, ivory-tower concepts detached from the concrete, everyday realities of how people live together. They are the foundations of a just and equitable common life.

The sages invite young and old to take these teachings to heart. They address the "simple" and the "young" (1:4). The "simple" (*pĕtā'yîm*) are youth who are inexperienced and naive but capable of learning (e.g., 8:5; 22:3). Without instruction, they are wayward, prone to the tendencies of fools (1:32; 14:15), and may even esteem their gullibility (1:22). Similarly, the "young" (sg. *na'ar*) are boys, presumably adolescents, who lack maturity, and without tutoring may act senselessly (22:15); in Proverbs 1–9, they are arguably of marriageable age (5:18; 7:7).

The sages also address the "wise" and "discerning" (1:5). Lest anyone believe the book is only for novices, the sages abruptly interrupt the string of infinitives (1:2-4) and call the wise to attention also. The study of wisdom, it seems, is a lifelong endeavor. The Egyptian *Instruction of Ptahhotep* aptly captures this:

4

> Don't be proud of your knowledge,
> Consult the ignorant and the wise.
> The limits of art are not reached,
> No artist's skills are perfect. (*AEL* 1:63)

The young are promised that Proverbs will teach them "shrewd-ness and prudence" (1:4). The former term denotes cleverness, cunning, and trickery (e.g., Exod 21:14; Josh 9:4). Such cleverness is attributed to personified wisdom (8:12) and the strategies of the wise (cf. "craftiness," Job 5:13). The latter term refers to discretion, private thoughts (e.g., Job 21:27-28; Ps 10:4), and plots or plans devised in secret. Such scheming may be regarded positively (e.g., 2:11; 5:2; 8:12) or negatively (12:2; 14:17; 24:8). Both terms, therefore, have to do with the capacity to think and plan freely, creatively, even cunningly to get things done. The sages acknowledge the value of that capacity when practiced in the context of "wisdom and discipline" (1:2, 7); with proper guid-ance, cleverness and plotting might be used to legitimate, worthy ends. The prologue offers *disciplined* cunning to the youth, perhaps with the hope that the youth might then refuse to join in the dangerous schemes of others (e.g., 1:18-22; 7:16-20). The sages preempt the mystique of "hatching a plan" and put the skill of autonomous thinking firmly under the thumb of wisdom's correction.

The prologue also promises, perhaps particularly for the wise and discerning (1:5), the honing of interpretive skills (1:6). Apart from "words of the wise," a phrase that anticipates later sections of the book (cf. 22:17–24:22; 24:23-34), the terms in verse 6 refer to genres: wisdom is about content (e.g., justice, shrewdness) *and* form. Two of the terms are rather cryptic. The first, a "figure" (*mĕlîṣâ*), is presumably some sort of crafted speech—perhaps a proverb or parable (cf. Hab 2:6; Sir 47:17). The second, "riddles" (*ḥîdôt*), are enigmatic expressions that require explanation or par-ticular skill to decipher (cf. Num 12:8). Often they are what we would call riddles (e.g., Judg 14:14-19; Ezek 17:1-21). Recall the "hard questions" the Queen of Sheba posed to Solomon: "There was nothing hidden from the king that he could not explain to her" (1 Kgs 10:1-3 // 2 Chr 9:1-2). Although proper riddles are extremely rare in Proverbs (arguably 23:29-30; there is debate as to their extent), use of the term *ḥîdôt* in the prologue suggests the book provides an "inside scoop"—access to what is otherwise unknowable. Not only is that sure to pique readers' interest, but they are more likely to pay careful attention to what follows (Fox 2000, 66). The sages might just pull one over on you.

Excursus on "Fear of the LORD" (1:7)

The climax of the prologue is the "motto" of Proverbs (1:7). Without question, the phrase "the fear of the LORD" is the book's resounding refrain; it is found fourteen times (1:7; 2:5; 8:13; 9:10; 10:27; 14:2, 26-27; 15:16, 33; 16:6; 19:23; 22:4; 23:17), and the imperative "fear the LORD" is found twice (3:7; 24:21). The idiom also forms an *inclusio*—a frame of a word, phrase, or idea repeated at the beginning and conclusion of a literary unit—around Proverbs 1–9 (1:7; 9:10) and the book as a whole (1:7; 31:30).

In Proverbs, "fear of the LORD" refers variously to dread of God's disapproval or punishment, trepidation in the presence of the holy, and a conscience defined by obedience to God. At times, "fear of YHWH" is nearly synonymous with "knowledge of God" (1:7, 29; 2:5; cf. 9:10; 30:3) and "instruction in wisdom" (15:33). These proverbs explicitly identify fear of God with cognition, with a worldview that recognizes God's sovereignty and the posture of humanity (our capacities and limitations) before God and creation. M. V. Fox rightly notes: "This is fear of God as *conscience*" (2000, 70)—a state of mind that engenders humility (e.g., 3:5-8, 34; 22:4; cf. 15:33; 18:12) and is equated with hatred of evil (8:13; cf. 14:16; 16:6).

At other times, however, what motivates "fear of the LORD" is dread of certain consequences, such as trouble (15:16), harm (19:23), and deadly snares (14:27; cf. 10:27). "Fear the LORD and the king," the sages admonish, "for . . . who knows the ruin that both can bring?" (24:21-22). These proverbs caution that, at least in Proverbs, we should not draw too sharp a distinction between "fear of the LORD" and fear (e.g., Exod 20:19-21; 2 Sam

6:6-11; Job 1-2). Indeed, insofar as Proverbs depicts God as sovereign, mysterious, and free (e.g., 16:1-9; 19:21; 21:30-31), one might argue that *not* to feel "some stirring of fear would indicate a profound state of spiritual numbness" (Davis 2000, 28), an overly domesticated conception of the divine, or an exaggerated sense of self. This dread, then, is not unreflective or irrational but rather cognitive. It reflects certain beliefs, namely, that should one act wrongly, God has the capacity to act (including adversely); God will probably do so; and the wrongdoer is accountable and vulnerable.

Thus "fear" in "fear of the LORD" is used equivocally, to name an emotion and a more complex orientation in the world (i.e., conscience) of which that emotion is a part. It manifests itself on a continuum, so that to talk of "fear of YHWH" we need to include everything from obedience to moments of trembling. The whole gamut, which reflects certain beliefs about God, humanity, and the necessity of a relationship between the two, is, for the sages, "the beginning of knowledge" (1:7). And, like many fears that promote survival, "fear of the LORD" enables one to avoid certain perils, including the storms of panic that consume fools (3:24-26; cf. 1:33), and as a result affords health and long life (e.g., 3:8).

"Fear of the LORD" also motivates and informs right conduct. It demands just and gracious acts even when human laws and regulations are ineffective or silent. "Fear of the LORD" requires, for example, respect for and deference to the elderly (Lev 19:32), care for the physically disabled (Lev 19:14), support and protection of family and resident aliens (Lev 25:36), and fair business practices (Lev 25:17). Without it, the threads that weave together moral, equitable relations easily fray or unravel completely. When Abimelech asks Abraham why he introduced Sarah as his sister, Abraham says he feared he might be killed on her account because he thought, "There is no fear of God at all in this place" (Gen 20:11). Moses indicts hard-hearted Pharaoh who, despite the ten plagues, adamantly refused to release the Hebrews: "But I know that you and your officials still do not fear the LORD God" (Exod 9:30 NIV). Without "fear of the LORD," all other fears, including the fears of scarcity, ineptitude, irrelevance, and insecurity, run rampant.

The sages declare that "fear of the LORD" is the "beginning" (rē'šît) of knowledge (1:7a; cf. 9:10; 15:33). The term rē'šît has a range of possible meanings. It may be interpreted temporally as "beginning" or "starting point" (cf. Gen 10:10; Jer 26:1), suggesting that "the fear of the LORD" is the prerequisite or foundation for knowledge. It may also be read qualitatively, so that this fear is the "first," "best," or "epitome" (e.g., Jer 2:3; Amos 6:6) of knowledge. Understood this way, "the fear of the LORD" is the quintessential expression of what it means to be wise. This fear is the beginning and end, the best and fullest expression of wisdom. Either way (and the ambiguity may well be intentional) there is no wisdom without it. The sages would thus find strange, if not bewildering, our present-day understanding that we know apart from faith, that there are "categories of thought"—science or religion, reason or faith, fact or belief. For them, because the whole world and its mysteries belong to God, to "know" can be nothing less than to seek and be subject to God.

Theological and Ethical Analysis

Imagine a group of protesters marching about with signs that read variously "justice," "equity," "righteousness," and "wisdom." On the one hand, we recognize immediately the values the protesters promote; we might even grab a placard and rush to join them. On the other, were we to strike up a conversation with them, we might well discover that what they mean specifically by justice, equity, and so on varies—perhaps significantly—from our understandings. That is, moral terms like those that greet the reader of Proverbs (1:2-7) have, to borrow M. Walzer's terms, "thin" (minimal) and "thick" (maximal) meanings (Walzer 1994). They are at once common principles shared across cultures and continents ("thin") *and* values that particular communities elaborate differently ("thick"). For example, Chinese and Americans talk about "justice," but their understandings of the term probably reflect, respectively, the presuppositions of socialism and capitalism ("thick"). Should they engage in dialogue or conflict about

"justice" and search for common ground, any mutually acceptable and accessible notions of the term that emerge are typically
"thin" (not substantively minor or shallow but precisely the opposite—notions of justice that are most "close to the bone," cf.
Walzer 1994, 6). Such shared understandings are what prompt
people around the world together to condemn certain injustices,
mourn mutually recognized tragedies, celebrate commonly valued
accomplishments, and work toward shared goals.

Proverbs invites readers in by appealing to our "thin" understandings. The prologue portrays the book as a universally accessible morality, a resource for shaping individuals and communities
in a commonly advantageous, "clearly correct" manner. Other
aspects of the book reinforce this perception. Although Proverbs
was shaped at certain times and in particular places, for example,
it reveals very few indisputable sociohistorical markers (see
Introduction to this book). With the possible exception of 25:1,
there are no references to Israel and its history and few to its religious and political institutions. Personal names are either prominent (e.g., Solomon, Hezekiah) or obscure (e.g., Agur, Lemuel).
Further, the setting of chapters 1–9 is a household in an unidenti-
fied city (1:8, 20-21; 6:20; 7:6-12; 8:1-3; 9:1-3, 14-15). The setting eclipses particularities: "This is not a landed aristocrat
speaking, not a senior bureaucrat, not a member of the urban
middle class or a disenfranchised intellectual, but 'your father'"
(Newsom 1989, 144). As such, Proverbs appears to be a morality
for *everyone* because it is distinctive to *no one*.

Should we take up placards and start walking with the sages,
however, we soon discern "thicker" meanings, ways in which the
worldview of Proverbs resonates deeply with and differs significantly from our own. We are reminded that rival and at times
incompatible notions of terms such as "justice" and "equity" regularly compete for our allegiance. And we begin negotiating with
the sages as we nod or shake our heads at their claims. The conversation itself is formative. Proverbs, like other texts, evokes
our sensibilities, exposes our prejudices, and engages us in a
process by which our understandings are clarified, complicated,
and disciplined. Whether we embrace the sages' teaching or reject

it in whole or in part, we emerge from the encounter with greater insight into our cultures, communities, and selves. Our character is honed not only by what we accept—which placards we continue to shoulder as we go on our way—but by what we refuse.

Introduction to Proverbs 1:8–9:18

At 1:8, we step into a family home and, arguably, the hermeneutical guide for the book of Proverbs as a whole. Set in a household in a city (1:8, 20-21; 6:20; 7:6-12; 8:1-3; 9:1-3, 14-15), Proverbs 1–9 are the instructions of an anonymous father to his son(s) on the brink of adulthood. Readers, regardless of our actual identities (cf., young *and* old, 1:4-5), are asked to assume the identity of the silent, apparently amenable son. This starting point, even when we question its privileging of the father-son relationship as the authoritative context for learning, seems appropriate for a book about the formation of human character. Because most people have or have had a family, and families are where our identities are first fashioned, the household is the "natural," familiar domain for theological and ethical teaching. Families command loyalty and bear primary responsibility for initiating children into the moral beliefs, traditions, and institutions of the family and community. Similarly, the city is a bastion of human culture, a symbol of civilization purportedly at its most advanced. Both locations are conventional though certainly value-laden places for moral education.

As "virtually all talk," Proverbs 1–9 puts speech on center stage as a primary means by which character is formed (Newsom 1989, 142). The father seems keenly aware of the power of speech to embody and engender, to form and deform. He describes the world as an arena of conflicting discourses (e.g., the sinners, 1:10-19; wicked, 2:12-15; "strange" woman, 7:14-23). The youth are "hailed from many directions, offered subject positions in discourses that construe the world very differently" (Newsom 1989, 146), but always under the watchful eye of the father who "quotes," or gives voice to, the rival characters and disparages their points of view. Moreover, to bolster his already advantaged perspective, the father associates himself with Solomon, whose renowned wisdom bears the stamp of the royal office (1:1); personified wisdom, who speaks with communal and transcendent authority (1:20-21; 8:22-31); and God (e.g., 3:1-4, 11-12; 6:20-23). The father is, for the youth, their most immediate representative. With the force of paternal assurance and some urgency—perhaps the community believed its values were under attack (see Introduction to this book)—the father aims for his speech to win out as "truth" and for the youth to recognize and resist opposing discourses, some of which the father acknowledges are quite compelling (e.g., 1:10; 7:21).

Although the father talks about many things, it is significant that what he repeats most often are exordia, namely, appeals for attention and obedience. For example, the father repeats these exordia with only minor variation (the brackets indicate any variation from the underlined word or phrase in the second text):

Listen [Keep], my son, to your father's instruction [command], and do not neglect your mother's teaching (1:8; 6:20).

Listen, my son [sons], to your [a] father's instruction (1:8a; 4:1a).

My son, if you accept [keep] my words, and treasure up my commands within you (2:1; 7:1).

[My son,] making your ear attend [attend] to [my] wisdom, inclining [incline] your heart [ear] to [my] understanding (2:2; 5:1).

So now, my sons, listen to me, do not depart from [give heed to] the words of my mouth (5:7; 7:24).

Bind them [i.e., my teachings] on your throat [fingers]; inscribe them on the tablet of your heart (3:3bc; 7:3).

My son [   ], do not let them [i.e., my words] escape your eyes (3:21a; 4:21a).

Keep my commands and live (4:4c; 7:2a).

Repetition of particular verbs (e.g., listen, hear, keep, bind, attend) and direct objects (e.g., discipline, commandment, teaching, my words), coupled with imperatives and direct address, suggest the father's priority is to foster an attentive, receptive posture—the orientation most advantageous for becoming wise (see, e.g., 2:1-5). With each exordium, the pitch of the father's urgency intensifies such that it becomes progressively more difficult for the youth and readers to refuse to listen and observe. The father is persistent. He never takes the youth's attention for granted. And apparently his efforts pay off: at the conclusion of Proverbs 1–9, the father addresses the youth as ready to instruct others (9:7-9).

The father also models "right" use of proverbs. When he quotes what appear to be preexisting, self-contained two-line proverbs, he nestles them in literary contexts—long didactic poems or instructions—that directly inform their interpretation (e.g., 1:17; 2:21-22; 6:10-11). The proverbs appeal to communal consensus and function as capstones for the larger story and its lessons. By providing these appropriate contexts of use, the father demonstrates for the youth when and how proverbs "make sense."

Finally, the father orients the youth in a world of strongly qualified horizons. He paints in vivid, memorable brushstrokes, characterizing life as a journey, introducing a lively cast of characters (e.g., the sinners, righteous, wicked, scoffers, strangers), and situating the youth at the intersection of two paths and two mesmerizing women, personified wisdom and folly, with their respective households. This is a world marked by moral polarities and little ambiguity, of desires and limits, choices and apt consequences. Moreover, as God carved a limit for the sea (8:27-29; cf. 8:15), the boundaries and bifurcations of this worldview are carved into creation, chiseled into its very foundations (3:19-20; 8:22-31). To embrace wisdom is to live in accordance with God's handiwork. To reject knowledge leads, inevitably, to peril. Thus, for the father, the youth's choices—the path he takes, the "woman" he desires and ultimately loves—determine his fate. They are matters of life and death. Subsequent chapters (10:1–31:31) reinforce this moral and theological framework, even as they complicate and widen its purview.

PROVERBS 1:8-33

Literary Analysis

At 1:8, the mode of communication changes to instruction by a father ("I") to his son ("you"). The father-to-son setting is common in ancient Near Eastern Wisdom literature. For example, the epilogue of the *Instruction of Anii* is presented as a dialogue between a father and son (*AEL* 2:144-145); the Sumerian *Instructions of Shuruppak* are lessons offered by Shuruppak to his son (*BWL* 92-95). Elsewhere in the Old Testament, Ecclesiastes addresses "my son" (12:12 NIV). In Proverbs, the father-to-son setting continues through chapters 1–9 and is assumed occasionally elsewhere in the book (cf. 19:27; 23:15, 19, 26; 24:13, 21; 27:11). Twice, the father associates his teaching with that of the youth's mother (1:8 and 6:20), but she never speaks directly to the son.

Two major literary units follow. The first is the father's warning not to get involved with the wrong crowd (1:10-19). The second is an address by personified wisdom (1:20-33). Each unit attends particularly to how the primary characters—the "sinners" and wisdom—speak to the son. The units are concerned with and presented as speech: the sinners "entice" with their words (1:10) while wisdom "cries out" and "raises her voice" so that the boy might heed her reproof and counsel (1:20-21, 23). The son, in turn, is charged to listen (1:8, 33). His challenge is to learn how to navigate astutely through the competing discourses. His survival depends on the ability to do so.

Exegetical Analysis

A Warning about Hanging Out with the Wrong Crowd (1:8-19)

This unit is the first of many warnings about the dangers of getting involved with the wrong people (1:8-19; see, e.g., 4:14-19; 7:1-27; 22:24-25; 24:1-2). The father presents the son with a choice between two options, two ways of living in the world (cf. 1:15): either the boy may be loyal to his parents and their teaching and over time enjoy the benefits of honor and power, or he may align himself with a gang that seeks to acquire riches quickly by illegal, violent means. The father lays out the alternatives in competing discourses, different (moral) "languages," each vying to define what it means to live wisely and well. He exhorts the youth to heed parental guidance (1:8-9), introduces the "sinners" and quotes their invitation to the youth (1:10-14), and, finally, highlights the irony of the criminals' words. Their own speech reveals and condemns them (1:15-19).

The father opens with an appeal to pay attention to parental teaching (1:8-9). Referring to the youth as "my son" (NRSV: "my child"; 1:8, 10; cf. 1:15), he calls on a ready relationship, an affiliation that associates the boy with him. Echoing the prologue, the father promises discipline (*mûsār*) while the mother offers instruction. The father then compares their words to a fair garland and a necklace—signs of wealth, favor, and power. For example, when Pharaoh designates Joseph his successor, he puts his signet ring on Joseph's finger, clothes him in fine linen, and places a gold chain around his neck (Gen 41:42). King Belshazzar promises that whoever deciphers the mysterious handwriting on the wall shall be adorned in purple and a necklace of gold, and rule as third in the kingdom (Dan 5:7; cf. 5:16, 29). And personified wisdom bestows a fair garland on those whom she favors (4:9).

The father's ethic here, and in Proverbs 1–9 more broadly, legitimates the favored status of the upper class, placing value on material wealth and social esteem as evidence of wisdom's favor. This ethic reminds us immediately that families are not ideologically "innocent." Indeed, when we look more closely, it is likely Proverbs 1–9 was intended for young men of relatively privileged circumstances, perhaps the sons of affluent and moderately wealthy members of an urban commercial class. Note, for example, that the father assumes the youth has ownership of or access to agricultural production (3:9-10) and money (5:10; 6:35). The youth needs guidance about the proper management of that money, including the dodging of get-rich-quick schemes (1:11-19), responsible giving (3:9-10; cf. 3:27-28), and the avoidance of certain financial risks (6:1-5). Further, the father uses money to motivate the youth to choose wisdom. He compares personified wisdom favorably to silver, gold (3:14; 8:10, 19), and costly jewels

(3:15; 8:11). Once acquired, she is a perpetual source of merchant profits and revenues (3:14), riches (3:16b; cf. 8:18, 21a), and filled treasuries (8:21b). Money is thus an objective means to evaluate human worth: economic success is the mark of superior moral character, whereas poverty signifies moral deficiency.

The father immediately distinguishes the parents and their instruction from the gang and its discourse (1:10). He introduces them as "sinners" and cautions that they "entice," a word for persuasion that is rarely, if ever, used positively (e.g., 16:29; 24:28; 2 Sam 3:25; Ps 78:36). The father thereby raises early warning flags for the youth and sets up a sharp dichotomy between "us" (which includes the boy) and "them."

As quoted by the father, the sinners' invitation to the youth offers him camaraderie and the promise of fast, easy money (1:11-14). Their speech suggests that they are a unified group; there is a spirit of solidarity, a sense of belonging to something bigger than oneself. "Come with *us*," they cry. "Let *us* lie in wait. . . . Let *us* wantonly ambush the innocent. . . . Let *us* swallow them alive. . . . *We* shall find all kinds of costly things. . . . *We* shall fill *our* houses. . . . *We* will all have *one purse*." Repetition of the first person plural underscores the group's cohesion, while imagery of all kinds of costly things—houses filled with loot, and a shared purse—suggests that the youth can get more with them, and get it more quickly, than he ever could by his own efforts. Just when the youth is captivated, they say, "Throw in your lot [with] us" (1:14). "Lots" are stones that are cast to get a decision. They were commonly used to determine the division of spoils (e.g., Ps 22:18 [Heb. v. 19]; Nah 3:10). In this sense, the gang's invitation implicitly promises rewards to come. The term "lot" may also refer, however, to a person's fate or destiny (cf. Ps 16:5; Isa 57:6; Dan 12:13). As such, the criminals are saying simultaneously, "Share our fortune!" and, "Be known as one of us!" Should the youth consent (1:10), he becomes a full partner in their criminal pursuits and reaps his share of their successes. With his fate bound to theirs, though, he can never turn them in without also incriminating himself.

When the father "quotes" the criminals' speech, he includes words and phrases that he later uses or alludes to in his admonition to his son (1:15-19). The effect is an ironic one: the sinners' own words reveal and condemn them. The father echoes the language and syntax of the gang's call, "Come/Walk [ḥālak] *with us*" (1:11), to admonish the youth: "Do not walk [ḥālak] on the way *with them*" (1:15 AT). At the center of the father's warning is the proverb: "For in vain [ḥinnām] is the net [spread] while the bird is looking" (1:17). The robbers use the same word, ḥinnām, in their invitation to "ambush the innocent without cause [ḥinnām]" (1:11 AT). With wordplay, the father reminds the boy that the sinners themselves identified their actions as gratuitous and for naught. Indeed, they describe their potential victims as innocent (1:11). Similarly, the father repeats the robbers' phrases "lie in wait for blood" and "lie in wait" (1:18; cf. 1:11) but adds the twist that the sinners set a deadly ambush not for the innocent but for themselves. They wait for their own blood; they lie in wait for their own lives (1:18). They fall into their own trap (Ps 35:4-8). Therefore, the thieves foreshadow their own fate when they compare their voracious greed to the insatiable appetite of Sheol, the underworld, for human lives (1:12; cf. 27:20; 30:16; Isa 5:14; Hab 2:5). Those greedy to gobble up illegal, quick profits find themselves instead swallowed up by an untimely and violent demise (1:19). Their violence is, quite literally, a dead end.

Interpreters puzzle over the meaning of the father's bird proverb (1:17). On the surface, the proverb declares the futility of trying to ensnare a creature when it knows about the trap. An obvious ploy never works. Use of the proverb in this context, however, prompts the question of who or what the bird may represent. Two possibilities are equally compelling: the youth and the thieves. If the youth is the bird (cf. 7:23), then the proverb asserts that the youth should see and avoid the verbal snare prepared right in front of him, especially now that the father has pointed it out. If, however, the bird is a metaphor for the thieves, the proverb furthers the father's diatribe about the gang's stupidity. Despite plotting and spreading out the net themselves, the muggers rush—indeed run (1:16)—to plunge into it. They hurry to destroy themselves. In this case, the bird proverb dramatizes with ironic flourish the proverb "The words of the wicked are a deadly ambush" (12:6a; cf. Ps 10:7-10). Should the son pay attention, he can avoid the snare. The foolish cutthroats will not be so lucky.

The father thus presents the youth with competing voices that offer radically different approaches to life (1:8-19). The first approach is marked by fidelity to parental discipline and promises the rewards of legitimately gained wealth and influence. The second approach is characterized by the lure of belonging and the pledge of quick, illicit gain. That approach, the father contends, is a deadly trap. No fortune, honor, or power comes from that way. The son must decide to whom he will listen.

The Call of Personified Wisdom (1:20-33)

Another competes for the youth's attention: wisdom personified as a woman. Personification is the "attribution of personal form, nature, or characteristics; the representation of a thing or abstraction as a person, particularly as a rhetorical figure or type of metaphor" (Oxford English Dictionary, 11:604). Whereas the personification of wisdom is more detailed than most, the personification of places, things, and abstract qualities is fairly common in the Old Testament, particularly in the poetic literature. Cities and lands, for example, are personified as women—Zion (e.g., Isa 52:1-2; 54:1-8; Jer 4:31; Lam 1:1–2:22); Babylon and Chaldea (e.g., Isa 47:1-15); Samaria and Jerusalem (Ezek 23:1-49). Heavens and earth, mountains and hills, seas and rivers are witnesses (e.g., Deut 32:1; Isa 1:2; Mic 6:1-2). The glory of God is a rear guard (Isa 58:8). Kindness and truth are divine heralds (Ps 89:14 [Heb. v. 15]), justice and peace kiss (Ps 85:10 [Heb. v. 11]), and elsewhere in Proverbs wine is a mocker and strong drink a brawler (20:1).

This, wisdom's self-introduction, is the first of three addresses the father ascribes to her in Proverbs 1–9 (cf. 8:1-36; 9:4-6, 11). As with the criminals' invitation, wisdom's speech takes center stage. She is introduced as one who "cries out . . . raises her voice . . . cries out . . . speaks" (1:20-21). Wisdom exhorts the simple, scoffers, and fools to listen to her counsel and reproof (1:22-23). She warns of the disaster that awaits those who refuse her instruction

(1:24-31), and concludes with a contrast between the fates of complacent, self-confident fools who deny her and the life of security enjoyed by those who listen to her (1:32-33).

In contrast to the thieves, wisdom takes her stand publicly, in the midst of a city (1:20-21; see also 8:1-3). There are town squares (1:20; 5:16; 7:12), bustling corners (1:21; cf. 7:8, 12), and intersections (8:2). Streets (1:20; 7:8, 12), roads (8:2), and pathways (e.g., 1:15; 3:17) crisscross. Houses line the streets (9:14-15). Wisdom, the embodiment of all that is virtuous and valuable, locates herself at those places most symbolic of communal power, authority, and justice ("at the entrance of the city gates," 1:21; cf. Deut 21:19; 25:7; Ruth 4:1-12). She is in plain sight. She is a public persona, a public voice. She stands right in the middle of the hustle and bustle of everyday commerce, civic, and social happenings. And because she speaks from there, no one can claim they do not know her, have not seen her, or somehow missed her call.

Yet the simple, scoffers, and fools refuse to heed her. Wisdom explains why: their affections are badly misplaced (1:22). The "simple" (*pĕtā'yîm*, cf. 1:4) love their simplicity. They cling fondly to the notion that ignorance is bliss. Similarly, "scoffers" (*lēṣîm*) delight in their mocking. Arrogant and contentious, cynical and insolent, they refuse instruction, ridiculing and even striking back at those who try to teach them (cf. 9:7-8a; 13:1; 15:12; 21:24; 22:10). Finally, "fools" (here *kĕsîlîm*) hate knowledge. They prefer to live complacently and carelessly, trusting their misguided wits (e.g., 14:16; 28:26; 29:11). Wisdom's question, "How long?" chastises (e.g., 6:9; Exod 10:3; 1 Sam 16:1; 1 Kgs 18:21; Jer 4:14) those with such imprudent sentiments.

On the offhand chance that the obstinate may yet listen to her, however, wisdom calls out: "turn to [NRSV: 'give heed to'] my reproof" (1:23). "Turn to" is a summons to attention, a call to turn back (literally and/or metaphorically) in the direction from which one came (e.g., Gen 18:33; Deut 20:5-8; Josh 1:15). Wisdom exhorts her listeners to abandon their misdirected affections and return to her reproof and counsel, her words, and her *rûaḥ* (NRSV: "thoughts," 1:23; cf. 1:25, 30), a term used to refer

18

broadly to a person's frame of mind, temperament, or spirit (e.g., 11:13; 14:29; 16:19, 32; 18:14). In short, she offers to "pour out" her discourse and disposition in order to (re)orient theirs.

For those who refuse, wisdom warns, disaster inevitably comes (1:24-27; see Theological and Ethical Analysis of Proverbs 3). Wisdom unleashes a torrent of terms to describe what happens: calamity, panic, distress, and anguish (1:26-27). She compares the disaster to a sudden, violent storm and a whirlwind (cf. 10:25). Moreover, her words, when read in Hebrew, pelt the listener with sharp, staccato sounds (k, b, p, ts). Wisdom whips up a rhetorical tempest to make her point masterfully: one who refuses her call unleashes a deluge of disasters upon oneself. Wisdom does not cause the storm but rather laughs the scoffers' derisive laughter when it overwhelms those who ignore her entreaties. Her unnerving response may perhaps be best understood as a reaction to "the absurdity of those who flaunt reality, who 'spit into the wind' and are puzzled when they get wet. It is also, perhaps, a fierce joy that the goodness of the world order and justice have been vindicated when the wicked reap what they have sown" (Van Leeuwen 1997, 41).

Shifting from second-person to third-person address, wisdom asserts that the simple, scoffers, and fools receive their just reward for hating knowledge, for spurning her counsel and "the fear of the LORD" (1:28-33). Her use of the image of eating and being sated by the fruit of their dispositions and plans conveys an act-consequence worldview (cf. 13:2; 14:14; 18:20-21). That is, persons experience the effects of their actions and choices. They reap what they sow. Just as wisdom once called and they did not listen (1:24), now, on the day of disaster, they will call and she will not answer; they will seek but not find her. Their fates are grim. The turning away (NRSV: "waywardness") of the simple and the fools' complacency destroy them (1:32). In contrast, wisdom concludes, those who "turn back" to her live securely, without anxiety or fear of disaster (cf. 31:11).

Many interpreters point out that personified wisdom's address in 1:20-33 is analogous to a prophetic judgment speech. Like the prophets, wisdom calls to a specific community (1:22), announces judgment against it (1:26-28), and enumerates the reasons the judgment is justified (1:24-25, 29-32). Wisdom's speech, for example, shares striking similarities with those of Jeremiah (esp. chs. 7, 20) and Zechariah 7. Whereas Jeremiah bemoans that everyone "laughs" and "mocks" him (Jer 20:7), wisdom "laughs" and "mocks" those who refuse her counsel (1:26). Just as Jeremiah associates "obeying" YHWH with "dwelling" in the land (7:7; cf. 7:3), so those who "obey" wisdom "dwell" securely (1:33). Moreover, wisdom's complaint that she speaks but the people do not listen, that she calls but the people do not answer, echoes God's complaint (1:24-25; cf. Jer 7:13; 7:24-27; Zech 7:13). Wisdom thus draws on prophetic language to admonish obstinate individuals. Perhaps her discourse would stir up cautionary memories of "stiff-necked" people who found themselves in exile.

Theological and Ethical Analysis

A view dominant since the Romantic period is that maturity is "found" by probing independently and inwardly for the "real me." It involves sweeping away whatever elements we deem not our "true selves," such as family, church, social, and cultural assumptions and expectations, so that we eventually uncover the bedrock of our "authentic selves" and thereby gain autonomy (Booth 1988, 237). From the beginning, Proverbs challenges this notion of maturity. The book introduces the youth (and reader) into a web of present and possible relationships—parents, sinners, personified wisdom, the "strange" woman, God—that together, for good and ill, shape the youth's character. The youth matures in relation; community forms the youth. So the sages would caution us that the very elements we try to sweep away as somehow not "true" self are, in fact, the bedrock of our identities.

Thus the company we keep really matters. Note that the parent and personified wisdom devote considerable energy to cultivating relationships with the young, even as they identify opposition to their efforts. They implore the youth to embrace their "way": to see himself as *like* them and *not like* the others, namely, the sinners, scoffers, and fools. Moreover, they caution the youth to avoid the others altogether because they will corrupt him—make him like *them*—and lead him down the wrong path. At the heart of their efforts is the question, whom do you want to be like? And their implicit understanding is that the young are impressionable, easily tempted to take on every bad habit that comes along, while at the same time capable of virtuous behavior if it is taught and modeled for them. Such thinking continues to prompt parents to move to a "better" neighborhood so their kids will meet "better" friends.

This conception of the human helps us understand Proverbs' emphasis on obedience to authority, a potential stumbling block for those of us in cultures marked by erosion of the same. A vestige of modernity is the elevation of doubt as our most important intellectual activity: we are responsible for building and ordering our own thoughts, so our knowledge is genuine only when we think it out for ourselves. Hence, we tend to suspect whatever is "authoritative," whether person, tradition, or institution. In contrast, the sages extol the role of authority, particularly authoritative instruction. Indeed, as the parent portrays it, the youths must *first* commit their allegiance to authority figures (e.g., parents, personified wisdom) and *then* persevere in a search, the goal and benefits of which they do not yet fully comprehend (see Prov 2). This can be bewildering for those of us trained to listen and then, and only then, if we like what we hear, commit. At the same time, it invites us to reflect on how we understand the responsibility of each generation to guide and accompany the next.

The sages' understanding of the human also sheds light on the parent's use of the term "sinners." Sin in Proverbs is not an innate characteristic of all humans but a descriptor for abandoning the path forged by God and the community. As the Hebrew term connotes, sinners "miss the mark"—and in this case brutally so. The youth must decide whether or not to join them ("do not consent," 1:10b). We dare not downplay the gravity of that decision, as some interpreters have, by construing the parent's depiction of the threat as exaggerated or extreme. Although street-gang violence may seem remote to some readers (though perhaps to fewer than even a decade ago), R. C. Van Leeuwen rightly observes that the parent, who we ought to remember is likely affluent, calls attention to the pervasive and invasive power of violence. The parent knows that *anyone*, including his own children, may be "enticed" to cross the line—as individuals and as members of institutions, communities, and larger systems. The parent regards the threat as proximate and anticipates that the youth will face it more than once (e.g., 2:12-15; 3:31; 4:14-16). So, whereas the parent may have had in mind particular "gangs" of the early Persian period, his graphic warning resonates readily—and widely—today (Van Leeuwen 1997, 38).

Finally, it is striking that chapter 1 and Proverbs as a whole abounds with language about emotions: greed (1:19), love and delight (1:22), hate (1:22, 29, 30), terror, distress, and anguish (1:26-27, 33). Furthermore, this emotional language often occurs in contexts that refer to bodily appetites (1:31; e.g., 5:15; 6:30; 9:5) and desires (e.g., for companionship and quick profits, 1:10-19; for sex, 6:25), phenomena that, while often considered distinct from emotions, have been grouped and analyzed with them since Aristotle. The nature and extent of this language suggest the sages engage the emotions as forms of perception and judgment, advocating certain patterns of emotions, which they deem may be taught, as characteristic of mature and flourishing lives. So Proverbs encourages emotions directed "rightly," such as love of wisdom or "the fear of the LORD," and discourages affections directed "wrongly," such as delight in scoffing and hatred of knowledge (1:7, 22, 29). Emotions are taken seriously as another way the young learn to map the world and themselves in it (Nussbaum 2001, 206-7).

Thus the sages advocate a holistic understanding of the human. Absent is the crisp, modern, Western distinction between the rational and the emotional (see excursus in Proverbs 2) that engenders an educational system devoted largely to the former. The attention to emotions in Proverbs suggests, as M. V. Fox writes, that "more is required than sententious warnings and somber maxims or even a logical demonstration of cause and effect, for by themselves these are abstract and lack rooting" in people's experiences (2000, 349). It is not enough to proclaim but not evoke; to teach but not enable affective participation; to appeal to the intellect and not care for the body. Proverbs reminds us that the formation of moral, faithful individuals and communities urgently depends on our capacities to engage human pathos and to cultivate people of passions—people captivated by beauty and goodness, disgusted by wickedness, and devoted fiercely to God, wisdom, and the welfare of others.

PROVERBS 2

Literary Analysis

This chapter describes the search for wisdom as a collaborative effort between humans and God. Parents have responsibility to teach (2:1). The young must be ardently receptive (2:1-4). And God grants wisdom and protects its recipients (2:6-8). As the father presents it, the endeavor has an encouraging certainty about it: *if* the youth seeks wisdom, *then* God will grant it to him.

Structured as one long conditional sentence of twenty-two lines, the number of consonants in the Hebrew alphabet (cf. 31:10-31), the chapter has four main movements: a protasis ("if you," 2:1-4), an apodosis ("then," 2:5-11), a description of wisdom's protection ("to save you," 2:12-19), and a purpose clause ("so that," 2:20-22). The protasis specifies in three phrases what the search for wisdom requires (2:1, 3-4). Should the youth commit to the search, the apodosis promises results—he will gain understanding (2:5-11). Two parallel units (2:5-8, 9-11), each of which begins with the phrase "then you will understand" (2:5, 9) and includes an explanation ("because," 2:6-8; 10-11), then characterize the nature of that understanding.

As a result, wisdom saves the youth from the wicked (2:12-19). Two units that open with the infinitive of purpose "to save you" (2:12, 16) depict the parallel evils of "wicked men" (2:12-15) and the "strange" woman (2:16-19). The chapter concludes with a purpose clause ("so that . . . ," 2:20; NRSV: "therefore") followed by a motivating promise and warning (2:21-22).

Exegetical Analysis

If You Seek Wisdom (2:1-4)

The youth has to commit to the search for wisdom *before* he can attain it. Allegiance precedes understanding (Newsom 1989, 147). The father offers his "words" (2:1a) and, as the parallel term "commandments" suggests (2:1b; cf. 3:1; 4:4; 6:20; 7:1-2), those words are authoritative: "commandments" are made by God (e.g., Num 15:39; Deut 4:2; 1 Kgs 18:18) and by persons of power and status, such as kings (e.g., 2 Kgs 18:36; Neh 11:23; Esth 3:3) and leaders (e.g., Moses in Josh 22:5; 2 Chr 8:13). The youth, in turn, is charged to accept and treasure up the words as he would precious valuables (2:1). He begins by listening and "inclining [his] heart" (2:2) to all wisdom, including that of his father. It is a matter of attitude. To "incline the heart" is to make a choice, to commit to something (e.g. Judg 9:3; 1 Kgs 11:2-4; Ps 119:36). The youth has to choose to accept his father's guidance.

The youth must also act. The father urges him to call out for wisdom (2:3), to seek her as he would silver and hidden treasures (2:4; cf. 3:14-15; 8:10-11, 18-19). Job describes the exceptional focus and persistence involved in the search for silver and other precious metals:

> Miners . . . search out to the farthest bound
>   the ore in gloom and deep darkness.
> They open shafts in a valley away from human habitation;
>   they are forgotten by travelers,
>   they sway suspended, remote from people. . . .
> They put their hand to the flinty rock,
>   and overturn mountains by the roots.
> They cut out channels in the rocks,
>   and their eyes see every precious thing.
> The sources of the rivers they probe;
>   hidden things they bring to light. (Job 28:3-4, 9-11)

Whereas Job contends that mortals, even with such skill, do not know and cannot find the way to wisdom (28:12-28), the father envisions the search for wisdom as such a treasure hunt—a quest demanding tenacity.

The father hints that seekers of wisdom do well to imitate wisdom herself. Recalling elements of her self-introduction (1:20-33), he urges the youth to pursue wisdom as eagerly as she summons him. As wisdom "stretches out" her hand to the "attentive" (1:24), so the son is to make his ear "attentive" and "stretch out" (NRSV: "incline") his heart to wisdom (2:2). As wisdom "cries out" (1:21, 24) and "lifts her voice" (1:20) to those who will listen, so the youth is to "cry out" and "lift [his] voice" (2:3) to beckon her.

Excursus on "the Heart"

Translation of the Hebrew term *lēb* (2:2, also *lēbāb*, cf. 4:21; 6:25) as "heart" can be misleading. At times, as in English, the term means the physical organ in a person's chest (e.g., 2 Sam 18:14; 2 Kgs 9:24). In other instances, however, *lēb* refers metaphorically to the inner self, the locus of thoughts and feelings. This contrasts sharply with the modern, Western distinction between the "head" as the source of cognition and the "heart" as the wellspring of emotions. Hebrew *lēb* encompasses both. The *lēb* is the seat of understanding, reason, and imagination (e.g., Exod 9:14; 1 Kgs 3:9; Ezek 13:2). It is the conscience (1 Sam 25:31; 2 Sam 24:10). It is the font of emotions (e.g., Exod 4:14; Judg 16:25; Isa 35:4), determination, and courage (e.g., Gen 42:28; 1 Sam 17:32; 2 Sam 17:10). Accordingly, *lēb* is translated variously depending on context, most commonly in the NRSV as either "heart" (e.g., 2:2, 10) or "mind" (e.g., 16:1, 9; 17:16).

The "heart" figures prominently in Proverbs. Wisdom is said to enter the heart (2:10; cf. 23:15), and there all wise teaching is kept (e.g., 3:1; 4:4; 6:21). The heart perceives and learns (e.g., 16:21; 17:16), plans (e.g., 16:1, 9), and emotes (e.g., 5:12; 12:25; 13:12; 14:10, 13; 15:13, 15). The heart also gives rise to speech (e.g., 16:23; 23:33; cf. Job 8:10). Intricate and mysterious—with purposes like deep water (20:5) and weight known only to God (e.g., 21:2; 24:12)—the heart, like the mysterious cosmos, is known by God, and God refines it (15:11; 17:3). No wonder the father admonishes the youth to guard his heart with all vigilance (4:23). Not to do so is to risk becoming a fool—literally, a person who "lacks heart" (e.g., 6:32; 7:7; 9:4; 10:21; NRSV: "without sense").

Then You Will Understand (2:5-11)

The father promises that the search will generate understanding that orients the youth rightly with God and the community (2:5, 9). First, the youth will know "the fear of the LORD," that is, reverence for God that is the foundation and epitome of wisdom and motivates just and generous acts (see excursus in Proverbs 1). Second, he will find "the knowledge of God" (2:5). Although knowing God is a significant concept in the Old Testament, the exact phrase "the knowledge of God" occurs only here and in Hosea (4:1; 6:6). In Hosea, "knowledge of God" is parallel to human faithfulness, loyalty (Hos 4:1), and steadfast love (Hos 6:6). For Hosea, "knowledge of God" is manifest in moral societies; it is absent when "swearing, lying, and murder, and stealing and adultery break out; bloodshed follows bloodshed" (4:2; cf. 6:7-9). Other prophets concur. Jeremiah, for example, praises Josiah for doing justice and righteousness, for judging the cause of the poor and needy, saying "Is not this to know [God]?" (Jer 22:16); and Isaiah distinguishes nations that know God's ways by their practice of righteousness and obedience to divine ordinances (Isa 58:2). Intimately associated with "fear of the LORD" (e.g., 2:5, 9:10), "knowledge of God" is thus an appreciation for God's purposes and ways and a commitment to act accordingly. Finally, the youth will understand the patterns of behavior essential to a just, common life: "righteousness and justice and equity" (2:9; cf. 1:3). Juxtaposition of the three words with "every good path" (2:9b) suggests that although they define moral conduct, there are various ways to practice it (2:10-11).

The seeker of wisdom gains understanding because God acts (2:6-8). The Hebrew emphasizes this by moving the subject before the verb: YHWH gives wisdom (2:6a). For all the youth's efforts, he cannot attain wisdom on his own. Wisdom is divine gift. As

God's mouth declares what is sure (e.g., Isa 1:20; 40:5; 45:23), exhales the life-breath (Ps 33:6), and speaks the sustaining word (Deut 8:3), so God's mouth gives the human knowledge and understanding (2:6b; cf. Job 32:8). God alone is wisdom's source. This assertion is not unique to Proverbs, of course. Ecclesiastes observes: "To the one who pleases [God] God gives wisdom and knowledge and joy" (Eccl 2:26; cf. Isa 11:2). God grants a discerning heart to Solomon (1 Kgs 3:12; 2 Chr 1:10-12) and wisdom (NRSV: "skill") to the artisans of the tabernacle (Exod 31:6; 36:1-2).

Attaining wisdom is about more than learning the rules. It is a transformation of the self, a reorientation of the heart (2:10). The father speaks of such a transformation here in individual terms. Elsewhere, God is said to transform the heart of the community. In Ezekiel, for example, God restores Israel by replacing their "heart of stone" with a "heart of flesh" so that they might follow divine ordinances (Ezek 11:19; cf. 36:26). Similarly, in Jeremiah, God covenants to inscribe the law on the hearts of Israel so that everyone will know God without instruction or reminder (Jer 31:31-34). The New Testament echoes this language of transformation when it describes new life in Christ as a renewing of the mind that enables one to discern the will of God (Rom 12:2). Because God pours God's love into the human heart—indeed, because Christ dwells there (Gal 4:6; Eph 3:17)—believers are reconciled to God and have hope in a world of suffering (Rom 5:1-5). So Paul writes to the Ephesians:

> I pray that . . . God . . . may give you a spirit of wisdom and revelation . . . so that, with the eyes of your heart enlightened, you may know what is the hope to which [God] has called you, what are the riches of [God's] glorious inheritance among the saints, and what is the immeasurable greatness of [God's] power for us who believe, according to the working of [God's] great power. (1:17-19; cf. 2 Cor 4:6, 16)

Inherent in wisdom is a promise of divine protection. God stores up "sound wisdom," the capacity to act with good sense, confidence, resourcefulness, and resilience (2:7; cf. 3:21). God puts aside, even hides away, an abundant supply because good sense is a shield for the upright (2:7b; NRSV erroneously identifies the shield with God). Similarly, discretion (cf. 1:4) and understanding will stand guard over the youth (2:11). The father thereby pledges that *if* the youth seeks wisdom (2:1-4), *then* God will grant it, and God and wisdom will protect him along the right paths (2:5-11).

Excursus on "the Path(s)"

Proverbs 2 contains twelve references to "path(s)" or "way(s)" (2:8 [2x], 9, 12, 13 [2x], 15 [2x], 18, 19, 20 [2x]). Common in Proverbs 1–9 (e.g., 3:6, 17, 23; 4:11, 14, 19, 26; 8:2, 13, 22, 32) and the book as a whole (e.g., 10:17; 12:28; 15:9-10; 16:2), the metaphor occurs occasionally elsewhere in Old Testament Wisdom literature (e.g., Job 22:15; 23:10-11). Egyptian wisdom also taught about the "way" (specifically, "the way of life"); for example, the *Instruction of Amenemope* aims "to direct [the reader] on the paths of life" (*AEL* 2:148; cf. *AEL* 2:156).

The sages use "path" as a metaphor for a pattern of behavior, a person's approach to life. The evident concern is not only where one is but where one is going. The metaphor is suggestive. First, whatever their starting point, people choose a path; our lives have direction. Second, taking that path entails movement. Every step advances or hinders movement ahead; we constantly progress or digress from our destination. Third, paths are carved out and worn down by many people over time: most, if not all, of the hazards are eventually removed, the debris cleared, and trail markers set in place to prevent confusion. As such, when we choose a path we implicitly trust those who have walked it before us. We rely on the tradition of "going this way." And because a path is public, we are likely to encounter other travelers. Fourth, a path directs movement but does not control it. We decide with each step whether to stay on a path. At the same time, after we start down a path, it is easier to stay on it than to find a different path or blaze a new trail altogether. Finally, a path does not necessarily reach its destination in the most direct way. It may wind, twist, or backtrack for the sake of progress. Stretches of seeming

28

idleness and regression may in fact be vital for renewed forward movement.

In Proverbs, the sages speak about two paths and multiple paths. The two paths are, broadly, those that lead to life and to death. The way of life is the bright, straight, level highway associated with discipline, wisdom, justice, and uprightness (e.g., 2:8, 13, 19-20; 4:11, 18; 6:23; 8:20; 9:6; 15:19). The way of death is dark, crooked, and riddled with obstacles; it is marked by wickedness, arrogance, and distorted speech (e.g., 2:13, 15; 4:19; 8:13; 15:19; 22:5). The dichotomy of the two paths is mirrored in the two basic types of people who travel them: the wise and just take the path of life, while the wicked, foolish, and lazy tread the way of death. If we imagine that there are only two possible destinations in the world—two absolutes—then the multiple paths are various and relative ways of traveling to them (e.g., interstates, back roads). A person may take one of the multiple paths (e.g., 3:6, 17; 4:26-27; 5:21; 8:20, 32) and still be considered en route on one of the two.

The Wicked Men and the Strange Woman (2:12-19)

In two parallel units that begin with the phrase "to save you from" (2:12, 16), the father elaborates on the protection wisdom affords: wisdom will save the youth from the "way of wickedness," specifically the perils of the "wicked men" (2:12-15) and the "strange" woman (2:16-19). The father presents these figures as equally threatening and describes them with the same general characteristics. They distort their speech (2:12, 16), they abandon honorable commitments (2:13, 17), and their paths are crooked and perilous (2:13, 15, 18). These qualities distinguish the wicked generally. Indeed, insofar as the father speaks of male and female, plural and singular, it is likely that the "wicked men" and the "strange" woman represent all wicked people.

The father's description of the "wicked men" (2:12-15) recalls his warning about the "sinners" (1:10-19) but with much less detail. Everything about the wicked men is corrupt. They speak "perversely," sowing discord and stirring up trouble (2:12b; e.g., 6:14; 16:28). They abandon paths of honesty for ways of darkness

(2:13a; cf. 4:18-19), a realm of anguish and alienation from God (e.g., Job 15:20-30; Ps 88:4-5; 107:10-11). Their paths twist and wander (2:15; NRSV: "who are devious in their ways"; cf. 22:5; 28:6); they are on the wrong track (cf. 3:31-32; 14:2). Finally, their affections are misdirected. Like the naive and the scoffers who delight in their misconduct (1:22), the wicked rejoice in doing wicked things, even in evil itself (2:14).

Wisdom also saves the youth from the "strange" woman (2:16-19). This is the first of five times in Proverbs 1–9 that the youth meets her (5:1-23; 6:20-35; 7:1-27; 9:13-18; cf. 22:14; 23:27). The father introduces her with two key terms (2:16). The first is zārâ (NRSV: "loose"), a word that elsewhere in the Old Testament designates "outsiders," people not of one's family (e.g., Deut 25:5), tribe (e.g., Num 1:51; 18:4, 7), or community (i.e., "foreigners," e.g., Isa 1:7; Hos 7:8-9). These "strangers" are often considered enemies (e.g., Isa 29:5; Jer 30:8), illegitimate (e.g., Hos 5:7), or forbidden (e.g., Jer 2:25). The second term is nokrîyyâ. Contrary to the NRSV translation ("adulteress"), the term most commonly denotes a "foreigner," usually a non-Israelite (e.g., Deut 17:15; Judg 19:12; 1 Kgs 8:41) but at times anyone outside a person's family (e.g., Gen 31:15); it may also refer figuratively to someone one knew formerly (e.g., Job 19:15). With zārâ and nokrîyyâ the father identifies the woman as "other" without specifying exactly what makes her so (just as he introduces vaguely the parallel male threat as "the way of evil," 2:12). She is "strange"— someone "outside" socially accepted categories, whether ethnic, legal, social, or sexual. Her ambiguous identity suggests that she represents such women generally, just as the "wicked men" represent male evildoers broadly.

Like the "wicked men," everything about the "strange" woman is awry. Her speech is "smooth" (2:16; cf. 5:3; 6:24; 7:21), that is, at once pleasurable and dangerous. "Smooth words" are slippery and deceitful, flattering but false (cf. 26:23, 28; Ps 12:2; Isa 30:10; Dan 11:32). She abandons the 'allûp nĕ'ûrêhā (2:17a; NRSV: "the partner of her youth"). The phrase 'allûp nĕ'ûrêhā may be interpreted two ways. The first and most common proposal is that the 'allûp, which typically means "close friend" (cf. 16:28; 17:9), refers to the "strange" woman's husband (cf. Mic 7:5), and the parallel phrase, "the covenant of her God" (2:17b; NRSV: "her sacred covenant"), refers to her marriage agreement. Thus the "strange" woman is an adulteress (so NRSV, 2:16b). Interpreters compare 2:17 to Malachi's rebuke of Israelite men for divorcing their wives to marry foreign women: "YHWH was a witness between you and the wife of your youth, to whom you have been faithless, though she is your companion and your wife by covenant" (Mal 2:14). The covenant is God's because God serves as its witness. God ensures and protects its integrity. Interpreted this way, 2:17 indicates that the "strange" woman is unfaithful to her husband, an aspect of her character developed more fully later in Proverbs 1–9 (esp. Prov 7). Her ethnicity, however, cannot be determined: she could be an Israelite or a foreign woman married to an Israelite man (e.g., Ruth; cf. Ruth 1:16: "Your God [will be] my God").

The second possibility is that the 'allûp is God and "the covenant of [her] God" refers to divine law, as it does nearly everywhere else in the Old Testament (e.g., Deut 31:26; Josh 3:3; 2 Sam 15:24). The phrase 'allûp nĕ'ûrîm ("companion of youth") occurs only once elsewhere in the Old Testament—in Jer 3:4, where the referent is God. Notably, Jeremiah is portraying God as the husband of Israel in that context, a motif fairly common among the prophets (3:1-5; e.g., Isa 54:1-8; Ezek 16; Hos 2:16-20 [Heb. vv. 18-22]). Marriage can be a metaphor for covenant fidelity. The father may play on this motif with 2:17, signaling at once the "strange" woman's adultery (specifically) and utter law-lessness (generally). Those who abandon God—"the companion of [their] youth"—reject God's authority and commandments (e.g., Judg 2:12; 1 Kgs 9:9; 2 Kgs 21:22). As Jeremiah describes it, they are wanton and lustful, without fear of God:

Your wickedness will punish you,
  and your apostasies will [rebuke] you.
Know and see that it is evil and bitter
  for you to [abandon] the LORD your God;
  the fear of me is not in you, says the Lord GOD of hosts.
  (2:19; cf. 2:24; 22:1-10)

Likewise those who forget "the covenant of [their] God" (2:17b) are stubborn and rebellious, preferring lives of deceit, murder, theft, adultery, and violence (Hos 4:2; cf. Deut 4:23; Ps 78). Interpreted this way, 2:17 identifies the "strange" woman as completely irreverent and immoral. This reading is consistent with the concern about wickedness generally in 2:12-19. Note that the parallel charge about the wicked men is similarly broad: they abandon "paths of uprightness" (2:13; cf. 4:11; 14:2).

Finally, the "strange" woman treads a deadly path. Her house (NRSV: "her way") sinks to the "shades," the spirits of the dead who inhabit Sheol, the underworld (2:18). Like many ancients, the Israelites believed the underworld to be the gated, dark, silent, and dusty place where people descend after death (e.g., Num 16:30; Job 17:13-16; Ps 31:17-18; Isa 5:14; 38:10). Imprisoned there, the shades pass their days in a sort of reclined stupor, stirring only to welcome new arrivals (e.g., 9:18; 21:16; Ps 88:11-12; Isa 14:9-10, 19; 26:14). Escape is impossible: "[Whoever goes] down to Sheol [does] not come up" (Job 7:9; cf. Isa 38:11). Such is the fate of those who "go to" the "strange" woman (2:19), an expression that may be interpreted literally and as a euphemism for sexual intercourse (e.g., Gen 16:2; 38:8; 2 Sam 16:21). Those who go to her never come back.

So That You May Live Long and Well (2:20-22)

What the NRSV translates as a closing exhortation, "Therefore walk" (2:20), is more accurately read as a purpose clause ("*so that* you will walk"). The chapter's flow of logic, then, is this: *if* you seek wisdom eagerly, *then* you will understand "the fear of the LORD," "the knowledge of God," and "every good path," which will *save you* from wicked men and women, *so that* you may walk in the ways of the good and just. The saying that follows (2:21-22; cf. 10:30) reaffirms the dichotomy between the upright and the wicked by pointing out the status of each vis-à-vis the land. The phrase "the land" (2:21) may denote a specific geographical area (e.g., the promised land in Deut 4:10; 5:33; 16:20), the whole world (Isa 18:3), or some unspecified region (e.g., 10:30); it may also refer metaphorically to "this world," namely, the land of the living (e.g., Ps 37:8-11). The ambiguity of "the land" invites the youth to make a number of connections, all of which bode very well for the security and longevity of those who are upright. In contrast, the wicked are cut off and torn away (2:22; NRSV: "rooted out").

The association of land tenure with separation from the "stranger" (also "outsider" or "foreigner") evokes the conflict over land tenure that arose in the Persian period (when Prov 1–9 was likely shaped, see Introduction to this book) between the returning exiles and the "people(s) of the land" (ethnic nondeported Judeans and neighboring ethnic foreigners) they found inhabiting the land. After the Babylonian deportation, poorer Judeans who were left behind (2 Kgs 25:12; Jer 52:16) took possession of many of the exiles' landholdings (Jer 39:10), properties that had been passed down in families for generations. They justified their new ownership on the grounds that the deportees had been expelled from the community and thereby forfeited any claim to property (Ezek 11:15). When the exiles returned and found their land expropriated, struggles over land tenure ensued.

The returnees saw repossession of the land as their right, ideologically and legally. Because God's judgment on them was devastation of the land and exile, God's restoration of them was their return and recovery of the land: a new exodus and conquest (e.g., Ezra 9:10-11; Jer 32:42-44; Ezek 33:23-29; 36: 8-12). Opposition to this restoration by the heterogeneous mix of "people(s) of the land" fueled sharp divisions within the community. By the time of Ezra and Nehemiah, that division was a chasm. Ezra denounced the "people(s) of the land" and urged the returnees to separate from them (Ezra 9-10; Neh 10:20-31). Drawing on the exodus tradition, Ezra declared: "Never seek their peace or [well-being], so that you may be strong and eat the good of the land and leave it for an inheritance to your children forever" (9:12b; cf. Deut 7:1-6). Of specific concern for Ezra and Nehemiah in this conflict over land and legitimacy was the intermarriage between returnees and "strange" women (cf. also 5:1-14).

Theological and Ethical Analysis

We talk about the "pursuit of truth." The notion is that if we keep after truth, our efforts move us ever closer to it until, one day, we find it. Truth is "out there," so to speak; we need only endeavor to grasp it. Whereas the parent of Proverbs 1–9 would agree that truth—here wisdom—is initially beyond the self (e.g., 2:6, 10), he would disagree that we can attain it on our own. For the parent, the attainment of wisdom is a convergence of human effort and divine gift. Seekers of wisdom do their part through discipline, receptivity, deliberation, and inquiry (2:1-4) but, in the end, neither determination nor talent guarantees knowledge. God, the bearer of wisdom, grants it (2:5-11). In effect, the search for wisdom is a search for God. Proverbs thus encourages us to take responsibility for our learning and, at the same time, rejects any arrogance and relieves any anxiety that what we learn is solely our doing. Ultimately, it is God's generosity, not human striving, that bridges the gap between humans and wisdom. We pursue wisdom. Wisdom finds us.

The chapter immediately and repeatedly associates wisdom with protection and security (e.g., 2:7b-8, 11-19). The implied context is one of instability and uncertainty, a situation rife with dangers from which the parent, by means of instruction and discipline, hopes to "save" the youth (2:12, 16). In the early Persian period, when Proverbs was likely finally compiled, Judah was such a context. As the community worked to rebuild itself as a small colony on the edge of a vast empire, it faced internal and external conflicts, economic volatility, physical vulnerability, and struggles over identity within a pluralism of cultures. That the parent of Proverbs 1–9 would seek recourse in the (re)affirmation and inculcation of the community's wisdom is not surprising. Didactic material like Proverbs "appeals to the need for certainty, stability, and unity . . . it affirms absolute truths, absolute values" (Suleiman 1993, 10). It conveys the "building blocks" of a culture—its core commitments and convictions—and thereby affords a sense of order amid disorder. Perhaps that is why people share proverbs during periods of trauma and disorientation, for example, during wakes in the West Indies (Davis 2000, 13), and why some communities, such as the Akan in West Africa, regard knowledge and right use of proverbs as essential for good leadership.

The parent in this chapter continues to define danger primarily in terms of other people—here the "wicked." By doing so, the parent dramatizes communal boundaries; he teaches who we *are* by pointing to who we *are not*, a move that also fosters communal solidarity and accountability. The wicked in this chapter are little more than stock figures whose general "crookedness" in speech, life direction, and so on signals the existence of disorder, and also the possibility that people can dance along the edges or step outside the moral and theological worldview the parent advocates—but to certain peril. The parent's claim is categorical: *this* wisdom roots and protects us in the land, in God's promise, in life itself, indeed in reality, while *that* wickedness, that contorted, chaotic worldview cuts us off from all of it (2:21-22). The wicked have no place. They are expelled. Note, however, that the parent does not say how or by whom. Subsequent chapters develop more fully the anchoring of wisdom in the fabric of reality (e.g., Prov 3, 8) and the respective fates of the righteous and wicked.

Readers may find the parent's categorical language unsettling. Many of us hesitate to invoke such broad, polarizing terms (e.g., "evildoers," "upright") to describe people. Perhaps our reticence has something to do with our inclination, in a culture shaped by individualism and notions about human rights, to distinguish between the quality of people's actions or values and the quality of their personhood. Perhaps we are also keenly aware that categorical—indeed, stereotypical—labels of individuals and groups dehumanize them, too often prove wrongheaded, and provoke considerable harm, violence, and at times death. That said, the parent's use of categorical language invites us to think carefully about when we, individually or communally, reach for such terms and find it difficult to separate the quality of a person from his or her behaviors and beliefs. At times, it may be a matter of survival, as when we counsel young children never to talk to strangers. At

others, however, it exposes our ignorance or misunderstanding—
even our hate.

PROVERBS 3

Literary Analysis

This chapter masterfully weaves together the topics of wisdom,
piety, and human relationships. It opens with six two-verse commands (3:1-2, 3-4, 5-6, 7-8, 9-10, 11-12), five of which are negative (all but 3:9-10). Each includes a motivational clause (3:2, 4,
6b, 8, 10, 12). The first two commands summon the youth to
embrace parental instruction (3:1-4). The remaining four urge
obedience to God (3:5-12; the divine name occurs five times). The
unit is framed by two commands that begin "my son, do not"
(3:1-2, 12 NIV).

A tribute to personified wisdom follows (3:13-18). Framed by
the word "happy" (or "blessed," 3:13, 18), it heralds the value of
wisdom by pointing to the prosperity and well-being of those who
find her. Such a teaching strategy is common. "Happy" proverbs,
also called beatitudes, occur elsewhere in the book (8:32, 34;
14:21; 16:20; 20:7; 28:14; 29:18), in the Psalms (e.g., 1:1; 2:12;
32:1-2; 33:12; 112:1), and in the New Testament (e.g., Matt 5:3-
12; Luke 6:20-22).

At 3:19, the object of praise shifts suddenly from personified
wisdom to God. The father signals the shift by inverting the
expected Hebrew word order (verb-subject) so that YHWH, the
subject, is first. Wisdom, in turn, becomes an instrument or agent
with which God created the world ("*by* wisdom"). Reference to
wisdom and two of its synonyms—understanding and knowledge—in so brief a unit (3:19-20) highlights wisdom's cosmologi-
cal significance.

The final unit of the chapter (3:21-35) has three sections. The
first charges the youth to keep good sense and discretion and
extols their benefits (3:21-26). The second is a series of negative
commands about how to treat others (3:27-31). The third motivates that conduct by contrasting God's devotion and generosity

to the upright with divine disgust and punishment of the wicked (3:32-35).

Exegetical Analysis

Trust and Honor God (3:1-12)

The chapter opens with another exordium (3:1-2; cf. 1:8-9; 2:1-2; 6:20; 7:2). As God and wisdom guard the upright (2:8, 11), the father urges the youth to guard (NRSV: "keep") parental commandments (3:1b; cf. 2:1; 6:20-23). Doing so brings long life and prosperity (3:2a; cf. 3:16; 4:10; 9:11).

Interpreters debate two matters with regard to 3:3. The first is whether one of the three lines (instead of the expected two) was not part of the text originally. Many argue that the first syntactically awkward line (3:3a) is a later addition. They note that in 6:20-21 and 7:1-3, which are similar to 3:1-3, what is tied around the neck and written on the heart is parental instruction; thus "them" in 3:3bc would refer back to the father's teachings and commandments (3:1) not to "loyalty and faithfulness" (3:3a). Verse 3a, that is, interrupts the flow of 3:1-3bc. Other interpreters contend that the third line (3:3c) was added later on the basis of the parallel in 7:1-3. To support this claim they point to the absence of 3:3c in some significant ancient Greek manuscripts of the Septuagint (LXX). Given the mixed evidence, the debate is not resolved easily.

With the text as it stands, the second matter is how to interpret 3:3a. The word pair "loyalty and faithfulness" (cf. 14:22; 16:6; 20:28) is a common expression for a gracious and trustworthy manner of relating to others. Both people (e.g., Gen 24:49; 47:29; Josh 2:14) and God (e.g., Gen 32:10; Exod 34:6; Pss 86:15; 117:2; 138:2) are known to demonstrate it. As such, one reading of 3:3a ascribes "loyalty and faithfulness" to the youth—he should be steadfast and honorable. A second and more compelling reading attributes "loyalty and faithfulness" to God. This makes better sense of the verb ("do not *let* [abandon] you"); if "loyalty and faithfulness" are the youth's virtues, we would expect instead "do not abandon." Moreover, concern that God's graciousness may forsake a person occurs elsewhere (e.g., Gen 24:27; Ruth 2:20). Verse 3:3a thus elaborates on 3:2. The benefits of parental instruction (3:1-2) are possible because of God's "loyalty and faithfulness" (3:3a).

With reference to a necklace and "the tablet of the heart," the father urges the youth to embody wisdom (3:3bc). Outwardly, the youth is to wear (figuratively? literally?) parental instruction tied around his neck (3:3b; cf. 1:9; 6:21). Adornments (e.g., necklaces, rings, frontlets) symbolizing what is to be remembered and cherished are found elsewhere in Proverbs (e.g., 6:21; 7:3) and in the Old Testament. Moses, for example, tells the people to "Bind [God's commandments] as a sign on your hand, [let] them [be] as [a symbol] on your forehead" (Deut 6:8; cf. 11:18). Moses also declares that the consecration of the firstborn serves figuratively "as a sign on your hand [and] an emblem on your forehead" that God brought the people out of Egypt (Exod 13:9). Such ornaments on the body are, in effect, mnemonic devices that keep what they symbolize physically at hand.

Inwardly, the youth is to write the teachings on "the tablet of [his] heart" (3:3c; cf. 7:3; Jer 17:1). To inscribe something on a tablet ensures its clarity and permanence (e.g., Exod 34:1, 28; Deut 10:1-5; Isa 30:8; Hab 2:2). To write on the heart is to make an indelible mark on the center of one's being, to etch the instruction onto the innermost parts of oneself (cf. 2:1-4)—to know (probably memorize) wisdom teaching so well it becomes innate. Hence God declares: "I will put my law within them, and I will write it on their hearts. . . . No longer shall they teach one another, or say to each other 'Know the LORD,' for they shall all know me" (Jer 31:33-34a). With parental teachings encircling the youth's neck and incised on his heart, there is no dissonance between the external appearances and internal commitments—a consistency of character that is honored by God and humanity (3:4; compare the theme of exteriority and interiority in the book of Job, e.g., 1:5; 2:10).

With two parallel commands (3:5-6, 7-8), the father implores the youth to trust God rather than the youth's own insight. The youth is to trust God completely ("with all your heart," 3:5). Trust in God dispels fear, inspires happiness, and enables patience (e.g., 16:20; 28:25; 29:25; Pss 28:7; 32:10; 37:3; 40:4; 84:12; 112:7). The patience is not idle, however. The psalmist, for example, exhorts us to "trust in YHWH and do good" (37:3). Elsewhere, Hezekiah is said to trust in God as he institutes religious reforms, observes the commandments, and even wages war (2 Kgs 18:1-8). Should the youth put his confidence in God, the father promises, God will "make straight [his] paths" (3:6b; cf. Isa 45:13), a phrase that evokes God's remolding creation—elevating valleys, hewing down mountains, and leveling uneven ground—so that God's people might safely journey home (Isa 40:3-4).

Picking up the image of the path (3:6b), the second command (3:7-8) urges the youth to "turn . . . away" from wickedness, a hallmark of wisdom (4:27; 13:19; 14:16; 16:6, 17; cf. Job 28:28). Blameless and upright Job is introduced repeatedly as "one who fears God and turns away from evil" (Job 1:1, 8; 2:3). To turn from evil is "a drink for your bones" (NRSV: "refreshment for your body," 3:8b). Bones, perhaps because they comprise the human frame, may represent the whole person. Moist bones are a source and indication of vitality (Job 21:23-24; Isa 58:11). Conversely, dry bones signify hopelessness and despair (17:22; Ezek 37:1-14).

Both commands urge the youth never to rely solely on his wits (3:5-6, 7-8). Just as Proverbs 2 asserts that God gives wisdom and wisdom enters one's heart (2:6, 10), 3:5-8 emphasize that wisdom does not originate with the self. Rather, God is the source of human insight (3:5, 7). The beginning and epitome of wisdom is "fear of the LORD," recognition of God's authority in all things and humanity's potential and limitations as part of God's creation. Humility, not hubris, is a hallmark of wisdom (e.g., 11:2; 15:33; 22:4; 26:12; 28:11, 26; cf. Jer 9:23-24).

The father next instructs the youth to put his money where his heart is, to demonstrate his devotion to God by practicing a discipline of faith: the offering of first fruits (3:9-10; cf. Dan 11:38; Isa 43:23). For the ancients, the firstborn and symbolically the best of their animals, families, and soil were holy and dedicated to God. "First fruits" (3:9) refers variously to grain, oil, new wine, dough, wool, and honey (e.g., Num 15:17-21; Deut 18:4) and, more generally, to "all the produce of the field" (2 Chr 31:5) and "the fruit of every tree" (Neh 10:37 [Heb. v. 38]). The community dedicated "first fruits" to God in thanksgiving (Exod 23:15c-16, 19; Lev 23:9-14; Deut 26:1-11) and then used them to support the priest-hood, widows, orphans, and aliens (e.g., Deut 18:4; 26:12; Neh 10:35-39 [Heb. vv. 36-40]). The father enjoins the youth to par-ticipate in this communal event. Although this is the only com-mand in Proverbs to participate in religious practices, they are fairly common in other ancient Near Eastern wisdom texts. The Egyptian *Instruction of Anii*, for example, urges: "Observe the feast of your god, / And repeat its season, / God is angry if it is neglected" (*AEL* 2:136), and "Offer to your god, / Beware of offending him" (*AEL* 2:141); the *Instruction of Ankhsheshonq* charges similarly: "Make burnt offering and libation before the god; let the fear of him be great in your heart" (*AEL* 3:170); and the Babylonian *Counsels of Wisdom* exhorts: "Present your free-will offering to your god. . . . Prayer, supplication, and prostration offer him daily" (*BWL* 105).

Should the youth offer his first and best to God, he is assured enormous returns (3:10), a promise that may be construed literally or metaphorically (see similar assurances of material gain from personified wisdom, e.g., 3:14, 16; 8:18-19, 21). His storehouses will be filled with plenty (*śābā*ʿ), a term that denotes not simply sufficiency but abundance or excess. In Genesis 41, the word is used several times to describe the seven years of plenty (*śābā*ʿ, 41:29-31, 34, 47, 53) in Egypt when Joseph stored up grain in "very large amounts—like the sand of the sea—until he stopped measuring it; for it could not be measured" (41:49 AT). As a result, when seven years of famine came, the people had plenty to eat. Indeed, "the whole world" came to buy grain from Joseph (41:57). The youth's vats will similarly "burst" with wine. They will split open and break apart as a result of the surplus (e.g., Gen 28:14; 30:30, 43; Exod 1:12; Isa 54:3). The father's choice of words and use of the plural (storehouses and vats) emphasize that God provides the faithful with abundance. It is a blessing for their obedience. The gain is a benefit, not the goal. Wrenched from this covenantal understanding, the claim prompts the question, posed sharply by the *haSatan*, or accuser, in the book of Job, whether the faithful offer gifts to God solely for material gain (Job 1:9). Elsewhere, Ecclesiastes also cautions there is a downside to "plenty." The śābā' (NRSV: "surfeit") of the rich makes them sleepless. They toss and turn all night, unable to sleep due to their full bellies, and worry about their financial investments (Eccl 5:12 [Heb. v. 11]).

The father concludes with a word about divine discipline (3:11-12; cf. Deut 11:2). The notion that God disciplines God's people is not unique to the sages, of course. The prophets warn repeatedly about God's reproach (e.g., Jer 2:30; 5:3; Ezek 5:15-16), and many in the community understand such difficult and pivotal experiences as the wilderness wandering and Babylonian exile to be God's reproof at work (e.g., Deut 8:1-5; Neh 9). Suffering as a means by which God educates is considered a positive thing, warranted (e.g., Jer 30:14) and, in the end, restorative (e.g., Job 36:10-12; Isa 53:5). Those who consent to it are happy (Job 5:17) and draw near to God (e.g., Zeph 3:2, 7). Those who refuse it turn their backs on God (Jer 32:33); they are stiff-necked (Jer 17:23; cf. Jer 5:3), wicked (Ps 50:16-17), and eager to act corruptly (Zeph 3:7). Accordingly, the youth is to receive God's discipline (NRSV: "do not despise," cf. 1:22, 25, 29-30) as readily as he celebrates overflowing storehouses and wine vats.

The reason, the father argues, is that divine discipline, like the discipline of a father, is an act of love (3:12). Throughout Proverbs the sages claim that a primary way parents demonstrate love for their children is by disciplining them strictly (e.g., 19:18; 29:17), including, at times, physically (e.g., 13:24; 23:13-14). The aim of the correction is to teach children how to navigate well in the world. Its intent is to be beneficial and life preserving. God's discipline is understood similarly (e.g., Deut 8:5). So Eliphaz declares to Job:

> How happy is the one whom God reproves;
>   . . . do not [reject] the discipline of the Almighty.
> For [God injures], but [God] binds up;
>   [God] strikes, but [God's] hands heal.
> [God] will deliver you from six troubles;
>   in seven no harm [will] touch you. (Job 5:17-19)

Elihu affirms this view, saying that God terrifies people with warnings to

> turn them aside from their deeds,
>> and keep them from pride;
> to spare their souls from the Pit. (33:17-18a; cf. 33:1-22)

It is important to note that the sages wrestle with facile interpretations of human suffering as necessarily indicative of God's reproof. Despite the friends' certainty that God is disciplining Job, for example, Job, God, and the reader know otherwise (e.g., 1:1, 8; 6:24-30; 9:13-35). And Proverbs is well aware that suffering may be the result of violence, extortion, or deceit (e.g., 11:1, 16, 13:23; cf. 1:10-19). Nonetheless, the parent of Proverbs 1–9 finds God's loving devotion expressed as much by the abundance God provides (3:9-10) as by the discipline God renders (3:11-12).

Tribute to Wisdom (3:13-18)

The word "happy" frames this tribute to wisdom (3:13, 18). It opens with the seek-and-find motif (3:13; cf. 2:1-6; 8:17, 35). The verbs "find" and "obtain" emphasize that the youth must take initiative and search for wisdom. To find *personified* wisdom further suggests intimacy and courtship. In Proverbs, the verb is used for acquiring a bride: one who "finds a wife" (18:22; cf. 31:10). Elsewhere, a lover rejoices when she "finds" the one whom her soul loves (Song 3:1-4; cf. 5:6; 6:1; Hos 2:7 [Heb. v. 9]). In Proverbs 1–9 the father instructs the youth to seek intimacy with wisdom as he would marriage to a desirable bride. Once the youth finds her, he is to hold her fast (3:18; cf. Isa 4:1) and embrace her (4:8; cf. Song 2:6; 8:3). He is to love (4:6; cf. Gen 24:67; Hos 3:1) and never abandon her (4:6; cf. Isa 54:7). He is to call wisdom his "sister" (cf. 7:4), a term of endearment parallel to "bride" in the whisperings of a lover to his beloved (Song 4:9, 10, 12; 5:1). In turn, wisdom will place on the youth's head a garland and crown, items typically worn by a bridegroom (4:9; cf. Song 3:11; Isa 61:10).

The father extols wisdom's worth in economic terms (3:14-15; cf. 2:4; 8:10, 19; 16:6). Her income (*saḥar*) is better than silver and her yield is better than gold (3:14; cf. Job 28:15-19). The word *saḥar* refers to earnings made from trade (e.g., 31:18; Isa 23:3, 18), and the participle from the same three-letter Hebrew root (*sḥr*) is used for the merchant profession (e.g., Ezek 27:36; 38:13; 1 Kgs 10:28; 2 Chr 1:16; Isa 23:2, 8). What wisdom brings to her companion, that is, exceeds the value of fine metals. She is also more precious than *pĕnînîm* (NRSV: "jewels," 3:15; cf. 8:10; 31:10), a term that likely means "corals" and is associated with gold (20:15). The father puts an exclamation mark on her value when he declares that *no* treasure (cf. 8:11; NRSV: "nothing you desire") compares to her.

Wisdom offers significant benefits (3:16). With her right hand, she extends long life and, with her left, "riches and honor"—a word pair that recalls God's generosity to Solomon, the paragon of wisdom (1 Kgs 3:13; 2 Chr 1:11-12). Some scholars associate this image of wisdom with Ma'at, the Egyptian goddess of truth and justice, who is depicted holding in one hand a scepter representing wealth and power and in the other the Egyptian symbol of life. M. V. Fox, however, rightly cautions that the Egyptians portrayed a number of deities holding emblems of their powers and blessings; as such, in the background of wisdom's picture may be the Egyptian practice rather than Ma'at specifically (2000, 157). Whatever the case, wisdom offers benefits that are elsewhere attributed to God.

The tree of life (3:18) is a mythological image in the ancient Near East. Drawings of a sacred tree, arguably representations of the tree of life, are fairly common. Typically, gathered around the tree are animals or people who reverently touch and, in the case of the animals, perhaps eat from it. In the Old Testament, outside of Proverbs, the tree of life is found only in the Genesis account of the garden of Eden, where it is paired with the tree of knowledge (Gen 2:9). After Adam and Eve eat from the latter, God expels them from the garden and puts cherubim and a flaming sword to guard the tree of life lest humans eat from it and become immortal (Gen 3:22-24): the "tree of life" is off-limits. In Proverbs, by contrast, the tree of life, or wisdom, stands in the heart of the city (1:20-21; 8:1-3)—to be "grasped," not as a means to everlasting life, but for health and joy (3:18). Indeed, the sages use the metaphor elsewhere to describe various sources of well-being: the fruit (i.e., speech, behavior) of the righteous (11:30), a fulfilled desire (13:12), and a gentle tongue (15:4). The tree of life has similar health-giving properties in the New Testament, where it yields fruit in season and leaves "for the healing of the nations" in the city of God's new creation (Rev 22:2; cf. 2:7; 22:14, 19; cf. Ezek 37:12).

In many ways, this tribute to wisdom anticipates the portrait of a "woman of substance" at the end of the book (31:10-31; see Introduction to this book). Their descriptions share similar vocabulary. The noun *sahar* (NRSV: "income"), for example, occurs in Proverbs only in chapters 3 and 31: wisdom's income is more than silver (3:14) and a "woman of substance" knows her income is good (31:18). The youth is urged to "find" these women (3:13; 31:10), both of whom are more precious than "corals" (3:15; 31:10; cf. 8:10). What they hold or do with their "hands" is significant (3:16; 31:13, 16, 19-20). And they exude happiness: those who embrace wisdom are "happy" (3:13, 18) while the children of a "woman of substance" rise up and call her "happy" (31:28). The extent of these and other connections suggests that wisdom and a "woman of substance" are to be closely associated if not identified with each other.

The Cosmological Significance of Wisdom (3:19-20)

With a simple inversion of standard Hebrew word order (verb-subject), the father shifts the object of praise from personified wisdom to God: "*The* LORD by wisdom founded the earth" (3:19a). All eyes now on God, wisdom becomes an instrument or agent by which God created the world (3:19-20). This cosmogony, or theory of the origin of the cosmos, resembles others in the Old Testament (cf. 8:18-31; Job 28:25-27). Ancients believed that the earth was a flat, solid mass that God "set" (e.g., Pss 102:25; 104:5; Isa 51:13) atop "the pillars of the earth" (e.g., 8:29; Ps 75:3; cf. Job 38:4-7). God similarly spread out, or "fixed," the heavens as a dome on "the pillars of heaven" (e.g., Job 26:11). So that the earth might flourish, God provided water, splitting the rock of the deep to release the waters of the abyss, and commanding the clouds to shower rain and dew (e.g., Job 38:27, 37; Ps 78:23; Isa 45:8). God continues to control the waters that flow from below and above: God restrains them (cf. 8:28-29; Job 38:8; Ps 78:15) and God releases them, as when God opened wide the fountains of the deep and the windows of heaven to flood the earth (Gen 7:11; cf. Gen 8:1-5).

Although the claim that God formed the world with wisdom is found elsewhere in the Old Testament (Ps 104:24; Jer 10:12; 51:15; cf. Isa 40:12-17), the father's placement of it after the tribute to wisdom (3:13-18), coupled with his use of *three* terms in 3:19-20—wisdom, understanding, and knowledge—leaves no doubt that wisdom is cosmically significant, authoritative, even elemental. As the means by which God created the world, wisdom is woven into the fabric of the universe. To "find" her is to embrace the rhyme and reason of God's handiwork.

The Interweaving of Divine and Human Relationships (3:21-35)

The father encourages the youth to hold on to good sense (NRSV: "sound wisdom") and discretion (NRSV: "prudence," cf. 2:7 and 1:4, respectively) by promising the benefits of life, esteem, and security (3:21-26). He makes a pun when he promises that they are "life for your *nepeš*" (NRSV: "soul," 3:22a). The *nepeš* is the "throat" or "neck"—the windpipe through which one breathes—and, by metonymy, the "life" or "self." As such, the father signals that good sense and discretion are "life for your spirit" and, as indicated by the parallel "[favor or charm] for your neck" (3:22b; cf. 3:3), vitality for the throat. They afford security (3:23-26). The youth can move ahead without stumbling. And his sleep will be pleasant, undisturbed by night terrors or haunting visions (e.g., Job 7:13-14; 27:20; 30:17; Ps 91:5). The youth will not know the panic and calamities that overcome the wicked (e.g., 1:26-27), for God keeps the upright from tangling their feet in snares and coming to ruin (cf. 1:17-18; Pss 35:8; 91).

A series of negative commands follows concerning how the youth should treat others (3:27-31). The term *rēaʿ* occurs twice

(NRSV: "neighbor," 3:28a, 29a) and *'ādām* once (NRSV: "anyone," 3:30a). In Proverbs, *rēa'* denotes anyone with whom one lives or interacts as a result of life circumstances—a friend, neighbor (e.g., 14:20; 17:17; 27:10), or simply another person (e.g., 11:9, 12; 16:29; 24:28). The term *'ādām* is more generic and inclusive. It may designate humanity as a whole (e.g., 8:31; 16:1) or any individual (e.g., 8:34; 19:3; 27:19). The commands therefore address how to behave with everyone. How one lives with and for others is significant. Moreover, one's moral actions need be neither global nor grandiose to matter. Moral agency begins locally. What people do in their neighborhood matters—so much so that God responds definitively, with blessing or curse (3:31-35).

The first two admonitions charge the youth to treat others justly and without delay (3:27-28; cf. 11:24). He is not to withhold good "from its owners," that is, people with a right to it (NRSV: "those to whom it is due"). Several proverbs in the book suggest this includes people in need of charity: "Whoever closes his [or her] ear to the cry of the poor / will also cry out and not be answered" (21:13 AT) and "the righteous know the rights of the poor" (29:7), meaning that they consider those rights legitimate and respond appropriately (cf. "do good" in Deut 15:7-11; Pss 14, 37; Sir 4:1-4). The father cautions against overdoing it, however. The parallel phrase "when it is in your power" (3:27b) indicates the youth should "do good" not to the point of personal harm but according to ability and means (cf. 2 Cor 8).

The second two admonitions prohibit plotting harm against others (3:29-30). Both sayings contrast the initiative and malevolence of the schemer with the innocence of his victims. With wordplay, the father warns the youth not to devise *rā'â* ("evil" or "wickedness") against his *rēa'* ("friend" or "neighbor," 3:29). For the sages, scheming is nearly always reprehensible (e.g., 12:20; 14:22), but particularly so against someone who trusts you. Similarly, if no *rā'â* has been done to the youth, he must not start a quarrel—whether verbally, physically, or by lawsuit. There is no reason for it (3:30). Whereas some disputes are warranted (e.g., 25:9), quarrels without cause cannot be justified.

The father characterizes those who commit such wrongdoings as "violent" (3:31). Their ways are marked by the intent and action to injure others, whether by selfishness (3:27-28) or personal attack (3:29-30). They rend the fabric of a community; so the youth must not envy them (e.g., 23:17; 24:1, 19; Pss 37:1, 7). Envy is a painful, even bitter awareness that another enjoys a particular advantage, coupled with desire to have the same. According to the sages, envy prompts self-destructive behavior. It sparks consuming fury and competitiveness that threatens a person's well-being (6:34; Eccl 4:4; cf. Isa 11:13). Envy overwhelms (27:4), makes the body rot (14:30), and destroys (Job 5:2). To envy the violent distorts and contorts a person in ways that are loathsome and misguided: loathsome because their ways are brutal, and misguided because their advantages prove illusory (3:32-35; e.g., Pss 37:1-2; 73:17-20; Jas 4:1-2).

The chapter closes with a contrast between the fates of the wicked and the upright (3:32-35). That the contrast immediately follows the admonitions about how to treat others (3:27-31) suggests a person's fate and relationship with God depends in no small way on whether that person behaves toward others honorably. The crooked are an "abomination of YHWH," what God finds disgusting and repulsive (3:32). Proverbs reiterates several times God's loathing for the wicked—their sacrifices, their ways (cf. 15:8-9; 21:27). God curses, namely, sends distress or disaster (cf. Deut 28:20; Mal 2:2-3) on the "house" of the wicked, a term that refers variously to the physical structure, its inhabitants, one's property, and descendants (3:33; e.g., Gen 7:1; 1 Sam 27:3). The whole family of the wicked suffers. God also treats the scornful according to their own action (3:34): God scoffs at the scoffers just as wisdom laughs at their calamity (1:26-27; Ps 18:25-26 [Heb. vv. 26-27]; cf. Jam 4:6 and 1 Pet 5:5, which quote LXX of 3:34). In the end, the wicked inherit disgrace (3:35). In contrast, God takes the upright into God's confidence (3:32b), a circle that includes prophets and angels (e.g., Ps 89:7 [Heb. v. 8]; Amos 3:7). There, they are privy to God's words and plans (Ps 25:14; Jer 23:18, 22). Moreover, God blesses their household, grants them favor (3:33-34), and bequeaths them honor (3:35).

Excursus on "Abomination of the LORD"

The phrase "abomination of YHWH," which occurs only in Proverbs and Deuteronomy, designates what is repugnant to God. The expression thus circumscribes boundaries for human behavior. The phrase occurs eleven times in Proverbs (3:32; 11:1, 20; 12:22; 15:8, 9, 26; 16:5; 17:15; 20:10, 23). In addition, the sages list six things YHWH hates, seven that are an "abomination to [God's] self" (6:16-19). Among these referents are certain attitudes (e.g., crooked hearts, 11:20; 15:26), persons (the arrogant, 16:5), dishonest practices such as false weights (11:1; 20:10, 23), lying (12:22), corrupting justice (17:15; cf. 16:12), scoffing (24:9), and, more broadly, "the way of the wicked" (15:9). In contrast to Deuteronomy, Proverbs invokes the phrase only once for a cultic practice—the sacrifices offered by the wicked (15:8; cf. 21:27)—but this is not surprising given the book's general lack of concern with cultic matters (cf. Deut 12:31; 17:1; 18:12; 23:18; 27:15). In many instances, the wrongs that the sages term "abominations of YHWH" are underhanded, and reparation is difficult to obtain.

Theological and Ethical Analysis

For those of us used to thinking of wisdom simply as a human characteristic, the parent's claim at the heart of Proverbs 3 is stunning: wisdom is how God made the world. Wisdom is woven into the fabric of creation, giving it shape, meaningful order, and a coherence that God continues to uphold. To "find" wisdom, then, is to glimpse this divine handiwork, to align oneself with it, and, as a result, to prosper. The wise live well and long. They enjoy ease and abundance (3:10, 21-26; cf. 1:33), health and happiness (3:2, 8, 16, 18), riches and honor (3:4, 16, 35). In contrast, the foolish and wicked are "out of place" in the world (cf. 2:22), and are therefore expelled from it variously by calamity, disgrace, and premature death (e.g., 1:26-27, 32; 2:22; 3:25, 33). Indeed, that the sages regularly describe this expulsion in passive language leaves open every possibility for it (Boström 1990, 116).

But experience readily challenges this worldview. Everyone can give countless examples to the contrary—situations when good people suffer terribly and, conversely, wickedness thrives. The ancient sages certainly could too (e.g., 24:10-12; 31:8-9; Eccl 3:16; 7:15; 8:14; Job). So why would the parent devote such time and energy to teaching this worldview to the next generation? What makes it "true"?

The worldview is, as C. Newsom observes, an "iconic narrative": a community's expression of how it understands the foundational structures of reality and the nature and tendencies of the world—in short, how the world "works" (Newsom 2003, 122-23). Iconic narratives ring "true" not as lawlike guarantees or failsafe formulas but as affirmations of deep structures at work even when particular circumstances may suggest otherwise. Such narratives explain a community's values and commitments and give meaning to behaviors and dispositions, encouraging some (e.g., as wise and righteous) and discouraging others (e.g., as foolish and wicked). In turn, people's participation in and avoidance of those behaviors reinforces belief in the narratives. For the parent, the wise prosper and the wicked perish because that is how God created and sustains the world. The world is not neutral. So if the wicked prosper from time to time, it is an exception—not the rule. The wise may take heart.

The chapter (and Proverbs as a whole) invites us to identify and consider our own iconic narratives. What do we believe and teach the next generation about the way the world "works"? Do we think there is predictability or "order" to the world? What, if any, is God's relationship to it? In practice, of course, we assume a certain degree of "order," whether on basic matters (e.g., we touch a hot stove, we burn ourselves; we lose our balance, we fall) or more complex ones (e.g., we are wronged and believe things will somehow be made right). Our convictions about "order" tend to fall somewhere on a spectrum. At one end is *legalism*. Legalism asserts a certainty about the "natural" (divinely mandated) order of things and prescribes how to live accordingly. Legalism errs, the sages would argue, because it too readily identifies human conventions with God's will. It leaves no room for divine mystery and freedom or for human discretion. At the other end of the spectrum is *atomism*. Atomism imagines each person to be a sovereign, self-made individual, a "free unfettered agent" not bound to any authority. Atomism rejects the sages' conviction that we are creatures "embedded in a structured creation that has its own say" and to which we are accountable (Brueggemann 1989, 37; cf. Taylor 1989, 192-98). For the parent of Proverbs 1–9, both extremes are cautionary tales of hubris and folly.

As part of the youth's quest for wisdom, the parent insists on participation in communal rituals, specifically here a religious one (3:9-10). Today we often associate the term "ritual" with practices we experience as obligatory, perfunctory, and perhaps obscure. But the parent reminds us that rituals embody meaning in flesh-and-blood acts. They constitute us as individuals and communities by ordering our lives; enacting and affirming particular meanings and relationships; forming and transforming our identities, thoughts, and behaviors; and, particularly in the case of religious rituals, pointing us beyond the ordinary to the extraordinary. Through rituals we locate ourselves in the world. Certainly, the power of rituals cuts both ways—they may be liberating or oppressive, life-giving or deadly—but that they have power is apparent. So we find that, particularly during critical moments in Israel's life, prophets and leaders sought to (re)form the community by means of its rituals (e.g., Neh 13:1-22; Jer 17:19-27; Heb 4:1-11).

Finally, Proverbs 3 defines moral units as communal. The households of the wicked and the righteous reap divine curse or blessing for their actions (3:33). This may strike readers as objectionable, even excessive, given our modern, Western emphasis on individual rights and responsibilities. Post-Enlightenment moralities tend to view justice as primarily an individual matter: each person alone bears the fruit of what he or she does. So while we might not oppose benefiting from the righteous deeds of others, we object to the idea of suffering for their misconduct (Kaminsky 1995, 187). In contrast, the parent underlines human interconnectedness—that the consequences for our deeds, whether blessing or curse, are borne by those around us. Experience would seem to confirm the point. Consider how parents rejoice or suffer as their children do, how generations benefit or suffer from the deeds of those before them, how nations celebrate the success or share the guilt for the conduct of some of their citizens. The parent highlights this corporate dimension of justice, just as personified wisdom earlier emphasized the individual (1:31-32). Both understandings recur throughout the Bible (e.g., Gen 9:20-27; Deut 29:14-21 [Heb. vv. 15-22]; 2 Kgs 21:10-15; Jer 31:27-30; Ezek 18; Matt 23:29-36; John 9:2).

PROVERBS 4

Literary Analysis

Chapter 4 opens with a third tribute to personified wisdom (4:1-9; cf. 1:20-33; 3:13-18). The father begins with an exordium or summons to heed his instructions (4:1-2; e.g., 1:8-9; 3:1-2). This time, however, he speaks in the plural, addressing "sons" (4:1a; NRSV: "children") rather than the singular "my son" (e.g., 1:8, 10, 15; 2:1; 3:1, 11, 21). A shift from singular to plural addressees is not unusual in Proverbs 1–9 (5:7; 7:24; 8:32-33) and is found in the wisdom book Sirach (e.g., 39:13; 41:14). Evidently a literary convention, it signals that the father's guidance of his son is intended also for a wider audience.

The father quotes *his* father to make an urgent appeal for the youth to "get wisdom" (4:3-9). The grandfather's speech starts with an exordium (4:4), a tactic his son clearly learned well. He continues with a series of imperatives that direct the youth to "get" wisdom (4:5-9). Repetition associates the father and grandfather with personified wisdom: "I *give*" (4:2a) and "she will *give*" (4:9a; NRSV: "she will place"), "*do not forsake* my teaching" (4:2b) and "*do not forsake* her" (4:6a), and "*keep* my commandments" (4:4c) and "she will *keep* you" (4:6a).

Verses 10-19 encourage the youth (sg. "my son," 4:10) to stay on the way of wisdom by further contrasting the two paths—here the path of the upright and that of the wicked (cf. 2:5-11). The phrase "your life" frames the exordium (4:10, 13), reinforcing the notion that acceptance of instruction is a life and death matter. The father then characterizes the way(s) of the wicked (4:14-17) and concludes with two sayings that employ vivid light and dark imagery to emphasize the difference between the two paths (4:18-19). The motif of "stumbling" weaves the unit together (4:12, 16, and 19).

An "anatomy" of a wise person follows (4:20-27). This head-to-toe description focuses on five principal organs of the body: the ear (4:20), eyes (4:21, 25), heart or mind (4:21, 23), mouth (4:24), and feet (4:26-27). At the center of the image is the heart or mind, the seat of human thought and emotion (4:23; cf. 2:2).

Exegetical Analysis

As My Father Told Me So I Tell You: Get Wisdom (4:1-9)

The father tries a new teaching strategy. He appeals to tradition, quoting the words his own father used to encourage him to accept parental discipline and pursue wisdom. He begins by remembering what he was like when he was in the care of his parents (4:3), a move that emphasizes his affinity with the youth, as if to say "once I was like you, and one day you will be like I am." The father describes himself as "weak," "delicate," or "soft" (4:3b; NRSV: "tender"), a characteristic commonly ascribed to youth (e.g., Gen 33:13; 1 Chr 22:5; 29:1). He was also *yāḥîd*, a term that means "alone" or "only one" (4:3b; NRSV: "favorite"). One who is *yāḥîd* is treasured, whether or not he or she is an only child (Isaac is *yāḥîd*, cf. Gen 22:2, 12, 16). Indeed, the prophets compare the devastation and bitterness of "the day of the LORD" to mourning for a child who is *yāḥîd* (Jer 6:26; Amos 8:10; cf. Zech 12:10). The father's self-description acts as a mirror for the youth, reflecting the father's perception of and love for him.

When the father refers to and quotes his father (4:3-9), he signals that the authority of his teaching rests not primarily on his life experience or position in the family but on the generations before him. The father passes on information, beliefs, and customs that the community has tested and reclaimed time and again. The Egyptian *Instruction of Ptahhotep* explains the cycle:

It goes well with [a son] when he has heard.
When he is old, has reached veneration,
He will speak likewise to his children,
Renewing the teaching of his father.
Every man teaches as he acts.
He will speak to the children,
So that they will speak to their children. (*AEL* 1:75)

For individuals and communities, such a deep reservoir of wisdom can be reassuring. It provides perspective because others have weathered similar situations and, based on their experiences, offers possible ways forward.

Insisting four times that the youth "get" wisdom (4:5, 7), the (grand)father interweaves economic and erotic terms to describe her (4:5-9). He appeals to monetary and sexual desires simultaneously. On the one hand, the verb *qānâ* (4:5, 7; NRSV: "get") commonly means "to acquire" or "buy" with cash or the exchange of goods (e.g., Gen 47:19; 1 Chr 21:24-25; Isa 43:24; Jer 32:9; cf. Prov 17:16; 23:23). On the other, it is used for marriage, as when Boaz "acquires" Ruth as his wife (Ruth 4:5, 10). The latter sense of the verb resonates with the language of intimacy in 4:6, 8-9. The youth is to love and cherish wisdom, to embrace and never abandon her. Wisdom should be his most intimate companion (cf. *qānâ* in 8:22).

In return, wisdom will protect and bring honor to the youth (4:6, 8-9). She will "exalt" and "honor" him (4:8), meaning she will raise the esteem with which others regard him. This may include increasing his material worth (e.g., Num 22:17-18; 24:11-13; 1 Sam 2:7), a benefit frequently ascribed to wisdom (e.g., 3:16; 8:18, 21). Moreover, wisdom will adorn him with a garland and crown (4:9; cf. 1:9)—symbols of favor, nobility (e.g., Isa 62:3; Jer 13:18), and marriage (Song 3:11; Isa 61:10). Thus the relationship between the youth and wisdom is reciprocal: a business transaction in which there is an exchange of goods and services (so the economic overtones) *and* a marital relationship (so the erotic). The youth "gets" her and pledges his devotion to her above everything else, and she in turn cares for him in ways that elevate his personal well-being and standing in the community.

Descriptions of brides and marriage contracts from the ancient Near East illuminate the (grand)father's intertwining of erotic and economic language to characterize personified wisdom (cf. 3:13-18). Song of Songs, for example, depicts a bride in highly erotic terms: she arouses her lover's desire (Song 4:1-15; 6:5) and seeks him eagerly (e.g., 3:1-4; 5:6-8); she is beautiful, perfumed, and bejeweled (e.g., 4:1-15; 6:4-10); she is chaste and sexually mature (Song 4:12-16). An Egyptian male lover celebrates his beloved likewise:

> She looks like the rising morning star
>> At the start of a happy year.
> Shining bright, fair of skin,
>> Lovely the look of her eyes,
> Sweet the speech of her lips,
>> She has not a word too much.
> Upright neck, shining breast,
>> Hair true lapis lazuli;
> Arms surpassing gold, fingers like lotus buds.
>> Heavy thighs, narrow waist,
> Her legs parade her beauty.
>> With graceful step she treads the ground,
> Captures my heart by her movements.
>> She causes all men's necks
> To turn about to see her;
>> Joy has he whom she embraces.
> He is like the first of men! (AEL 2:182)

Other Old Testament narratives highlight the erotic desirability of brides, though with notably more restraint (e.g., Gen 24:16; Isa 61:10).

In contrast, the language of marriage was largely economic. Commonly negotiated by the groom and the bride's father, marriage was a sort of business deal between two families. A marriage contract, if there was one, specified the economic arrangements of the union: the dowry from the bride's family and, in some cases, a monetary gift to the bride's family from the groom or his family. The predominant feature of the contract was the inventory of the dowry; the greater its value, the greater the perceived "value" of the bride (cf. 31:10-31). As the (grand)father personifies wisdom, she is an extremely "valuable" spouse. She is worth more than costly jewels (3:15; 8:11; cf. 31:10b), and she brings to the youth wealth (e.g., 3:14, 16; 8:18-19, 21), security (4:6; e.g., 1:33), and status (4:9; e.g., 8:15-16).

The Two Paths (4:10-19)

In the next exordia, the father identifies his teaching as dynamic, as orientation to and leadership down a "way" that, hopefully, the youth will soon walk of his own volition (4:11; see excursus in Proverbs 2). The father in the Egyptian *Satire of the Trades* similarly describes his efforts:

> Lo, I have set you on god's path. . . .
>   Praise god for your father, your mother,
> Who set you on the path of life!
>   This is what I put before you,
> Your children and their children. (*AEL* 1:191)

What follows in 4:12-19, in fact, teems with language of movement—walk, run, stumble, enter, avoid, go, turn away, and pass by. On the way of wisdom the youth can move freely and safely; whether he walks or runs, his steps will not be hampered nor will he stumble over obstacles (cf. 3:21-26; Job 18:5-12). Thus the father urges holding fast to "discipline" (*mûsār*, 4:13; NRSV: "instruction"). Notably, although *mûsār* is a masculine noun, he refers to it in the feminine: "guard *her*, for *she* is your life" (4:13b). This suggests it is another name for personified wisdom. Just as the youth must accept the father's words to enjoy a long life (4:10), so the youth must cling fiercely to discipline (i.e., wisdom) to savor freedom and well-being (4:13; cf. 3:18).

The father cautions again about the wicked in general terms (cf. 2:12-19). With terse, staccato imperatives, he implores the youth to avoid their path at all costs (4:14-15). To explain, the father points to how the wicked live—their sleep habits, food, and drink. Whereas other Old Testament writers describe the wicked lying awake in their beds scheming future plans (Ps 36:4 [Heb. v. 5]; Mic 2:1), the father attributes their lack of sleep to the fact that they have *not* done wicked deeds, namely, made others stumble into wickedness with them. So they are restless. They toss and turn in their beds, preoccupied and unsatisfied with their failure to do harm. Their diet is similarly telling. Like the old adage "you are what you eat," the sages identify people with their food and drink: they speak of the "bread [or food] of the stingy" (23:6), the "deceptive food" of rulers (23:3), and the "bread of idleness" (31:27; cf. 9:5, 17). Here, the wicked are said to consume "bread of wickedness" *and* quench their thirsts with "wine of violence" (4:17; cf. Job 15:16; 34:7). The use of both verbs (to eat and to drink) intensifies the point; the wicked satiate themselves with malice and cruelty. They swallow violence again and again so that very soon they have internalized it. Wickedness is intrinsic to who they are.

Food and drink often serve metaphorically for the human condition. The psalmist, for example, describes mourners as eating "the bread of tears" and drinking tears in full measure (Ps 80:4-5), and those who do not rely on God as eating "the bread of anxious toil" (Ps 127:2). Isaiah speaks of "the bread of adversity and the water of [oppression]"—meager rations given by God to the people in judgment (Isa 30:20)—and Jeremiah refers to "the wine of wrath" (Jer 25:15-18; cf. Isa 51:21-23). In the New Testament, Jesus identifies himself as the "bread of life" (John 6:22-59) and exhorts his disciples to partake regularly of the Eucharistic bread and wine (e.g., Mark 14:22-25; Luke 22:14-23). And the Egyptian *Instruction of Ptahhotep* warns that the fool "lives on that by which one dies, / His food is distortion of speech" (*AEL* 1:75).

The father summarizes with two sayings that contrast the way of the just with that of the wicked (4:18-19). The former path is like dawn, when the world grows increasingly bright until the full light of day spills over the horizon. On such an illumined way, people can walk and even run with confidence (4:12). In contrast, a deep and murky darkness—the kind of darkness a person can feel (Exod 10:21; cf. Isa 8:22)—engulfs the path of the wicked. Their way is so dangerous and riddled with hazards that the wicked who thrive on making others stumble (4:16), stumble themselves. The scene is described well in Job 18:8-11:

> [The wicked] are thrust into a net by their own feet,
>   and they walk into a pitfall.
> A trap seizes them by the heel;
>   a snare lays hold of them.
> A rope is hid for them in the ground,
>   a trap for them in the path.
> Terrors frighten them on every side,
>   and chase them at their heels.

Even worse, the wicked do not know over what they trip. Other proverbs herald the ignorance of the wicked about their path and its perils: the street gang does not recognize they set a deadly snare for themselves (1:10-19); the ways of the "strange" woman wander and "she does not know it" (5:6); those who accept personified folly's invitation "do not know" that the dead are her guests (9:18); and a person trying to get rich quickly "does not know that [poverty] is sure to come" (28:22). For the sages, ignorance is the inevitable consequence of refusing to accept discipline and thereby gain knowledge; the wicked have no sense of how the world "works" (e.g., 3:19-20; cf. Theological and Ethical Analysis of Proverbs 3). Ignorance is never bliss. Indeed, it is often deadly.

The Anatomy of a Moral Life (4:20-27)

The chapter concludes with a portrait of the moral self that, much like an abstract painting, features five principal body parts: the ear (4:20), eyes (4:21, 25), heart or mind (4:21, 23), mouth (4:24), and feet (4:26-27). Just as we might say, "He's got shifty eyes," about someone we distrust, the sages contend that, metonymically, parts of the body may represent the whole self (cf. the Egyptian proverb "A man's character is one of his limbs,"

AEL 3:168). The self is fully invested in each part, any of which may work for its benefit or harm. At the center of this portrait literarily is the heart or mind (4:23; see excursus in Proverbs 2), which the father urges the youth to guard vigilantly because from it flow the "outgoings of life" (NRSV: "springs of life"). The heart is the source of life. Not surprisingly, then, the youth is to keep his father's teachings there "for they are life to [the one] who find[s] them" (4:22; cf. 4:13). To "guard the heart" is to be prudent about the heart's "outgoings," to tend with diligence and discretion to how one expresses one's thoughts and feelings. Other ancient writers urged similar caution. The *Instruction of Ankhsheshonq*, for example, exhorts "Do not say right away what comes out of your heart" (*AEL* 3:165), and the *Instruction of Anii* warns:

Do not empty your belly to everyone,
    And thus destroy respect of you;
Broadcast not your words to others,
    Nor join with one who bares his heart. (*AEL* 2:159)

The chapter concludes with practices that reveal and enable a heart rightly guarded (4:24-27). The father teaches that actions are a discourse. Actions speak as loudly as words about a person's thoughts and convictions. Every part of the body is a mouthpiece. So the father urges the youth to assume a wise deportment and, in turn, to learn how to interpret the behavior of others (e.g., 6:12-15). First, the youth should speak honestly (4:24). Control of one's lips (speech) is a significant concern in Proverbs (e.g., 10:19; 12:18-19; 13:3; 15:23) and in other ancient Near Eastern Wisdom literature. The Babylonian *Counsels of Wisdom*, for example, urges: "Let your mouth be controlled and your speech guarded; / Therein is a man's wealth—let your lips be very precious" (*BWL* 101); and the *Instruction of Anii* cautions: "A man may be ruined by his tongue, / Beware and you will do well" (*AEL* 2:140). Second, the youth should fix his eyes straight ahead on where he is going (4:25). He should neither look aside at inevitable distractions along the way, nor squint his eyes in concentration while he schemes to make trouble like the wicked do (6:13; cf. 10:10; 16:30). Finally, he should move his feet straight ahead (4:26-27).

The youth dares not turn a toe to the right or left, even for an instant, lest he wind up wandering like the "strange" woman (5:6) and the wicked (6:18).

Theological and Ethical Analysis

How do we understand the role and importance of tradition? Our answers likely vary depending on the matter and tradition in question. At one extreme, we may regard traditions as ultimate, unchanging, self-evident norms; accordingly, we acclaim and preserve them as sacrosanct—impervious to the ebb and flow of history. At the other extreme, we discount and ignore traditions because we consider them outdated rivals to our autonomy and freedom. The former extreme extols the value of generations of time-tested understanding; the latter, the worth of individuals and personal judgment.

The sages stand firmly on tradition. They "rarely appeal to their own authority or even their personal experience. They are not celebrities offering their philosophies of life, but rather anonymous 'sons,' passing on the lessons their own devoted parents taught them. . . . Time-tested understandings of the past are far more valuable than the fresh opinions of today's headliner" (Davis 2000, 48). So the parent teaches the youth as his father taught him (4:3-9).

At the same time, however, the parent portrays traditions as dynamic, as "*the way* of wisdom . . . *the paths* of uprightness" (4:10-11). The metaphor suggests that whereas the young must learn time-tested understandings, they neither circumscribe nor exhaust wisdom. Instead, as the language of movement conveys (4:10-19), traditions are a means for navigating life. Tradition is not a static, universally applicable set of settled conclusions, but a trusty, worn map, a framework and language, which enables the young to recognize terrain that is new to them as familiar, even well known, to others (e.g., "nothing new under the sun," Eccl 1:9-10) and, where it is not, to better cope with the new situation. Thus the sages embrace and pass on traditions but are not captive to them. Indeed, the wisdom tradition itself requires discernment of what is prudent in particular circumstances (e.g., 25:11; 26:9).

At times the map may be clear; at others, the lay of the land may require an informed, thoughtful, and creative revision.

Other biblical texts caution against the extreme views of tradition. Some warn against idolizing it. In Isaiah, for instance, God rebukes the Israelites for so elevating tradition that they miss God altogether: "These people draw near with their mouths and honor me with their lips, while their hearts are far from me, and their worship of me is a human commandment learned by rote" (29:13). Later, Jesus quotes Isaiah's words when he chastises the Pharisees for abandoning God's word for the sake of tradition (Mark 7:1-13; cf. Matt 15:8-9). Other texts warn that the disregard of tradition is perilous. The book of Judges, for example, recounts history as a seemingly endless cyclical pattern driven by the community's failure to remember God and God's work on their behalf (e.g., Judg 2:10-15; 3:7-15; 8:33-35).

By tradition and circumstance, what do we counsel one another to "get . . . with all you possess, get" (4:7 AT)? What do we consider vital for well-being? And how do we communicate that to our children? The grandparent's urgent instruction (4:4b-9) reveals a prioritization of "goods" or virtues. Wisdom, the highest good, enables the realization and enjoyment of other goods, such as wealth, honor, security, health, and happiness (e.g., 3:13-18). To "find" wisdom is to attain a plurality of goods, to savor the "good life." To strive instead for any of the other goods first—to regard them as ends in themselves—is folly and leads to vice, shame, and despair (e.g., 11:1, 28; 15:16-17, 27; 16:8, 16, 19; Eccl 4:7-8; 5:12). For the sages, those goods are not means to happiness but benefits of virtue. Such conviction challenges our present-day preoccupation with goods such as money, power, and fame as keys to happiness.

PROVERBS 5

Literary Analysis

Having just compared personified wisdom and the wicked (4:5-9, 13-19), the father turns to the "strange" woman and "the wife of one's youth." Highlighting the dangers of the former and delights of the latter, he aims to teach the importance of fidelity to one's spouse, community, and, more broadly, wisdom. The chapter opens with an exordium, or call to attention (5:1-2; cf. e.g., 1:8-9; 3:1-2; 4:1-2, 20-22), followed by a description of the "strange" woman that focuses on her lips and speech and her wayward, deadly path (5:3-6; cf. 2:18). After a second exordium (5:7, this time to plural "sons," cf. Literary Analysis of Proverbs 4), the father charges the youth never to go near her and enumerates the grave consequences of doing so (5:8-14). At 5:15 the father shifts the spotlight from the "strange" woman to the "wife of one's youth," whom he describes with a series of erotic water and animal metaphors (5:15-20). Finally, the father summarizes the fate of one who foolishly chooses the wrong woman (5:21-23).

The chapter is a study in contrasts. Foremost is the juxtaposition of the "strange" woman (5:3-14) and the "wife of one's youth" (5:15-20) who, like oil and water, simply do not mix. Repetition highlights other differences, including the *lips* of the youth (5:2) and of the "strange" woman (5:3), the capacity of the youth to guard *knowledge* (5:2) while the "strange" woman *does not know* "her ways wander" (5:6), and the failure of the "strange" woman to *observe* her path (5:6) while God *observes* every path (5:21). Repetition also invites certain associations, such as the "strange" woman's steps that *hold fast* to her deadly descent (5:5) and the fetters that *hold fast* the wicked (5:22), and, relatedly, the fate of the "strange" woman ("her end," 5:4) and that of her foolish companion ("your end," 5:11; NRSV: "at the end"). The chapter concludes with play on the verb "to stagger" or "stray" (5:19-20, 23).

Exegetical Analysis

A Pit of Despair: The "Strange" Woman (5:1-14)

The father opens with an exordium (5:1-2). For the first time, however, he charges the youth to attend to "my wisdom . . . my understanding" (5:1). This is striking for two reasons. First, use of the possessive with "wisdom" (and its synonym "understanding") occurs only here in Proverbs. Elsewhere, "wisdom" is always a comprehensive term; it is never specific to someone or something. Second, the father ordinarily urges attention to "my teaching," "my words," or "my commandments" (e.g., 2:1; 3:1; 4:1-2, 20-21), that is, the various ways by which he communicates wisdom. The expression "my wisdom" thus conflates the comprehensive and the particular: what the father teaches is universal in scope ("wisdom") and particular in expression ("my"). Should the youth pay attention, he too will speak wisely. His "lips will guard knowledge" (5:2).

The lips and speech of the "strange" woman (NRSV: "loose") are a different story (5:3; cf. 2:16-19). The father describes them vividly and erotically, with imagery similar to that found in the Song of Songs. That her lips drip with honey echoes the male lover's praise of his beloved ("Your lips drip honey" [NRSV: "distill nectar"], Song 4:11a). That her "palate" (NRSV: "speech") is oily smooth recalls his plea, "[May] your kisses [be] like the best wine that goes down smoothly" (Song 7:9a [Heb. v. 10a]; cf. Song 5:16a). The "strange" woman's lips promise the sweet smoothness of such intimate pleasures.

But there is more to the imagery of honey and oil. Consumed alone, neither satisfies hunger and thirst nor provides sufficient sustenance (e.g., Deut 32:13-15; 2 Sam 17:27-29). Although honey is sweet and good for you (e.g., 16:24; 24:13), it is also sticky, a ready golden trap for the unsuspecting. Too much of it makes a person nauseated and sick (25:16, 27). Similarly, oil is a household staple (e.g., 1 Kgs 17:12), but it is slippery (27:16) and stains with a greasy permanence. An excess of it leaves one bloated and sluggish (e.g., Isa 28:1, 4). The images of honey and oil, therefore, are ambivalent. They are liquids of delight *and* danger.

In the end, the "strange" woman's allure proves the latter (5:4). Her lips and speech turn bitter as wormwood. Wormwood is a small shrub with gray, fragrant leaves and small flowers that produces extremely bitter oil. In the Bible, wormwood nearly always occurs parallel to something poisonous, suggesting its hazardous, potentially lethal effects (e.g., Deut 29:18 [Heb. v. 17]; Jer 9:15

[Heb. v. 14]; 23:15; Lam 3:19; Amos 6:12). The (after)taste of the "strange" woman's mouth, it seems, has a sharp, vicious bite, one that devours with the piercing swiftness of a two-edged sword, literally, "a sword with two mouths" (5:4b; cf. Judg 3:16; Ps 149:6). "Her end" (5:4a) overturns expectations: what one anticipates will be an intimate, sugary smooth kiss instead pierces with violent fury.

In 5:7-14, the father calls attention back to *his* mouth and speech before enumerating the consequences of crossing her threshold. The father paints the youth's potential loss in thick brushstrokes: it is comprehensive (honor, years, wealth, labors, and health) and particularly grievous because everything goes to faceless "others," "strangers," "a cruel one," "a foreigner"— those not in the youth's family (5:9-10). That all the terms in Hebrew are masculine singular or plural suggests the beneficiaries are unknown men (cf. 5:17). Should the youth associate with the "strange" woman, the consequences ripple far beyond the two of them, their families, and perhaps their immediate community. What the youth loses will end up the gain of undeserving strangers.

The (after)taste of wormwood ("her end," 5:4) endures for a lifetime, the father contends, so that "your end" (5:11; NRSV: "at the end of your life") is bitter with regret and public disgrace. The youth's would-be cry of remorse is clear that there will be no one to blame but himself: "*I* hated. . . . *My* heart despised. . . . *I* did not listen. . . . [*I* did not] incline *my* ear" (5:12-13). It further reveals that the remorse is about more than sexual transgression. The youth confesses his utter failure to seek wisdom: "I hated *discipline* (*mûsār*, e.g., 1:2-3, 7). . . . despised *reproof*. . . I did not listen to the *voice of my teachers*. . . . [I did not] incline my ear to *my instructors*." The father's pragmatic instruction about avoiding sex with strangers is more broadly about choosing the wrong path (cf. 4:26-27) and ending up utterly ruined in front of everyone (5:14).

The description of the consequences associated with the "strange" woman suggests the father's concern is (at least in part) exogamy or marriage to someone outside one's group. Insofar as Proverbs 1–9 likely dates to the Persian period (see Introduction to this book), recent studies by H. C. Washington, J. Blenkinsopp, and others argue that the father's warnings about her in 5:7-14 (and 2:16-19) resonate with Ezra and Nehemiah's campaign against exogamy (Ezra 9–10; Neh 10:30; 13:23-27; cf. Mal 2:10-16; cf. Washington 1994b; Blenkinsopp 1991). As the community sought to rebuild itself after the exile, some believed such marriages threatened moral and religious purity and, given the inheritance and property rights of women, economic stability. Ezra recounts that he convened the male heads of households to identify publicly who had married outside the group (Ezra 10:16-17) so that their wives and children might be sent away (Ezra 10:3). Failure to attend the proceedings meant expulsion from the community and confiscation of one's property (Ezra 10:8)—"utter ruin in the public assembly" (5:14). For Ezra and Nehemiah, the survival of the community necessitated the exclusion of "strange" women and their children (but notably not "strange" men). To the extent that the father's polemic against the "strange" woman resonates with that conviction, it is a reminder that communal survival can, and often does, come at an extremely high cost.

A Wellspring of Joy: The Wife of One's Youth (5:15-20)

Liquid imagery continues here but it is no longer honey and oil. To advocate for marital fidelity, the father uses the metaphor of water to describe the "wife of one's youth" as a wellspring of joy and satisfaction. His teaching overflows with terms for water and various means by which it is contained or channeled. Water is primeval and essential for life (Gen 1–2). It is the purest, most effective means to quench thirst and cleanse oneself. Water is also limited and precious, particularly in a desert clime such as Palestine. Water's considerable value is indicated by the extent to which people argue and rejoice about it (e.g., Gen 21:25-26; 26:17-22; Num 21:16-18; Pss 104:10-13; 114:8).

The association of water and women is not unique to Proverbs. The lover in the Song of Songs calls his bride "a sealed cistern" (4:12 AT)—"a garden [spring], a well of [fresh] water, and . . . streams from Lebanon" (4:15)—and the Egyptian *Instruction of Anii* describes a "stranger" woman as a "deep water whose course is unknown" (*AEL* 2:137). Moreover, meeting a woman—often a future wife—at a well is a recurrent motif. Recall, for example, the stories of Rebekah (Gen 24), Rachel (Gen 29), Zipporah (Exod 2:15-22), and the Samaritan woman (John 4:6-15).

The father likens "the wife of one's youth" to an array of waterworks. Cisterns are hollows cut into the ground to store runoff rainwater. Because cistern water often contains sediment and pollution, it was used primarily for irrigation and livestock but occasionally also for drinking (e.g., Deut 6:10-11; 2 Kgs 18:31; Neh 9:25; Isa 36:16). To "drink water from your own cistern" is, like eating from one's own vine and fig tree, an indication of prosperity (e.g., 2 Kgs 18:31; Isa 36:16). Wells are shafts dug to tap into fresh, flowing aquifers (e.g., Gen 26:18, 32). Because well water is of higher quality and requires more effort to draw, it is used mainly for drinking and watering livestock (e.g., Gen 24). Springs running above ground are prized because of their rarity, convenience, and purity; indeed, they are symbols of God's goodness (e.g., Ps 107:35; Isa 41:18). Finally, the father calls the wife a "fountain" (5:18), that is, a surging spring or source; "fountain" may also refer to a woman's reproductive capacity, namely, to her menstrual blood (Lev 20:18) and the blood of childbirth (Lev 12:7). Elsewhere in Proverbs wisdom is a "fountain" (18:4; cf. 16:22), and wise teaching (13:14; cf. 10:11) and "the fear of the LORD" (14:27) are "fountains of life," a list to which Jeremiah adds YHWH (Jer 2:13; 17:13; cf. Ps 36:8-9 [Heb. vv. 9-10]). This catalog of waterworks presents "the wife of one's youth" as a vital source of life, health, blessing, and posterity that is associated intimately with wisdom and the divine.

Interpreters debate about how best to construe 5:16 ("Let your springs be scattered outside, streams of water in the streets"). The statement appears contrary to the father's aim to teach the youth to restrict his sexual activity to his wife. Three ways of addressing this contradiction are most common. First, the statement is a result clause ("so that") that extols the rewards of marital fidelity; "streams" allude to the husband's virility (specifically semen; cf. Isa 48:1) and perhaps its realization in numerous, legitimate children who, like springs, flow into the streets. Second, the statement is a caution against infidelity. Proponents of this view also understand "streams" to refer to semen but add an initial negative particle (e.g., "*Lest* your streams . . .") or read a negative rhetorical question ("*Should* your streams . . . ?"). The third, and in my view most likely, proposal also construes the statement negatively but understands "springs" to refer to "the wife of your youth." That is, if the husband does not drink from his "cistern" (i.e. his wife), then other men who are "outside" and "in the streets" will.

The third interpretation is compelling for several reasons. It is consistent with water as a metaphor for the "wife of one's youth" in the surrounding verses, a use made explicit in 5:18b. Moreover, the following verse: "Let [the streams] be for yourself alone and not for sharing with [strange men]" (NRSV: "strangers"; cf. 5:10) makes little sense if "streams" refer to the husband's semen or to his children (indeed, water is never used elsewhere for descendants). Finally, the verb "scattered" is typically negative (e.g., Gen 11:4, 9; 49:7; Deut 28:64; but cf. Zech 1:17), making it unlikely that water dispersed in the streets is a positive expression for children. The sense of 5:16, therefore, is that if the husband does not observe sexual exclusivity, neither will his wife. Whether by choice or by force, she will abandon him. Ironically, should she do so, she becomes a "strange" woman herself (cf. 2:17).

A husband's sexual behavior thereby has a profound impact on his wife's. The assumption, which is common in a patrilineal culture, is that he has charge of his wife's sexuality much as her father would have prior to her marriage (e.g., Deut 22:13-21, 28-29). Repetition of the possessive pronoun ("your") underscores the husband's exclusive claim to her, as do the metaphors of water contained: she is "*your* cistern," "*your* well," "*your* springs," "*your* fountain," "for *yourself alone*" (5:15-18). Should he be unfaithful, suddenly that same water is released—"scattered outside" and flowing "in the city squares" (5:16-17). The image is one of broken boundaries and immediate chaos. According to the father, the husband's loyalty is necessary to preserve sexual and social order. Similar logic is found in the Egyptian *Instruction of Ptahhotep*:

When you prosper and found your house,
  And love your wife with ardor,
Fill her belly, clothe her back,
  Ointment soothes her body.
Gladden her heart as long as you live.
  She is a fertile field for her lord.
Do not contend with her in court,
  Keep her from power, restrain her. . . .
Thus will you make her stay in your house. (*AEL* 1:69)

The father highlights the wife's sexual desirability. He describes her as "a lovely deer, a graceful [mountain goat]" (5:19a). Animal imagery is common in ancient erotic speech. Song of Songs, for example, likens a woman's breasts to "two fawns, twins of a gazelle" (4:5; 7:3), her eyes to doves, her hair to a herd of goats, and her teeth to a flock of freshly shorn ewes (4:1-2; 6:5-6); similarly, the male lover is a gazelle and young stag (2:9, 17; 8:14). The father next makes a pun (5:19b). He talks of her *daddîm* ("breasts" or "nipples"), a word that is remarkably similar to *dōdîm* ("sex-making," cf. 7:18). *Dōdîm* refers to sexual encounters between people who may or may not be in love—everything from kissing and embracing to intercourse (e.g., Song 1:2, 4; Ezek 23:17). The father charges the husband to let his wife's breasts or sex-making so "quench" his thirst (NRSV: "satisfy")—an image that recalls the liquid images of 5:15-18—that he "staggers" about as if intoxicated (5:19; e.g., 20:1; Isa 28:7). Interestingly, with this verse as the only apparent exception, the verb "to stagger" is negative, meaning "to stray," "make a mistake," "do wrong" (e.g., 19:27; 1 Sam 26:21; Ps 119:21, 118). That is certainly its sense when the father asks why the youth would "stagger" with a "strange" woman and cling to *her* breasts (5:20). So why does the father say to "stagger" or "stray" with one's wife? As M. V. Fox suggests, it may be brilliant pedagogy: rather than admonishing a young man never to stray despite all the excitement and passion that connotes, the father encourages him to do so and regularly ("at all times," 5:19)—with his wife (2000, 203-4).

Closing (5:21-23)

With the question, "Why would you stagger with a 'strange' woman?" still in the air (5:20), the father describes the fate of the man who chooses the wrong woman (5:21-23). Shifting from second-person ("you") to third-person masculine singular ("he/his/him"; NRSV: "they/their/them"), the father puts distance between the youth and "that man." If the youth heeds instruction, he need not suffer the same fate. The father emphasizes, first, that God watches which paths a man chooses. In contrast to the "strange" woman who does not observe the way ahead (5:5), God's eyes observe a person's ways in detail (5:20). One cannot get away with infidelity. Should a man choose that path nevertheless, the father continues, his iniquities inevitably ensnare him (cf. 1:17-19). Fetters of his own making bind and hold him fast, as tenaciously perhaps as the steps of his partner, the "strange" woman, hold (NRSV: "follow") her on the descent to death (5:5). His lack of discipline ends up killing him (an echo of the remorseful cry in 5:12). He staggers not from intoxicating sexual pleasures but utter foolishness (5:23). The man suffers, and fatally so, for choosing the wrong woman, the wrong path.

Theological and Ethical Analysis

History abounds with portraits of erotic love as dangerous coupled with efforts to control and repress it. Some philosophers would eliminate erotic love, at least as part of an ethical life. Plato, for example, argued that people are freed from the "frenzy" of sex, an "unnecessary" pleasure, when they direct their desire to such higher goods as truth and beauty (*The Republic*, 403a, 559cd). The Greek Stoics believed that the attainment of virtues brought about freedom from passions. Paul encouraged believers not to marry unless they lacked self-control ("It is better to marry than to be aflame with passion," 1 Cor 7:9). And I. Kant argued that sexual desire leads to "using" people and thereby degrading their humanity—a tendency that only marriage with its promises of mutual concern might limit (1980, 163-64). Time and again, we find considerable effort devoted to "reform or educate erotic love, so as to keep its creative force while purifying it of ambivalence and excess, and making it more friendly to general social aims" (Nussbaum 2001, 469).

In conjunction with Proverbs 6–7, this is the parent's most fervent attempt to do precisely that. As the references to water and "staggering" indicate, the parent regards sexual desire as a potent, indeed intoxicating, power. Expressed within certain bounds, like the waters to which God assigns limits (8:29), it can be joyful and life-giving. Expressed outside those bounds, it becomes chaotic and destructive—devastating not only the people involved but others in the community. The descriptions of passions and appetites elsewhere in the book resonate with this understanding. Passions and appetites are vital to human flourishing, but one must channel them "rightly" or risk being burned (cf. 6:20-35; see Theological and Ethical Analysis of Proverbs 1 and, e.g., 12:16; 14:17a, 29; 17:27; 19:11a).

Today many talk similarly about sex, but we tend to motivate sexual fidelity differently. We appeal to the damage wrought by sexual transgression on the two people involved and their immediate families, on self-esteem, and on emotional, psychological, and physical health. By contrast, the parent appeals to the youth's (but not the woman's) honor. The parent teaches that the youth's desire for esteem should outweigh his desire for sex, that shame and ostracism are the real nightmare. Honor is a highest good and functions much like a contract: people seek honor by exemplifying the community's values and the community, in turn, bestows honor as affirmation on those who do. To violate the contract is to absent oneself from the community, to step "outside" the bounds of its expectations and traditions ("I hated discipline. . . . I did not listen," 5:12-13) and, as such, to face loss (5:9-10), public rejection, and personal guilt (5:11-14). It is to become in effect a "stranger"—not unlike the woman whom the parent's discourse keeps "outside" as little more than an object of sexual desire. The parent says nothing about what circumstances might prompt the woman's behavior or what consequences she likely endures for it—a silence indicative of sexism.

PROVERBS 6

Literary Analysis

The chapter has two main units (6:1-19 and 20-35), each of which begins "my son" (6:1, 20). The first is comprised of four subsections (6:1-5, 6-11, 12-15, and 16-19), the initial two of which concern behaviors that threaten personal and communal welfare: guaranteeing the loan of a stranger (6:1-5) and laziness (6:6-11). Both feature second-person address ("my son," 6:1, 3; "you lazybones," 6:6, 9), comparisons to animals (gazelle and bird, 6:5; the ant, 6:6-8), the human hand (6:1, 3, 5, 10), and a need to stay awake (6:4, 9-10).

The second two subsections are portraits of the wicked—the "good-for-nothing" (6:12-15) and seven abominations of YHWH (6:16-19). These are, like the earlier subsections, closely associated. Both refer to parts of the body: the mouth (6:12, 17 [tongue]), eyes (6:13, 17), hands (6:13 [fingers], 17), heart or mind (6:14, 18), and feet (6:13, 18). They share the verb "to devise" (6:14, 18) and culminate with the phrase "to send out discord" (6:14 [so Kethib, or the written tradition], 19). Read together, the "good-for-nothing" illustrates what God despises.

Verses 16-19 comprise a numerical proverb. In such proverbs, two numbers typically occur in parallel (x, x+1), and the second number governs the content. Numerical proverbs figure prominently later in Proverbs (cf. 30:15-16, 18-19, 21-23, 24-28, 29-31) and are found occasionally elsewhere in biblical wisdom (e.g., Job 5:19-22; Sir 25:7-11) and other ancient Near Eastern wisdom texts (e.g., the Aramaic *Proverbs of Ahiqar*, TAD 3.1.1.187-188).

The second main unit returns to the subject of sexual conduct to warn against committing adultery (6:20-35; cf. 5:1-20). In 6:20-24, the father claims that parental instruction and wisdom protects the youth from the "strange" woman, here identified explicitly as a married woman (6:26; cf. 6:29, 34-35). He cautions about her enticing beauty (6:24-25), argues that she poses a deadly threat (6:26-31), and concludes with a summary warning (6:32-35).

Exegetical Analysis

Money Matters (6:1-5)

Turning to money issues, the father cautions against providing surety to a neighbor for the debt of a stranger (6:1b; NRSV: "another"). In ancient Israel, there were several ways to guarantee a loan. The borrower might offer an item of value as collateral (e.g., Deut 24:6, 10-13; Exod 22:25-26); pledge fields, houses, and even children (Neh 5:1-5); or request that another person, often in exchange for a small fee, serve as guarantor. If one became a guarantor, all of one's property (and oneself if necessary) was subject to seizure if the debtor failed to repay the loan. Calling such responsibility senseless (17:18) and unsafe (11:15), the sages of Proverbs urge avoidance of it altogether, whether the debtor is a stranger (11:15; 20:16; 27:13) or a neighbor (17:18). The personal and financial risks are *always* prohibitive (cf. 22:26-27; but cf. Sir 8:13) but extremely so in the case of surety for strangers who purportedly have less social pressure to honor their commitments. Indeed, the sages tell creditors that they might as well "take the garment of one who has [stood] surety for a stranger" (20:16; cf. 27:13) because strangers will almost certainly renege on their loans. To guarantee the debt of a stranger is in effect to forfeit everything, including the shirt on one's back.

The father describes the agreement to provide surety as a deadly snare that is set with a flurry of words and a handshake. What the youth says to negotiate the arrangement binds him (6:2; as firmly, it seems, as a written contract), while his handshake ("striking the hand") with the stranger seals the deal (6:1b). The father refers three times to "hands" (6:1b, 3b, 5b), a term that in Hebrew may refer metaphorically to a person's "power," much as the English expression "the matter is in your hands" means you have control over it (e.g., Deut 32:36; Josh 8:20). As the father tells it, when a person shakes hands with a *stranger* as guarantor of his loans (6:1b), he ends up in his *neighbor's* hand (6:3b), a position the father likens to that of trapped animals: a gazelle in the (hand of) a hunter and a bird in the hand of a fowler (6:5b). A misguided

71

handshake with one person, that is, puts the youth firmly in the grasp of another who then wields power over him and his possessions. This precarious position distorts the equitable relations neighbors ought to enjoy, establishing instead an economic hierarchy. Much as the schemes and iniquities of the wicked ensnare them (e.g., 5:22-23; 11:6), the poor judgment of a guarantor ensnares him.

Twice the father implores, "Save yourself!" from such an entanglement (6:3, 5). He also tells the youth how. Go to the neighbor (the creditor), "trample on" oneself (i.e., be humble), and beg to be released as guarantor (6:3). The instruction makes clear the matter is of utmost import and urgency. Forsaking all pride, the youth is to grovel relentlessly—not stopping for sleep (6:4). Like prey caught tightly in a predator's grip (6:5), he must do whatever is necessary to free himself quickly, even at the risk of pain and injury. For the father, it is better to humiliate oneself completely than endanger one's financial security and relationship to a neighbor. Perhaps the father hopes that such a graphic, demeaning portrait of how to escape the role of guarantor may deter the youth from ever assuming it.

The father's conservative financial advice may have been the best way he knew to navigate the risky economic circumstances of the Persian period. What had been a largely barter economy (cf. Ezek 27:12-25) shifted under the Persian administration to a monetary one. As goods and services were increasingly assigned monetary values, the demand for cash rose quickly, creating an environment rich with opportunities for economic advancement and exploitation (Seow 1996, 171-89). As people borrowed to get ahead or merely to survive, the business of granting loans of cash or goods flourished. Annual interest rates were high, varying from 20 to 40 percent in Babylon to an astounding 60 to 120 percent at a Jewish military garrison in Egypt, and the penalties for default were severe. A creditor could seize all of the debtor's property (house, land, slaves, food, grain, and even children) and, if that was not sufficient, consign the debtor to a "house of detention" to work off the remainder of the debt. Moreover, if debtors died before the debt was repaid, their children inherited it along with its interest. Nehemiah describes the grim consequences of such economic realities for some in Jerusalem:

> There were those who said, "We are mortgaging our fields, our vineyards, and our houses so that we may get grain during the famine." And there were those who said, "We have borrowed money for the king's tax on our fields and vineyards. Now, we are of the same flesh as our kin and our children are as their children. But we are at the point of selling our sons and daughters into slavery—indeed some of our daughters are enslaved. We are powerless, for our fields and our vineyards belong to others." (Neh 5:3-5 AT)

Perhaps, looking around at such a scene, the father thought the best advice for his children's welfare and that of the community was never to get involved with loans in the first place.

Go to the Ant (6:6-11)

To teach about industriousness and sloth, the father presents two contrasting figures: the ant and the slacker (6:6-11). "Go to the ant," he urges, and *look*. Consider one of the smallest, most familiar of creatures and learn something new about self-reliance, initiative, and hard work (6:6-8). A hallmark of the wisdom tradition is the belief that the natural world is revelatory. Solomon, the quintessential sage of Israel (see 1:1), would "speak of trees . . . animals, and birds, and reptiles, and fish" (1 Kgs 4:33). Job similarly expounds:

> But ask the animals, and they will teach you;
>   the birds of the air, and they will tell you;
> [Talk to] . . . the earth, and [it] will teach you;
>   and the fish of the sea will [tell] you.
> Who among all these does not know
>   that the hand of the LORD has done this?
> (Job 12:7-9; cf. Isa 1:3; Jer 8:6-7; Luke 12:22-31)

The ant is mentioned in the Old Testament only in Proverbs—here and in 30:25, where it is listed as one of four creatures that are small yet exceedingly wise. Both 6:6-8 and 30:25 highlight the ant's preparation of food in the summer. In Palestine, there are two primary seasons: the wet, cool months (October–April) and the dry, warm season (May–September). Harvest typically takes place in the latter (e.g., Jer 8:20; 40:10, 12; Amos 8:1; Mic 7:1). The ant apparently knows this instinctively because without instruction, order, or coercion, it makes ready its food in the summer, storing it up for the rainy season when sustenance is scarce. By doing its work at the appropriate time, the ant is prepared and never hungry. Foresight saves the ant (cf. 10:5; 20:4; and the *Instruction of Ankhsheshonq*: "He who does not gather wood in summer will not be warm in winter," *AEL* 3:167).

The contrast to the ant is the lazybones to whom Proverbs devotes, in addition to 6:9-11, two longer units (24:30-34 and 26:13-16) and individual proverbs (10:26; 13:4; 15:19; 19:24; 20:4; 21:25; 22:13). The father's opening question, "How long?" signals his reproach (6:9; cf. 1:22; Exod 10:3; 1 Sam 16:1; 1 Kgs 18:21; Jer 4:14). Unlike the diligent ant, the slacker lies around, snoozing the day away (cf. 26:14). The father details the idler's recipe for disaster (6:10; cf. 1:26-32): a dash of sleep, a pinch of snoozing, a dollop of hands folded in rest (cf. 24:33; Eccl 4:5). And, soon enough, poverty attacks. It springs on the lazybones with the swift aggression of a vagabond or warrior (6:11). Like the onset of the rainy season, the fate of the slacker is predictable and certain. He ends up with nothing (cf. 20:4, 13). Proverbs 6:11 recurs later in Proverbs after a description of the lazy person's field as overgrown with thorns and nettles, its stone wall in shambles (24:30-34).

It is possible, of course, to construe 6:9-11—the only proverb in Proverbs 1–9 to mention "poverty"—in reverse, namely, that poverty indicates laziness. Experience teaches, however, that although that may be true in some cases, it is not in many others. Even a cursory look at proverbs concerned with wealth and poverty elsewhere in Proverbs reveals that the sages also regarded poverty as a complex phenomenon (e.g., 10:15; 13:7, 18, 23; 22:9; 28:3, 19; 31:7).

The Good-for-Nothing (6:12-15)

In a manner reminiscent of the "anatomy" of a moral life (4:23-27), the father next describes the "good-for-nothing," noting his speech (6:12b), body language (6:12b-13), thoughts (6:14a), effect on the community (6:14b), and fate (6:15). "Good-for-nothings," persons of questionable character who are prone to wickedness, include apostates (Deut 13:13 [Heb. v. 14]), rapists (Judg 19:22; cf. 20:13), slanderers (1 Kgs 21:10, 13), perjurers (19:28), and rebels (2 Sam 20:1; 2 Chr 13:7). Counted among them are Abigail's ill-mannered husband Nabal (whose name means "fool," 1 Sam 25:17) and Eli's sons, who flagrantly disregard God and their priestly responsibilities (1 Sam 2:12).

An observant eye should never miss a ne'er-do-well. His mouth is "twisted," meaning it is contorted physically and his speech is distorted and false (6:12b); elsewhere, the sages compare a scoundrel's lips and speech to scorching fire (16:27). The ne'er-do-well's eyes are narrowed (6:13a; NRSV: "winking"), which suggests he looks on others with envy, disdain, or hatred (cf. Ps 35:19) or squints as he conspires to make trouble (10:10; 16:30). His feet shuffle back and forth, signaling his shiftiness and unease. His fingers point in the air, perhaps showing the way to his crooked path (16:29) or attributing blame to others (cf. Isa 58:9). Finally, his mind or heart "devises" (*ḥōrēš*) wickedness (6:14a). In Proverbs, the verb *ḥāraš* refers several times to the abstract notion of "devising" or "crafting" (e.g., 3:29; 12:20; 14:22). Elsewhere, however, the verb most commonly means "to plow" or "cultivate" (e.g., 20:4; Deut 22:10; 1 Sam 8:12; 1 Kgs 19:19; Isa 28:24; and its cognate in other languages). That the immediate literary context of 6:14a includes harvest imagery (6:6-8) evokes this latter sense: while the ant diligently harvests her food, the good-for-nothing "cultivates" wickedness. The NRSV and other translations (e.g., RSV, NJB) capture this nuance when they render the parallel line "continually sowing discord" (6:14b; NJB: "he sows dissension"). The yield of the good-for-nothing's cultivation is controversy and conflict—the breakdown of community.

For that reason, the ruin of the good-for-nothing comes (6:15; cf. 1:26-31; 3:25; 24:22). The father offers little detail about the agent or nature of the disaster. What he does say is that, much like poverty's attack on the slacker, the ruin of the good-for-nothing is sudden (6:14), absolute ("shattered," a verb that connotes extreme physical and/or psychological harm, e.g., 29:1; 1 Sam 4:18; Isa 8:15; Ezek 30:8), and final ("beyond healing," 6:15b).

Seven Abominations (6:16-19)

The enumeration of seven abominations to God is associated closely with the prior description of the "good-for-nothing" (6:12-15). When the two units are read in succession (6:12-15, 16-19), the ne'er-do-well is reframed as one who exemplifies what God hates. The youth should therefore avoid him not only because the father says so, but because God finds his conduct repulsive (cf. 3:32-35). Various proverbs elsewhere reiterate the seven abominations identified here (e.g., 11:20, 12:22; 15:26, 16:5) and add others, such as cheating with false weights and measures (11:1; 20:10, 23), false justification or condemnation (17:15), and the sacrifices of the wicked (15:8; cf. 21:27). For more on "abomination (of YHWH)" in Proverbs, see the excursus in Proverbs 3.

The father ascribes the first five abominations to parts of the body and moves systematically from head to toe (6:17-18). "Haughty eyes" signal arrogance, a willful disregard for humility and respect (6:17; cf. 21:4; 30:13). Given humanity's limitations, propensity to "miss the mark," and radical dependence on God, such overinflated pride is reckless. Indeed, God is said to "bring down" those with lofty eyes (e.g., Ps 18:27 [Heb. v. 28]; Isa 2:11; Sir 23:4). A "lying tongue" similarly spurns reality. It twists and ignores the truth at will. Liars wield their mouths like weapons (25:18; cf. Ps 64:2-4), whetting their tongues like swords, bending them as bows (Ps 64:3; Jer 9:3 [Heb. v. 2]), and unleashing bitter words as a barrage of arrows (Ps 64:3-4). Their every word drips with hatred for truth and for their victims (10:18; 26:28; Ps 109:2-19). "Hands [or arms] that shed innocent blood" are guilty of murder, not an accidental killing (e.g., Deut 19:10-13; 21:1-9; 27:25; Jer 7:5-7). With forethought and deliberateness, they take the life of another violently (cf. 1:10-19). Finally, a devising heart (see 6:14) concocts wicked plans while feet that "hurry to do evil" ensure that those plans are carried out quickly (6:18; cf. Isa 59:7).

The last two abominations are types of people (6:19). The first is the false witness who literally "breathes out" deceit (cf. 14:5), whether in court or in everyday conversation (e.g., 12:17; 25:18; Deut 19:18-19; Ps 27:12). The second "sows discord between brothers" (NRSV: "in a family"; cf. 6:14). In Hebrew, "brothers" may refer to blood relations (e.g., Gen 4:8; 44:20; Hos 12:3 [Heb. v. 4]) and more generally to companions (e.g., Job 30:29), members of one's tribe or nation (e.g., Gen 31:32; Exod 2:11; Lev 19:17; Judg 9:18). The sower of discord sparks conflict with abandon, in intimate and distant relationships alike.

Warning against Adultery (6:20-35)

The exordium (6:20-23) appeals to the youth to keep his father's "commandment" (*miṣwôt*) and his mother's "teaching" (*tôrâ*). In Proverbs 1–9, both terms always designate parental instruction (*miṣwôt*, cf. 2:1; 3:1; 4:4; 7:1-2; *tôrâ*, cf. 1:8; 3:1; 4:2; 7:2). Elsewhere in the Old Testament, however, they commonly refer to divine law. Verbal and thematic parallels between 6:20-23 and Deut 6:1-9 and 11:18-20 associate the two. Note, for example, Moses' instruction:

> You shall put these words of mine in your *heart* and soul, and you shall *bind them* as a sign on your hand, and fix them as an emblem on your forehead. Teach them to your children, talking about them when you are at home and when you are away, *when you lie down* and when you rise. (Deut 11:18; cf. Deut 6:7-8)

Moreover, the description of parental instruction as a "lamp" and a "light" (6:23) evokes the psalmist's praise of the divine word as the same (Ps 119:105). The father thus suggests (again) that parental guidance is consonant with divine law.

Given that the subject of 6:20-23 is plural (parental instructions), the feminine singular in 6:22 (contra NRSV: "they") is surprising: "*She* will lead you. . . . *She* will [keep] you. . . . *She* will talk with you." Parental instructions are personified as a woman who tends to her companion day and night. She guides him on his way. She watches over him as he sleeps (compare wisdom as protector; cf. 2:11; 4:6). And, when he wakes, she "talks" with him; the verb used refers to emotionally laden speech such as praise (Judg 5:10; Ps 105:2), lament (Job 7:11; Ps 55:17 [Heb. v. 18]), and taunting (Ps 69:12 [Heb. v. 13]). She talks passionately with him, that is, whatever the subject. Insofar as the father turns next to warn about the adulterous woman (6:24-33), he again juxtaposes a "desirable" woman, whose speech is compelling, with a "dangerous" one (cf. 5:1-23). If *this* woman is your companion, why would you ever desire *that* one?

Parental instruction protects (6:24; cf. 6:22) the youth, in particular, from the "strange" woman, who is portrayed here as married (6:24-33; esp. 6:26, 29). The father anticipates what is alluring about her (6:24-25): her "smooth tongue" or "slippery talk" (cf. 2:16) and her beauty, which he associates specifically with her eyes or (batting?) eyelashes (the Hebrew term can mean either). Ben Sira cautions similarly: "A woman's harlotry may be recognized by her haughty eyes and her eyelids" (26:9 AT; cf. Prov 6:17). Elsewhere in the Old Testament, beauty is portrayed as an attribute that captivates and elicits the desire of others. Beauty is a pleasing, even inspiring, quality of wise women (1 Sam 25:3), leaders (e.g., Gen 39:6), and kings (e.g., 1 Sam 16:12; 2 Sam 14:25, 27). Occasionally, there is an implicit assumption that people cannot resist the pull of beauty; that gazing upon someone who is beautiful renders people helpless with desire, perhaps to the point of losing control in inappropriate or violent ways, as in the case of Sarai (Gen 12:10-20), Joseph (Gen 39:6-20), and Tamar (2 Sam 13:1-22). The father's worry that the "strange" woman will "capture" the youth with her eyelashes (6:25) suggests such thinking, as does an Egyptian lover's celebration of his beloved: "She casts the noose on me with her hair, / She captures me with her eye" (*AEL* 2:187). An insidious inference, of course, is that that youth temporarily loses moral agency; transfixed by the woman's attractiveness, he is not fully responsible for his actions.

The father then explains why the youth must avoid married women. Whereas the fee for a prostitute is a loaf of bread—an item of subsistence (e.g., 1 Kgs 17:11-16; 18:4, 13)—the cost of adultery (defined in the ancient world as sex with a married or betrothed woman; the marital status of her partner is inconsequential) is a man's very life. Indeed, the woman is said to hunt (NRSV: "stalks") for him, much as the wicked lie in wait to ambush the innocent (1:10-19; cf. Mic 7:2).

The father gives two explanations for why the penalty is so high (6:27-31). First, adultery has dire, unavoidable consequences (6:27-29). As predictably as a person who takes fire to her chest burns her clothes (6:27) or who walks on burning coals scorches his feet (6:29), a man who "comes to" his neighbor's wife incurs blame (6:29). The expression "to come to" a woman is a euphemism for sexual intercourse (so NRSV: "sleeps with"; e.g., Gen 16:2; 30:3; 38:8); the parallel "touching her" (6:29b) confirms that the issue is physical contact (e.g., Gen 20:6; Ruth 2:9). In sum, play with fire and you get burned. Second, the consequences exceed and endure far longer than any perceived gains (6:30-31). Look at the thief, the father says, whom no one hates for stealing to satisfy his hunger (an appetite not unlike libido), but when he is caught, that bellyful costs him "sevenfold" or all the wealth of his house. Imagine how much worse the penalty will be for a man who commits adultery— who rends the fabric of fidelity that safeguards family and communal relationships.

Verses 32-35 summarize the warning. The adulterer is said to be without sense (he "lacks heart," cf. 7:7; 9:4, 16; 10:13) and to destroy himself (6:32). For his stupidity, he suffers affliction and shame (6:33). The term "affliction" refers to bodily harm caused by disease (e.g., Lev 13; 1 Kgs 8:37) or physical violence (e.g., 2 Sam 7:14; Ps 39:10 [Heb. v. 11]; 89:32 [Heb. v. 33]). Given the description of the husband's rage as unrelenting—he shows "no restraint" and will accept no amount of compensation or "hush money"—it seems certain that the husband and perhaps others beat the adulterer. The adulterer's humiliation is public and enduring (6:33).

The husband's retaliation is called "a day of vengeance" (6:34b; NRSV: "revenge"), a phrase elsewhere attributed only to God (Isa 34:8; 61:2; 63:4). Unlike the English word "vengeance," which carries negative or pejorative connotations, "vengeance" in the Old Testament typically refers to punishment inflicted justly for an injury or offense. The Hebrew root for "vengeance" occurs most frequently in judicial texts and others concerned with fair compensation (e.g., Exod 21:20-21; Josh 10:12-13; Isa 59:15-19; Jer 15:15; Ezek 25:13-14). Although the adulterer's punishment here is (apparently) not death as legally prescribed (Deut 22:22; Lev 20:10), use of the phrase suggests that the husband acts justifiably, perhaps in a manner consistent with everyday legal practice.

Theological and Ethical Analysis

It is easy in a culture of individualism to read this chapter as largely self-interested advice—about what is good for *me*. What financial commitments are too risky? What relationships should I avoid? How do I balance work and rest? And so on. The parent challenges us, however, to step back for a moment and consider such matters from a wider perspective. Who has a stake in our attitudes and behaviors? Whom do they affect? The parent points first and repeatedly to the neighbor (6:1, 3, 29; cf. "brothers" [NRSV: "family"], 6:19 and "another," 6:26). Granting surety creates economic disparity (6:1-5); laziness requires others to do more work (6:6-11); plotting harm and stirring up conflict puts others at risk and frays social harmony (6:14, 18-19); murder unjustly and violently takes another's life (6:17); false testimony injures a neighbor's reputation and imperils his or her future (6:17, 19); and adultery enrages one's neighbor beyond hope of reconciliation (6:24-35). The parent calls for an ethic of neighborliness, the recognition that we are entwined in a complex web of social relationships that we sustain, strengthen, or shred.

The parent points second to God. The juxtaposition of 6:12-15 and 6:16-19 at the heart of the chapter makes clear that behaviors the community recognizes as destabilizing and destructive are offensive to God. There is essential continuity between the community's values and God's moral standards (e.g., Lev 19). God is fiercely, indeed passionately ("God hates," 6:16), concerned with matters of neighborliness and justice—not only on a grand scale, but in everyday decisions and actions (see excursus in Proverbs 3).

"Go to the ant" (6:6-8) affirms that nature contributes to our moral understanding. The parent urges the youth to look at a familiar creature in a new way, to see its existence as one with dignity and purposes that disclose something about the God who, by wisdom, created it. Considered as such, nature is valuable for far more than its utility. Nature teaches us about existence as creatures of God (e.g., Matt 6:25-34). In today's consumer culture, "going to the ant" highlights how distorted is our demand for instant gratification ("buy now, pay later") given the rhythms of the world. The ant gathers its food "in season," during harvest when there is abundance, so that it has enough when, *inevitably*, food is scarce. In contrast, many of us "gather" perpetually, with little to no regard for the ebb and flow of resources and the needs of others. Such "out of season" consumption threatens far more egregious scarcities.

PROVERBS 7–8

Literary Analysis

The two women about whom the father has interwoven speeches to this point in Proverbs 1–9—the "strange" woman and personified wisdom—stand now back-to-back: chapter 7 is the fourth and most extensive teaching about the "strange" woman (2:16-22; 5:1-23; 6:20-35), and chapter 8 is personified wisdom's self-revelation (1:20-33; 3:13-18; 4:5-9; 7:4-5). The juxtaposition sets the stage for invitations from both women in Proverbs 9 (9:1-6, 11; 13-18). It also casts in sharp relief the father's depiction of women as either "bad" or "good." Ancient Egyptian sages portray women analogously. Women are either "bad," namely, outside the family (prostitutes and potential adulteresses), or "good," inside the family (wives, mothers, or widows). The *Instruction of Anii*, for example, cautions:

Beware of a woman who is a stranger,
    One not known in her town;
Don't stare at her when she goes by,
    Do not know her carnally.
A deep water whose course is unknown,
    Such is a woman away from her husband.
"I am pretty," she tells you daily,
    When she has no witnesses;
She is ready to ensnare you,
    A great and deadly crime when it is heard. (*AEL* 2:137)

And later encourages:

Do not control your wife in your house,
    When you know she is efficient;
Don't say to her, "Where is it? Get it!"
    When she has put it in the right place.
Let your eye observe in silence,
    Then you recognize her skill;
It is a joy when your hand is with her,
    There are many who don't know this. (*AEL* 2:143)

The dichotomy between "good" and "bad" women continues in Proverbs (see Theological and Ethical Analysis and 12:4, 14:1; 18:22; 19:14; 22:14; 23:27-28; 30:20).

Following an exordium (7:1-5), the heart of chapter 7 is the father's depiction of a street scene that features two principal characters: a naive youth and the "strange" woman (7:6-23). Told as an eyewitness account (cf. 24:30-34; Job 5:3-5) observed from a latticed window, the scene abounds with suspense and dramatic detail. The father sets the stage by identifying the young man, his whereabouts, and the time of day (7:6-9). Then, abruptly, he shifts attention to "a woman" down the road who approaches the youth (7:10). He describes her appearance, character, and actions (7:10-13) and "quotes" her words to the boy (7:14-20). Her speech is effective. The youth follows her without hesitation—a decision with deadly consequences (7:21-23). The chapter concludes with a summary warning (7:24-27).

In the wake of the "strange" woman's compelling speech (7:21), the father directs the youth's attention back to personified wisdom (8:1-5), who now offers her longest, most self-revealing speech to persuade the youth—indeed, everyone—of her desirability.

Wisdom extols first the integrity of her speech (8:6-11). She structures this section of her appeal with four imperatives: "Learn!" (8:5 [2x]), "Hear!" (8:6), and "Take!" (8:10). Pointing repeatedly to her mouth—the parting of her lips (8:6; cf. 8:7b), her palate (8:7a), and mouth (8:8)—she asserts the trustworthiness of her words with three interrelated claims (8:6-7, 8-9, 10-11). Repetition of the Hebrew root yāšar ("right" or "straight," 8:6, 9) emphasizes her point. At 8:11, wisdom abruptly shifts into third-person speech and repeats 3:15 nearly word for word; the verse is likely a later addition.

Wisdom moves on to celebrate her character and benefits (8:12-21). She describes her nature (8:12-14) and identifies herself as the source and means of human governance (8:15-16). For those who love her, wisdom promises she will reciprocate their affection and bestow wealth upon them (8:17-21, framed by an *inclusio* of "love"). Her testimony abounds with first-person singular speech: the first-person pronoun (8:12, 14, 17), first-person singular verbs (i.e., "I find," 8:12; "I hate," 8:13; "I love," 8:17; "I walk," 8:20; "I fill," 8:21), and first-person singular object and possessive suffixes (marked in Hebrew by a long *i*, e.g., "by me," 8:15-16; "with me," 8:18; "love me," 8:17, 21; "seek me," 8:17; "find me," 8:17; "my fruit," "my yield," 8:19). The inundation of "I language" conveys wisdom's inimitability.

Then, in perhaps the most renowned and contested verses of Proverbs 1–9, wisdom claims her preeminence and association with God (8:22-31). With syntax that evokes other creation accounts ("when . . . when . . . then," e.g., Job 28:25-27), she describes her origins before (8:22-26) and presence during God's formation of the world (8:27-29), and is evocative about the nature of her relationship with God and humankind (8:30-31).

Finally, echoing her earlier command to "listen" (8:6), wisdom charges her audience to listen to her (8:32-36), repeating the verb "to listen" three times (8:32, 33, 34) and "to keep" twice (8:32b,

34c). Her exaltations about her speech, nature, preeminence, and roles (8:6-31) provide ample motivation for doing so. But wisdom is not yet finished. She reminds everyone she is also the bearer of happiness (8:32b, 34a; cf. 3:13-18), long life, and divine favor (8:32-35). Those who miss her surely do so at their own peril (8:36).

Exegetical Analysis

Keep Parental Instruction So That It May Keep You (7:1-5)

"Keeping" parental instructions and wisdom (7:1-4), the father promises in this exordium, "keeps" the youth from the "strange" woman (7:5; cf. 2:16; 6:24). So the youth must be wholly devoted to wisdom. The father's "commandments" (cf. 2:1) should be the "pupil of [the youth's] eye" (7:2b)—the center and means of his vision (cf. Sir 3:25) and that which he loves deeply and fiercely protects (e.g., Deut 32:10; Ps 17:8). Parental instructions must be inscribed on the "tablet of [the youth's] heart" and bound around his fingers (7:3; cf. 3:3; Deut 6:8; 11:18), namely, known so well (probably memorized) that the teaching is innate. Moreover, the youth must call wisdom "my sister" and "companion" (7:4; see Ruth 2:1 for the only other use of the latter). Both terms suggest kinship, familiarity. "Sister" may also refer to a female lover. In Song of Songs, "sister" is synonymous with "bride" in the whisperings of a man to his beloved (4:9-10, 12; 5:1-2) and, in Egyptian love songs, lovers address each other as "brother" or "sister" (*AEL* 2:181-193).

The Illicit Encounter (7:6-23)

If the youth is not devoted to wisdom, the father continues, his fate is surely that of the "youth without sense" introduced in 7:6-9. A master storyteller, the father ushers the imagination of the youth (and readers) up to a latticed window to observe an unnamed boy on the street. In the Hebrew, the father speaks in the first-person singular ("my house . . . I looked down. . . . I observed," 7:6-7). In LXX, by contrast, the narrator speaks in the third-person feminine singular ("her house . . . She looks down.

. . . She observes"), referring apparently to the "strange" woman. The shift in perspective may be influenced by a type-scene in the Old Testament of (royal) women looking out a window, such as Sisera's mother (Judg 5:28), Michal (2 Sam 6:16; 1 Chr 15:29), and Jezebel (2 Kgs 9:30). However, the scene is not exclusive to women (e.g., Abimelech in Gen 26:8; the eunuchs in 2 Kgs 9:32), and a change in narrative voice at 7:6 is too abrupt. Moreover, by speaking autobiographically, the father heightens the believability and hence the severity of his warning. He speaks as an eyewitness. (Implicit may also be caution that, should the youth disobey the instruction, someone is sure to see).

The father's initial description of the youth raises alarm (7:7-9). First, the youth is one of the "simple" (*pĕtā'yîm*, cf. 1:4)—the inexperienced and naive who are capable of learning but, without tutoring, tend to behave foolishly (e.g., 1:32; 8:5). He is also a "youth," an adolescent who "lacks sense," a characteristic ascribed elsewhere to adulterers (6:32), slackers (24:30), guarantors of loans (17:18), and so on (e.g., 11:12; 12:11; 15:21). Second, the youth is on the "strange" woman's street, near her corner, on the road to her house—outside, in transitional spaces where one is vulnerable. He is precisely where he has been warned repeatedly not to go (2:17-19; 5:8-14); indeed, he "strides" there, a verb that indicates he walks with purpose and conviction. Finally, the time of day passes from early evening (7:9a) to the deep of night (7:9b). This is a time of vulnerability and life-changing encounters (e.g., Gen 32; Job 4:12-17), when lovers seek each other (e.g., Gen 30:15-17; Song 3:1-4; 5:2; cf. Ruth 1:12), when one can move discreetly, without fear of being recognized (e.g., Exod 10:22-23). According to Job, the "eye of the adulterer [watches] for . . . twilight, saying 'No [one] will see me'; and he disguises his face" (24:15).

With a sudden *hinnê* ("Look!"), the father turns to the other principal character—"a woman" (7:10). She "approaches" the young man; he has come to her part of town, but she initiates their encounter (cf. 7:15). The father describes her (7:10-13) in a manner reminiscent of his anatomical descriptions of the moral person (4:20-27) and the good-for-nothing (6:16-19). Though a married woman (7:19-20), she wears the garments of a prostitute, suggesting perhaps that a veil covers her face (Gen 38:14-15; cf. Job 24:15). She is "guarded" (NRSV: "wily") of heart so she does not readily reveal her thoughts and intentions (cf. 4:23). She is noisy (cf. 9:13), rebellious (NRSV: "wayward," cf., Deut 21:18; Isa 30:1; 65:2), and restless (7:11b). Her "feet"—which may also be a euphemism for her genitalia (cf. Deut 28:57; Ezek 16:25)—do not stay at home. Instead, she is out and about, "in the street . . . in the squares, [near] every corner" (7:12), exactly where a married woman should not be (5:16). She is where lovers seek each other (Song 3:2), where prostitutes wait (Jer 3:2; Ezek 16:30-31). She is also where personified wisdom speaks (cf. 1:20-21; 8:1-3). But whereas wisdom takes her stand *at* the corners, this woman lingers *near* them, "lying in wait" like an animal on the hunt (e.g., Ps 10:9; Lam 3:10), an army ready to attack (e.g., Josh 8:4; Judg 9:34), and a street gang out to ambush the innocent for profit (1:11, 18; cf. 24:15). There, she grabs hold of the youth and kisses him, a public display likely viewed with disdain (cf. Song 8:1). Her brazenness is written across her "hardened" face (NRSV: "impudent," 7:13), an expression used for people who lack appropriate sensibilities, such as circumspection (21:29), respect (Deut 28:50), and humility (Dan 8:23). She is not bothered by what others may think. Rather, she does whatever it takes to have a moment "face-to-face" with the young man (cf. her face in 7:13b and his in 7:15b: "I have been eagerly seeking *your* face").

The father "quotes" what she says (7:14-20). Her opening words represent her as a pious person who observes cultic obligations and is true to her word (7:14). Just "today," she says, "I made sacrifices of well-being and fulfilled my vows," practices that together denote religious devotion (e.g., Ps 50:14; 66:13; 116:17-18; Isa 19:21; Jon 2:9). She immediately puts at ease any religious sensibilities the youth may have. To offer "sacrifices of well-being," people brought unblemished animals from their herds or flocks (oxen, sheep, goats, or rams) to just outside the temple and slaughtered them. Priests then dashed the blood of the animals against the altar, burned the fat (Lev 3:1-19; 7:15-17), and returned the meat for consumption that day or, at the very latest, the next (Lev 7:15-17; 19:5). It seems the youth could not have run into the "strange" woman at a more fortuitous time. Because of her sacrifices, she has fresh meat for dinner—a rare treat. Moreover, if the youth partakes of it, he helps her fulfill her religious responsibility; he, so to speak, "does his duty." The woman thus begins with an implicit, seemingly innocuous summons to a feast. She appeals to his appetite. At the same time, the summons establishes her capacity to kill, and foreshadows the outcome of their meeting: the youth hastening to his death "like an ox to the slaughter" (7:22b).

As the woman continues, she flatters the young man by recounting her tenacious pursuit of him (7:15). Although the father describes her as constantly "in the street, in the squares," she speaks to the youth as though he alone is the object of her desire and the reason she is still about: "I have come out to meet *you* . . . to seek *your* face eagerly . . . and now I found *you*." The verb "to seek eagerly" always has a clearly defined object, whether it is God (e.g., Ps 63:1 [Heb. v. 2]; Isa 26:9), a particular person (cf. Job 7:21), or personified wisdom (1:28; 8:17). The woman keeps a lookout for him, it seems, as earnestly as others search for God and wisdom. And whereas the youth must seek and find wisdom (1:28; 3:13; 8:17, 35), he need not pursue the "strange" woman. *She finds him.*

The woman has made elaborate preparations in anticipation of their meeting (7:6-7). As she recounts what she has done, her wealth and intentions become increasingly evident. She made ready her "couch," or bed (e.g., Job 7:13; Pss 6:6 [Heb. v. 7]; 41:3 (Heb. v. 4]; 132:3; Amos 6:4)—a place of lovemaking (Song 1:16). She spread on it thick, quality blankets ("coverings") and multi-colored or embroidered cloths made of Egyptian linen. An imported product, linen was a luxury of wealth and royalty (e.g., 1 Chr 15:27; Isa 3:23; Ezek 16:10, 13). She also perfumed her bed with imported, fragrant spices. Myrrh, aloe, and cinnamon are counted among the most erotic spices (Song 4:14). Myrrh, whether solid or liquid in form (cf. Song 5:5, 13), was a prized perfume to wear and to scent garments (Ps 45:9); women may have worn myrrh in a bag suspended between their breasts (Song 1:13;

cf. a woman's breast as "the mountain of myrrh" in 4:6), and mixed it with oil for purposes of skin treatment or massage (Esth 2:12). Aloe, imported from India to Palestine, and cinnamon from Sri Lanka were similarly renowned for their intense fragrances (e.g., Exod 30:23; Ps 45:9). With her every word, the woman enfolds the youth in a bed of soft, luxurious fabrics and sensual aromas.

The woman then makes explicit what feast she proposes: "Come! Let us drink our fill of lovemaking; let us together taste love" (7:18). Echoing the sinners' opening cry, "Come!" (1:11), she offers a nightlong banquet of sexual pleasures the youth may savor with her until he is satisfied, perhaps even staggering (5:20). Eating and drinking can be euphemisms for sexual intercourse. For example, a lover entreats, "Eat . . . drink, and be drunk with love" (Song 5:1; cf. 4:16), and an adulteress "eats, and wipes her mouth, and says, 'I have done no wrong' " (30:20). The youth may satisfy his appetite for hours, the woman assures him, without fear of being caught by her husband. The "strange" woman emphasizes that her husband's absence is long-term and that she knows exactly when he will return: he is away on a long journey, he took a bag of money with him, and he will come back at the full moon (7:19b-20). She further distances herself (and the youth) from her husband by calling him "the man" (7:19) and their home "his house" (7:19-20). As she describes it, her husband could not be more insignificant. So the youth need not worry about suffering his jealous wrath (6:34-35).

The situation is nonetheless perilous. The "strange" woman's speech at an end, the father shifts the spotlight back to the naive adolescent. Her "smooth words" have force, he declares; they are "moving." Her slippery instructions "turn him aside" (NRSV: "persuade," cf. 21:1). Her smooth words "shove" (NRSV: "compels") him. Indeed, she is so enticing that the youth goes after her "suddenly" (7:22), without hesitation, without protest. The term "suddenly" recalls earlier warnings about the calamity that descends on the wicked "suddenly" (6:15) and their equally "sudden" panic (3:25). In an instant, the youth is like them. In a moment, he is rendered subhuman, an animal rushing heedlessly to the slaughter (7:22-23). The father compares the young man to three creatures: an ox on its way to the slaughter, a stag that "bounds" toward the trap (the verb suggests movement that is unthinking, even joyful; cf. Isa 3:16), and a bird that hurries headlong into a snare (cf. 1:17-19). As the father lists them, 7:23a seems out of place—why would a hunter shoot a stag with an arrow if it was already rushing into a trap? Most interpreters therefore read 7:23a as the conclusion: "He does not know that it will cost him his life [until an arrow pierces his liver]." The youth hurries off to become her "fresh meat" and does not know it until his wound is fatal (cf. Jer 11:19).

Conclusion (7:24-27)

Finally, the father urges his "sons" (see Literary Analysis of Proverbs 4) not to turn aside their hearts to her ways, nor "wander about in" (NRSV: "stray," cf. Gen 21:14; 37:15; Ps 107:4) her paths (7:25). Contrary to what the "strange" woman implies, the youth is not the only young man in her sights. Rather, she is a proficient, experienced killer: *many* are those she has brought to ruin and *numerous* are those she has slain (7:26). Not only is she deadly but her house (in contrast to "his house," 7:19-20) is the way to the underworld itself (2:18-19). The *Instruction of Ankhsheshonq* warns similarly, "He who makes love to a married woman is killed on her doorstep" (*AEL* 3:177).

The Setting (8:1-3)

The "strange" woman's invitation still resonant in the night air (7:14-20), the father asks, "Does not wisdom call?" (8:1). His rhetorical question, which assumes an affirmative answer, invites the youth to listen closely for wisdom over the compelling speech of folly and amid the clamor around him. With that, the father ushers the imagination of the youth (and readers) down from the latticed window (7:6) and into the hubbub of the city streets to find her. The city is unnamed, its details vivid yet common, suggesting it represents every city (8:2-3; cf. 1:20-21). The father first guides the youth to the top of the "high places," a reference to the elevated portions of a city (8:2; cf. 9:3, 14). Such locations were typically administrative centers, home to the palace, temple, storehouses, markets, and army encampments. There, wisdom is alongside the roads and takes her stand in the intersections. The father then leads the youth down to the gates, the door of the city ("the mouth of the city," 8:3a). There, wisdom stands in the center of jurisprudence (e.g., Deut 21:19; 25:7; Ruth 4:1-12) and is among those entering and leaving the city. It seems wisdom takes her stand and is on the move. She is at the centers of political, military, and religious power; the hubs of commerce, justice, and social exchanges. She is alongside the paths where people come and go, heads down, feet hurried. She is in the doorway, at the threshold between the city and the outside world. In sum, wisdom stands in the middle of the community, in the heart of everyday life, and raises her voice in the cacophony of noise. She calls out to people where and as they are, from the very place it is hardest to be heard: amid the clamor and commotion of an ordinary day in the city.

The Integrity of Wisdom's Words (8:4-11)

Wisdom calls out to everyone (8:4; cf. 1:22). Disrupting standard word order to get everyone's attention ("To you!"), she summons "people" and "humans" (NRSV: "all that live"), terms that together denote the whole of humanity, male and female (e.g., Num 23:19; 2 Sam 7:14; Jer 49:18). She next addresses specifically the naive (*pĕtā'yîm*, cf. 1:4), who are inexperienced but capable of learning, and fools, who are notoriously obstinate (8:5; cf. 1:22; 23:9). She commands both groups to learn: the simple, "cleverness" (cf. 1:4) and the fools, "heart" (NRSV: "intelligence," see excursus in Proverbs 2). The latter is a plea for fools to open themselves to wisdom (e.g., 14:33; 15:7). Fools notoriously resist all instruction, choosing instead to trust and take pleasure only in their own "hearts"—their thoughts and sensibilities (e.g., 18:2; 28:26). The situation is so dire that the sages ponder: "Why should fools have a price in hand / to buy wisdom, when they have no mind [or heart]?" (17:16). Wisdom thus commands fools to "come to their senses," to pay attention to her, so that they too might be wise (cf. 3:10-11).

Wisdom testifies to the honesty of her speech (8:6-11). She describes her words twice as "right," that is, accurate and just (8:6, 9; cf. 1:3; 2:9; 23:16), as "truth" (8:7; cf. "just" in 8:8), and as "straightforward" or honest and accessible (8:9; cf. 24:26). They are also *nĕgîdîm* (8:6a), a term used in this sense only here in the Old Testament; a plural form apparently derived from *nāgîd* "prince" or "official" (NRSV: "noble things"), it suggests her words have dignity and authority (cf. her association with royalty, 8:15-16). The extent and forcefulness with which wisdom certifies the reliability of her speech differentiates her sharply from the "strange" woman and the wicked who are renowned for enticing, deceptive speech (e.g., 1:10; 2:12, 16; 4:24; 5:3; 6:12, 24; 7:5, 21). Indeed, wisdom's specific references to her lips and palate (8:6-7) counter key aspects of the "strange" woman's allure, namely, lips that drip honey and an oily smooth palate (5:3).

Wisdom's forcefulness may be due, in part, to her awareness that not everyone is able to distinguish true from false speech. She acknowledges that her words are straightforward to "one who understands" and right to "those who find knowledge" (8:9). Recognizing the value of her discourse is a matter of perception. So that those listening might perceive her words "rightly," therefore, wisdom commands them to "take [i.e., learn] discipline" (*lāqaḥ mûsār*, cf. 1:2-3) and knowledge (8:10; cf. 4:10), a charge that evokes the book's prologue (*lāqaḥ mûsār*, 1:3; NRSV: "for gaining instruction") and the father's repeated urgings to "take" (*lāqaḥ*) his teachings (2:1; 4:10). Wisdom also reiterates prior claims that discipline and knowledge are worth more than such valuables as silver and choice gold (8:10; cf. 2:4; 3:14). Verse 11 follows with a refrain that speaks of wisdom in the third person: "Wisdom is better than corals, and all desires do not compare with her" (cf. 3:15; 31:10; see above Literary Analysis). It is as though the father in his enthusiasm cannot help interrupting his quotation of wisdom's speech to make the point.

Wisdom's Character (8:12-14)

Wisdom frames the description of her character with two phrases of self-naming ("I [am] wisdom" [8:12a] and "I [am] understanding" [8:14b]; cf. 8:1; 4:5) that resemble biblical and extrabiblical self-identifications of royalty and of the gods. In the Old Testament, for example, we find, "I am Pharaoh" (Gen 41:44), "I am YHWH" (e.g., Gen 15:7; 28:13; Exod 6:6-8), and "I am El Shaddai" (e.g., Gen 17:1; 35:11). Likewise, certain ancient Near Eastern royal inscriptions and divine self-revelations begin, "I am Mesha," "I am Kilamuwa," and "I am Zakir" (*ANET* 320-321, 500-502). Such phrases are associated typically with claims about the speaker's identity, roles, or benefits, as in the case of "I, YHWH, am first and will be with the last" (Isa 41:4); "I, YHWH, speak the truth, I declare what is right" (Isa 45:19); and "I, YHWH, test the mind and search the heart" (Jer 17:10; e.g., Gen 15:7; Isa 41:17; 43:3; 45:5; 60:22; 61:8; Jer 32:27). We find *inclusios* of self-naming like that of wisdom elsewhere (e.g., Isa 45:5-6).

Not surprisingly, wisdom's attributes and values are precisely those that the book of Proverbs aims to teach (8:12-14). She embodies what she gives. She abides in the "cleverness" she summons the naive to learn (8:12; cf. 1:4; 8:5). Like those who perceive her words rightly (8:9), she finds knowledge (cf. 1:4b, 7; 2:5-6, 10; 5:2) and cunning (cf. 1:4b; 5:2). She epitomizes "the fear of the LORD" (see excursus in Proverbs 1), hating "the way of evil" (cf. 2:12) and characteristics associated with it—every form of pride and twisted speech (8:13). Finally, she offers counsel (cf. 1:25, 30), wisdom, and power (8:14), a combination of traits elsewhere attributed only to the messianic king (Isa 11:2) and God (Job 12:13).

Wisdom and Human Governance (8:15-16)

Wisdom establishes and empowers just, ordered societies (8:15-16). Beginning both verses with "by me," wisdom emphasizes that she alone grants power and enables rulers to fulfill the duties of their offices. Solomon apparently recognized this. When God asked what he desired, Solomon requested only "an understanding mind [or heart] to govern your people" (1 Kgs 3:9). Wisdom's influence is not exclusive to the ruling class of Israel, however. She speaks here generally and in the plural ("kings," "rulers," and "nobles"), signaling that her reach is global. She also makes clear that the power she grants is recognized as justice. Twice she employs the Hebrew adjective ṣedeq ("righteous" or "just"): by her, rulers establish just laws; by her, judges make just decisions. Indeed, it was Solomon's justice that the people recognized as evidence of the wisdom of God in him (1 Kgs 3:28).

Wisdom Bestows Wealth (8:17-21)

To those who love her, wisdom promises her love. She demonstrates this reciprocity, at least in part, by granting them wealth. Verses 17-21, a unit framed by an *inclusio* of the word "love" (8:17, 21), highlight in four ways the desirability of her riches. First, they are of the highest *quality*. Confirming the father's prior assertions (8:11; cf. 3:14), wisdom states that her "fruit" and "yield" (in context, references to her wealth) are worth more than fine gold and choice silver—precious and rare metals (8:19; e.g., Ps 21:3 [Heb. v. 4]; Isa 13:12). Second, her riches *last* (8:18a, 21b). Wisdom describes them as enduring (8:18), an adjective apparently derived from the Hebrew root meaning "to advance" or "move forward." Her wealth "advances." It is passed on, a point wisdom confirms when she says that she gives her riches "as an inheritance" (8:21; cf. 13:22). Third, wisdom's wealth is *legitimate*. Unlike the sinners who ambush the innocent to fill their purse (1:10-19), wisdom never strays from paths of righteousness and justice to acquire her gain. She comes by it and gives it away fairly and honestly (8:20-21; compare the Egyptian *Instruction of Ptahhotep*:

> Great is justice, lasting in effect,
> . . . Baseness may seize riches,
> Yet crime never lands its wares;
> In the end, it is justice that lasts. (*AEL* 1:64)

Finally, her wealth is *abundant*, enough to fill treasuries (8:21). In the ancient world, treasuries were associated with royalty and holy places (e.g., 2 Kgs 14:14; Neh 7:70; 10:39; 13:12-13; Ezek 28:4; Dan 1:2). They were economic centers, repositories of cash and valuable goods. Full treasuries signaled prosperity and power. To impress the Babylonians, for example, Hezekiah showed off his treasuries teeming with silver, gold, spices, precious oils, and weapons (Isa 39:2). That wisdom promises to fill not just one treasury but *many* offers a stunning visual image of the magnitude of her wealth and an indication of the status her lovers enjoy (e.g., "kings," "nobles," "princes," 8:15-16).

Wisdom's Preeminence and Role in Creation (8:22-31)

Wisdom declares her preeminence. In 8:22-26, she establishes her existence *prior* to God's creation of the cosmos through the use of various prepositions ("before," 8:25), negative expressions (e.g., "when there were no," 8:24; "when God had not made," 8:26), and phrases such as "at the beginning" (8:22a), "at the start of God's works of old" (8:22b; NRSV: "the first of"), "from ancient times" (8:23a; NRSV: "ages ago"), and "at the first, at the origin of the world" (8:23b). Then wisdom asserts her presence *during* God's creative work (8:27-29). "I was there" (8:27), she declares, a claim she develops more fully in 8:30-31: she was at God's side daily; she was before YHWH "at all times." Wisdom leaves no room for dispute. From the beginning, she was. And she was always in the presence of God.

Wisdom makes clear that God originated their association. She describes God as the subject who acts and herself as the one acted upon, but she leaves mysterious exactly *how* God initiated their relationship. Questions begin with 8:22a: "YHWH 'created' (*qānâ*) me." The verb *qānâ* has a wide range of meaning. Most commonly, it means "to acquire" or "buy." That is its sense everywhere else in Proverbs, often with wisdom as its object (cf. 1:5; 4:5, 7; 15:32; 16:16; 17:16; 18:15; 19:8; 20:14; 23:23). Thus some interpreters and ancient witnesses (e.g., the Vulgate) render 8:22a, "YHWH 'acquired' me," a translation that suggests wisdom was coeval with God. At the same time, *qānâ* can mean "to create" or "give birth," particularly when God is the subject. Melchizedek, for example, blesses Abram in the name of "El Elyon, Creator (*qānâ*) of heavens and earth" (Gen 14:19), an epithet Abram then promptly ascribes to YHWH (Gen 14:22;

cf. Deut 32:6; Ps 139:13). Similar epithets are found elsewhere in the ancient Near East, such as the Phoenician "El, the creator (*qānâ*) of the earth" and the Ugaritic "Asherah, creator (*qānâ*) of the gods." Wisdom's assertion that she was "brought forth" (8:24-25), a verb often associated with childbirth (e.g., Job 15:7; Ps 51:5 [Heb. v. 7]), further suggests God "birthed" or "created" her. In short, the verb *qānâ* is ambivalent. Its two senses may overlap, such that God's creation of wisdom is, at the same time, an acquisition of her (e.g., Eve at the birth of Cain: "I have created/acquired [*qānâ*] a man with [the help of] God," Gen 4:1 AT). Whatever the case, wisdom leaves obscure exactly how God initiated their relationship.

The mystery continues with 8:23a: "I was 'formed' " (NRSV: "set up"). The Hebrew is "I was 'poured out' (*nāsak*)," possibly a reference to the pouring of oil to anoint a king; in Ps 2:6, for example, God says: "I have 'poured out' (*nāsak*) my king on Zion." As such, God appointed (and anointed?) wisdom to her position in the very beginning. Some interpreters contend, however, that in light of wisdom's claims that she was "brought forth" (8:24-25), the verb in 8:23a is more appropriately understood as *sākak* ("to weave" or "form"). Elsewhere the psalmist and Job speak of God "knitting together" (*sākak*) a child in the womb, forming the innermost parts (Ps 139:13b) and weaving bone with sinew, skin with flesh (Job 10:11). Interpreted this way, God "crafted" wisdom. Both readings of 8:23a are compelling.

Thus wisdom heralds that God originated their relationship at the very beginning but leaves mysterious how God did so. Although she is explicit and repetitive about her preeminence and distinction from God, she is comparatively vague about exactly what happened. It is as though the details of her beginnings lie just beyond her words, that the multiple metaphors she evokes—birthing, establishing, anointing, creating—point variously to what is otherwise ineffable. The effect is certainty about God's initiation of their association before the creation of anything else and absolute wonder as to how. Wisdom is self-revelatory, yet mysterious.

Wisdom locates herself at the beginning of God's "way" or "works," namely, at the start of God's creative activity (8:22). She speaks of God having a "way," a pattern of behavior, a history. The same term, and the metaphor more broadly, refers frequently in Proverbs to a person's course in life (e.g., 1:15, 31; 2:8, 12-13, 20; 3:23; cf. 2:15-19); wisdom and the "strange" woman have their respective "ways" (e.g., 3:17; 5:6; 7:25; 8:20). Here, it seems, God also has a "way," at the beginning of which is wisdom and then the creation of the world.

Framing her words with "earth" (8:23b, 29b), wisdom describes God's creation in broad and sweeping terms. She begins "when there were no depths" (8:24a), before the primeval waters existed over which the spirit of God hovers in Gen 1:2. From there, she ascends to the springs that flow to the earth's surface (8:24b; cf. Job 28:11); to the mountains and hills with their pillars sunk in the depths (8:25); to the land (8:26); and to the heavens (8:27-28a). She then descends slowly to the horizon (the "circle" inscribed on the face of the deep, 8:27b; e.g., Job 26:10); to the clouds (8:28a; NRSV: "skies"); to the seas and its shores (8:28b-29; cf. Ps 104:9; Jer 5:22); and finally to the foundations of the earth (8:29b). Her brushstrokes are long and full, drawing her audience's imagination through God's work systematically, from the bottoms of the abyss to the highest reaches of heaven and back again. Throughout, God is the Creator, the one who establishes (8:27a), inscribes (8:28b), makes strong (8:28; cf. 8:29), and sets boundaries (8:29). That wisdom can so testify to God's work emphasizes again her preeminence. She is the eyewitness.

With God's creation writ large, wisdom turns to her role within it (8:30-31). She first declares: "I was at God's side (*'āmôn*)" (8:30). This locates her with respect to God (at the divine side) but leaves her exact role, like her origins, obscure. The word *'āmôn* confounds interpreters. Three proposals, all with ancient witnesses, garner the most support: (*a*) "artisan" (so Vulgate, Syriac, LXX), (*b*) "faithful" or "trusted" (so the Targum and the Greek translators Symmachus and Theodotion), and (*c*) "nurtured one" or "child" (the Greek translator Aquila). Proponents of the first typically emend *'āmôn* to *'ommān* ("artisan," cf. Song 7:1 [Heb. v. 2]) and associate the term with the Mesopotamian mythological *apkallū* and *ummānu*, preflood and postflood semidivine sages, respectively, who brought culture to the world. In 8:22-29, however, wisdom neither demonstrates their traits nor assigns herself an active role in God's creative activity. (Wisdom of Solomon later identifies wisdom as the "fashioner of all things" and the one who teaches the arts, philosophy, natural science, and so on; but such is not the case in Proverbs, e.g., Wis 7:15-22; 8:1-9). Proponents of the second proposal understand ʾāmôn to derive from the root ʾmn ("to be faithful" or "trustworthy"), but the verbal stem of ʾāmôn (Qal), if so, is not what we expect (Niphal). Finally, proponents of the third derive ʾāmôn from the root ʾmn ("to nurture" or "nurse") and read it variously as a passive participle ("one who is nurtured") or as an infinitive absolute ("nurturing" or "growing up," so Fox 1996a, 699-702). Though not without complications, this reading is appealing in that it requires no emendation of the Hebrew and resonates with the metaphors of "birthing" or "creating" in 8:22-25, and the portrait of wisdom "playing" (NRSV: "rejoicing") before YHWH and on earth with humanity (8:31). Wisdom, that is, matured at the side of God throughout creation.

Wisdom elaborates on her relationship with YHWH (8:30b-31). Her words form a chiasm that binds God's delight in her with her delight in humanity:

> I was *delight(s)* [NRSV: "his delight"] day by day
> *rejoicing* before [YHWH] at all times
> *rejoicing* in [YHWH's] inhabited world
> My *delight* is in humanity (cf. 8:4).

Echoing her earlier self-identifications (8:12a, 14b), wisdom names herself "delight" itself (8:30b). The parallel phrase "rejoicing before [YHWH]" implies that she is *God's* delight specifically. God revels in her. Elsewhere, Jeremiah describes Ephraim as the child in whom God "delights" (Jer 31:20); Isaiah says Judah is the "planting of [God's] delight" (5:7). Wisdom is a source of God's joy. She "rejoices" before God, a verb that refers broadly to "making merry": playing (Job 40:20; Zech 8:5), singing and dancing (1 Sam 18:6-7; 2 Sam 6:5, 21; 1 Chr 15:29), and telling jokes or performing tricks (e.g., 26:19; Ps 104:26; Jer 15:17). That wisdom's merriment is at once "before [God] at all times" and "in the world" associates God's delight with God's creation (e.g., the refrain "God saw that it was good" in Gen 1). While God delights in her, wisdom delights in humanity—the very audience she beckons in 8:4.

Now . . . Listen! (8:32-36)

Wisdom commands the response of her audience (8:32-36). "Now, [my] sons," she begins, invoking for the first and only time the father's earlier summons (cf. 5:7; 7:24) and thereby assuming the intimacy of parent and teacher. "Listen [to me]," she commands (cf. 8:6). *Listen* to "discipline" (mûsār, cf. 1:2) and *be wise* (8:32a, 33). Wisdom interweaves these commands with motivations to obey (8:32b, 34-36). Twice she uses "happy" sayings: happy are those who observe her ways (8:32b); happy is the one who watches her doors (8:34a; cf. 3:13-18). The latter "happy" saying portrays the one attentive to wisdom as a lover who waits expectantly outside the home of his beloved. The motif occurs elsewhere. Job, for example, denies having ever been enticed by a woman and having lain in wait at his neighbor's door (Job 31:9). The female lover in the Song of Songs points to her beloved, exclaiming:

> Look, there he stands
> behind our wall,
> gazing [through] the windows,
> [peering] through the lattice. (Song 2:9)

And, in the closest analogy to 8:32-34, Ben Sira writes:

> Happy is the person who meditates on wisdom,
> and reasons intelligently . . .
> pursuing her like a hunter,
> and lying in wait on her paths;
> who peers through her windows,
> and listens at her doors;
> who camps near her house,
> and fastens his tent peg to her walls;
> who pitches his tent near her
> and so occupies an excellent lodging place. (Sir 14:20, 22-25)

If people wait eagerly at wisdom's door, they cannot be at the door of the "strange" woman (cf. 9:13-14; 5:8). That they wait "day by day" (8:34b) further suggests that they are as persistent as wisdom, who "day by day" is God's delight in creation (8:30). Finally, wisdom's command to keep watch at her doors anticipates the description of her house and invitation to enter it (9:1-6, 11).

Wisdom closes with a comparison between the one (m. sg.) who finds her and the one (m. sg.) who does not (8:35-36). The one who "finds" her—language that suggests intimacy and courtship (cf. 3:13)—attains her benefits: life (cf. 1:33; 3:16, 18; 4:13; cf. 9:6, 11) and divine favor (8:35). A relationship with wisdom delights God (cf. 11:20; 12:2, 22; 14:9; 15:8; 18:22). In contrast, the one who "misses" (ḥāṭāʾ) wisdom suffers harm at his own hands (8:36). The verb ḥāṭāʾ can mean "to miss" something (as in "to miss the mark," e.g., Job 5:24; Isa 65:20), a suitable translation given the parallel "to find" (8:35). Most commonly, however, it means "to wrong," "offend," or "sin" (e.g., 2 Kgs 18:14; Neh 6:13). This range of meaning permits wisdom to simultaneously name the undesired action (i.e., to miss her) and condemn it as an offense—one that does harm to the perpetrator. He "does violence to himself." To "miss" wisdom is a form of self-hatred and injury (e.g., 15:32).

Theological and Ethical Analysis

The diptych of Proverbs 7–8 highlights for modern readers a disturbing yet not unfamiliar aspect of the sages' pedagogy: women are either "bad" or "good." The "strange" woman, lurking about in the streets at twilight, symbolizes folly and vice. To cross her threshold is death. Personified wisdom, in turn, signifies knowledge and virtue. Anchored in the divine realm, woven into creation itself, she stands unabashedly in the city square. Mirror opposites, these women have much in common. Both use speech to persuade (e.g., 7:14-21; 8:4-36). Both have houses and offer luxuries (7:8, 16-17, 27; 8:18-21; 9:1-6). And both seek the attention and affections of the young man, whose choice renders him either victim (the "strange" woman entraps him, 7:22-23) or beneficiary (wisdom makes him happy, e.g., 8:32-34). To direct the behavior of young men, then, the parent uses women as pedagogical devices. Women stand at polar ends of the youth's world: bad and good, death and life, folly and wisdom.

What models, images, or roles of women inspired these figures? To date, there is no consensus among interpreters—a fact that underscores the complexities of the metaphors (for summaries of the main proposals, see, e.g., Camp 1985, 23-68; Whybray 1995, 71-78; Fox 2000, 333-41). Proposals typically point to either divinities and abstract concepts or persons. The "strange" woman has been construed as representing a foreign goddess or such "real" women as outsiders, foreign devotees of a foreign god, foreign or native prostitutes, or wives of other men. Recently, R. J. Clifford argued that the woman (and Prov 7 in particular; cf. 9:13-18) might be influenced by an epic type-scene in which a goddess deceptively offers love or marriage to a young man (1993, 61-72). Examples are Anat in the Ugaritic epic *Aqhat* (*KTU* 1.17.VI.2-45), Ishtar in *Gilgamesh* (VI.1-79), and Calypso and Circe in *Odyssey* (V.202-209; X). Although the proposal is suggestive, several of the primary features of the type-scene do not correspond with the "strange" woman and the scene in Proverbs 7. Most notably, the "strange" woman proposes one night of sexual indulgence, not a long-term relationship or marriage. And whereas the epic hero recognizes the goddess' offer as deceitful and rejects it, the youth of Proverbs 7 goes after the "strange" woman without hesitation—"an ox to the slaughter" (7:22b).

Although the tendency is to posit "real" women as the background of the "strange" woman, the opposite is true of personified wisdom—who many contend was shaped wholly or mainly as an Israelite parallel to goddesses in other ancient Near Eastern cultures (e.g., Ishtar, Maʿat, Isis, Asherah). (Note the assumption that negative female figures are derived from real women, whereas positive, powerful female figures are not; women, it seems, may be that "bad" but not that "good.") But only two of the five passages about personified wisdom in Proverbs 1–9 indicate explicitly some sort of divine or mythological status, and both texts subordinate her to God (3:13-20; 8:22-31): she is an instrument or agent of divine action ("*by* wisdom, God created," 3:19), and she is preeminent "at the side" of God during creation (8:22-31). Furthermore, none of the proposed goddess parallels corresponds consistently with personified wisdom. Some interpreters explain this variously—wisdom is "semidivine," a goddess demythologized over time, or an incompletely developed hypostatization (independent entity) of God's wisdom. More recently, others, including myself, argue instead that personified wisdom reflects roles of actual women (e.g., Camp 1985; Yoder 2001). The pedigrees of the "strange" woman and personified wisdom remain elusive; it seems likely the figures reflect multiple and varied images of women—mythological and real.

Whatever their precise origins in Proverbs, both women have significant "afterlives" in communities of faith. Their development across centuries cautions against speaking of them as static figures, as some recent conversations do about personified wisdom (or, as in the Wisdom of Solomon, *Sophia*). In the Jewish tradition, the "strange" woman is interpreted frequently as a symbol or allegory for "bad" wisdom—including heresies (particularly Christianity), foreign philosophies, and doctrines—and/or for physical desires, the body, and worldly pleasures (Fox 2000, 254-55). Conversely, personified wisdom becomes identified with Torah (Bar 3:9–4:4; Sir 24:23-34) and, in the Wisdom of Solomon (7:7–10:18), is the *pneuma Sophias* (spirit of Sophia): the breath of the power of God, a pure emanation of divine glory, a reflection of eternal light, a flawless mirror of divine workings, and an image of God's goodness (Wis 7:25-26). She renews and orders all things (Wis 7:27; 8:1). The author calls her alternatively the *Logos* ("Word") of God. Cosmic and immanent, she touches "heaven while standing on the earth" (Wis 18:15-16).

Personified wisdom is also important in the Christian tradition. Scholars agree that early Christians drew on language and imagery associated with her to describe the person and work of Jesus Christ (e.g., Luke 7:35; 11:49; John 1:1-18; 17:5; 1 Cor 1:18-31; 8:6; Col 1:15-20; Heb 1:1-3). Indeed, Proverbs 8:22-31 was a point of contention in the fourth-century CE controversy between orthodox and Arian Christians about the nature of Christ's relationship to God. Orthodox Christians read 8:22a as

"YHWH 'possessed' [qānâ] me," insisting that Christ is the eternal Word and Wisdom of God. In contrast, Arian Christians interpreted 8:22a with LXX ("YHWH 'created' [qānâ] me") and argued Christ is the first creation of God—a unique, perfected creature but, by virtue of having been created, one subject to God and not eternal. The controversy led ultimately to the condemnation of Arius and his thinking by the Council of Nicaea (325 CE).

Many readers today find the "stranger" woman and personified wisdom at once compelling and dangerous. On the one hand, in personified wisdom the sages arguably elevate and theologically legitimate activities and attributes of women and/or evoke certain female divinities. As "God-talk," wisdom figured as a woman in Proverbs and subsequent literature prompts vital reflection about female imagery and God. On the other hand, the parent's depictions of personified wisdom and the "strange" woman reinforce values and customs of a context patriarchal in structure and androcentric in bias. The parent objectifies women (e.g., the youth should "acquire" personified wisdom as the most valuable of his possessions, 4:5, 7), and their juxtaposition perpetuates the stereotyped polarization of women as either wholly good or wholly evil (e.g., Madonna/Whore, Bad/Good)—with men as either their beneficiaries or victims. The parent's pedagogy thus offers no respite to women. Rather, it serves as strong caution: such gender assumptions and mythic conceptions of women are woven deeply into Western culture and persist today (cf. Newsom 1989, 157-58).

Mindful of the promise and peril of the parent's pedagogy, we note certain convictions. First, wisdom and folly are "out there," beyond the self. Whereas wisdom beckons to all people and must be pursued intently, folly waits for and seizes the naive and unsuspecting (cf. sin "lurking at the door" in Gen 4:7). This sense of temptation as aggressive, enticing, and ever present ("in the streets ... in the squares and at every corner," 7:12) makes the continual teaching of wisdom—as a powerful and life-preserving alternative—necessary and urgent ("Does not wisdom call?" 8:1). Second, God created in the company of wisdom; wisdom was there before and during God's crafting of every detail, God's setting of every boundary. To be wise, then, is to be a witness to

God's handiwork in the world and, in turn, to appreciate the limits of our knowing. Third, inasmuch as wisdom guides all rulers in ways of justice, the wise are attentive to the insight and knowledge of other nations (e.g., 30:1-33; 31:1-6). Finally, and perhaps most strikingly, wisdom is utter delight. God and humanity revel in wisdom and she in them. Far from being burdensome or tedious, learning here is a joy-filled, love-inspiring, playful relationship with knowledge and God. And wisdom offers that relationship to everyone—not solely a privileged few.

PROVERBS 9

Literary Analysis

The concluding chapter of Proverbs 1–9 presents two invitations—one from personified wisdom (9:1-6, 11) and the other from personified folly (9:13-18; i.e. the "strange" woman). A series of five proverbs addressed to advanced wisdom students (9:7-10, 12) separate the two.

Wisdom's invitation opens with a past-tense narration of her house-building (9:1) and elaborate preparations for a feast (9:2-3a). At 9:3b, the tense switches suddenly to the present ("she calls"), lending immediacy to the invitation that follows in 9:4-6 and, arguably, verse 11. As many interpreters observe, the inexplicable shift in 9:11a to the first-person singular ("for by me") is awkward. Who is the speaker? However, if we read 9:11 as a (misplaced) conclusion to wisdom's invitation, the first-person singular speech is expected (cf. 9:5). Moreover, the phrase "by me" recalls wisdom's refrain in 8:15-16, and the benefit of long life is ascribed elsewhere to her (3:16; cf. 8:35).

Five sayings counsel the advanced wisdom student (9:7-10, 12). Because the sayings "interrupt" the invitations of wisdom and folly, many consider them an early addition to the chapter. Yet the interlude helps frame Proverbs 1–9 and connect it to what follows (10:1–22:16). Repeating vocabulary and concepts from Proverbs 1, the proverbs create a thematic *inclusio*, a frame formed by repetition of a word, phrase, or idea at the beginning and conclusion of a literary unit, around Proverbs 1–9. Note, for example, that 9:10 reiterates the "motto" of the book (cf. 1:7). Verses 7-8 and 12 evoke personified wisdom's warning to the scoffers and fools about their misplaced affections and solitary fate (cf. 1:22-29). And 9:9 reasserts that, when taught, the wise "gain instruction" (cf. 1:5). At the same time, the juxtaposition of the wicked and the righteous in 9:7-10, 12 anticipates a predominant theme of the next main unit of Proverbs (10:1–22:16) and, as such, points readers onward.

The chapter concludes with the invitation of personified folly (9:13-18). The father describes her character (9:13), her preparations (9:14-15), and quotes her invitation (9:16-17) before issuing one last warning (9:18).

Exegetical Analysis

The Invitation of Personified Wisdom (9:1-6)

The father's tributes to personified wisdom lead ultimately to her doorstep (1:20-33; 3:13-18; 4:5-9; 8:1-36; cf. 7:4). That wisdom builds her house (cf. 14:1; 24:3-4) indicates her capacity to provide stability and prosperity (Isa 65:21; Jer 29:5, 28; Ezek 28:26; cf. Ezek 11:3). And hers is not just any house; it is a mansion with seven pillars, a round number (much like our "dozen") that signifies completeness or wholeness (e.g., 6:16-19; 24:16; 26:16). Interpreters propose various symbolic meanings for the pillars, including the first seven chapters of Proverbs, the seven sacraments of the church, the seven gifts of the Holy Spirit, the seven preflood sages in Mesopotamian mythology, the seven days of creation, and the seven liberal arts. In this context, however, the number highlights the size and elegance of her home. Archaeological evidence demonstrates that the number of pillars in a house was an indication of wealth and status. Wisdom's affluence is suggested further by the presence of servant girls (pl.), likely female freeborn slaves who do primarily domestic labor. To have even one servant was a mark of privilege. In the Old Testament, women with servants are royalty or from well-to-do families, such as the daughter of Pharaoh (Exod 2:5), Esther (Esth 4:4, 16), and Rebekah (Gen 24:61).

In anticipation of her guests, wisdom prepares a lavish feast of meat (a delicacy) and wine likely mixed with spices (Song 8:2). Her arrangement of the banquet signals her hospitality—a celebrated virtue. When three unexpected visitors come to Abraham at Mamre, for example, he orders the slaughter and preparation of a calf (Gen 18:7-8); similarly, when Joseph sees that his brothers have returned with Benjamin, he orders the slaughter of an animal for the noon meal (Gen 43:16). In contrast, the callousness of the rich fool Nabal is demonstrated by his refusal to extend such hospitality to David and his men. When his wife Abigail learns of his surliness, she hurries with a spread of bread, wine, cooked meat, grain, raisins, and figs to intercept the vengeful David—an action of "good sense" for which David praises her (1 Sam 25:2-35). Unlike these others, however, wisdom makes ready her table of rich fare *before* she issues her invitation—before there are guests at her front door. As such, wisdom acts not out of social expectation or obligation but her own generosity. She seems confident that guests will come and take seats at her table.

Biblical narratives often describe the table as a place of discernment, where host and guests may glimpse God and learn about God's activity in the world. Abraham's three mysterious visitors, for example, reveal that Sarah will bear the long-awaited child of God's promise (Gen 18:1-16). Following ratification of the covenant at Sinai, Moses, Aaron, Nadab, Abihu, and seventy elders "[saw] God, and they ate and drank" (Exod 24:11). God is the quintessential host, providing water, manna, and quail in the wilderness; preparing a table in the presence of enemies; and stirring creation to yield food and wine to strengthen and delight the human heart (e.g., Exod 16-17; Pss 23; 104; cf. 2 Kgs 4:42-44). Indeed, the prophets describe the future reign of God as an unending banquet (e.g., Isa 25:6-8; Joel 3:18; Amos 9:13-15), a claim that Jesus echoes (Matt 8:11; 22:1-14 // Luke 14:16-24; Mark 14:17-25). Throughout Jesus' ministry the table continues as a place of discernment—of generous hospitality, radically new social configurations, and of happenings yet to come (e.g., Matt 26:20-25; Mark 2:15-17; 6:35-44; 8:1-10; Luke 14:7-14; 15:1-2; John 13). It is not surprising, then, that after Jesus' death and resurrection, two of the disciples recognize him first at the table in the breaking of bread (Luke 24:13-35).

Wisdom extends her invitation broadly (9:3-6). She sends her servant girls out to herald her words ("she calls," 9:3b) from the "highest places in town," where wisdom is known to take her stand (8:2). Addressed to the "simple" (*petî*, cf. 1:4) and to "those without sense" (e.g., 6:32; 7:7; 9:16), the invitation unfolds in four moves. First, she urges them to "turn aside" (cf. 1:23) and come into her house to enjoy her food and wine (9:5). Wisdom's guests must change their direction and enter. Second, she charges them to "abandon" naiveté, that is, to leave behind a central aspect of their character (9:6a; cf. Isa 55:1-3, 6-7). That naiveté is a matter of choice resonates with wisdom's prior characterization of the naive as loving their naiveté (1:22); if so, perhaps they can fall "out of love" with it. Third, she commands them to live and walk in the new way of understanding (9:6, 11; cf. 3:16; 7:2). Paradoxically, wisdom's house is the destination for those who love wisdom, and a reprieve "on the way." Acceptance of her invitation requires one to choose a new direction and lose an attitude.

Counsel for the Advanced Wisdom Student (9:7-10, 12)

Verses 7-9 instruct advanced students of wisdom—which, by this point, readers of Proverbs presumably are—about whom they should and should not teach. Those who teach scoffers and the wicked suffer shame, "hurt," and the scoffer's derision for their efforts (9:7-8a; cf. "Do not instruct a fool, lest he hate you" in the *Instruction of Ankhsheshonq, AEL* 3:165). The term translated "hurt" refers most frequently to physical impairments, such as blindness, lameness, broken limbs, skin blemishes, and distorted features (Lev 21:17-23; 24:19-20; 2 Sam 14:25; Song 4:7; cf. Dan 1:4); on rare occasions it is also used for moral injury (Deut 32:5; Job 11:15; cf. Job 31:7). The father thereby cautions that teachers of scoffers and the wicked endure public disgrace and physical injury (that may itself lead to disdain and exclusion; cf. Lev 21:17-

23), likely at the hands of one's own hateful students (9:8a). In contrast, those who teach the wise and righteous are loved by their students and know that their teaching is effective because their students "grow even wiser" (9:8b-9).

Verse 10 provides the rationale for the counsel of 9:7-9. Forming an *inclusio* around Proverbs 1–9, it repeats the "motto" of the book as a whole: wisdom begins with "the fear of the LORD" (see excursus in Proverbs 1). Before students can learn, they need an innate awareness of and reverence for "the Holy One" (9:10b; cf. 30:3; Hos 12:1); religious piety is the soil in which instruction sinks its roots and bears fruit. Without it, scoffers contend with their teachers, arrogantly resisting any discipline (e.g., 1:22-25; 12:1; 15:12).

The section ends with a proverb about the personal consequences of being wise or a scoffer (9:12). Whichever way people choose to be, they reap the blessings or misfortunes of their decision. The father makes a distinction, however: whereas the consequences for scoffing are exclusive to the scoffer ("you alone"), the benefits of wisdom are enjoyed by, but not necessarily limited to, its possessor ("for yourself"). Indeed, that the immediate context is about teaching suggests the importance of sharing one's wisdom with others so that they, too, might benefit (cf. Sir 37:22-23; 24:34).

The Invitation of Personified Folly (9:13-18)

Whereas the description of personified wisdom in 9:1-3 focuses on the preparations she makes for her guests (i.e., building, slaughtering, mixing wine, setting her table), the parallel depiction of personified folly attends primarily to her character (9:13-15). She is "loud" (cf. 7:11). She is "thoughtless" (*pĕtayyût*; NRSV: "ignorant"), a word derived from *pĕtî* ("simple" [sg.]; cf. e.g., 1:4, 22, 32; 7:7 [pl.]). Ironically, folly is the embodiment of naiveté, a reality that compounds the danger of the situation. She is, moreover, comparatively lazy, sitting at the door of her house (cf. 5:8) and on a seat at the high places (9:14). She takes such positions so that she might easily get the attention of those "crossing by" and "making straight" their paths (9:15; cf. 7:8). The latter reference evokes the father's instructions in 4:25-26 (cf. 3:6):

> Let your eyes look directly forward,
> and your gaze be straight before you.
> Keep straight the path of your feet,
> and all your ways will be sure.

It seems that folly seeks the attention of *any* gullible passersby (cf. 9:16)—including (perhaps especially) those trying to stay on the "straight and narrow." Unlike wisdom, who requires her guests to abandon naiveté (9:6), folly aims to capitalize on it.

Personified folly's invitation has two parts (9:16-17). She begins with a call to the naive that is—to a word—exactly the same as wisdom's (9:16; cf. 9:4). Apparently, the two women are not always readily distinguishable from each other; one must pay attention to more than their first words. Folly then describes her feast. Whereas wisdom issues a series of commands (e.g., "Come!" "Eat!" "Drink!" 9:5) to accept her gracious hospitality (*"my* food," "the wine *I have mixed*"), folly speaks abstractly about "stolen water" and "food eaten secretly" (9:17). Her offer of water (rather than wine) recalls the use of water as a metaphor for a woman or wife in 5:15-20 (cf. Song 4:12, 15); "stolen water" is any woman who "belongs" to another. Hers is an illicit, erotic banquet—one enjoyed furtively, without right or permission. Its forbidden nature makes it particularly satisfying. Getting away with something can make it "taste" all the more delicious.

The father concludes with a warning about the deceptiveness of her invitation and the ignorance of the youth (9:18). What the naive boy does not know is that her house is the underworld, not a haven in which one savors a feast of delights (cf. 2:18). In her house, the shades dwell. Her guests inhabit the "depths of Sheol," a claim that emphasizes just how far down they descend (e.g., Deut 32:22; Ps 86:13). To turn aside at her beckoning is to choose a "dead end" (cf. 21:6).

Theological and Ethical Analysis

Much ink has been spilled about the nature of choice. The question has long captivated theologians, ethicists, and philosophers, and more recently has sparked research by neuroscientists, physicists, and computer scientists. Are we free moral agents? Or are we pre-disposed or "programmed" to respond in particular ways? For many, at stake in these questions is ethical responsibility. Stated simply, if we have free will, we are accountable for our actions. If not, we are not, or at least not to the same degree.

Proverbs 1–9 culminates at a crossroads. Standing there in the twilight, the youth hears voices beckoning him home for supper. Two invitations. Two houses. Two hosts. The parent's description compels a choice and suggests certain convictions about it. First, the youth will choose between wisdom and folly not once but many times. The invitations are present and persistent, and the youth is responsible for which he accepts each time. Second, the youth does not choose in a vacuum. The decision at the crossroads follows chapters of instruction, time and investment by parents and the community, and indications that the youth can distinguish between wisdom and folly—at least enough to teach others (9:7-9, 12). The parent implicitly trusts that a good upbringing will predispose the youth to continue on the "way of wisdom" (4:11) and "turn in" at wisdom's house. Subsequent chapters will complicate this view in light of God's sovereignty (e.g., 16:1-3, 9).

Finally, the youth will be required to distinguish between wisdom and folly. As the parent describes and interweaves speeches about them throughout Proverbs 1–9, the two in many ways resemble each other. Both seek the youth's attention, persuade with their words (e.g., 1:20-33; 7:14-21; 8:4-36), move about in the city streets and squares (1:20-21; 7:10-12; 8:2-3), have houses (7:8, 27; 9:1), and offer wealth and luxuries (e.g., 3:7, 16; 7:16-17; 8:18-19). Now they call with the same initial invitation (9:4, 16). The ambiguity necessitates that the youth not make snap judgments but be patient, attentive to details, and shrewd in discernment. What is foolish can at first appear wise (e.g., 14:12).

The crossroad quandary is a striking conclusion to the opening chapters of the book. By content and arrangement, it raises the question: which will the youth choose? The spotlight centers on the youth as the parent slowly exits the stage. Moreover, the lack of an explicit answer to the question leaves it perpetual. Readers, like the youth, must decide anew whether to "turn in" to folly's house and put the book down, or choose wisdom and step over the threshold into its next major section (10:1–22:16)—a decision that, as the parent tells it, remains one of life and death.

PROVERBS 10:1–22:16: "THE PROVERBS OF SOLOMON"

Introduction to Proverbs 10:1–22:16

The superscription at 10:1a, "the proverbs of Solomon," announces the beginning of the second section of the book: 10:1–22:16. Though the superscription is familiar (1:1; cf. 25:1), readers who cross its threshold encounter a markedly different literary landscape. Like many other ancient Near Eastern wisdom texts, Proverbs 10:1–22:16 consists largely of two-line proverbs, each of which may stand on its own and each of which—at least initially—appears disconnected with the proverbs that precede and follow it. On the heels of the longer didactic poems of Proverbs 1–9, this seemingly haphazard arrangement is disorienting. No longer is the father in evident control of the discourse, nor is personified wisdom at the crossroads. No longer do proverbs occur hand in glove with lengthy instructions that inform their meaning. No longer is the reader even directly addressed (until 14:7). Instead, proverbs follow one after the other in no apparent order of priority.

This literary arrangement abruptly shifts responsibility for making sense of the proverbs from the father of Proverbs 1–9 to readers—those with whom responsibility must finally reside given the book's aim to form wise people (1:2-7). Moreover, the arrangement initiates a process of deliberation—inviting those whom the father has instructed to participate now in wisdom-making themselves. Apparent lack of prioritization among the proverbs compels us examine and test each one. And, ironically, the extent to which the proverbs seem for the most part disconnected from literary and oral contexts sharpens the significance and effects of context itself. So-called decontextualized proverbs require readers to imagine appropriate contexts of use based on their own experience. As such, "The single line [a proverb comprised of two parallel sections] often enough makes higher claims and demands a greater degree of intentional participation than a developed didactic poem" (von Rad 1972, 27).

Borrowing a metaphor from E. B. White, we may say that 10:1–22:16 reads like a literary mosaic: a text crafted with small pieces of variously colored proverbs, each a polished entity unto itself, placed next to other equally polished and vibrant proverbs (White 1984, 40). Viewing the mosaic up close, we focus on each proverb, then on those immediately around it, noting ways the colors are distinct from one another and how they interact with one another. From a step or two back, however, we notice that the bits of polished color blur into something different from what any of the pieces standing alone resemble. Proverbs 10:1–22:16 thus generate "patterns of experience" that, in conjunction with its content, teach about the ways of wisdom.

First, the sages' use of genres requires increasing dexterity on the part of readers. Indeed, 10:1–22:16 may be divided into two roughly equivalent smaller units distinguished principally on the basis of genre: 10:1–15:33 and 16:1–22:16. The first unit is comprised predominantly of antithetical proverbs, a genre that, coupled with its redundant use, continues the worldview of moral polarities and strongly qualified horizons established by Proverbs 1–9. In the second unit, by contrast, antithetical proverbs are but one genre of many, including a wealth of synonymous and synthetic proverbs; more than twice as many "better than" proverbs (e.g., 16:8, 32; 17:1; 19:1); more rhetorical questions (17:16; 18:14; 20:6, 9, 24; cf. 14:22); and the introduction of "not fitting" or "not good" proverbs (e.g., 16:29; 17:7). Although a morally bifurcated worldview persists in 16:1–22:16, this variety of genres affords greater elaboration, nuance, and expression of relative values.

Readers further discover that, absent the father's firm mediation, conflict and contradiction exist not only between the wise and foolish, the righteous and wicked, but within wisdom itself. Divergent proverbs occur side by side, or nearly so, without reflection. Some proverbs, for example, speak of wealth as an unqualified good (e.g., 10:15, 22; 14:20; 22:4, 7), others speak of it as a liability (see 11:4, 28); some attribute poverty to laziness (e.g., 10:4; 12:24; 20:13; cf. 6:10-11 // 24:33-34), others attribute it to violence, extortion, and deceit (e.g., 11:1, 16; 13:23; 21:6; cf. 1:10-19). The sages' interweaving of countering claims, none of which they discount or trivialize, reveals that wisdom does not afford only one perspective on wealth or poverty or, for that matter, many things; indeed, "The first to present one's case seems right, / until one's opponent comes and cross-examines" (18:17 AT). This in turn points readers to a claim larger than the proverbs in question: wise communities and mature moral persons hold an amalgam of multiple and often conflicting views from which they draw to address their particular circumstances wisely. A ready reservoir of divergent proverbs, in fact, makes it more likely one can both "accommodate the many fine distinctions and qualifications to which each particular life situation is subject" (Kirschenblatt-Gimblett 1973, 826) and respond as the sages urge—with perceptiveness and good timing (e.g., "Apples of gold in a setting of silver," such is a word spoken at the right time [25:11; cf. 25:12; 26:7, 9]).

The sages' use of repetition reinforces wisdom's plasticity. Whereas what the father repeated in Proverbs 1–9 was largely exordia (calls to attention), what the sages repeat from 10:1 to the end of the book is comparatively indiscriminate; in most cases, there are no apparent thematic or structural indications for why some proverbs or lines are repeated while others are not. Yet readers quickly learn that word-for-word repetition cannot be equated with identity of meaning(s), that "every new use entails deviant use, every repetition a variation. For the original is rooted in its native ground—tone, genre, situation—so that even to reiterate it word for word is to uproot and transplant it" (Sternberg 1985, 390). For example, we first encounter "The words of a [gossiper] are like delicious morsels; they go down into the inner parts of the body" (18:8) after a proverb pair about the trouble fools get themselves into by talking (18:6-7). Emphasis on speech in that context focuses attention on the words of whisperers (18:8)—how, like junk food, they taste delicious but are harmful when swallowed. Later, when the same proverb recurs (26:22), it is nestled between proverbs that reflect on the power of words to spark conflict (26:20-21) and the deceptive cruelty of the gossiper (26:23-26). The new context invites reconsideration of the proverb in light of the gossiper's malicious disposition (compare also, e.g., 20:16 and 27:13; 21:9 and 25:24; and 22:3 and 27:12).

In turn, proverbs and lines repeated nearly verbatim highlight the durability and adaptability of proverbs themselves. Consider the following examples:

1. A false witness will not go unpunished,
    and a liar *will not escape* (19:5).
    A false witness will not go unpunished,
    and [a] liar *will perish* (19:9).
2. A wise son gives joy to a father,
    and a foolish son, *grief* to his mother (10:1bc AT).
    A wise son gives joy to a father,
    but a fool *of a man despises* his mother (15:20 AT).

Elements of the proverbs persist even as the sages take poetic license to revise. This suggests the wisdom tradition is inherently dynamic, "subject to reexamination and complication, to a further process of thought" (White 1984, 152). The sages, and ultimately readers, play with its elements (e.g., metaphors, genres, exact wording) for varied effects.

Finally, repetition also teaches readers something about what it is to be human: we are incapable of holding on steadily to what we know. Seemingly inexorable is the human capacity to forget even the most significant of lessons. A climatic scene in book ten of Homer's *Iliad*, White argues, demonstrates this similarly. There, on a corpse-strewn battlefield, Patroclus's passionate appeal on behalf of the Achaeans so strongly evokes the reader's sympathies that she (momentarily) forgets what she learned at the poem's beginning about the equal humanity of those who die—Achaean and Trojan alike. White notes, "We learn something in the early books, we forget it, and learn it again; and this time we learn something else as well, about our own susceptibility to circumstance, our own incapacity to keep solidly to what we know" (1984, 52). So too repetition after 10:1 reminds us that human learning is inescapably repetitious: we learn, forget, and relearn. This steady erosion of our knowledge means that we must discover or be told what we "know" again and again. By reminding us of the human disposition to forget, the sages underscore our lifelong need for wisdom and pedagogy of the sort Proverbs offers to us (e.g., 1:2-7; 8:4; 9:9; 12:1a; 14:12).

Proverbs 10:1–15:33

Theological and Ethical Overview

When we cross the threshold of 10:1, the door does not close on the household; but the position of the implied reader shifts with regard to it. The sages of 10:1–15:33 (and 16:1–22:16) urge the once silent son, whose parents instructed him (Proverbs 1–9), to embrace, from an arguably more mature stance (9:7-9), the value of building and maintaining a good household. As the sages tell it, the welfare of families and individuals is tightly coupled: the fate of a household hinges on the character and conduct of its inhabitants and vice versa. So readers are encouraged to find a good spouse (12:4) and to discipline their children (13:24). A child's wisdom or folly brings honor or shame to the household (10:1, 5; 15:20). Women are wise or foolish depending on whether they build up or tear down the household (14:1). Character types are described as "sons" (10:5; 13:1; cf. 15:5). Consequences are measured in households (e.g., 12:7; 14:11). The sages condemn those who trouble the home (11:29; 15:27) and honor those who provide for its future (13:22; 14:26; cf. 15:6). The sages further underscore the value of a good home theologically: God destroys the house of the proud and stakes out boundary markers for the widow (15:25). The household remains the primary social context and, alongside the individual, the predominant moral unit (wisdom is even said to be "at home" in the wise heart [14:33] and the attentive ear "lodges" among the wise [15:31]). City and nation are comparatively peripheral (11:10-11, 14; 14:34-35; cf. Brown 2004, 159).

The sages continue to sketch the moral self principally in physical terms (see Theological and Ethical Analysis of Proverbs 1). The proverbs teem with references to the body, its postures and movements, emotions and appetites—making clear that moral formation is about orienting the whole body, not merely educating the mind. Walking a path remains the metaphor for life (e.g., 10:9, 17; 11:5; 12:26, 28; 14:2, 8; 15:9, 19, 21). Parts of the body represent by synecdoche the moral orientation and well-being of the whole person (e.g., 10:4, 10; 12:4, 24-25; 15:30). Desires and emotions signal moral commitments (e.g., 10:23; 12:1; 13:5, 13, 24; 15:10, 12, 20-21). Discipline is defined spatially as staying away from the foolish and wicked (e.g., 14:7) and drawing close to the wise (13:20; cf. 15:12). And consequences are often expressed bodily: the wise and righteous enjoy full bellies (e.g., 10:3; 12:11; 13:25); the wicked go hungry, stumble, and fall (e.g., 11:5; 13:25). Their names rot (10:7). Most prominent in all this "body talk" are organs of speech—lips, mouth, tongue, and the heart or mind (liars also "breathe out" lies, 12:17; 14:5, 25). And the words they release have physical effects. Words are consumed as food and nourish or deplete the body (10:21; 12:14; 15:1-2, 14); they pierce and wound (e.g., 12:18; 15:4); they delight and heal (12:18; 13:17; 14:38; 15:4, 23). Given the potency of speech, the sages urge caution and restraint as the implied reader matures from silent son to adult (e.g., 10:19; 11:12; 12:23; 13:3).

Relative confidence continues about the connection between acts and dispositions and consequences. The conviction that people "reap what they sow" resonates in 10:1–15:33, bolstered by the prevalent genre of antithetical proverbs: choices are ultimate—good or evil, wisdom or foolishness—and everyone is accountable. (The sages consider more questions and exceptions to the rule after 16:1.) There is no allowance made for "It doesn't really matter what I think," or "To each his or her own." Related and equally resonant is the iconic narrative that the wise and righteous prosper while the foolish and wicked suffer (see Theological and Ethical Analysis of Proverbs 3). The wise enjoy long life (e.g., 10:2, 16-17, 27; 11:4; 12:19, 28; 13:9, 14); security and permanence (e.g., 10:9, 25, 30; 12:3, 7); honor and a lasting reputation (e.g., 10:7; 13:15); health and happiness (10:24). The foolish, in contrast, experience dread, destruction, and premature death (e.g., 10:21, 24-25, 27-29; 11:3, 5-6). Their names are rancid and soon forgotten (e.g., 10:7b, 30; 11:7). Descriptions of the fates of the wise and foolish remain largely in the passive voice, leaving open the agents of their prosperity or imperilment. The sages' direct and repeated assertions of the iconic narrative coupled with their exhortation to "be assured" of its veracity (11:21) drives home a worldview of predictability woven together by rightness.

The world is not neutral because God, its creator, is not (14:31; cf. 3:19-20; 8:22-31). The sages of 10:1–15:33 highlight God's attention to and investment in the human situation. Their description, particularly the occasional use of language about the body, suggests there is consonance between the moral self and God. God is viscerally repulsed by the wicked and their deeds (e.g., 11:20; 12:22a; 15:8a, 9a, 26)—at times, God is "far away" from the wicked (15:29). By contrast, God is delighted by the righteous (e.g., 12:22b; 15:8b, 9b). God's responses are paralleled by God's protection of and provision for the wise and righteous and God's opposition to the foolish and wicked (e.g., 10:3, 29; 12:2; 14:26-27; 15:25). God is an agent of favor and retribution. God acts to ensure justice. And to that end, a few proverbs indicate God's particular concern for the vulnerable in society (e.g., 11:1; 14:31; 15:25; cf. 14:21). The sages base their appeal for generosity to the poor on God's creation of everyone (14:31). God's work in creation defines who is worthy of concern. God's work inspires the social ethic; in turn, our behavior toward the poor reveals our embrace or rejection of God and that ontology. Indeed, the sages readily associate one's behavior with one's disposition toward God: the devious despise God (14:2); the wise "fear the LORD" (10:27; 14:2; 15:16; see excursus in Proverbs 1). Finally, near the end of 10:1–15:33, the sages herald God's sovereignty and knowledge (15:3, 11)—themes they will develop more fully in 16:1–22:16.

God's concern for the poor is part of a larger conversation about wealth and poverty in 10:1–15:33. Wealth is a mixed bag. On the one hand, wealth is a reward and sign of divine blessing for the diligent, wise, and righteous (10:4b, 22; 13:22; 14:23; 15:6). It affords them protection and public esteem (e.g., 10:15; 14:21). On the other hand, wealth is clearly not a good to be pursued for its own sake (15:16-17); the sages caution against hoarding it (11:24, 26), putting one's trust in it (e.g., 11:4, 28), and acquiring it quickly and dishonestly (10:2a; 11:1, 4, 16; 13:11; 15:6, 27). Money is a benefit, not an end in itself. As for poverty, the sages—like the parent of Proverbs 1–9 (cf. 6:9-11)—attribute it primarily to laziness (10:4; 14:23). Only occasionally do they acknowledge the reality of injustice (11:1, 16; 13:23). Poverty is an indication of folly and, as such, invites shame and ostracism (10:15; 13:18; 14:20). The sages at the same time commend generosity (e.g., 11:24-25; 14:21).

PROVERBS 10

Literary Analysis

A new superscription ("the proverbs of Solomon," 10:1a; cf. 1:1; 25:1) signals the beginning of the second section of the book (10:1–22:16). As before (1:1), the proverbs that follow are attributed to Solomon, the second and last king of the united monarchy (ca. 966–926 BCE) and the quintessential sage of Israel (cf. 1 Kings 3-11). Notably, the Hebrew consonants in the name Solomon (*šlmh*) have the numerical value of 375 (300 + 30 + 40 + 5), the number of proverbs in 10:1–22:16.

Comprised mostly of antithetical proverbs (all but 10:18, 22, and 26), the chapter is a study in contrasts: righteous and wicked (10:2-3, 6-7, 11, 16, 20, 24-25, 28, 30, 32; cf. 10:27); wise and foolish (10:1, 8, 13-14, 23; cf. 10:18); prudent and shameful (10:5; cf. 10:19); diligent and lazy (10:4; cf. 10:26); persons with integrity and those of crooked ways (10:9; cf. 10:29). Spilling out one after another, the positive terms begin to blur as do the negative, so that readers learn to associate, on the one hand, righteousness, wisdom, insight, integrity, and diligence, and on the other, wickedness, folly, laziness, and shameful and crooked behavior. Indeed, the sages make such associations. They eventually juxtapose the righteous with fools (10:21) and the crooked (10:31), not with the wicked as we anticipate.

Interpreters debate whether and how to divide the chapter into smaller units. Repetition of the word "son" (NRSV: "child") provides an *inclusio*, or literary frame, around 10:1-5. Catchwords link some of the proverbs, such as "blessing" (10:6-7), "conceals" (10:11-12, 18), "ruin" (10:14-15), "to life" (10:16-17), "heart" or "mind" (10:20-21), and "perverse" (10:31-32). Two lines are repeated verbatim just a few proverbs apart (10:6b // 10:11b; 10:8b // 10:10b). And certain themes figure prominently, such as speech (e.g., 10:11, 13-14, 18-21, 31-32) and the fates of the righteous and wicked (10:24-30, except 10:26). Overall, however, Proverbs 10 resists delineation into smaller units. Some of the connections are tenuous, and there is a lack of consensus about their significance.

Exegetical Analysis

The Wise Life (10:1b-5)

What had been a talking *to* is now a talking *about*. At 10:1b, the reader's assumed position shifts from that of a silent son being instructed by his father (as in Proverbs 1–9) to an unspecified, arguably more mature stance (cf. 9:7-9). The shift is signaled when "son" occurs not as part of the familiar direct address "my son" but as a common noun (e.g., "a wise son," "a foolish son," 10:1bc, 5). Indeed, after 10:5, the word "son" disappears altogether until 13:1 (cf. 13:22, 24) and "my son" does not recur until 19:27. Thus while the context of 10:1bc clearly remains the household ("father," "mother," cf. 1:8; 4:3; 6:20), the reader's location with respect to it is different.

Framed by repetition of "son," 10:1b-5 may be diagrammed as a chiasm (a concentric structure in which elements are repeated in reverse) around verse 3:

   (A) A wise son (v. 1bc)
       (B) The profit of righteousness (v. 2)
           (C) YHWH sustains the righteous (v. 3)

(B') The profit of diligence (v. 4)
(A') A wise son (v. 5)

The structure highlights what it means to be wise: to make good decisions, behave justly, and work hard (10:1bc-2, 4-5) while recognizing one's reliance on God (10:3). God is the source and heart of the wise life.

The outer frame of the chiasm contrasts wise and foolish youth (A and A', 10:1bc, 5). Verse 1bc asserts that a youth's choice between wisdom and folly affects his or her parents (10:1b // 15:20a). That the parents react—and with profound emotions (joy, grief)—reveals the intensity of their investment in the youth's decisions (cf. "My [son], if *your heart* is wise, *my heart* too will be [happy]; *my* [*innards*] will rejoice when *your lips* speak what is right," 23:15-16). Stories elsewhere illustrate this intensity, such as those concerning David, Amnon, and Absalom (2 Sam 13:21; 18:33); Saul and Jonathan (e.g., 1 Sam 20:24-34); and Hosea's depiction of God's agony at the prospect of punishing God's "child," Israel (Hos 11). The sages frequently invoke the parent-child relationship to motivate certain behaviors (e.g., 17:21, 25; 19:26; 23:24-25; 27:11; 28:7; 29:3) much as they extol the importance of good marriages (e.g., 12:4; 14:1; 18:22). Of high value is the building and maintenance of a happy household, and essential to that is the choice of wisdom by its inhabitants.

Proverbs 10:5 (A') distinguishes wise and foolish children on the basis of their conduct at harvest time. Alliteration and assonance reinforce the contrast. The "wise son" (*bēn maśkîl*) gathers "in the summer" (*baqqayiṣ*) while the "disgraceful son" (*bēn mēbîš*) sleeps "in the harvest" (*baqqāṣîr*). Palestine has two primary seasons: the wet, cool months (October–April) and the dry, warm season (May–September). Harvest typically occurs in the latter (e.g., Jer 8:20; Mic 7:1). A wise youth, like the ant (6:8; cf. 30:25), is mindful of the rhythms of the world and works hard at the appropriate time, gathering food when it is abundant so there will be enough in the season of scarcity. The shameful son, in contrast, not only sleeps, but sleeps *soundly*, like Jonah on the ship to Tarshish (Jon 1:5-6), oblivious to the happenings—and urgencies—of the world around him.

The next level of the chiasm (B and B', 10:2, 4) considers what profits a person in life. Verse 2 is one of several cautions in the book about wealth acquired dishonestly (e.g., 1:8-19; 15:6; 21:6; 28:16b; cf. Sir 5:8). That which "does not profit" is contrary to God's instruction, including idols (e.g., Isa 44:9-10; 57:12; Jer 16:19; Hab 2:18), deceptive words (Job 15:3; Jer 7:8), and false prophets (Jer 2:8; 23:32). By contrast, righteousness "delivers from death" (cf. 11:4, 6), a phrase that occurs most frequently in contexts of imminent threat (e.g., Josh 2:13; Pss 33:19; 56:13 [Heb. v. 14]). Whereas ill-gained money proves no gain at all— and may invite death (21:6; 28:16b)—righteousness profits even in the face of peril.

Proverb B' (10:4) connects monetary profit with diligence:

> A poor person acts with (or "makes") a slack hand,
> A diligent hand makes rich.

The first line is ambivalent. On first read, it claims that the poor have lazy hands (so NASB, "Poor is he who works with a negligent hand"). But the second line invites a rereading that switches the verb's subject and object: slack hands make a poor person (cf. Clifford 1999, 112-13). That is, wealth or poverty is in a person's "hands" (in Hebrew, as in English, "hand" may also mean "power"). The sages elsewhere connect idleness and poverty (e.g., 6:10-11 // 24:33-34; 12:24; 19:15), even as they acknowledge poverty has other causes (e.g., 1:10-19; 11:1; 13:23).

Finally, proverb C (10:3), a YHWH proverb, asserts the sovereignty of God by its content and placement at the center of the chiasm (10:1-5). Lest people believe that their own wisdom, righteousness, and diligence ensure well-being, the proverb declares God's charge over and provision for human life, represented here by the most basic of appetites: hunger. Israel had an abiding sense of God as host and provider for all of creation (e.g., Exod 16–17; Pss 23, 104; Isa 25:6-8). Whereas some texts concur that God always provides for the righteous (e.g., Ps 34:10; 37:19, 25; Matt 6:11), others wrestle with circumstances that suggest otherwise (e.g., Job; Pss 10, 13). The second line includes a pun: *hawwâ* can mean "craving" or "disaster" (e.g., Job 6:2; 30:13;

cf. Prov 19:13). God may push away the "craving" of the wicked (13:4; Ps 112:10) or push toward the wicked the "disaster" that is coming to them (e.g., 1:26-27).

10:6 The word "blessing" and comparison of the righteous and wicked link the next two proverbs (10:6-7). A blessing signals a positive relationship between parties and, to the recipient, conveys certain benefits such as power, security, or material goods. A blessing *reveals* favor—the recipient and others recognize the value and desirability of the relationship (e.g., Job 42:12). That the blessings are "on the head" (10:6a; cf. 11:26) recalls the blessings of Joseph by Jacob ("May [the blessings of your father] be on the head of Joseph," Gen 49:26) and by Moses (Deut 33:16). In Proverbs parental instruction is also metaphorically "on [one's] head" as a fair garland, a sign of wealth, favor, and power (1:9; cf. 4:9). The mouth of the wicked, in contrast, *conceals* violence (10:6b // 10:11b). The wicked obscure their brutal inclinations; their speech is intentionally misleading, "hatred covered by deception" (26:26). Although the sages acknowledge that the concealment of something is necessary at times, even prudent (cf. 11:13; 12:16, 23; 17:9), they unequivocally condemn the masking of ill will (e.g., 10:18; 26:26).

10:7 This proverb contrasts the *zēker* (NRSV: "memory") of the righteous with the *šēm* (NRSV: "name") of the wicked. Both Hebrew terms refer to a person's name and reputation. For the sages, to have a good name is better than great riches (22:1) and fine ointments (Eccl 7:1; but cf. Eccl 2:16); the Egyptian *Instruction of Amenemope* teaches similarly, "Better is praise with the love of men / Than wealth in the storehouse" (*AEL* 2:156). Both terms may also refer to one's posthumous name, how a person is remembered after death (cf. Exod 17:14; Deut 32:26; Ps 9:6; Isa 26:14; 55:13). The verb "rot" in 10:7b evokes this meaning (e.g., Ps 49:14 [Heb. v. 15]; Isa 40:20). Isaiah celebrates a lasting reputation as "better than sons and daughters" (Isa 56:5), and as Ben Sira exhorts, "A human body is a fleeting thing, but a reliable name will never be cut off. Take care of your name, for it will remain for you longer than a thousand stores of gold; the goodness of life lasts only for a few days, but the goodness of a name lasts forever" (Sir 41:11-13 AT). Whereas the name or memory of the righteous endures (Ps 112:6), the name or memory of the wicked decomposes or is wiped out, as Bildad describes to Job:

By disease their skin is consumed,
    the firstborn of Death consumes their limbs. . . .
In their tents nothing remains;
    sulfur is scattered upon their habitations.
Their roots dry up beneath,
    and their branches wither above.
Their memory perishes from the earth,
    and they have no name in the street.
They are thrust from light into darkness,
    and driven out of the world.
They have no offspring or descendant among their people,
    and no survivor where they used to live. (Job 18:13, 15-19; cf. Pss 9:5-6 [Heb. vv. 6-7]; 34:16 [Heb. v. 17])

<u>10:8</u> Whereas the wise accept guidance and thereby presumably benefit (10:8a does not mention the consequences for "taking commandments"), fools chatter on and pay for it. The wise heed "commandments," a term that in Proverbs typically refers to parental instruction (e.g., 2:1; 3:1; 4:4; 6:20). Indeed, 10:8a recalls many of the father's exordia in chapters 1–9 (e.g., 3:1-2; 6:20-21; 7:1-3). By contrast, a babbling fool is too busy talking nonsense to hear, much less heed, instruction (e.g., 18:6b). As a result, the fool "comes to ruin," a verb used only here, in 10:10, and in Hos 4:14, where it describes the fate of those who lack knowledge. Ecclesiastes observes:

[The] words [from the mouth of] the wise bring . . . favor,
    but the lips of fools consume them.
The words of their mouths begin in [folly],
    and their talk ends in [terrible] madness;
yet fools talk on and on. (Eccl 10:12-14a).

<u>10:9</u> A gentle rhythm and repetition of sounds in 10:9a— *hōlēk battōm yēlek beṭaḥ* ("Whoever walks in integrity walks

securely")—sway readers back and forth in a manner suggestive of the proverb's primary image: walking. Juxtaposition of that physical activity with moral language ("integrity") highlights again that wisdom (and foolishness) are embodied (e.g., 4:20-27; 6:12-15, 16-19). Proverbs esteems those who "walk in integrity" (19:1; 20:7; 28:6) and promises that they do so with (divine) protection and security (2:7; 13:6; 28:18; cf. Ps 26), a promise challenged by Job who, though "blameless and upright, one who feared God and turned away from evil" (Job 1:1, 8; 2:3), found himself imperiled as victim of a divine wager. Conversely, those who "twist their ways," who act wrongly and deceitfully (e.g., 2:15; cf. Isa 59:8) "are found out." The passive verb leaves open how this happens and the consequences that follow, thus heightening the ominous tone (cf. 28:18).

10:10 Body imagery continues with reference to the one who "narrows" the eye (NRSV: "winks"). As in 6:13, the expression suggests the person looks on others with envy, disdain, or hatred (Ps 35:19), or squints as he or she conspires to make trouble for others (cf. 16:30; Sir 27:22). In MT, the parallel line (10:10b) repeats 10:8b ("a foolish babbler will come to ruin," cf. NIV, NASB). Interpreters often consider this a scribal error: the line breaks the pattern of antithetical proverbs, and the connection between 10a and 10b is not clear. Accordingly, many translations follow LXX and read "but the one who rebukes boldly [or openly] makes peace" (e.g., NRSV, NJB, REB). The eye-squinter sows discord (so 6:14); those who rebuke engender goodwill. The sages celebrate the value of reproof throughout Proverbs (e.g., 1:23; 3:11-12; 5:12-13; 6:23; 10:17; 13:18; 17:10; 25:12; 27:5-6). That a rebuke "makes peace" speaks to its rightful intent (to foster good relationships) and its impact (when one heeds a rebuke, peace should eventually follow).

10:11-12 The catchword "conceals" links 10:11-12, the first two of four proverbs concerned with speech (10:11-14). "A fountain of life," a particularly vivid metaphor given the desert climate of Palestine, suggests that the words of the righteous flow like fresh, life-giving waters from a deep reservoir (cf. 18:4b). The metaphor is used elsewhere in Proverbs for the wife of one's youth

(5:18), the teaching of the wise (13:14), fear of the LORD (14:27), and wisdom (16:22)—a list to which Jeremiah adds YHWH (Jer 2:13; 17:13; cf. Ps 36:10). By contrast, the speech of the wicked conceals their violent intentions (cf. 10:6b).

To conceal something is not necessarily wrong, however (e.g., 11:13; 12:23). Hatred rouses conflict (e.g., 6:16-19; cf. 29:22) while love makes it possible "to conceal" an offense—not in the sense of condoning the wrong, but forgiving (cf. Ps 78:38) or overlooking it (cf. 17:9). Love enables people to excuse the transgressions of others; it does not permit them to conceal their own (28:13). The proverb is echoed by 1 Pet 4:8b: "Love covers a multitude of sins" (cf. Jas 5:20); and similar sentiments are suggested by Col 3:13-14: "Bear with one another and, if anyone has a complaint against another, forgive each other. . . . Above all, clothe yourselves with love."

10:13 The first line speaks to the perennial question about the location of wisdom (e.g., Job 28:12; Bar 3:15, 31–4:1; Sir 24:1-12), which Proverbs answers by pointing to wisdom personified (1:28; 3:13; 8:17, 35), a parent's instruction (4:20-23), and here the lips and speech of anyone with understanding (10:13a). Those who seek wisdom find it (and, implicitly, its many rewards) in the words of the wise. Fools, however, ignore wise speech (e.g., 1:22-25) and, as such, find only the disciplinary sting of a rod on their backs (e.g., 13:24; 17:10; 19:25; 22:15; 23:13). It is not clear whether they learn anything from it; the sages later compare fools to stubborn animals that can only be motivated by brute force (26:3).

10:14 Whereas the wise accumulate knowledge to the benefit of themselves and others (e.g., 2:1; 7:1; 10:21), the talk of fools threatens everyone (e.g., 13:3; 18:6-7).

10:15 The term "ruin" links this proverb to the previous one, but the topic now is money. Wealth, like a fortified city, affords security, protection from attack, and a stable supply of goods and social connections. Poverty renders people defenseless, exposed to the elements, and bereft of means and support. The juxtaposition of a rich man (sg.) with the poor (pl.) heightens the contrast. Other proverbs caution against investing too much in the claim (e.g., 10:29; 11:4; 18:10-11; 23:4-5; 28:6; cf. Eccl 5:13-16; 6:1-2). Proverbs 18:11a repeats 10:15a.

10:16-17 The phrase "to life" connects these two proverbs. The first (10:16) continues with the topic of money, comparing what happens to wages in the hands of the righteous with what happens to wages in the hands of the wicked (no mention is made of how the wages were earned). The righteous put their money "to life"—to foster well-being (cf. 19:23)—and the wicked put their earnings not "to death," as we expect, but more jarringly "to sin." The Hebrew term *hattā't* refers to "missing the mark" or "sin" (e.g., Lev 4:3; Num 5:7) and to its consequences, such as penance, recompense, or sin-offerings (e.g., Exod 29:36; Lev 4:8, 20; 2 Kgs 12:16 [Heb. v. 17]). This suggests that the gain of the wicked may go toward perpetrating sin and precipitating its consequences, including punishment and death (e.g., 1:10-19; 5:22-23; 11:18-19; cf. Paul's claim that "the wages of sin is death" in Rom 6:23).

The second proverb (10:17) describes a person who keeps discipline (*mûsār*, cf. 1:2) as a path to life. He or she will guide others in the right direction. In contrast, those who ignore a rebuke "mislead" others—the form of the verb is causative (i.e., "to cause others to err" or "lead astray," cf. 12:26b; Isa 3:12; 9:16 [Heb. v. 15]; 30:28).

10:18 Interpreters debate the subject of the first line: "lying lips" (e.g., NRSV, NJB, REB) or "[the one] who conceals" (e.g., NASB, NIV, TANAKH). Given the subject in the parallel line ("the one who finds"), the latter provides a better antithesis. The proverb thus sets up a contrast between "concealing" (10:18a) and "finding" (10:18b), understood here in the sense of "revealing," namely, uttering (NJB) or spreading (NASB, NIV) a rumor. The sages repeatedly commend consistency of character—consonance between one's thoughts, speech, and actions (e.g., 4:20-27; 6:12-19)—even as they warn about people who obscure their intentions (cf. 10:11; 26:24).

10:19 The concern is the sheer number of "many words." Less is more in matters of speech. Ecclesiastes observes that fools "talk on and on" (10:14) and that "there are many words that increase vanity" (6:11); Elihu claims that Job opens "his mouth with empty talk and . . . multiplies words without knowledge" (Job 35:16). In contrast, the wise choose their words carefully and speak sparingly (cf. 12:23; 17:27-28; Eccl 5:2). Compare the Egyptian *Instruction of Ptahhotep*:

> Your silence is better than chatter.
>   Speak when you know you have a solution. . . .
> Speaking is harder than all other work,
>   He who understands it makes it serve. (*AEL* 1:70)

10:20 Parallel use of tongue and heart or mind (see excursus in Proverbs 2) signals the intimate connection between the two (e.g., 16:1; 17:20; Ps 45:1 [Heb. v. 2])—which the psalmist describes aptly: "My *heart* [was] hot within me. [In my thoughts,] fire burned; then I spoke with my *tongue*" (Ps 39:3 [Heb. v. 4]). Speech is an "outpouring of the heart" (e.g., 16:23; 23:33). Though the sages frequently compare the value of things to silver (3:14; 8:10; 16:16; 22:1), the standard of "choice silver," or silver refined by fire, occurs only here and in 8:19 with regard to wisdom's revenues. R. C. Van Leeuwen notes the wordplay: a "tongue" is also the shape of a bar of precious metal (1997, 111-12; e.g., "tongue of gold," Josh 7:21, 24).

10:21 The association between speech and the heart or mind continues. The lips of the righteous "feed" many. The verb "to feed" or "to protect as a shepherd" (*rāʿâ*) is used to describe the work of caring for and protecting people, particularly by kings and others in power (e.g., Jer 23:1-6; Ezek 34; cf. the metaphor used for God, e.g., Gen 48:15; Ps 23; Ezek 34:11-22). The righteous are able with their words to nourish many (cf. Jer 3:15), while fools, without sense ("lack of a heart [or mind]"), cannot keep themselves alive.

10:22 Whereas the first line emphasizes its subject with the insertion of a pronoun ("the blessing of YHWH, *it* makes rich"), the subject of the second is ambiguous: (*a*) "YHWH does not add sorrow to it" (e.g., NRSV, NIV, NASB, REB) or (*b*) "toil does not add to it" (e.g., NJB). Both translations are possible and have significant theological implications. According to (*a*), the wealth that God gives comes without sorrow, unlike ill-gained wealth that brings trouble and suffering (e.g., 10:2; 13:11; 15:6; 16:8; 21:6). As Ecclesiastes observes, however, people who earn their money honestly may suffer even so (e.g., Eccl 4:7-8; 5:13-16). According to (b), no amount of work can add to the wealth God gives. God is ultimately responsible for human welfare. The claim curbs over-valuation of human effort—including proverbs that draw a straight line from toil to wealth (e.g., 10:4; 14:23).

10:23 The objects of our affections matter. For fools, doing "wrong," a term that can mean unspoken scheming (21:27; 24:9) and egregious behavior (e.g., adultery in Jer 13:27; Ezek 16:43; murder in Hos 6:9), is not only their tendency—it is their joy (cf. 1:22; 2:14; 15:21; 26:19). Doing wrong is the fool's sport. Those with understanding, on the contrary, find their delight in wisdom and behaving justly (e.g., 21:15). What gives people pleasure and satisfaction reveals much about their values and character (cf. "Where your treasure is, there your heart will be also," Matt 6:21).

10:24-25 These two proverbs turn to the fates of the righteous and wicked (cf. 10:27-30). Like the storm that personified wisdom predicts for scoffers and fools (1:24-27), 10:24 does not specify agency. Whatever sparks fear in the wicked *comes* whereas the desire of the righteous *is given*—apparently inevitably. The claim is poetic justice: the wicked and righteous receive their just deserts as a matter of course (e.g., Ps 34; Isa 66:4).

After the storm, the wicked "are not" (10:25a). R. Alter notes the proverb denies the wicked "a proper predicate," while the righteous are "so substantial" they are established as a foundation wall, something neither storm nor adversity can sweep away (Alter 1985, 175; cf. 10:30; 12:3, 7; Ezek 13:13-16; cf. Matt 7:24-27). Job echoes this notion of the wicked as insubstantial, describing them as "straw before the wind, / and like chaff . . . the storm carries away" (Job 21:18). He later describes their fate:

> Terrors overtake [the wicked] like a flood;
>> in the night a whirlwind carries them off.
> The east wind lifts them up and they are gone;
>> it sweeps them out of their place.
> It hurls at them without pity;
>> they flee from its power in headlong flight.
> It claps its hands at them,
>> and hisses at them from its place. (Job 27:20-23)

10:26 Sharp, overpowering irritants interrupt the series of anti-thetical proverbs to describe how employers experience the "slacker," a figure of scorn to whom the sages devote longer units (24:30-34 and 26:13-16) and individual proverbs throughout the book (6:6, 9; 13:4; 15:19; 19:24; 20:4; 21:25; 22:13). "Vinegar" refers broadly to any strong acidic drink made from grapes (25:20; cf. Num 6:3); this "sour wine" may be revitalizing (Ruth 2:14) but is utterly distasteful (the term is parallel to "poison" in Ps 69:21 [Heb. v. 22]). Like the bite of vinegar on teeth and the sting of smoke to the eyes, the lazy are agonizing for those who entrust work to them.

10:27 "Fear of the LORD" occurs here for the first time in 10:1–22:16 (see excursus in Proverbs 1; also 14:26-27; 15:16, 33; 16:6; 19:23; 22:4). "Fear of the LORD" is a hallmark of the wise and righteous. Prolonged life is among the many gifts of wisdom (e.g., 3:2, 16; 4:10; 8:35; 9:11; 19:23), while premature death is a consequence of wickedness and folly (e.g., 1:29-33; 5:22-23).

10:28 The expectations of the righteous and wicked also have different ends. The NRSV, informed by 10:28b, reads 10:28a as, "The hope of the righteous *ends in* gladness." But the Hebrew is, "The hope of the righteous *is* joy." This implies that the hope of the righteous is itself a source of joy even before that hope is (eventually) fulfilled (as implied by 10:28b; cf. 10:24). The claim is challenged by 13:12a ("Hope deferred makes the heart sick") but echoed by Paul: "Rejoice in hope" (Rom 12:12). The hope of the just persists (23:18; 24:14). That of the wicked perishes (cf. 11:7; Job 11:20).

10:29 The first line may be interpreted three ways. If it is trans-lated, "A stronghold for the upright is the way of YHWH" (cf. NRSV), the subject—"the way of YHWH"—may refer to God's "way" of being and acting (cf. 8:22; usually the "ways" of YHWH; e.g., Exod 33:13; Hos 14:9 [Heb. v. 10]) or to the "way" God invites people to live, namely, by obedience to the covenant (e.g., 2 Sam 22:22; Ps 18:22; Jer 5:4-5) and the practice of justice (Gen 18:19). The phrase thus compares to the "way of wisdom" (e.g., 3:17; 4:11). The first line might also be translated: "A refuge for the upright of way [i.e. those whose ways are honest] is YHWH" (e.g., REB). Although "the way of YHWH" is found nowhere else in Proverbs, the phrase "upright of way" occurs in 13:6 (cf. 11:20 [NRSV: "those of blameless ways"]; Job 4:6; Ps 119:1; Ezek 28:15). This translation resonates with claims that God is a "stronghold" (e.g., Pss 27:1; 28:8; Jer 16:19), a refuge for those who walk uprightly (e.g., Ps 37:39). Proverbs 21:15b repeats 10:29b.

10:30 The first line reiterates that the righteous are unshakable ("will not be made to totter," cf. 10:25; 12:3, 7; Pss 15:5; 62:2 [Heb. v. 3]; 112:6). The second line connects that immovability to residence "in the land" (cf. 2:20-22), a phrase that may denote a specific geographical area (e.g., the promised land in Deut 4:1; 5:33; 16:20), the whole world (Isa 18:3), some unspecified region (e.g., 10:30) and, metaphorically, "this world"—the land of the living, divine blessing, and abundance (cf. Ps 37). "The land" thus invites a number of connections, all of which bode badly for the wicked.

10:31-32 Translated woodenly, the chapter concludes:

| Mouth of righteous | brings forth (*yānûb*) wisdom | tongue of wicked | cut off |
| Lips of righteous | know what is pleasing | mouth of wicked | perverse |

The verb *nûb* (10:31a), which has the sense of "growing" or "sprouting" (cf. Ps 92:14 [Heb. v. 15] and its cognate in other languages), evokes descriptions of the righteous as thriving trees (11:28, 30; cf. Pss 1:1-6; 92:12, 14 [Heb. vv. 13, 15) and of speech as fruit (12:14; 13:2; 18:20; cf. 15:4). In contrast, the tongue of the wicked is "cut off" (cf. Ps 12:3 [Heb. v. 4]), a verb used elsewhere for the felling of a tree (cf. Job 14:7). The harsh language of disfigurement parallels the twisted mouth and speech of the wicked in 10:32b, and calls to mind the ancient Assyrian practice of tearing out the tongues of rebels (*ANET* 288). The Aramaic *Proverbs of Ahiqar* enjoins similarly: "El will twist the mouth of the twister (= treacherous) and tear out [his] tongue" (*TAD* 3.1.1.156). The tongue may also by synecdoche represent the whole, so the wicked are "cut off" from the community and land (2:22; 10:30).

PROVERBS 11

Literary Analysis

"Delight" or "pleasure" (*rāṣôn*) connects 11:1 with 10:32, and the predominance of antithetical proverbs continues (except 11:7, [16], 22, 25, 29). The chapter develops the theme of fates, particularly those of the righteous and wicked (11:3-8, 17-21, 23; cf. 10:24-30), and highlights the effects of the righteous and wicked on their communities (cf. "neighbor," "city," and "people" in 11:9-14). The chapter tends also to economic matters (11:1, 15, 16), including generosity and stinginess (11:24-26).

A couple of smaller units are evident. Verses 3-6 are linked by the Hebrew roots "to be upright" (11:3, 5, 6), "to be complete" or "blameless" (11:3, 5), "to deliver" (11:4, 6), "to be righteous" (11:4, 5, 6), and the plural noun "wicked" (11:3, 6). Similarly, verses 9-12 share the catchwords "neighbor" (11:9, 12), "city" (11:10, 11), and "mouth" (11:9, 11), and each line, except for 11:12b, begins with the Hebrew letter *bêt* (*b*). Catchwords associate other proverbs, such as "delivered" (11:8-9), "only" (11:23-24), and "blessing" (11:25-26), and there are a few proverb pairs (11:5-6, 10-11, and 12-13). The chapter concludes with two proverbs that compare the righteous to flourishing trees (11:28, 30).

Exegetical Analysis

<u>11:1</u> Three of the book's eleven "abomination of YHWH" proverbs (see excursus in Proverbs 3) concern false weights and measures (11:1; 20:10, 23; cf. 16:11). Abomination proverbs typically address wrongs that are unnoticed and for which reparation is difficult to obtain. Until rather late in Israel's history, lack of precise standards made fraudulent use of weights (called "stones," 11:1b) and measures such a wrong. Although biblical law denounces this deception (e.g., Lev 19:35-36; Deut 25:13-16), frequent prophetic indictments of the rigging of weights suggest it was a recurring problem. Amos, for example, admonishes merchants who "make [an] ephah small and [a] shekel

great, [and deceive] with false balances" (Amos 8:5), whereas Micah quotes God asking: "Can I [pardon] wicked scales and a bag of dishonest weights?" (Mic 6:10-11; cf. Ezek 45:10; Hos 12:7 [Heb. v. 8]). The Egyptian *Instruction of Amenemope* cautions similarly: "Do not move the scales nor alter the weights, / Nor diminish the fractions of the measure" (*AEL* 2:156). The term *rāṣôn* ("pleasure" or "delight") connects this proverb with 10:32.

11:2 Repetition of the verb "to come" (*bōʾ*) and assonance in the first line signals the coupling of pride (*zādôn*) with shame (*qālôn*): *bāʾ zādôn wayyābōʾ qālôn*. They are traveling companions; when one arrives so does the other. As such, 11:2a is a variation on the claim "pride precedes a fall" (cf. 15:33b; 16:18; 18:3, 12). By contrast, humility and wisdom are associated (e.g., 15:33; 22:4). The term *ṣĕnûʿîm* (NRSV: "humble") occurs only here in the Old Testament, but its use in Sirach suggests levelheadedness (Sir 34:22; 42:8), a realistic appreciation of one's gifts and limitations.

11:3 Along with 11:4-6, this proverb extols how certain virtues guide and sustain the upright while vices destroy the wicked. The verb "to guide" evokes the image of a way or path and is used similarly for parental instruction that orients and enables a person to navigate in the world (cf. 6:22). The "treacherous," a term that elsewhere is parallel to the wicked (cf. 2:22; 21:18) and occasionally translated by the NRSV as "faithless" (21:18; 22:12; 25:19), are people who break commitments and deal unfairly with others—including family members (e.g., Exod 21:8; Jer 12:6), business and political allies (e.g., Judg 9:23), and God (e.g., Jer 3:20; 5:11; Hos 5:7; 6:7). Deceivers and tricksters, they are utterly unreliable (cf. 11:6).

11:4 Compare this proverb to 10:2; the second lines are identical but the contrast here is not wealth acquired dishonestly but simply "riches." Money however gained, it seems, affords no advantage in the "day of rage." That said, the juxtaposition of "riches" with "righteousness" and the concern of other proverbs in the immediate literary context with money either illegitimately acquired (11:1) or relied on too heavily (11:7) suggests these "riches" may be somehow suspect. The phrase "the day of rage [of YHWH]" occurs also in Job 21:30; Zeph 1:15, 18; and Ezek 7:19. The latter two texts warn that on that day—when God judges all nations of the world and exacts punishment on a cosmic scale—neither the people's silver nor gold will save them. The psalmist echoes the sentiment: "Truly, no ransom avails for one's life, there is no price one can give to God for it" (Ps 49:7 [Heb. v. 8]; cf. Luke 12:15-21). "Day of rage" calls to mind the sages' other admonitions about a "day of disaster" (e.g., 27:10; Job 21:30; cf. Prov 1:26-27) and prophetic cautions about "the day of the LORD" (e.g., Amos 5:18-20).

11:5-6 This proverb picks up the theme introduced in 11:3 that the virtues of the righteous preserve them, while the wrongdoings of the wicked trip the wicked up. Just as integrity is a "guide" for the righteous (11:3), so righteousness "keeps straight" their way and "delivers" them. The second line contains a pun: *hawwâ* can mean "desire" (NRSV: "schemes") or "disaster" (e.g., Job 6:2; 30:13; cf. Prov 19:13). The wicked, that is, become entangled by their desire or disaster (cf. 10:3). They are notorious for stumbling on their way and falling into their own traps (e.g., 1:13-18; 4:19; 15:19; 22:5; cf. Ps 35:4-8).

11:7 Repetition of the verb "to perish" (11:7a and 7b; NRSV: "comes to nothing") emphasizes the fate of the wicked. The first line refers to *'ādām rāšā'* ("a person of wickedness"), not the terse *rāšā'* ("wicked one") typical of Proverbs; the phrase occurs twice elsewhere in Old Testament Wisdom literature, however (Job 20:29; 27:13). In the second line, *'ônîm* (NRSV: "godless") may be either of two nouns. The first, which means "mourning" (Gen 35:18; Deut 26:14; Hos 9:4), prompts the translation, "Any hope of mourning perishes" (11:7b). Any expectation the wicked harbor that others will mourn for them dies with them. The second noun has several possible meanings, including virility (e.g., Gen 49:3; Deut 21:17), physical power (e.g., Job 40:16; Hos 12:4; e.g., NIV, NEB, NAB), and wealth (e.g., Job 20:10; Hos 12:8 [Heb. v. 9]; e.g., NJB). The ambivalence of *'ônîm* underscores that death takes *all* hope from the wicked. No one will grieve them, and neither children, nor power, nor money will outlast them. So Job portrays the demise of the *'ādām rāšā'*:

If . . . children [of the wicked] are multiplied, it is for the
sword;
   and their offspring have not enough to eat.
Those who survive them the pestilence buries,
   and their widows make no lamentation.
Though they heap up silver like dust,
   and pile up clothing like clay—
they may pile it up, but the just will wear it,
   and the innocent will divide the silver.
They build their houses like nests,
   like booths made by sentinels for the vineyard.
They go to bed with wealth, but will do so no more;
   they open their eyes, and it is gone.
Terrors overtake them like a flood;
   in the night a whirlwind carries them off.
The east wind lifts them up and they are gone;
   it sweeps them out of their place. (Job 27:14-21; cf.
Prov 10:28)

11:8 Juxtaposition of a passive verb ("is delivered," 11:8a) with
an active one ("comes" or "enters," 11:8b) heightens this comparison of the righteous and the wicked. The word "trouble" is
literally "straits," or narrow, tight spaces. When the righteous
become trapped or stuck—in a pinch, so to speak—they are delivered, presumably by God (e.g., Pss 34:4, 19; 107; cf. Prov 21:18);
the righteous have difficulties, but they are temporary. The
wicked, in contrast, rush in and insert themselves into the very
same trouble: the wicked "enters beneath" or "instead of" the
righteous. The righteous can count on eventually getting *out* of
trouble. The wicked run headlong *into* it.

11:9 Contrary to the familiar "sticks and stones" adage, words
can destroy others (e.g., 15:4). The mouth of the "godless"
(ḥānēp)—a term that occurs only here in Proverbs but in other
texts is parallel to the wicked (Job 20:5), evildoer (Isa 9:17 [Heb.
v. 16]), and sinner (Isa 33:14)—inflicts devastating harm on neighbors. The contrast between "mouth" and "knowledge" suggests
that the godless speak ignorantly. They disregard God (e.g., Job
8:13; Isa 32:6) and, as such, lack the "knowledge" that characterizes

and saves the righteous. Inherent to that knowledge is appreciation for the power and perils of speech (cf. 11:12-13). The verb *ḥālaṣ* ("to deliver") in 11:9b connects this proverb to 11:8.

11:10-11 Just as the welfare of a neighborhood relies on the integrity of its members (11:9), so the vitality of a community depends on its citizens. This proverb makes the point by contrasting what inspires joy in the city: the prosperity of the righteous and demise of the wicked (cf. 28:12; 29:2). Both purportedly enhance the city's welfare. The city's outburst of joy at the downfall of the wicked is an expression of *Schadenfreude*, or enjoyment of another's troubles. Although some texts acknowledge and even encourage *Schadenfreude* by people and God, particularly when the wicked stumble (e.g., Job 22:19-20; Pss 37:10-13; 52:5-7; 58:10-11; Isa 14:3-21; Rev 18:20), others condemn it outright (e.g., 24:17-18; Job 31:29; Ps 35:11-16, 19). Sound links 11:10 to 11:9: the verb *ʿālaṣ* ("to rejoice," 11:10a) resonates with *ḥālaṣ* ("to deliver," 11:9b).

Verse 11 provides reasons for the city's joy. The upright "bless" the city. The term may refer to various manners of blessing (e.g., leadership, wealth), but its use parallel to "mouth" here suggests that the speech of the upright "builds up" the community. The mouth of the wicked, by contrast, tears the city down (cf. 11:9).

11:12-13 At times, as these two proverbs suggest, silence is smart (cf. 17:28). The first juxtaposes "remains silent" with "despises a neighbor" (cf. 14:21), implying the concern is the expression of hatred out loud. R. Alter notes the strangeness of this juxtaposition: "It brings us up short, makes us absorb what is for Proverbs a rather devious perception about humanity—that, all too often, one's fellow may in fact behave in a manner worthy of revilement, but that the prudent person will keep his mouth shut about what he sees" (1985, 175).

The second (11:13) builds on this perception by contrasting two types of people—the "gossip," a term derived from the Hebrew root meaning "to traffic" or "sell," who goes about to *reveal* secrets (cf. 20:19), and the "resolute in spirit" (NRSV: "trustworthy") who stands firm, as it were, and *conceals* matters (cf. 25:9). Slander is emblematic of personal and communal immorality, a mark of people who do not know God (e.g., Lev 19:16; Jer 9:3; Ezek 22:9).

11:14 The right word can be a matter of survival, a claim this proverb makes through a variety of possible readings, each dependent on how we interpret four of its terms. First, *taḥbūlôt* (NRSV: "guidance") has to do with the art of steering, as with a sailor navigating a boat; in Proverbs, the term is used for deliberation (12:5) and for wise counsel in military circumstances (20:18; 24:5-6). Second, *'am* (NRSV: "nation") may refer to any group of people (28:15; 29:18; metaphorically, 30:25-26), an army (e.g., 2 Kgs 13:7), or a nation (e.g., 24:24; 29:2). Third, *těšû'â* (NRSV: "safety") can mean deliverance, especially by God (e.g., Ps 119:41, 81), and in Proverbs is used particularly for military victory (21:31; 24:6b // 11:14b). Finally, *yô'ēṣ* (NRSV: "counselor") refers to professional counselors (e.g., advisers to the king, Ezra 7:28; Isa 19:11) and anyone who offers guidance (e.g., 12:20). Such a constellation of terms affords multiple interpretations, from the value of good advice for the welfare of any group (e.g., "For want of leadership a people perishes, / safety lies in many advisers," NJB) to the importance of deliberate military strategy for success in battle (e.g., "For want of skillful strategy an army is lost; / victory is the fruit of long planning," REB).

11:15 This proverb encapsulates the warning of 6:1-5 about guaranteeing the debt of a stranger. In ancient Israel, there were several ways to guarantee a loan. The borrower might offer as collateral an item of value (e.g., Exod 22:25-26; Deut 24:6, 10-13); pledge fields, houses, even children (Neh 5:1-5); or request that another person, often in exchange for a small fee, serve as guarantor. If a person became a guarantor, all of that person's property (and him or herself if necessary) was subject to seizure if the debtor failed to repay the loan. With striking assonance— *ra'-yērôa' kî 'ārab zār* (lit. "Suffering one will suffer if one stands surety for a stranger," 11:15a)—this proverb urges particular avoidance of serving as guarantor for strangers who purportedly have less social pressure to honor their commitments. Indeed, the sages tell creditors that they might as well "take the garment of one who has [stood] surety for a stranger" (20:16a; cf. 27:13a), because strangers will almost certainly renege on their loans. Only outright refusal to "strike the hand" (11:15b)—to shake hands and seal such a deal—ensures a person's safety.

11:16 This proverb may be translated:

> A charming woman (*'ēšet ḥēn*) attains honor,
> And/but violent men attain money.

Because the conjunction may be read as "and" or "but," the two lines may be construed as complementary or antithetical. Read as complementary ("and"), the proverb observes the effectiveness of charm and violence: a woman uses her *ḥēn* ("graciousness," "beauty," or "favor"; the *'ēšet ḥēn* is "beautiful" in Sir 9:8) to attain status and its benefits, whereas men use violence to get rich. The proverb so interpreted may implicitly warn about the fleeting nature of such gains (e.g., 10:2; 11:4; 21:6; 28:16b; cf. 31:30). Read as antithetical ("but"), the proverb contrasts a woman who achieves prominence by her graciousness with men who behave ruthlessly to get what they want. The disparity between them is heightened by use of the singular (woman) and plural (men). Whichever way the proverb is construed, it reinforces certain assumptions about gender, namely, that men use "muscle" whereas women use beauty and kindness to get ahead—assumptions with which present-day readers are likely familiar. The singling out of particular "types" of women is found elsewhere in the book, such as a "woman of folly" (9:13) and a "woman of substance" (31:10-31).

The NRSV reflects LXX and Syriac versions of this proverb, which add a second line to 11:16a and a first line to 11:16b. The additions were likely intended to clarify what was considered a problematic proverb.

11:17 The dispositions of people affect their well-being. This observation can be construed in at least two ways. First, that acts of kindness or cruelty toward others prompt similar acts in return (i.e., kindness begets kindness; violence begets violence). Second, that how one relates to others reveals how one regards and treats oneself. The proverb thus highlights how interconnected people are to one another.

11:18 A play on words emphasizes the contrast: the "empty" (šeqer, "false") wages of the wicked and the reliable "wages" (śeker) of the one who sows righteousness. Both receive rewards, but only those of the latter are trustworthy. Ill-gotten gains are notoriously fleeting (e.g., 10:2; 11:4; 15:6; 21:6; cf. 11:16). Compare the Egyptian *Instruction of Amenemope*:

> If riches come to you by theft,
>   They will not stay the night with you.
> Comes day they are not in your house. . . .
>   They made themselves wings like geese,
> And flew away to the sky. (*AEL* 2:152)

The metaphor of sowing and reaping appears frequently in the Bible to express the relationship between acts and consequences (e.g., 22:8; Job 4:8; Ps 126:5; Hos 8:7; 10:11-15; 2 Cor 9:6).

11:19 The first line begins with kēn, a term that may mean: (*a*) "thus," which couples the proverb to 11:18—perhaps as an elaboration of its claims—but provides an odd parallel to "one who pursues evil" in the second line, or (*b*) "justice" or "right," which is also awkward. Consequently, the NRSV (along with other translations) emends kēn to tikkōn from the Hebrew root "to be firm" or "established"; because the Hebrew letter *t* is the last letter of 11:18, a scribe may have unintentionally skipped over it as the first letter of 11:19, an error called haplography. This affords a contrast between one who is "firm" (NRSV: "steadfast") in righteousness and one who pursues evil (cf. 11:13). The proverb thus reasserts that righteousness is life-giving and wickedness death dealing (e.g., 10:3, 16, 27; 11:4; 12:28; 21:21).

11:20 This is one of eleven "abomination of YHWH" proverbs in the book (see excursus in Proverbs 3); four contrast an abomination to God—what God finds disgusting—with a source of divine delight (11:1, 20; 12:22; 15:8; cf. 15:9). Certain behaviors and attitudes, the sages argue, provoke strong reactions from God. In this instance, God's repugnance and joy is in response to general orientations in the world: crookedness and uprightness (cf. "blameless of way," 13:6). Parallel use of "heart" or "mind" and "way" is consistent with their association elsewhere (e.g., 7:25; 16:9; 23:19).

11:21 This proverb reasserts the inevitability of the fates of the righteous and wicked. "Assuredly" is literally "hand to hand"— an expression akin to "shake on it"; the exchange is trustworthy (cf. 16:5b). The phrase "will not go unpunished" condemns the wicked while leaving open the possibilities for their punishment (cf. 6:29; 16:5; 17:5; 19:5, 9; 28:20). The second line ("The seed [i.e., children] of the righteous will escape") is odd. Its meaning is perhaps twofold: the righteous will *have* children, unlike the wicked according to some traditions (e.g., Job 18:19), and their children will be *safe*, unlike those of the wicked (e.g., Exod 24:7).

11:22 A bejeweled pig, one of the most unclean of animals (cf. Deut 14:8; Ps 80:14), is a vivid metaphor for the incongruity of beauty without sense. The contrast here is not, as the NRSV suggests, between the pig and any beautiful but unintelligent woman. Rather, the second line is better translated "a beautiful woman who turns aside from good sense." The woman forsakes her discretion, she veers off the right path—and *that* makes her beauty disconcerting (cf. descriptions of the "strange" woman in Proverbs 1–9, esp. 6:25), like a pig decked out in the gold finery typical of the affluent (e.g., Gen 24:22, 30, 47; Job 42:11; Isa 3:21; Ezek 16:12). The proverb serves as a caution against the idolization of beauty (cf. 31:30) and suggests that the sages expect beauty and wisdom to go hand in hand.

11:23 Translated woodenly, the proverb is "the desire of the righteous, only good; the expectation of the wicked, wrath." It affords several interpretations insofar as "desire" and "expectation" may refer to an act, its object, and its result (NRSV: "ends in"; cf. 10:24, 28; 11:7). Moreover, the proverb leaves ambiguous whose wrath the second line refers to—that of the wicked themselves, others who act against the wicked, or perhaps God (cf. "day of wrath," 11:4). If "desire" and "expectation" are read as actions and/or their objects, the proverb is about the interests of the righteous and wicked; if the terms are construed as about results, the proverb describes the consequences of their actions.

11:24 This proverb is typically interpreted to be about generosity and stinginess: generosity rewards; tightfistedness depletes. The verb "gives freely" has the sense of scattering (e.g., Ps 147:16; Joel 3:2 [Heb 4:2]) and is used in Ps 112:9 for giving to the poor. Here the claim is a general one, however. It does not specify to whom one gives (cf. Eccl 11:1-2; Mark 4:24). The proverb may also be read as an economic paradox, namely, those who spend a lot become rich, and those who save aggressively wind up poorer. It thus encourages big spending, perhaps in the spirit that one reaps what one sows.

11:25 Food and drink serve to restate the paradox of generosity observed by 11:24a. A generous person "will be made fat" (NRSV: "will be enriched"; cf. 13:4; 28:25), an expression that denotes satiation and contentment (e.g., Job 36:16; Isa 30:23; Jer 31:14). In the second line, repetition of the verb draws a straight line from act to consequence: one who "quenches with water" will "be quenched." The proverb leaves open how the generous come to enjoy these benefits (e.g., 11:8, 21). It merely asserts their feast is inevitable.

11:26 The lessons of 11:24-25 are now expressed in commercial terms: hoarding and selling. The proverb appears concerned particularly with circumstances in which there is a scarcity of grain and much demand for it, as in a famine; the term that the NRSV translates as "the people" (*lĕʾôm*) typically refers to nations (e.g., 14:34; Gen 25:23; Ps 2:1; Isa 34:1). For the sages, hoarding in such circumstances—presumably to make a profit—is reprehensible and worthy of public scorn.

11:27 Playing on the "seek and find" motif (e.g., 1:28; 7:15; 8:17; 21:21), this proverb begs the question, what do you seek? by contrasting those who pursue "good" and "evil," terms that broadly encompass the moral and aesthetic.

> The one who *seeks* good   *seeks* favor
>
> The one who *seeks* evil   it comes to him.

Use of two different verbs for "seek" in the first line align the pursuit of good with a quest for "favor" or "delight"—from God (e.g., 8:35; 11:1, 20; 12:2; 18:22; cf. Matt 6:33; 7:7) and others (e.g., 3:4; 14:35; 16:15; 19:12). When we encounter yet a third verb for "seek" at the beginning of the second line, we anticipate a fourth. But the proverb surprises us. The subject and object shift suddenly: evil *comes to* those who seek it. It stops them in their tracks (cf. 11:19).

11:28 Although wealth can be an advantage (e.g., 10:4, 15), this proverb warns against trusting in it, presumably at the cost of trusting in God as Proverbs urges (cf. 3:5; 16:20; 28:5; 29:25). Those who trust in their riches "will fall," a claim that evokes the foolish and wicked who stumble and fall on their way (e.g., 4:19; 22:14; 28:10). The second line then invites a different image: falling leaves. Foliage as a metaphor in 11:28b prompts some to emend unnecessarily the verb in the first line from "fall" to "wither," a verb associated with leaves elsewhere (e.g., Isa 1:30; 34:4; Jer 8:13; Ezek 47:12). The righteous are often compared to flourishing trees. Of particular note here is Ps 1:3:

> [The righteous] are like trees
>   planted by streams of water,
> which yield their fruit in its season
>   and their leaves do not wither.
> (cf. 10:31; 11:30; Ps 92:12-14 [Heb. vv. 13-15])

11:29 A prevalent concern in Proverbs is care for one's "house," a term that refers variously to the physical structure, its inhabitants, one's property, and descendants. The sages encourage conduct that builds up the household (e.g., 14:1; 24:3; 31:27) and discourage anything that disrupts it (e.g., 6:31; 15:25, 27; 17:1, 13; 21:9). Those who trouble their home inherit "wind," a term used frequently as a metaphor for that which lacks substance and lasting value (e.g., Job 6:26; 8:2; 15:2; Eccl 1:14, 17; 4:16). Troublemakers end up with nothing. The second line intensifies the claim: fools not only lose everything—they end up servants, literally or figuratively, of the wise.

11:30 As in 11:28b, the righteous are likened to flourishing plants; they bear "fruit," a term that elsewhere in the book refers to speech (e.g., 12:14; 13:2; 18:20) and to the consequences of speech (18:21) and behavior (e.g., 1:31; 31:16, 31). In Proverbs, the tree of life (see commentary on 3:18) is a metaphor for sources of vitality and joy: so wisdom (3:18), a fulfilled desire (13:12), and gentle speech (15:4). The second line is puzzling: "A wise person takes lives." Some translations understand this to mean that the wise "win" or "captivate" people (e.g., NIV, *TANAKH*, NASB). But the expression "take life" in Hebrew, as in English, nearly always means "to kill" (e.g., 1:19b; 1 Kgs 19:4; Ps 31:13 [Heb. v. 14]; Ezek 33:6; Jon 4:3). The NRSV thus follows LXX and emends "wise person" (*ḥākām*) to "violence" (*ḥāmās*).

<u>11:31</u> Although this proverb is easily construed as yet another claim that the righteous are repaid for their righteousness (cf. 13:13, 21; 19:17) and the wicked for their wickedness, the phrase "how much more" signals progressive parallelism, a movement from lesser to greater or, said differently, to increasing certainty (e.g., 2 Sam 4:11). This suggests that what is repaid is the same in both lines: just as the righteous are repaid for their wrongdoing, *all the more so* are the wicked and sinners. Although the righteous transgress and are judged, their offenses and recompense pale in comparison to those of the wicked. First Peter 4:18 offers a loose rendering of this proverb, likely based on LXX.

PROVERBS 12

Literary Analysis

Antithetical proverbs continue (except 12:9, 14, [28]), as does the spotlight on the righteous and wicked. The chapter has a few thematic subunits. Verses 5-7 contrast the righteous and the wicked, moving from their thoughts (12:5), to their words and actions (12:6), to their respective fates (12:7). Verses 10-11 feature agricultural imagery. And 12:13-23 (except 12:21) concern speech.

Exegetical Analysis

<u>12:1</u> The objects of our affections matter. Proverbs repeatedly encourages the embrace of discipline (*mûsār*, e.g., 1:3; 4:13; 6:23; 8:10, 33; 23:23). To refuse reproof is "stupid," a term for brutish

(Ps 49:10 [Heb. v. 11]), subhuman (30:2), even animalistic (Ps 73:22) ways of being. To despise discipline is to hate oneself (15:32), to endure public disgrace, and, ultimately, to suffer disaster and death (5:14, 23).

12:2 "Good" is a sweeping term. Other proverbs refer to "good" people and actions that delight God, including those who find wisdom (8:35), engage in fair business practices (11:1), speak truthfully (16:13), and are upright (14:9). In turn, God condemns people of "schemes"—those preoccupied with private thoughts (e.g., Job 21:27-28; Ps 10:4) and plots devised in secret. Scheming is not inherently negative; indeed, the sages aim to teach it (1:4) and value craftiness when practiced with the guidance of wisdom (cf. 2:11; 5:2; 8:12). Juxtaposition of the term here with "good," however, suggests this is scheming with malicious intent (14:17; 24:8).

12:3 A good number of proverbs assert the permanence of the righteous and the impermanence of the wicked (e.g., 10:7, 25, 30; 12:7). The "root" of a person or thing is its foundation, that which anchors it to the world and provides nourishment. "The root of the righteous" suggests the flourishing tree metaphor associated often with the just (e.g., 10:31; 11:28, 30; Pss 1:3; 92:12-14 [Heb. vv. 13-15]). By contrast, the roots of the wicked "dry up beneath, / and their branches wither above" (Job 18:16; cf. Isa 5:24); they are "like chaff that the wind drives away" (Ps 1:4).

12:4 This is the first mention of the "woman of substance" ('ēšet ḥayil) to whom Proverbs pays tribute in 31:10-31 (cf. Ruth 3:11). The term ḥayil is weightier than "good" (NRSV) suggests. It typically means wealth (e.g., Gen 34:29; Ezek 28:5) and strength (e.g., Judg 3:29; 1 Sam 2:4; Eccl 10:10). Men with ḥayil are persons of influence—brave warriors, professionals, or managers of property (e.g., Gen 47:6; Judg 11:1; Ruth 2:1). Like them, a woman with ḥayil is a "crown" for her husband, a bearer of prominence and power akin to other "crowns" the sages mention: riches (14:24), gray hair (16:31), and grandchildren (17:6). Given the context of marriage, the metaphor also denotes the crowns worn by bridegrooms (4:9; Song 3:11; Isa 61:10).

Whereas a "woman of substance" builds up her husband's public stature, a shameful wife destroys his vitality from the inside out. The condition of a person's bones is diagnostic: moist bones indicate prosperity (3:8; cf. Job 21:23-24; Isa 58:11); dry bones indicate hopelessness and despair (17:22; Ezek 37:1-14). Rotting bones signify increasing weakness and ultimately ruin (cf. 14:30).

12:5 This proverb, the first of three that contrast the righteous and wicked (12:5-7), highlights the quality of their thoughts (e.g., 6:18; 16:3b; 19:21a, 20:18; Sir 37:17). Those of the righteous are just (e.g., 21:5). Those of the wicked are deceptive (e.g., 6:18; 15:26; 12:20).

12:6 From thoughts (12:5) to speech, the deception of the wicked is made more graphic: their words are an "ambush for blood," an expression that recalls the street gang that "lies in wait for blood," intending to ambush the innocent but ensnaring itself instead (1:10-19; cf. 12:13a; Ps 10:7-10). The mouth and speech of the upright, in contrast, rescues "them"; the ambiguous object suffix likely refers back to the upright (e.g., 12:13b) but may include others (e.g., 14:25). The second line is a variant of 10:2b and 11:4b, 6a.

12:7 From the speech of the righteous and wicked (12:6), this last proverb in the subunit turns to their respective fates (e.g., 12:3; 10:7, 25, 30). The "house" of the righteous stands—the physical structure, its inhabitants, one's property, and descendants (e.g., 15:6)—but the wicked "are overthrown." The verb, which also means "to collapse" or "demolish" and is used for the destruction of tents (Judg 7:13) and cities (e.g., Gen 19:21, 25, 29; Deut 29:22; 2 Sam 10:3), calls to mind the short-lived "house of the wicked" (cf. 14:11; 21:12). That the verb is passive leaves open the agents of their demise (but cf. 21:12).

12:8 This proverb connects understanding or lack thereof with public regard. Wisdom elicits praise (cf. 3:3-4) while wrongheadedness (NRSV: "perverse mind") is spurned. The strong reactions emphasize that the knowledge or ignorance of every person is a matter of public concern. Compare 13:15.

12:9 Public acclaim is not the goal, however. Anonymity and self-sufficiency are better than putting on airs and living beyond one's means. The verb qālâ can mean "to be dishonored" or "despised" (Deut 25:3; so NRSV) but often is merely "of little account" or "low esteem" (e.g., Isa 3:5; 16:14; 1 Sam 18:23), prompting such translations as "commoner" (NJB) and even "nobody" (NIV). Further, the first line may be translated two ways: (*a*) "Better to be of little account and have a servant" (e.g., NRSV, NIV, *TANAKH*) and (*b*) "Better to be of little account and a servant of oneself" (e.g., LXX). Both esteem the capacity to support oneself. Ben Sira teaches similarly: "Better is the worker who has goods in plenty / than the boaster who lacks bread" (Sir 10:27).

12:10 Agricultural imagery associates the next two proverbs (12:10-11). "To know the life" (NRSV: "to know the needs") is to understand and pay attention to the whole being, its requirements and desires. The righteous anticipate and tend to the well-being of their animals (cf. 27:23-27), care that is enjoined by biblical law (Exod 20:10; 23:12; Deut 5:14; 25:4). That they do suggests their mindfulness of all creatures, animal and human. The wicked, on the contrary, practice only cruel mercy—which is to say no mercy at all.

12:11 Language of abundance and scarcity drives home the import of hard work. The one who tills stays put, works his land, and is satiated with food. The Egyptian *Instruction of Amenemope* teaches similarly: "Plow your fields and you'll find what you need, / You'll receive bread from your threshing-floor" (*AEL* 2:152). The antithetical figure lacks sense, chases pipe dreams, and, implicitly, ends up with nothing. Proverbs 28:19 is a close variant of 12:11. For a critique of this as a general rule, see 13:23.

12:12 Obscure Hebrew complicates interpretation of this proverb. The first line reads, "A wicked person desires the *měṣôd* of the wicked." A *měṣôd* is a net, specifically the snare that a hunter spreads over the ground or a hidden pit to capture an animal or bird (e.g., 29:5; Ps 35:7); it may also refer figuratively to the net's entangled prey (Ezek 13:21; NRSV: "proceeds"). The term recalls descriptions of the sinners and the "strange" woman as setting traps and then lying in wait, eager to snare their reward (e.g., 1:10-19; 7:21-27; cf. Eccl 7:26; Sir 9:3; 26:22). Proverbs notes the irony of such nets: their ill-gotten gains are short-lived (e.g., 10:2; 11:4; 21:6; 28:16b), and they often trap the wicked themselves (e.g., 1:17-19; 5:22; 11:5-6). The second line of the proverb is abrupt—"the root of the righteous gives." Perhaps "gives" serves as a sort of shorthand for the expression "to give or bear fruit" used elsewhere of the ground and trees (NRSV; Lev 26:4, 20; Ps 1:3; Zech 8:12). The metaphor of a tree is used commonly for the righteous (e.g., 10:31; 11:28, 30; Pss 1:3; 92:12-14 [Heb. vv. 13-15]). The sense of the proverb may be that the wicked prosper only by ensnaring and imperiling others whereas the righteous generate their own well-being.

12:13 Ambiguity in the first line ("in transgression of lips, an evil trap [or trap of an evil person]") suggests false speech ensnares everyone, including the wicked (12:6; cf. 18:6-7; Eccl 9:12). The righteous evade capture, however, whether by their own agency or the help of others (e.g., 11:8; Pss 34:4, 19; 107).

12:14 This nonantithetical proverb continues the thought of 12:13a. What we say ("the fruit of the mouth") and do ("the labor of the hands") affects not only others but ourselves (e.g., 1:31; 11:17; 31:31). The NRSV reflects the Kethib, or written version, of the second line; the Qere, or vocalized tradition, implies that God "returns" or rewards our work. Both claims find support in Proverbs (e.g., 14:4; 16:7). Proverbs 13:2a and 18:20a are variants of 12:14a.

12:15 This proverb contrasts what the fool sees ("in his eyes"; NRSV: "thinks") with what the wise hear. Fools navigate life based solely on their own perceptions despite the sages' repeated warnings about being "wise in your own eyes" (e.g., 3:7; 26:5, 12, 16; 28:11; 30:12). They navigate as without a map; when their ways wander, they do not know it (e.g., 5:6). The wise, by contrast, heed the directions of others and, as a result, remain rightly oriented (e.g., 3:5-8, 21-26). Compare 17:24.

12:16 Guided by their wits alone (12:15), fools reveal their anger when they are provoked, signaling immediately the impact and magnitude of the offense and putting themselves on the defensive (cf. 18:2). The wise, however, conceal (NRSV: "ignore") an affront, presumably to consider whether and how best to respond (cf. 13:16). Several proverbs urge similar self-restraint (e.g., 14:17a, 29-30; 17:27; 19:11).

<u>12:17</u> Truth-telling should be as instinctive as breathing ("exhales"; NRSV: "speaks"). "False witness" may refer to dishonesty generally but is used often for testimony in court (e.g., Ruth 4:9-11; Jer 32:10, 12). Prohibited by the Ten Commandments (Exod 20:16; Deut 5:20) and condemned by the sages as an "abomination of YHWH" (6:19; see excursus in Proverbs 3), perjury is subject to stiff penalties (e.g., 19:5, 9; 21:28; Deut 19:18-19). Other proverbs about the importance of honesty include 14:5, 25; 19:5, 9; 21:28; 24:28; and 25:18.

<u>12:18</u> Thoughtless and dishonest speech, for the sages, is as dangerous as a weapon (5:4; 25:18; 30:14; cf. Ps 64:4). Like thrusts of a sword, gossip (NRSV: "rash words") cuts, wounds, and even kills its victims. In contrast, the "tongue" of the wise, a notably more pliant instrument, soothes and makes well (15:4; 16:24; cf. also *Proverbs of Ahiqar*: "Do not cover [= ignore] the word of a king; let it be healing for your heart," *TAD* 3.1.1.6). The word "tongue" associates this proverb with the next (12:19).

<u>12:19</u> The warning of 12:18a is followed by this more optimistic claim about truth and deceit. Wordplay with *'ad*, which may be a noun or a preposition, links the two lines:

Truthful lips	endure to eternity (*'ad*)
But until (*'ad*) I blink	is a lying tongue

Two interpretations are possible. First, true speech persists, but falsity survives a mere moment—an eye wink—before it is discovered and dismissed. Second, truth-tellers live a long time but liars do not ("lips" and "tongue" by synecdoche can represent the whole person), a claim that recalls proverbs about the durability of the wise and the impermanence of the fool (e.g., 10:7, 25, 30; 12:3, 7).

<u>12:20</u> Perhaps the deceptive do not live long (12:19) because their scheming affects them (e.g., 12:6, 13; cf. 18:6-7). It lodges "in [their] hearts [or minds]," distorting their self-regard and twisting their interactions with others (e.g., 6:12-19). Treachery wreaks havoc internally and externally. In contrast, those who

counsel peace—presumably because their heart or mind is so inclined—experience joy. The "heart" of one's thoughts and plans bears directly on one's welfare.

12:21 Sharp contrasts animate this description of the fates of a righteous person (sg.) and many wicked (pl.). The verb in the first line is passive. Trouble—*any* trouble—"is not allowed to meet" a righteous person; like an unwanted guest, it remains outside and distant, presumably because God holds it back. Compare the psalmist's use of the same verb: "Because you have made YHWH your refuge . . . no evil *shall befall* you, no scourge come near your tent" (Ps 91:9-10). In contrast, the verb in the second line is stative ("are filled"). Whether the wicked fill themselves or are filled with it by others (both are possible), they are bloated with wickedness. The wicked (*rĕšā'îm*) are filled with wickedness (*rā'*). It is intrinsic to who they are.

12:22 This is one of eleven "abomination of YHWH" proverbs (see excursus in Proverbs 3); three others similarly contrast an abomination to God—what God finds disgusting—with a source of divine "delight" (11:1, 20; 15:8; cf. 15:9). Certain behaviors and attitudes, here lying and truth-telling ("to do truth"; cf. John 3:21), provoke strong reactions from God. Compare the following from the Egyptian *Instruction of Amenemope*:

> Do not speak falsely to a man,
>   The god abhors it. . . .
> God hates the falsifier of words,
>   He greatly abhors the dissembler. (*AEL* 2:154)

12:23 The wise know when to keep their mouths shut (e.g., 11:13; 12:16). That they *conceal* knowledge does not mean they never speak (15:2); rather, they are shrewd about when, how, and with whom they share what they know. By contrast, fools *herald* their foolishness (10:14; 15:2b; 17:27, 28; Eccl 10:3)—a habit that is destructive to themselves and others (e.g., 10:8; 13:3; 18:6-7). The Egyptian *Instruction of Ankhsheshonq* similarly enjoins: "Muteness is better than a hasty tongue" (*AEL* 3:171). Compare also the *Instruction of Ptahhotep*:

Concentrate on excellence,
　　Your silence is better than chatter.
Speak when you know you have a solution,
　　It is the skilled who should speak in council;
Speaking is harder than all other work,
　　He who understands it makes it serve. (*AEL* 1:70)

12:24 Power distinguishes the diligent one from the sluggard. The diligent "rule"—they enjoy authority, agency, and relative autonomy—while the lazy are enslaved. Corvée, or forced labor, was used for menial and physically demanding work such as massive building projects (Gen 49:15; Exod 1:11-14; 1 Kgs 9:15-22); that it was imposed most frequently on racial and ethnic outsiders signals further its low social status (e.g., Josh 16:10; 1 Kgs 9:15-22). Other proverbs extol the benefits of hard work and the banes of laziness (e.g., 6:6-11 // 24:30-34; 10:4; 12:27; 13:4; 19:15; 21:25).

12:25 Worry debilitates. It "weighs down" (NRSV) or bends low the heart or mind—a term that refers to the physical organ in one's chest and, metaphorically, the wellspring of one's intellect, speech, and emotion (see excursus in Proverbs 2). The physical and metaphorical meanings together highlight the extent of damage that anxiety inflicts: it cripples a person in every respect. The incapacitating power of worry is described elsewhere in similar terms: "Hamath and Arpad [sway]. . . . Damascus has become feeble. . . . [Distress and pain] have taken hold of her, [like] a woman in labor" (Jer 49:23-24), and, "Anxiety brings on premature old age" (Sir 30:24). But a "good" word, one that is morally or aesthetically pleasing, brings joy; good news refreshes the body (15:30). True to its claim, the proverb plays with sound artfully: "it weighs it down" (*yašḥennâ*) and "it cheers it up" (*yĕśamměḥennâ*).

12:26 The Hebrew of the next three proverbs is problematic. In this case, the first line is obscure. The NRSV reads with the ancient Syriac version, and many other solutions have been proposed. If the lines are closely related, "lead astray" in the second suggests the parallel verb in the first line is about directing people rightly. Perhaps, then, the upright show their neighbor the way (e.g., "A righteous man gives his friend direction" *TANAKH*), while the wicked lead themselves and others off course (e.g., 2:12-19).

12:27 The meaning of the Hebrew is uncertain. The verb in the first line is a *hapax legomenon*, a word that occurs only here in the Old Testament, but it has the meaning "to burn" or "roast" in postbiblical Hebrew and cognate languages. That the sluggard "does not roast his game" suggests he leaves work unfinished—he fails to prepare the meat—and he does not take full advantage of available resources (e.g., 26:15). The order of words in the second line is obscure ("The wealth of a man is precious, diligent"), prompting various proposals for rearrangement and emendation. Other proverbs about the lazy or diligent include 6:9-11; 10:4, 26; 12:24; 13:4; 15:19; 19:24; 20:4; 21:25; 22:13; 24:30-34; and 26:13-16.

12:28 The Hebrew of the second line is problematic. The NRSV follows MT and interprets the relationship between the two lines as synonymous. The phrase "not death" is awkward, however. Found nowhere else in biblical Hebrew, it does not likely refer to "immortality" (e.g., NIV)—the concept is rare in the Old Testament and develops relatively late, sometime in the last two centuries BCE (e.g., Dan 12:1-3, ca. 164 BCE). With emendation, the line may read "but the way of wickedness is to death" (cf. 2:18). The proverb thus reasserts that righteousness is life-giving (e.g., 10:2; 11:4; 14:27) and wickedness death dealing (e.g., 11:19; 15:9).

PROVERBS 13

Literary Analysis

Proverbs 13, like chapters 10 and 12, opens with a proverb that recalls the reader's initial position in the book: a silent son at home learning from his father (Proverbs 1–9). Emphasizing yet again the importance of discipline, the proverb also introduces the chapter's dominant theme—the value of instruction—which it explores in another series of antithetical proverbs (except 13:14).

The young may mature, but they never outgrow the need to accept discipline. The chapter portrays the intensity of that need—and of the fool's error—in language of desire, emotions, and physical appetites, including *nepeš* ("throat," "life," "appetite," or "desire"), which is repeated seven times (13:2, 3, 4 [2x], 8, 19, 25); "craves" (13:4); "hates" (13:5, 24); "rejoices" (13:9); "despises" (13:13); "pleasing" (13:19); "abomination" (13:19); "food" (13:23); "love" (13:24); "to eat" and "belly" (13:25).

The chapter has a few subunits. Verses 2-4 are linked by repetition of *nepeš* (13:2, 3, and 4 [2x]) and "mouth" (13:2, 3). Verses 12-19 are a chiasm, or concentric structure, arranged by shared themes: 13:12 and 19a (realized desires), 13:13 and 18 (the consequences of accepting or ignoring instruction), and 13:14 and 17 (persons whose speech is life-giving or deadly); and at the center, two proverbs about good sense (13:15-16). Verses 7-8 and 21-22 are proverb pairs.

Exegetical Analysis

13:1 The sages never take attentiveness for granted. Lack of a verb in the first line ("a wise son, a father's discipline") suggests the verb in the second—"to listen" or "obey"—does double duty. The wise heed discipline while scoffers do not, ridiculing and even lashing out at those who attempt to teach them (cf. 1:22; 9:7-8a; 15:12; 21:24; 22:10).

13:2 The catchwords *nepeš* ("throat," "life," "appetite," or "desire") and "mouth" link this proverb to 13:3-4. Contrary to NRSV, the subject of the first line is indefinite ("From the fruit of a person's mouth, one eats good things," cf. 12:14a; 18:20a). Both the hearer (e.g., 13:1) and speaker may be understood to enjoy the benefits of good speech. In the second line, the "appetite" (*nepeš*) of the treacherous for violence may mean they relish speaking and acting brutally toward others (e.g., 10:11; 11:9) or that they consume the fruit of their violence (e.g., 4:17)—it returns to them.

13:3 If speech yields good or bad fruit (13:2; cf. 18:21), then one must be careful with the means of releasing it: the mouth. Indeed, this proverb makes restraint of the lips a matter of life (*nepeš*) and death (cf. 11:9; 18:21), a perception echoed by the psalmist, "Set a guard over my mouth. . . . Watch over the door of my lips" (Ps 141:3). The contrast is lips "opened wide," a verb that occurs only once elsewhere in the Old Testament—with Jerusalem as the metaphorical bride of God who promiscuously "opens wide" her legs for others (Ezek 16:25). At issue is both *quantity* (babbling) and *quality* (rude, reckless speech). R. C. Van Leeuwen recalls a similar proverb from World War II: "Loose lips sink ships" (1997, 131). Proverbs repeatedly calls for caution with speech (e.g., 10:14, 19; 11:13; 12:23; 15:2, 28; 17:27-28; 21:23).

13:4 Whether a desire is unfulfilled or fulfilled turns on hard work. The sluggard "craves" and has nothing. The verb "craves" is used broadly for bodily appetites (e.g., hunger, thirst, sex) and often has illicit connotations ("coveting," e.g., 21:26; Deut 5:21). The sluggard's discontent may thus result from indolence *and* imprudent longing. The desires (*nepeš*) of the diligent, however, are "fattened" (NRSV: "richly supplied"), presumably because the desires are appropriate, the diligent work hard for them, and God rewards their effort (cf. 28:25; 11:25). Fatness is a sign of blessing and prosperity (e.g., 15:30; 28:25; Deut 31:20). For other proverbs about the lazy and diligent see 6:6-11; 10:4, 26; 12:24, 27; 19:15; 21:25; and 24:30-34.

13:5 Language of passion continues in the first line of this proverb: the righteous *hate* false speech (cf. 6:17, 19; 8:13; 12:22). The relationship of that claim to the second line is not clear, however. The wicked "stink" (NRSV: "act shamefully"), a verb that may be construed (*a*) literally, as in the stench of rotting manna (Exod 16:24) or festering wounds (Ps 38:5 [Heb. v. 6]); (*b*) figuratively, as when Achish describes David as abhorrent to Israel (1 Sam 27:12); or (*c*) causatively, as when a dead fly spoils ointment (Eccl 10:1; cf. Gen 34:30; Exod 5:21). Similarly, the wicked "are shameful," which may refer to their character and to the disgrace they bring others (e.g., 19:26). Use of these multivalent verbs characterizes the wicked as utterly deplorable—a "stench" themselves and on anyone who comes in contact with them.

13:6 The abstract concepts of righteousness and sin are portrayed here as independent agents (on "sin" in Proverbs, see

Theological and Ethical Analysis of Proverbs 1). Righteousness "guards" the upright (e.g., 11:4-6) while sin "misleads" or "ruins" the wicked (cf. 1:10-19; 5:22; cf. Ps 23:6). Elsewhere in Proverbs the sages use the same verbs to assign the same roles to God (22:12; cf. 21:12).

13:7-8 The Hebrew roots for "rich" (ʿāšar) and "poor" (rûš) connect these two proverbs. The first—"One makes oneself rich, yet nothing at all; one makes oneself poor, yet much wealth"— may be read as about self-deception (e.g., 12:9; Rev 3:17-18) or deception of others. Appearances can be misleading (cf. 11:24). Implicit is an indictment of false pretense.

The relationship between the two lines of 13:8 is disputed. The first states that a person will give all of his money as kōper to save his life (e.g., Job 2:4). Kōper can be a "bribe" (e.g., 6:35; 1 Sam 12:3; Amos 5:12), which implies the person is innocent, or a "ransom to avoid punishment" (e.g., Exod 21:30; Isa 43:3), which denotes guilt. In short, wealth exposes a person to illegal and legal attempts by others to take it away (e.g., 1:10-19; 6:1-5), an ironic assertion on the heels of 13:7a. The poor, by contrast, "do not heed a rebuke" (cf. 13:1b). Parallel to the first line and given that "rebuke" can also mean "threat" (Isa 30:17), the claim may be twofold: the poor respond neither to reprimands that threaten to take away their wealth nor to threats of extortion.

13:9 The spotlight shines again on the stability of the righteous and impermanence of the wicked (e.g., 10:7, 25, 30; 12:3; 14:11; 15:6). A burning lamp indicates prosperity (e.g., 31:18; Jer 25:10). An extinguished lamp signifies impoverishment, guilt, and even death (e.g., 20:20; 24:20; Job 21:17). Bildad develops the second line of this proverb more fully:

> Surely the light of the wicked is put out,
>   and the flame of their fire does not shine.
> The light is dark in their tent,
>   and the lamp above them is put out. (Job 18:5-6)

13:10 The Hebrew of the first line is awkward ("only [raq] with arrogance, he makes strife"), prompting some to emend raq to rēq

(NRSV: "the heedless"). The contrast is between the arrogant, whose refusal to take advice leads to conflict (e.g., 9:7-8), and the wise, whose receptiveness to counsel avails them of more options and opportunities to find consensus—that is, to promote peace (cf. 11:2, 14; 15:22; 19:20).

13:11 "Wealth from vapor" (*hôn měhebel*) in the first line indicates the concern is money acquired without effort—easy cash— and most likely by dishonest means (cf. 21:6). The awkwardness of the phrase, however, prompts some versions (including NRSV) to emend it to "wealth hastily gotten" (*hôn měbōhāl*), a matter of concern in Proverbs (e.g., 20:21; 28:22; cf. 1:10-19). Both readings afford an appropriate contrast to wealth gathered "by hand" in the second line, an expression that denotes both industry (NASB: "by labor") and slow, steady accumulation (NRSV: "little by little"). Encouragement to work hard abounds in Proverbs (e.g., 12:11; 14:23; 28:19), as does caution about the fleeting nature of wealth gained without it (e.g., 10:2; 15:6; 16:8).

The Importance of a Good Education (13:12-19)

13:12 Immediately after a "slow and steady wins the race" proverb comes caution about the physical and psychological harm wrought by deferred hopes (13:12a; cf. 13:19). Fulfilled hopes, by contrast, are a "tree of life," a metaphor in Proverbs for sources of well-being: wisdom (3:18); the fruit of the righteous (11:30); a gentle word (15:4). The proverb presumably applies to everyone. Other proverbs, however, teach that the hopes of the righteous are realized while those of the wicked are dashed (e.g., 10:3, 24, 28; 11:7; 13:4, 25). This proverb and 13:19 share the theme of realized desires and comprise the outer frame of a chiasm (see Literary Analysis).

13:13 As elsewhere in Proverbs, "word" and "commandment" likely refer to parental instruction (e.g., 2:1; 3:1; 4:4; 6:20), but ambiguity does not preclude divine teaching and law. The sages, after all, associate the two (e.g., 3:11-12). The verb *hābāl* in the first line may mean "to fare badly" and "to bind" or "pledge"; to hate instruction is self-destructive (NRSV; e.g., 1:29-31; 5:12; Num 15:31) and puts one "in debt" to it (e.g., NASB). One must pay up or find the pledge is seized by other means. The NIV deftly conveys both meanings ("He who scorns instruction *will pay for it*"). Similarly, the verb šālam in the second line means "to be rewarded" or "to be repaid" (e.g., 11:31). Those who "fear" instruction enjoy good compensation (e.g., 3:2; 13:21). Compare 13:18.

<u>13:14</u> A "fountain of life," a potent metaphor given the desert climate of Palestine, suggests that the instruction of the wise flows like fresh, life-giving waters from a deep reservoir. The metaphor is also used in Proverbs for the wife of one's youth (5:18), the mouth of the righteous (10:11), fear of the LORD (14:27, a proverb nearly identical to this one), and wisdom (16:22). The contrasting image, "snares of death," evokes the cords of Sheol that entangle the imperiled (e.g., Ps 18:5; 116:3) and likely refers to any fatal snare (e.g., 1:10-19; 7:21-27; 12:13; 22:24-25; 29:6). Attention to persons whose speech is life-giving (and deadly) recurs in 13:17.

<u>13:15</u> At the center of the chiasm are two proverbs about good sense (13:15-16). Those with good sense enjoy the favorable regard of others and God (e.g., 3:3-4; 12:8a; cf. 1 Sam 25:3-38). The second line, "the way of the faithless (cf. 11:3) 'endures' ('êtān)," is surprising given Proverbs' repeated claims that the wicked are short-lived (e.g., 10:25, 30; 12:3, 7; 13:9). NRSV follows ancient versions to read, "is their ruin ('êdām)." The line thus reiterates that the ways of the wicked end in disaster (e.g., 1:26-27; 6:15; 17:5; 24:22; 27:10).

<u>13:16</u> Actions reveal dispositions. The first line, "every clever person acts with knowledge" (e.g., NIV, *TANAKH*), is a general claim that associates wise behavior with cleverness. One is a sign of the other (e.g., 1:4; 8:12). Similarly, fools "spread out" folly; they stretch it out like a covering, net, or garment for everyone to see. Other proverbs describe fools similarly making a public display of their foolishness (e.g., 12:23; 15:2; 17:12; 18:2; 26:4-5).

<u>13:17</u> Returning to persons whose speech is life-giving or deadly (cf. 13:14), this proverb focuses on messengers—those responsible for conveying another's words (e.g., 22:21, 25:13; 26:6). The contrast here is between "wicked" (not merely incompetent as "bad" [NRSV] may suggest) and "trustworthy" messengers. Lack of a

verb in the second line suggests "falls into" (13:17a; NRSV repoints the vowels to make the causative "brings") does double duty. That wicked messengers "fall into" trouble puts themselves and the one sending them at risk; they may distort the message, work against it, or fail to deliver it altogether. Trustworthy messengers, by contrast, provide peace of mind to their senders (cf. 25:13) and avoid trouble for themselves.

13:18 The companion to 13:13, this proverb is framed by the consequences of accepting or rejecting instruction. Poverty and "shame" (a noun based on the Hebrew root meaning "to be small," "light," or "insignificant") comprise the subject of the first line. The predicate of the second is kābôd (NRSV: "honored"), a verb based on the Hebrew root meaning "heavy." What stands between being "light" and a person of "weight"—one with a good reputation and wealth (e.g., 3:35; 11:16; cf. 5:10-12)—is a decision. Will one "ignore" discipline, a verb that suggests avoidance and neglect (13:18a), or embrace it (13:18b)? Paradoxically, the road to authority requires assent to the authority and wisdom of others.

13:19 The first line of this proverb returns to the topic of realized desires, thus closing the chiasm (cf. 13:12). The term nepeš may refer to the whole person (NRSV: "soul") and, more specifically, to a person's throat or appetite (e.g., 13:4, 25; 23:2; 27:7). Fulfilled longing thus tastes pleasing—like a delicious and satisfying meal. The fools' cravings, however, only get them into trouble; they esteem wrong things (e.g., 2:14) and detest right ones, such as "turning aside from evil" (e.g., 3:7; 4:27; 14:16; 16:6, 17). Other proverbs ascribe the joy of realized desires only to the righteous (e.g., 10:3, 24, 28; 11:7, 23; 13:4).

Walk with the Wise (13:20-25)

13:20 Repetition reinforces the affinity one has with the company one keeps: "Walk with the wise (ḥăkāmîm) and be wise (weḥĕkām); but the companion (rōʿeh) of fools suffers harm (yērôaʿ)." The *Instruction of Ankhsheshonq* concurs: "The friend of a fool is a fool; the friend of a wise man is a wise man. / The friend of an idiot is an idiot" (AEL 3:169). The sages emphasize repeatedly that one's community constitutes one's character (e.g.,

1:10-19; 14:7; 16:29; 22:24-25; 24:1-2; cf. Sir 6:34-36; 1 Cor 15:33). The Kethib, or written version, of the first line is a command; the NRSV follows the vocalized tradition (Qere), "Whoever walks with the wise becomes wise," presumably because it provides a more precise parallel to the second line.

13:21-22 The next two proverbs are linked by the repetition of "righteous" and a chiasm of the first and last words in each: sinners/good (13:21), good/sinner (13:22). The first personifies evil pursuing its pursuer (on "sin" in Proverbs, see Theological and Ethical Analysis of Proverbs 1). What people chase after catches up with them (e.g., 11:19, 27; 21:21; 28:19; cf. Ps 23:6). Lack of an explicit subject in 13:21b leaves open the possibilities—perhaps "good" similarly personified (NRSV) or God.

Verse 22 intensifies the notion of retribution described by 13:21. Not only is the good of the righteous passed down from generation to generation (13:22a), but the sinners' wealth is "saved up," or hidden away for the righteous as a ready reserve (cf. 28:8; Job 27:13-17; Eccl 2:26; but cf. Eccl 2:18-21).

13:23 Although Proverbs often holds the poor accountable for their plight, attributing it variously to laziness or wickedness (e.g., 6:10-11 // 24:33-34; 10:4; 11:18; 20:13), the sages also acknowledge the reality of injustice (e.g., 11:1, 16; 21:6). What the poor accomplish here is noteworthy: they produce "much" food by working "fallow ground," that is, soil left untilled and unsown after plowing (cf. Jer 4:3; Hos 10:12). They do not enjoy their hard-earned harvest, however, because it is "swept away," a verb that denotes devastation, typically by violent means (e.g., Gen 19:15, 17; Num 16:26; 1 Sam 26:10; 27:1). Silence as to who reaps the yield of the poor intensifies the proverb's description of their powerlessness.

13:24 The first line of this proverb lies behind the English adage, "Spare the rod, spoil the child." The second urges parents who love their children to "seek [them] eagerly" for discipline. Elsewhere, objects of the verb include wisdom (1:28; 8:17), the good (11:27), and God (e.g., Job 8:5; Ps 78:34; Hos 5:15). With the earnestness of such pursuits, parents should keep after discipline. It reveals their love for their children, whereas lax or nonexistent discipline exposes their "hate" (13:24). Although ready association of physical discipline with education offends (many) modern Western sensibilities, it was common in the ancient Near East. Compare a student's praise for his teacher in the Egyptian schoolbook *Papyrus Lansing*: "I grew into a youth at your side. You beat my back; your teaching entered my ear" (*AEL* 2:172), and the words of a father to his son in the Aramaic *Proverbs of Ahiqar*: "Do not withhold your son from [the] rod. If not, you will not be able to save him" (*TAD* 3.1.1.176). See also 10:13; 17:10; 19:25; 22:15; 23:13; 26:3.

13:25 Satiation and hunger again serve literally and metaphorically to distinguish the righteous, whose appetites (*nepeš*, cf. 13:2, 4, 19) are satisfied, from the wicked who waste away (e.g., 10:3, 24, 28; 11:7). A person's diet reveals divine blessing or lack thereof (e.g., 10:3; Deut 28:48, 57; Ezek 4:16-17). But the association must be made carefully. The verb "to eat" (*'ākal*, 13:25a) points back to 13:23 (where the noun of the same Hebrew root appears), prompting an immediate qualification: sometimes, through no fault of their own, people go hungry.

PROVERBS 14

Literary Analysis

The wise and foolish take center stage again in this series of largely antithetical proverbs. Interpreters debate whether and how best to delineate the chapter into subunits; the majority of its proverbs appear unrelated to those adjacent to them. At a minimum, we note some thematic connections, namely, attention to the wise and foolish in 14:15-18 (cf. repetition of "simple" and "clever" [14:15, 18], "folly" [14:17, 18], "wise" and "fool" [14:16]), and concern about relationships between people of different socioeconomic circumstances or moralities in 14:19-24. Catchwords or phrases associate some proverbs—"its end" (14:12-13); "the fear of the LORD" (14:26-27)—while others are paired thematically (14:20-21, 29-30). Finally, for the first time in 10:1–22:16, we encounter proverbs about the king (14:28, 35).

Exegetical Analysis

<u>14:1</u> The NRSV emends the Hebrew of the first line from plural ("wisdom of women") to singular ("the wise woman"). Interpreted as a straightforward comparison of two women, wise and foolish, the proverb complements others that emphasize the necessity of a "good" wife for the establishment and maintenance of a "house," a term that refers variously to the physical structure, its inhabitants, one's property, and descendants (e.g., 12:4; 18:22; 19:14; 21:9, 19; 25:24; 27:15-16; 31:10-31). At the same time, many interpreters emend further, removing "of women" as a later addition to read, "Wisdom has built her house"—the Hebrew consonants of which correspond to 9:1. The proverb so construed explicitly recalls the juxtaposition of personified wisdom and folly in Proverbs 1–9 and anticipates the portrait of wisdom's household in 31:10-31. Whichever way it is read, the proverb vividly portrays the opposition of wisdom and folly. Wisdom *builds* and it is *her* (cosmic) house. Folly *tears down* wisdom's house—with *her bare hands*. Wisdom constructs. Folly destroys.

<u>14:2</u> Because this proverb does not distinguish subjects and predicates, its two lines may be read as simple equations: "One who walks uprightly = one who fears the LORD; but one who is twisted in his ways = one who hates [the LORD]." The equivalences suggest that one's "path" (see excursus in Proverbs 2) and one's attitude toward God are interrelated and mutually reinforcing. For more on "the fear of the LORD," see the excursus in Proverbs 1.

<u>14:3</u> The first line is, "In a fool's mouth is a shoot (*ḥōṭer*) of pride." The noun *ḥōṭer* is found elsewhere only in Isa 11:1, where it refers to a shoot or branch that grows out of a stump (NRSV follows ancient versions that read *ḥōṭer* as "rod" and adopts the emendation "for their backs"). The mouth of a fool, that is, sp(r)outs arrogance, much as the mouth of the righteous "sprouts" wisdom (10:31). Pride, the sages warn, leads to trouble and a person's downfall (e.g., 11:2; 16:18; 18:12; 29:23). The lips and speech of the wise, by contrast, protect them (e.g., 6:20-24).

<u>14:4</u> The word *bar*, which can mean "clean" or "grain," affords two translations of the first line: "without oxen, a clean crib" and

"without oxen, a crib of grain." Juxtaposition of either with the second line reveals the concern is quantity: an empty crib or only one crib of grain (14:4a) compared with many (*rāb*) crops (14:4b). The difference between the two—what turns things around from *bar* to *rāb*—is oxen. In the ancient Near East, oxen were common draft animals (e.g., Deut 22:10). Farmers used wooden-frame "scratch" plows pulled by teams of oxen (typically two, but cf. 1 Kgs 19:19) to plow the fields in December and January, moving the second time at a right angle with the first so that the soil would be turned over. Without the "oxen's strength" (14:4b) the work was extremely difficult if not impossible. The proverb highlights the importance of good resources for productive work and, by implication, the care of those resources (cf. 12:10a).

14:5 Truth-tellers do not lie, presumably ever, whereas false witnesses "exhale" deceit (14:5b // 6:19a). Lying is as instinctive and regular to them as breathing (cf. 12:17a). The sages repeatedly underscore the value of honesty (e.g., 12:17; 14:25; 19:5, 9; 21:28; 24:28; 25:18) and condemn false testimony as an "abomination of YHWH" (6:19; see excursus in Proverbs 3).

14:6 The opening words of this proverb, "A scoffer seeks wisdom," are startling because scoffers are notorious for *not* doing so. Proverbs describes them as arrogant and contentious, cynical and insolent, refusing instruction, ridiculing and striking back at those who try to teach them (9:7-8a; 13:1; 15:12; 21:24; 22:10). Should they suddenly reverse course to pursue wisdom, however, this proverb claims—with one dismissive word—"[there is] none" (NRSV: "in vain"), presumably because their motivations and/or means are insincere. Personified wisdom foretells such a moment when scoffers and fools, overwhelmed by inevitable disaster, "will call upon me, but I will not answer; / they will seek me diligently, but will not find me" (1:28). Comparatively, those who understand the quest for knowledge find it "easy."

14:7 The imperative "Go!" interrupts the antithetical proverbs, giving urgency to the sages' counsel to walk away from a fool because he or she does not speak knowledgeably. The company we keep matters, for they constitute our character (e.g., 1:10-19; 4:14-19; 13:20; 16:29; 22:24-25; 24:1-2; cf. Sir 6:34-36; 1 Cor 15:33).

<u>14:8</u> Wisdom affords a road map of sorts. The clever look down the way, watch their step (14:15b), and plan their journey carefully. Although this foresight has limits (14:12), it is better than the fools' folly, which disorients them (e.g., 5:6; 12:15a) so that they conduct themselves in ways harmful to others and themselves.

<u>14:9</u> It is unclear what the subject is in the first line of this proverb, the Hebrew of which is obscure. If fools are the subject (NRSV), they mock *'āšām*, a term that means "guilt" (Gen 26:10; Ps 68:21 [Heb. v. 22]; Jer 51:5) or what a person offers as compensation for guilt, whether restitution (Num 5:7-8) or a "guilt offering" as for such transgressions as inadvertent sin (Lev 5:17-19), swearing falsely (Lev 6:1-7 [Heb. 5:20-26]), and misusing sacred items (Lev 5:14-16). Like the witness who "mocks justice" (19:28), fools ridicule the notion they are accountable for their actions *and* should compensate the people they wrong. By contrast, because the upright try to avoid wrongdoing and take responsibility for any harm they cause, they enjoy the favor of others.

<u>14:10</u> This proverb poignantly conveys the limits of communication and comprehension. It emphasizes personal ownership of one's experiences with possessive suffixes ("its own bitterness," "its joy") while the use of "stranger" (e.g., 5:3, 10; 7:5; 22:14) exaggerates the distance between oneself and others. Even with the best of intentions and efforts, no one can fully know the heights and depths of another's experience. This does not diminish the importance of community and empathy (e.g., 12:25; 27:9, 19) but frames it in such a way that we do not overestimate our capacities to express ourselves and understand others. For the sages, God alone is capable of knowing the human heart (15:11; 17:3; cf. Ps 44:21 [Heb. v. 22]).

<u>14:11</u> The stability of a "house"—the physical structure, its inhabitants, a person's property, and posterity—is not guaranteed by solid construction materials. For whereas the *tent* of the righteous "blooms" (cf. 12:7), the *house* of the wicked "is destroyed"; the passive verb leaves open the agents of their demise (but cf. 21:12). The verb "blooms" (NRSV: "flourishes") evokes the

righteous as a thriving tree (e.g., 11:28, 30; Pss 1:3; 92:12-14 [Heb. vv. 13-15]). This is one of many proverbs about the stability of the righteous and the instability of the wicked (e.g., 10:7, 25, 30; 12:3; 15:6).

14:12 Although wisdom affords a road map of sorts (14:8), the path a person takes does not always end where he or she anticipates. By juxtaposing "its end" (14:12b) with how straight the way seemed stretched out "before" a person (14:12a), the proverb delineates the limits of human knowledge and judgment. Wise and foolish alike misperceive, self-deceive, and are subject to happenings beyond their control that lead them to places they do not expect. Further, with hindsight, a path often looks quite different than it did at the beginning. Proverbs 16:25 is identical.

14:13 Not only may the end of a thing be different than its beginning (14:12; cf. 14:13b), but incongruities—joy and pain— coexist (14:13a). The sages recognize how closely interwoven are happiness and heartache: people die, passions wane, health declines, and loves end. Indeed, people's greatest joys often bring their greatest pain and, perhaps because we know this, laughter mingles with or anticipates sorrow (e.g., Eccl 7:1-4). The proverb may also caution against "judging a book by its cover." External appearances do not necessarily mirror internal sentiments.

14:14 On the heels of two proverbs about human limitation and vulnerability (14:12-13), this reassertion of character-consequence thinking—that the "wayward of heart" (NRSV: "perverse," e.g., Ps 53:3 [Heb. v. 4]) are sated by their ways as good people are by their deeds (e.g., 1:31-32; 12:21; 22:8; Isa 3:10-11; Hos 12:2)— seems particularly bold and optimistic. The effect highlights the tension between the sages' insistence on the limits of wisdom and their at times rather dogmatic claims about the way things work.

14:15 Wisdom requires good judgment. The naive (*petî*, cf. 1:4; NRSV: "simple") believe everything and, in their gullibility, wander off in the wrong direction (e.g., 7:6-9; 22:3). They readily allow whatever others say to guide them. Conversely, the clever take responsibility for their steps, exercising caution and discerning which way makes sense before moving ahead (e.g., 14:8a; 16:9). Proverbs aims to teach the naive such discretion (1:4).

14:16 "The wise fear and turn from evil" (14:16a). Wisdom inspires heightened awareness and caution in the face of malevolence (NRSV, NJB). "Fear" may also be an elliptical reference to "the fear of the LORD" (so NIV; see excursus in Proverbs 1) which entails turning aside from evil (e.g., 3:7; 8:13; 16:6). Fools are arrogant hotheads who instead rush headlong into trouble (e.g., 22:3; 28:26).

14:17 The quick-tempered, when provoked, reveal their anger, signaling immediately the impact and magnitude of the offense and putting themselves on the defensive—an act of folly (cf. 12:16; 14:29; 16:32; 17:27; 19:11). More insidious, however, are the schemers who devise in secret and conceal their wicked plans (cf. 12:2; 24:8). Others despise them.

14:18 The first line, which NRSV unnecessarily emends, is "the simple inherit folly" (cf. 3:35; 28:10). The "simple" (*pĕtā'yîm*) are inexperienced and naive; they are capable of learning but, without instruction, are prone to take on, or "inherit," foolish tendencies (cf. 1:4, 32; 8:5; 14:15; 22:3). The clever, in contrast, are crowned with knowledge—an image of royal dignity. Proverbs often describes abstract concepts or qualities as clothing or jewelry (e.g., 1:8-9; 3:3, 21-22; 31:25). Other "crowns" include a "woman of substance" (12:4), old age (16:31), and grandchildren (17:6). People "wear" indications of their disposition and commitments.

14:19 The superiority of good over evil is made tangible with this description of the wicked bowing down before the good and, perhaps as beggars, at their "gates." The latter image implies the righteous live well (cf. the gates of wisdom's seven-pillared house, 8:34; Luke 16:19-21).

14:20-21 "His neighbor" and reference to the poor associate the next two proverbs. The first (14:20) illustrates the social ostracism of the poor by: (*a*) juxtaposing singular ("neighbor") and plural ("lovers," "many"); (*b*) use of the particle "even," a marker of emphasis; and (*c*) placement of the passive verb ("is hated") between "his neighbor" and "the poor." Hatred literally separates the poor from even his friend (14:20a) while many admirers encircle the rich (14:20b).

Even by his neighbor	is hated	the poor
But	lovers of	the rich (are) many.

The proverb exemplifies common social tendencies; we disparage the poor and try to distance ourselves from them (perhaps because they remind us of our own vulnerability) while we surround the wealthy to curry favor or to live vicariously. Poverty brings shame; money brings fame (cf. 10:15; 19:4-7; Sir 6:10-12; 13:21-23).

The second proverb (14:21) promptly condemns those tendencies:

One who despises his neighbor	a sinner
One who shows favor to the poor	happy

The parallelism redefines "his neighbor" as "poor"—and hatred of one's neighbor is sin. Shame thus belongs not to the poor but to those who despise them. Those gracious to the poor, in contrast, are happy ("blessed," e.g., 3:13, 18; 8:32, 34; 16:20). Other proverbs enjoin generosity to the poor on the grounds that God created everyone, poor and rich alike (14:31; 17:5; 22:2; 29:13; cf. 21:13). Compare the *Instruction of Amenemope*: "God prefers him who honors the poor / To him who worships the wealthy" (*AEL* 2:161).

14:22 Those who devise wicked schemes "wander" (NRSV: "err") like lost animals (Exod 23:4; Job 38:41; Ps 119:176) and people who are misguided, confused (Ps 95:10; Isa 21:4), or intoxicated (Isa 28:7). Unable to stay on track, their plans fail. The second line, "Those who plan good, loyalty and faithfulness," may be read as a statement of action—they *do* loyalty and faithfulness (e.g., REB)—or outcome—they *find* loyalty and faithfulness, presumably from God and others (NRSV; e.g., 3:3-4).

14:23 Extolling the advantage of hard work over laziness (e.g., 10:4; 12:24, 27), this proverb defines the latter in terms of speech: "a word of the lips" (NRSV: "mere talk"). Talk is cheap without action.

14:24 The first line of this proverb is, "The crown of the wise is their *riches*" (NRSV follows LXX). Money is a celebrated benefit of wisdom (e.g., 3:16; 8:18). Other "crowns" in Proverbs include a "woman of substance" (12:4), knowledge (14:18), old age (16:31), and grandchildren (17:6). The second line, "The folly of fools, folly," is commonly considered a tautology, an unnecessary repetition of the same term; hence NRSV and many commentators emend the first "folly" to "garland," which occurs parallel to "crown" elsewhere (4:9). But the repetition of "folly" may well be the point: wisdom bestows a crown but folly confers just that—folly (14:18; cf. Murphy 1998, 106).

14:25 This is one of many proverbs about the power and perils of true and false speech (e.g., 12:17; 14:5; 19:5, 9; 21:28; 24:28; 25:18). Its second line repeats 12:17b.

14:26-27 "Fear of the LORD" (see excursus in Proverbs 1) associates the next two proverbs. Unlike fears that shatter confidence and render people weak, insecure, and doubtful about the future, "fear of the LORD" inspires a "strong confidence" that affords not only a bright future (children [pl.], 14:26b) but a secure one ("refuge"). It enables a person to "turn aside from deadly snares" (14:27b). The psalmist characterizes "fear of the LORD" similarly (esp. Pss 25 and 34) and often depicts God as a refuge (e.g., Pss 46:1 [Heb. v. 2]; 62:5-8 [Heb. vv. 6-9]; 91; cf. Jer 17:17). Implicit is the assumption that parents teach reverence to their children (e.g., 1:1–9:18; 20:7).

The metaphor of a refuge is paired with that of fresh water by 14:27, a proverb that is identical to 13:14 except for the replacement of "teaching of wisdom" with "fear of the LORD." A "fountain of life," a vibrant metaphor given the desert climate of Palestine, is used also in Proverbs for the wife of one's youth (5:18), the words of the righteous (10:11), and wisdom (16:22).

14:28 This is the first of many proverbs about kings in Proverbs 10–31 (e.g., 14:35; 16:10, 12-15; 19:12; 20:2, 8, 26, 28). It measures the "majesty" of a monarch by the number of people in his charge (e.g., 2 Sam 24:3): if many, the king is powerful; if few, the ruler is weak and may lose the throne. Implicit is the need to rule wisely so that one's citizens prosper and remain loyal.

14:29 Several proverbs urge self-restraint with regard to one's emotions (e.g., 12:16; 14:17; 15:18; 16:32; 17:27; 19:11). The contrast here is between the idioms "long of nostrils" (NRSV: "slow to anger") and "short of spirit [or breath]" (NRSV: "hasty temper"). The former is characteristic of the wise, the latter of fools. The *Instruction of Amenemope* mirrors the contrast in its descriptions of the "silent man" and his rival, the "heated man" (*AEL* 2:146-163). A restrained temper is also a celebrated attribute of God (e.g., Exod 34:6; Num 14:18; Neh 9:17; Pss 86:15; 103:8; 145:8; Jon 4:2).

14:30 But is self-restraint always better (14:29)? This proverb suggests that the harboring of emotions can be self-destructive. The term *qin'â* has more negative connotations than "passion" (NRSV) suggests; it refers variously to jealousy (e.g., 6:34; 27:4), rivalry (Eccl 4:4; Isa 11:13), and animosity and anger (Num 5:14, 30; Ezek 35:11)—emotions that eat away at people (cf. 12:4). By contrast, a serene heart or mind (see excursus in Proverbs 2) fosters good health. "Flesh" and "bones" by synecdoche may signify the whole person (e.g., 4:22; 16:24).

14:31 This proverb aligns God with the poor: how we behave toward one, we behave toward the other. To extort a poor person, an act condemned in the Old Testament (e.g., 22:16; Deut 24:14; Jer 7:6; Ezek 22:29; Amos 4:1; Zech 7:10), is to taunt "his [or her] maker" (cf. 17:5a). That the referent for "his" is ambiguous—it may be the oppressor or the poor—implies what 22:2 makes explicit: "A rich person and a poor person meet: / God is maker of them all" (AT; cf. 14:21; 19:17). In turn, those who honor God show favor to the poor.

14:32 The first line reiterates the notion of act-consequence: "A wicked person is thrust down by his wickedness" (cf. 13:6; 26:27). The second line is difficult: "But the righteous person seeks refuge 'in his death'"—presumably his own but possibly that of the wicked person. Portrayal of death as a refuge is startlingly contrary to the overwhelmingly negative depictions of death in Proverbs (i.e., as a consequence of folly and wickedness). Accordingly, NRSV follows LXX and Syriac and, with metathesis (the inversion of letters), reads "in [their] integrity." Whereas the wicked are overthrown by their temperament, the righteous are protected by theirs (e.g., 11:3, 5; 9; 13:6; 14:26; cf. Isa 30:2).

14:33 Although it is no surprise that wisdom "rests"—is at home—in the heart or mind of the wise (cf. 2:10 and excursus in Proverbs 2), the second line is puzzling: "Among fools, she is known [or 'makes herself known']." Like many other modern translations, NRSV follows LXX and the Syriac and inserts a negative: "[Wisdom] is *not* known." But the emendation is not necessary. The line may be read as a question ("But among fools will [wisdom] be known?") or as a statement ("But among fools [wisdom] makes herself known"). Both suggest wisdom's availability to fools while conceding that fools are not likely to pay attention (e.g., 1:20-33; 8:1-5; 9:1-6). The term *qereb* in the second line (NRSV: "the heart of") may mean "inward parts" or "entrails" (e.g., Gen 25:22; 1 Sam 25:37; Job 20:14), an apt parallel to "heart" or "mind" in the first line. It may also mean "among" or "in the middle of" (*TANAKH*, NIV; e.g., Gen 24:3; 1 Sam 16:13). Wisdom's challenge is to be known *in* the hearts of fools and to be recognized when she takes her stand *in the middle* of them.

14:34 The majesty of a king may be many citizens (14:28), but numbers do not guarantee national prosperity. As righteousness emboldens individuals (e.g., 10:2; 11:4, 19; 12:28; 13:6; 16:31; 21:21), so it builds up communities (e.g., 16:12b). Conversely, sin brings shame. The proverb plays with expectations. "Righteousness" in the first line prompts reading its parallel in the second, *hesed*, as "steadfast love" or "kindness." But "sin," the last word of the proverb, calls that into question, and invites rereading *hesed* as "shame" or "reproach," a secondary meaning of the noun (cf. Lev 20:17).

14:35 On the heels of 14:34, it is all the more understandable that a king has a vested interest in the conduct of his servants—so much so that he responds to them strongly, with favor or wrath. The king relies on their wisdom, as they do on his (e.g., 16:15; 22:11). Compare 14:35b to this proverb from the Aramaic *Proverbs of Ahiqar*: "[The king's] rage is swifter than lightning. You, watch yourself. Let him not show it because of your sayings lest you die prematurely" (*TAD* 3.1.1.86).

PROVERBS 15

Literary Analysis

This chapter marks the end of the first half of the Solomonic section (10:1–15:33). As if on cue, the antithetical parallelism so dominant in chapters 10–14 begins to give way to a diversity of proverbial genres. Most notable among them are YHWH proverbs, which comprise nearly a third of the chapter (15:3, 8, 9, 11, 16, 25, 26, 29, and 33), perhaps in anticipation of Proverbs 16.

Interpreters debate whether and how best to delineate the chapter into subunits. At a minimum, it may be observed that 15:1-2 and 4 are about speech. Strong emotions (delight, love, hate) and repetition of "way" connect the proverb pair 15:8-9 with 15:10, which is, in turn, linked to 15:11 by the image of death. Verses 13-17 are loosely associated by the theme of happiness and repetition of "heart" or "mind" (*lēb*) and "good" (*tōb*, cf. the verb of the same root in 15:13); included are two proverb pairs—15:13-14 and 15:16-17. A motif of joy (the Hebrew root *śāmaḥ*) dances through 15:20-21 (a proverb pair) and 15:23. And "sense and sensibility" draws the chapter to a close in 15:29-32, a unit woven together by repetition of the Hebrew root *šāmaʿ* ("to hear" or "heed") and a string of references to the body and its organs of perception. The last proverb of the chapter recalls 1:7, the "motto" of the book (15:33).

Exegetical Analysis

15:1 Irony flavors this proverb about the power of speech. "Soft" speech turns back *ḥēmâ*, a term that means "rage" or "fire," whereas hurtful (i.e., hard) speech enflames the situation. Other proverbs observe the potency of gentle speech (e.g., 15:4; 25:15b).

15:2 The wise speak in beneficial ways (cf. 15:1). They "do well" (NRSV: "dispenses") with their knowledge. Fools, by contrast, "pour out" folly—it streams from their mouths as from a fountain. The image of words as liquid that "pours out" of the mouth recurs in Proverbs (1:23; 15:28; 18:4) and in the Psalms (Pss 19:2 [Heb. v. 3]; 59:7 [Heb. v. 8]; 78:2; 94:4; 119:171; 145:7).

<u>15:3</u> God keeps watch. "The eyes of the LORD" observe everyone everywhere (5:21; 22:12; cf. 24:18; Ps 33:15; Sir 23:19). Indeed, in Zechariah's proto-apocalyptic visions, God's seven eyes range over the whole earth (Zech 4:10). The Egyptian *Instruction of Amenemope* speaks similarly of divine watchfulness. Thoth's eyes encircle two lands, and the Eye of Re watches for those who cheat with false measures (*AEL* 2:156-157).

<u>15:4</u> This proverb, like 15:1, is concerned with how speech affects others. Healing (NRSV: "gentle") speech is a "tree of life," a source of vitality (cf. 3:18; Gen 3:22-24; Rev 2:7; 22:2, 14, 19). Good words mend a person (e.g., 16:24). In contrast, crooked speech does harm (cf. 11:9)—literally, a "break in [the] spirit" (*šeber běrûah*). The Hebrew root *šābar* ("to break, crush") is used to describe physical injuries, such as fractured limbs (e.g., Lev 21:19; 24:20). Parallel to the "tree of life," it evokes the "breaking" of trees and boughs (Ps 29:5; 105:33; Isa 27:11; Ezek 31:12; cf. Job 24:20). Healing words restore. Harmful words cut down, leaving one in misery (cf. the nearly identical phrase *miššeber rûah*, "anguish of spirit," parallel to "pain of heart" in Isa 65:14).

<u>15:5</u> Fools hate discipline (e.g., 1:22; 9:7-9; 12:1; 13:1), which, the sages claim, leads inevitably to their downfall (e.g., 1:20-33; 5:12-14; 15:10). Those who accept reproof, however, become "clever" (NRSV: "prudent"). They have the capacity to think creatively, even cunningly, in any situation (cf. 1:4).

<u>15:6</u> This proverb paints vividly the material advantage of the righteous over the wicked. The righteous not only have a "house" in which they have "much" treasure, but that treasure is *hōsen*, namely, "treasure" or "stocks"—wealth that is stored (e.g., Jer 20:5; Ezek 22:25; cf. Isa 23:18). The wicked, by comparison, have no house, and their income is the comparatively short-lived *těbû'â*, or proceeds from harvest (e.g., 3:9; 10:16; Job 31:12). Further, because the wicked presumably acquired their income unjustly, it comes with "trouble" (e.g., 10:2; 15:27; 21:6). Economic prosperity is a celebrated benefit of wisdom (e.g., 3:16; 8:18), even as the sages recognize it is not guaranteed (e.g., 15:16-17; 16:8; Job 21:7-26).

15:7 Parallel use of "heart" or "mind" and "lips" signals their close association—the heart is the wellspring of speech (e.g., 10:20; 16:1; see excursus in Proverbs 2). The speech of the wise "scatters" (NRSV: "spreads") knowledge, a verb that connotes free, generous, and wide dispersal, as if blown about by the wind (Job 37:9; Isa 41:16). The second line may be translated "not so the minds of fools" (NRSV) or "the hearts of fools are not steadfast (i.e., righteous, honest)" (e.g., Job 11:13; Pss 57:7 [Heb. v. 8]; 78:37; 112:7). As a result, their speech is unreliable. Compare 15:2.

15:8-9 These two proverbs are a pair, joined by the contrast between what God hates ("abomination of YHWH," see excursus in Proverbs 3) and what God enjoys. The first is one of the few proverbs concerned with worship practices (3:9-10; 7:14; 15:29; 21:3, 27; 28:9). What induces God's disgust or delight is not the act of the worshiper (i.e., sacrifice or prayer) but his or her character. The prophets similarly caution against insincere worship (e.g., Isa 1:10-15; Amos 5:21-27; Mic 6:6-8).

The second proverb (15:9) widens the lens from worship to one's path in life (see excursus in Proverbs 2). God loathes the "way of the wicked." God loves those who pursue justice.

15:10 With its reference to "way" and strong emotion ("hate"), this proverb builds on 15:8-9. It affords different translations depending on how one understands "bad" (NRSV: "severe") and the relationship between the two lines. Those who forsake the way—implicitly the path of life (e.g., 2:13; 10:17)—consider discipline (*a*) "bad," as in *repugnant*, a distorted perception that proves deadly (e.g., *TANAKH*); or (*b*) "bad," as in *severe*, given that the parallel is "will die" (NIV, e.g., 1:32).

15:11 Continuing the image of death (15:10), this proverb points to the underworld to express in spatial terms the extent of divine knowledge (cf. 15:3). Sheol and Abaddon are a hendiadys (two nouns for the same referent) for the underworld—a remote, dark, and dusty place from which there is no escape (e.g., Job 7:9-10; Isa 38:10-11). If the vast underworld is "in front of" God (cf. Job 26:6; 38:17; Ps 139:8), then how much more so is the small human heart, even with its deep recesses (20:5; cf. Sir 42:18).

15:12 Scoffers despise anyone who rebukes them (e.g., 9:7-8a; 13:1; 21:24; 22:10). Their misplaced affection and its consequence frame this proverb: "The scoffer does not love. . . . [The scoffer] will not go." Repetition of the liquid Hebrew letter *lāmed* (l) six times reinforces the motif of movement.

15:13-14 The first word of the next two proverbs is *lēb* ("heart" or "mind," see excursus in Prov 2). The first proverb connects inward disposition with outward expression (Sir 13:25-26; but cf. 14:13). A joyful heart "does good" to the face, whereas heartache strikes the *rûaḥ*, a term that refers variously to the breath, spirit, and disposition. Despair, that is, defeats a person. Even taking the next breath is difficult. Other proverbs assert that a "defeated spirit" dries up the bones (17:22) and is worse than illness (18:14).

The second (15:14) contrasts the "understanding heart" with the "mouths of fools." The former seeks knowledge. The wise do not learn and then rest on their laurels. Rather, they search for knowledge their whole lives (e.g., 1:5; 10:14; 12:1; 18:15). Fools, in contrast, "pursue" folly; the verb, which is related to the noun "shepherd," refers to nourishing or grazing (NRSV: "feed on," e.g., Jer 50:19; Ezek 34:18-19) and, metaphorically, to busying oneself with or practicing something—that is, running after and tending to it as a shepherd does a flock (e.g., Ps 37:3; Hos 12:1 [Heb. v. 2]). This proverb pair is similar to 18:14-15.

15:15 If we read each line of this proverb as an absolute statement, the poor are never cheerful, a claim experience calls into question. More likely, the second line modifies the first: a "good" heart (15:15b) enables those in "bad" circumstances (15:15a) to experience joy. A person's inward disposition can transform how he or she lives in any situation, even one of extreme adversity (e.g., 2 Cor 4:8; Heb 10:34).

15:16-17 Both of these "better than" proverbs extol living reverently and conclude with *bô* ("with it"). A little with "fear of the LORD" (see excursus in Proverbs 1) is preferable to much treasure with "tumult"—provoked by the treasure or otherwise. The contrast is between reverence and dismay or panic (e.g., 1 Sam 5:9; 14:20); implicitly, the former does away with the latter. The proverb also challenges the notion that prosperity is an inevitable reward for wisdom and faithfulness (e.g., 1:33; 3:16; 8:6, 32-34). Indeed, faithful people may have little.

Talk about money turns to talk about food (15:17), and the contrast between a modest meal (a "portion" or "allowance" of greens or herbs, e.g., 2 Kgs 25:30 // Jer 52:34) enjoyed with loved ones and a lavish feast of fatted ox (cf. 1 Kgs 4:23) with people who hate one another. What makes a meal "better" is not the food but good companionship. The Egyptian *Instruction of Amenemope* teaches similarly: "Better is bread with a happy heart / Than wealth with vexation" (*AEL* 2:152).

15:18 This proverb describes how anger affects others. The hot-tempered "stir up" conflict—they inflame the situation—whereas those who are slow to anger "soothe" it. Their calm demeanor invites and enables others to calm down and settle their differences. For the sages, emotional self-restraint is a virtue (e.g., 14:29; 16:32) whereas sowing discord is a vice (e.g., 6:14; 16:28; 22:10; 26:21; 28:25; cf. Sir 28:8-12). The contrast here between the "hot-tempered one" and the one who is "slow to anger" is mirrored by the juxtaposition of the "silent man" and his rival, the "heated man," in the *Instruction of Amenemope* (*AEL* 2:146-163). Slowness to anger is also a celebrated attribute of God (e.g., Exod 34:6; Num 14:18; Pss 86:15; 103:8; 145:8; Jon 4:2).

15:19 Comparison to a "hedge of briers" suggests the sluggard's way is nearly impassable; any attempt to move along it inflicts harm, and its overgrown condition is because the sluggard refuses to clear it (cf. 24:30-31). The lazy thus thwart their own progress (e.g., 6:9-11; 19:24; 20:4; 21:25). By contrast, the way of the "just" (the Hebrew root means "straightforward" or "right," cf. 15:21) is a highway. In the ancient Near East, highway construction was associated with securing peace. Nebuchadnezzar II of Babylon, for example, declared: "I cut through steep mountains, I split rocks, opened passages and [thus] I constructed a straight road. . . . I made the inhabitants of the Lebanon live in safety together and let nobody disturb them" (*ANET* 307; cf. *ANET* 320-321). Similarly, highways in the Bible make way for security and goodwill (e.g., Isa 40:3-5; 45:13; 57:14; 62:10; Jer 31:9; Luke 3:4-6; Heb 12:13).

15:20-21 Concern with the fool's misplaced affections and repetition of the Hebrew root meaning "to rejoice" (śāmaḥ) connect the next two proverbs. The first line repeats 10:1a exactly: a wise child "makes glad" (yĕśammaḥ) his father. The second line, which we expect to assert the mother's reaction to the foolish child (so 10:1b), turns instead to the *child's* hatred of *her*, a grave offense in ancient Israel (e.g., 20:20; 30:11, 17; Deut 21:18-21; 27:16; Ezek 22:7). The divergence suggests another facet of a mother's heartache over a foolish child (10:1b); in part, it is the anguish of unrequited love.

The fools' "joy" (śimḥâ) is similarly misdirected—to folly (15:21a). The proverb conjures up an earlier scene at a street corner. There, the "one who lacks heart" turns aside, enticed by the strange woman's "smooth words." His joy misplaced, he goes to his demise—an ox to the slaughter (7:6-23). The wise, by contrast, stick to their path and walk right by (15:21b; cf. 4:25-27; 7:25).

15:22 The wise seek advice (e.g., 11:14; 13:10; 19:20; 20:18). The word *sôd* refers to *counsel* (NRSV, e.g., 11:13; 20:19; 25:9) and, as the parallel "many advisers" suggests, to a *council* of friends or others who offer guidance (e.g., 3:32; Job 19:19; Ezek 13:9). Availing oneself of both makes the difference between plans that are "broken" or "destroyed" (NRSV: "go wrong") and those that are "built up" or "established" (NRSV: "succeed"). Lest we think too highly of our well-advised plans, however, the sages caution elsewhere that, in the end, God's plan is "established" (19:21).

15:23 The theme of "joy" resumes (cf. 15:20-21). The first line indicates that a person finds joy in the "answer of his mouth," namely, in the *content* of his response to others (e.g., 12:14). The second line then celebrates good *timing*, a word spoken "in its time" (e.g., 25:11). Both inspire delight. The NRSV interprets the first line in light of the second—the "answer of his mouth" is "apt" (cf. NIV). But the first line does not include the term. Similarly problematic is to interpret the lines as comparative:

"Someone may be pleased with his own retort; how much better is a word in its season!" (REB). As for timing, the Egyptian *Instruction of Ankhsheshonq* similarly admonishes: "Do not say something when it is not the time for it" (*AEL* 3:169).

15:24 The path of life traverses upward—in exactly the opposite direction as the downward path to Sheol (cf. 15:11). The ascent is not to some sort of heavenly existence but to everyday well-being. Language of high and low, top and bottom, amplifies the difference between wise and foolish living (2:18; 5:5-6; 10:17; e.g., Deut 28:13).

15:25 The up-and-down motif continues (cf. 15:24). God *tears down* the house of the *risen up* (NRSV: "proud"), but God *sets up* the boundary of the widow, one of the *lowest* in the social hierarchy. Exceedingly vulnerable without a husband, widows were frequent victims of oppression, extortion, and violence. Indeed, Job characterizes the wicked as those who

remove landmarks;
  they seize flocks and pasture them.
They drive away the donkey of the orphan;
  they [seize] the widow's ox [as] a pledge.
(Job 24:2-3; cf. 22:9; 31:16)

Such injustice is condemned by biblical law and the prophets (e.g., Deut 24:17-21; Isa 1:23; Mal 3:5), and here by the sages who point to God as the one who stakes out the widow's property, who provides for and protects her socioeconomic welfare. Removal of any boundary marker was illegal (Deut 19:14; 27:17)—but how much more so when God established it (e.g., 22:22; 23:10; cf. Ps 68:5 [Heb. v. 6]). The Egyptian *Instruction of Amenemope* teaches similarly:

Beware of destroying the borders of fields. . . .
  One pleases god with the might of the lord
When one discerns the borders of fields. . . .
  Beware of the Lord of All;
Do not erase another's furrow. (*AEL* 2:152)

15:26 This proverb associates the language of divine delight and revulsion ("abomination of YHWH," see excursus in Proverbs 3) with the ritual categories of clean and unclean. Whereas evil plans are repugnant, gracious words are "pure"—clean and, accordingly, precious (cf. Ps 12:6 [Heb. v. 7]). The use of cultic language in a moral sense blurs distinctions one might make between standards for religious rituals and everyday behaviors (i.e., speech): both are deemed by God as acceptable or not. The sages elsewhere describe "gracious words" as honeycomb: sweet to the taste and good for you (16:24).

15:27 The first line identifies the "greedy for gain," such as the street gang in 1:19 (cf. Hab 2:6-11), as troublemakers for their households (cf. 11:29). The verb ʿakar (NRSV: "make trouble") has a range of meaning, from stirring up confusion and disorder (e.g., 1 Kgs 18:17-18) to causing disaster and death (e.g., Josh 7:25-26). The parallel "will live" (15:27b; cf. 28:16b) suggests the more extreme sense. Proverbs repeatedly warns that ill-gotten gains are troublesome, even deadly (e.g., 10:2; 15:6; 17:23; 21:6; Eccl 7:7; but cf. 21:14).

15:28 This proverb is similar to 15:2, but now it is the wicked who "pour out" wickedness (cf. "There [the wicked] are, pouring out with their mouths, with sharp words [swords] on their lips," Ps 59:6-7 [Heb. vv. 7-8]). Conversely, the wise think carefully before they answer (e.g., 10:14, 19; 11:13; 12:23; 13:3; 17:27-28; 21:23).

15:29 That God "hears" the prayers of the upright, a source of divine delight (15:8b), suggests God is proximate and attentive. Conversely, that God is "far from" the wicked denotes God is remote and inaccessible (e.g., 22:15; 27:10). The proverb leaves open why. Perhaps God finds the prayers of the wicked abhorrent and refuses to listen (e.g., 15:8a); God is "near in their mouths / yet far from their hearts" (Jer 12:2). Or perhaps, as the psalmist describes, the wicked distance themselves from God, claiming God is inattentive and ineffective: "The wicked say, 'God will not seek it out.' / . . . 'There is no God'" (Ps 10:4); "God forgets, / God hides God's face, / God never looks" (Ps 10:11 AT); "[God] will not call us to account" (Ps 10:13).

15:30 Verbal and nonverbal communication profoundly affects others (e.g., 15:1, 4, 18, 23). "Light of the eyes" is frequently considered a divine gift (e.g., 29:13; Ezra 9:8; Ps 13:3 [Heb. v. 4]; 19:8 [Heb. v. 9]; but cf. 1 Sam 14:27) and evokes the shining countenance associated with wisdom (Eccl 8:1). To *see* a bright face inspires joy (16:15). To *hear* good news "makes one's bones fat" (NRSV: "refreshes the body"; cf. 25:25)—it generates health and prosperity (11:25; 13:4; 28:25; cf. Deut 31:20). "Bones" by synecdoche may represent the whole person (e.g., 3:8; 12:4; 14:30; 16:24; 17:22).

15:31-32 "Hearing reproof" (NRSV: "heed admonition") links these two proverbs. Anyone seeking the "discipline of life" stays near the wise (15:31). The company we keep matters (e.g., 1:10-19; 13:20; 14:7). Conversely, to stay far from discipline—to avoid or neglect it—is to hate oneself (15:32; cf. 19:8a). It leads to calamity and anguish (1:25), poverty and shame (13:18), and even to death (5:23; 8:36).

15:33 This proverb, which concludes the first half of this Solomonic section, begins by identifying discipline (cf. 15:31-32) with "fear of the LORD." One is tantamount to the other. The second line then invites a rereading of the first. As humility precedes honor (cf. 18:12; 22:4) so "fear of the LORD" precedes wisdom. It is the prerequisite. The proverb thus reuses the vocabulary of the book's "motto" and echoes its assertion that reverence for God is the *rē'šît* of knowledge (1:7)—the fullest expression of wisdom *and* its starting point (see excursus in Proverbs 1). The proverb points us back to the beginning even as it anticipates a dominant theme of Proverbs 16: humility in the face of divine freedom.

PROVERBS 16:1–22:16

Theological and Ethical Overview

The second portion of the Solomonic collection (16:1–22:16) shares much in common thematically with the first (see Theological and Ethical Overview of Proverbs 10:1–15:33). The household figures prominently, its fate hinging on the character and conduct of its members (e.g., 17:6, 13, 21, 25; 19:13, 16); the sages extol the value of a good wife (described now as a gift from God, 18:22; 19:14) and urge again the discipline of children (e.g., 19:18; cf. 19:27; 20:11, 20; 22:6). The moral self is sketched largely in physical terms (e.g., 16:2, 26, 29-30, 32; 19:24; 20:7), including for the first time a "crown" of gray hair (16:31; 20:29), and the spotlight remains squarely on organs of speech (e.g., 16:1; 17:4, 20; 18:6, 21; 21:23). Acts and dispositions have consequences (e.g., 16:17-18, 20; 17:2, 20; 18:3). The importance of attentiveness and reproof animates every page (e.g., 16:20; 18:15; 19:2, 8, 16, 20, 25, 27). The sages depict God as invested in the human situation—repulsed by injustice (e.g., 16:11; 17:15; 20:10, 23; 21:3) and at work protecting and defending the righteous and most vulnerable (18:10; 19:17; 20:4, 22; 21:12-13). And creation continues to motivate appeals for generosity and respect for human dignity (17:5; 22:2). The steady, rhythmic pulse of these themes throughout 10:1–22:16 leaves no doubt as to their importance. They are essential elements of the sages' worldview.

We observe, at the same time, certain thematic developments. The sages widen the circle of moral concern. In addition to the family, there is greater emphasis on friends (16:28; 17:9, 17; 18:24; 19:4, 6-7; 22:11), who are occasionally favored over family (e.g., 17:17; 18:24), and we greet a more diverse cast of characters, including personal enemies (16:7), nobles (17:7, 26; 19:6), princes (19:10), warriors (16:32; 21:22), contenders (18:18), lenders (22:7; cf. 19:17), and hagglers (20:14). The sages stress the value of reliable and trustworthy companions, an ethic of neighborliness, and the preservation of social boundaries, even as they acknowledge that wisdom may at times disrupt the status quo (e.g., 17:2). So high is their esteem for community, they denounce anyone isolated from it as self-indulgent and hostile (18:1)—a stinging indictment of our present-day pervasive individualism.

Particularly noteworthy in this broadening moral purview is the king who, though mentioned in 14:28 and 35, steps to the forefront in 16:10-15 and remains a significant figure thereafter (19:12; 20:2, 8, 26, 28; 21:1; 22:11). Indeed, his appearance prompts many interpreters to call 16:1–22:16 "The Royal Collection." Although we in the modern West do not share the Israelite political ideology of a king appointed and invested with authority by God, the sages' ideal portrait of political leadership (which they complicate later in the book) invites reflection about what we hope for in our own. For the sages, the king manifests and defends the values of God and the community. Drawing again on physical language, the sages herald the power of the king's favor and wrath (16:14-15; 19:12; 20:2); his inspired speech (i.e., lips, 16:10); his delight in and love for honesty (16:13); his abhorrence of evil (16:12); his eyes that winnow the wicked (20:8; cf. 20:26); his affection for the pure and righteous (22:11); and his heart and mind as directed by God (21:1; cf. 16:10). Above all else, they argue, the king embodies and promotes justice. His throne is established on it (16:12-13; 20:28; cf. 16:11) and, implicitly, will fall in its absence. Such an understanding assumes good government is necessary for a community to prosper; leaders are subject to very high standards; and wise citizens should rarely experience conflicted loyalties (i.e., subject to God or authorities, e.g., John 19:11; Rom 13:1-2).

As if to help readers navigate in the expanded moral arena, the sages pay greater attention to the complexities of human relationships. Concern for justice (*mišpāṭ*) figures more prominently—the term is found ten times as compared to only twice in 10:1–15:33 (cf. 12:5; 13:23)—and judicial contexts are more often explicit or implied (e.g., 17:15; 18:5, [17]; 19:5, 9; 21:28). Conflict rears its head: two terms for "strife" (*mādôn* and *rîb*), previously only in 15:18, recur frequently (*mādôn*, 16:28; 17:14; 18:19; 21:19; 22:10; *rîb*, 17:1, 14; 18:6, 17; 20:3); the verb "to divide" or "alienate" (*pārad*) is found only in this section of Proverbs (16:28; 17:9; 18:1, 18; 19:4); and "quarrels" or "controversies" (*midyānîm*) are taken up for the first time since 6:14 (18:18, 19; 19:13; 21:9). The sages also engage the ambiguous topic of gifts and bribes (17:8, 23; 18:16; 19:6; 21:14; elsewhere only in 6:35; 15:27).

In this contested space the sages commend certain behaviors and attitudes. Their recommendations safeguard relationships and social order, frequently above the interests and desires of the individual. First, because the company we keep shapes us, avoid troublemakers—gossipers (e.g., 16:28; 20:19), the violent (16:29; 19:19), the quarreling spouse (21:9). If one stays away, one cannot be drawn into what the sages assume are unnecessary and harmful conflicts. Second, practice self-restraint, attentive listening, and openness to advice (16:32; 17:14, 28; 20:3, 18; 21:23, 28). Recognize that there may be many sides to a story (18:17). Third, if one needs to speak, tell the truth with thoughtful and persuasive words (e.g., 16:21, 23, 24) and an appreciation for one's social standing (17:7; 18:23). It matters what we say *and* how we say it. Fourth, err on the side of friendship. The sages extol loyalty and forgiveness over "being right" (17:9, 17; 19:22); they condemn *Schadenfreude* (e.g., 17:5b), or joy at another's suffering, and assign to God the work of vengeance (20:22). Lastly, the sages urge the wise to reprove, shame, and even send away those who, in speech or action, chip away at individual and communal well-being (e.g., 19:25, 29; 22:10).

In conjunction with a greater variety of genres (see Introduction to Proverbs 10:1–22:16), the sages also nuance some of the convictions they asserted straightforwardly in 10:1–15:33. Several proverbs, for example, acknowledge that, contrary to the iconic narrative (see Theological and Ethical Analysis of Proverbs 3), the righteous may suffer and the wicked prosper. A wise person may be poor (e.g., 16:8, 19). Concurrently, the sages occasionally reframe poverty—which in 10:1–15:33 was nearly always a culpable offense—as a good relative to ("better than") injustice (16:8), arrogance (16:19), strife (17:1), and lying (19:1, 22). Such expressions of contrary narratives and relative values highlight the limits of wisdom and remind readers that humility, not hubris, marks a "fearer of the LORD" (e.g., 15:33).

The point is underscored further by heightened attention to God's sovereignty and its corollary, the limits of human ingenuity and resolve (e.g., 16:1-7, 9, 33; 17:3; 19:21; 20:24, 27; 21:30-31). The sages elaborate on divine scrutiny and highlight, in particular, the transparency of humans to God—who is said now to test and weigh their character (16:2; 17:3; 20:27; 21:2; 22:12; cf. 15:3, 11). As YHWH proverbs follow one after the other in 16:1-9, readers find themselves, to borrow a metaphor from E. Gilbert, "like circus performers balancing on two speeding side-by-side horses"—one foot on the horse of divine power and freedom and the other on the horse of human autonomy—or, variously, straddling divine determination and human freewill (see Theological and Ethical Analysis of Proverbs 9). Half of life "you have no control over," Gilbert writes, "half of it is absolutely in your hands, and your actions will show measurable consequence": mortals are neither wholly puppets of God nor captains of their own destinies (2006, 177). For the sages, the balancing act is inherent to "fear of the LORD"—to taking responsibility for one's life (e.g., Deut 30:15-20; Sir 15:11-14), recognizing the human capacity for wrongdoing and self-distortion (16:2, 25; 20:9; 21:2), and acknowledging the incomparability of God's majesty and wisdom. Yet even the sages occasionally wrestle with how best to understand the balancing act and its implications (e.g., "A person's steps are decided by the LORD; what does a person know about his [or her] way?" 20:24 AT; cf. 19:3).

The sages weave together different views on God's activity in human lives. One thread speaks of God's "purpose" broadly, as the goal and/or frame of our efforts (e.g., 16:4; 21:31). This view resonates with those who consider God to be the architect of human lives, who seek divine direction in grand terms—vocations, relationships, and so on—and strive to carry out what they prayerfully understand to be God's "master plan" for them. We are accountable, that is, for life's particulars. A second thread is the inverse: we choose our way and God is "in the details" (e.g., 16:1, 3, 9). Just as the parent in Proverbs 1–9 urges the youth to choose her path in life (cf. "Choose life!" Deut 30:19), this view holds us responsible for the big picture, for asking and deciding about such questions as, what kind of life is worth living? How do I best use my gifts and talents? What are my goals? How do I envision my life? God delights when we choose wisely (16:7) and is proximate in the journey, directing our steps (16:9). The two interwoven threads hold us accountable for decisions in every aspect of our lives and, at the same time, underscore that our fate is not solely up to us.

PROVERBS 16

Literary Analysis

From 15:33 we step into the central chapter of Proverbs. Chapter 16 is an important crossroad: it introduces the second half of the first Solomonic collection (10:1–15:33, 16:1–22:16) and of Proverbs as a whole, even as portions of it recall Proverbs 1–9 (esp. 16:16-19, 26-32). Moreover, the chapter introduces readers to a greater complexity of theological content and literary forms. In lieu of the antithetical proverbs so prevalent in 10:1–15:33, one finds a mix of proverbial forms, including YHWH proverbs (16:1-7, 9, 11, 20, 33), synonymous or reiterative proverbs (e.g., 16:4-7, 10-15), and "better than" proverbs (16:8, 16, 19, 32).

The first subunit spotlights the sovereignty of God (16:1-9). Every proverb, with the exception of 16:8, is a YHWH proverb; that several are also antithetical heightens the contrast between God and humankind (16:1, 2, 9). Verses 1 and 9 frame the unit with repetition of "heart" or "mind" (*lēb*) and "humanity" (*'ādām*) and with Hebrew roots that mean variously "to plan" or "arrange." Repetition of "all" (*kōl*) connects 16:2, 4 (it is the first word in each), and 5, and reinforces the comprehensiveness of divine power.

The king—the earthly representative of God in ancient Near Eastern thought—takes center stage in 16:10-15. This is Proverbs' first extended description of the king, and it is a rather ideal one. (To this point, the king is mentioned only in superscriptions [1:1; 10:1] and three proverbs [8:15; 14:28, 35].) The description is comprised of three proverb pairs: verses 10-11 (linked by the catchword "justice"), 12-13, and 14-15. The unit celebrates the king's intimate association with YHWH (compare 16:12-13 with 16:5, 7; cf. also 24:21-22); at the same time, its placement after 16:1-9 reminds readers that the king, like every human, is subject to God.

The third subunit is at the heart of Proverbs (16:16-19). Indeed, the Masorah, the textual apparatus provided by medieval Jewish scribes, identifies 16:17 as the book's central verse. Numerous echoes of Proverbs 1–9 connect this midpoint of the Solomonic collection back to Proverbs 1–9, the hermeneutical guide to the book as a whole. The heart of the book, that is, recalls what is "at the heart" of the book. Verses 18-19 are a proverb pair.

Key words and attention to insight and speech tightly weave the fourth subunit together (16:20-24). The Hebrew root meaning "to have insight" or "understanding" (śākal) recurs in 16:20, 22-23. Verses 21 and 23 are linked by the expression "the wise of heart" (16:21a) and its inverse "the heart of the wise" (16:23a); 16:21b is also nearly identical to 16:23b. Lastly, the Hebrew root "sweet," or "sweetness" (mātaq) connects 16:21 and 24.

The chapter concludes with proverbs about certain paths in life—particularly those with bleak "ends" (16:26-32; but cf. 16:31-32). The unit is held together by repetition of "way" (derek, 16:25, 29b, 31b), "person" or "man" ('îš, 16:25a, and the first word in 16:27, 28, and 29), and various terms for "mouth" (16:26, 27b, 30b), as well as linguistic and thematic connections to 6:12-15. Verse 33, with its reassertion of God's freedom and sovereignty, forms an inclusio, or literary frame, with 16:1 and 9.

Exegetical Analysis

God's Sovereignty, Human Capacity, and Limitation (16:1-9)

<u>16:1</u> This proverb and 16:9 form a literary and theological frame that heralds God's activity precisely where humans believe we have control: our words (16:1) and our actions (16:9). The intimate connection between the heart and tongue (e.g., 10:20; 16:23; 17:20; 23:33; see excursus in Proverbs 2) highlights God's immediacy; mortals do not move from thought to speech without God. Because the waw that links the two lines may be conjunctive ("and") or disjunctive ("but"), the proverb may be construed as a celebration of God's proximity, even mutuality ("and"), and as a caution lest we forget it ("but"). The Egyptian Instruction of Amenemope teaches similarly: "The words men say are one thing, / The deeds of the god are another" (AEL 2:157; see also AEL 3:179).

16:2 Given the human capacity for self-deception—to be pure "in [one's] own eyes" (e.g., 3:7; 14:12)—God alone determines who is upright (15:11; 17:3; 21:2; 24:12). That God "weighs" the human spirit evokes depictions of Thoth, the Egyptian god of the scribes, who questioned the deceased about their deeds in life and weighed their hearts on a scale against the feather of Ma'at. If their hearts were "light as a feather," not burdened with wrongdoing, Thoth declared the dead righteous and ready for eternal life. If their hearts were heavy, Ammut consumed their souls. So *Papyrus Insinger* declares: "The great god Thoth has set a balance in order to make right measure on earth by it. / He placed the heart hidden in the flesh for the right measure of its owner" (*AEL* 3:188).

16:3 This proverb shifts abruptly to direct address ("Commit *your* work . . . *your* plans") and reverses the familiar sequence of plans then works. "Commit" is literally "roll away to," as when shepherds roll the stone off the top of a well to water their flocks (Gen 29:3, 8, 10) or people roll stones over the mouth of a cave or pit (26:27; Josh 10:18). The idiom "roll away to God" is found also in Pss 22:8 [Heb. v. 9] and 37:5. Paradoxically, moving works *from* oneself *to* God enables one's plans to "be established," presumably by God.

16:4 The referent for the third-masculine singular possessive suffix on "purpose" (or "answer") is ambiguous. It may be "everything" ("its purpose," e.g., NRSV, NASB) or God ("[God's] purpose," e.g., NIV, NAB). The sense either way is that God assigns to everything and everyone "purpose" (cf. "The LORD made everything for a purpose," *TANAKH*)—including the wicked. Such thinking prompts theological wrestling about God's justice, specifically God's relationship to the wicked. In Isaiah, for example, God creates light and darkness, well-being and evil (NRSV: "woe") so that nations will know "there is no other" God (45:6-7; cf. Ezek 38:22-23). Ecclesiastes emphasizes the mystery of it all (7:13-14). Ben Sira describes God's creation as balanced by opposites: good and evil, life and death, godly and sinner "come in pairs" (Sir 33:7-15; 42:24-25; cf. 39:16-35). For the sages of 16:4, God's creation and power over *all* creatures is good news: the wicked do not escape trouble.

16:5 On the heels of 16:4, this proverb names a particular kind of wickedness that God finds repulsive and judges accordingly (see excursus in Proverbs 3; cf. 8:13). "High of heart" (NRSV: "arrogant"; cf. 18:12; Ps 131:1; Ezek 28:2, 5, 17) is an expression similar to "high of spirit" (16:18; Eccl 7:8). The haughty are often described in physical terms: eyes lifted up (6:17; Ps 101:5; Isa 5:15) and snootiness (Ps 10:4). They elevate themselves and, as such, lack the humility of "fearers of the LORD" (22:4; cf. 15:33). "Be assured" (NRSV) is literally "hand to hand"—that is, "shake on it." The claim is trustworthy (cf. 3:3; 14:21-22).

16:6 "Loyalty and faithfulness" (3:3; 14:22; 20:28) refer to a gracious and trustworthy manner of relating to others; people (e.g., Gen 24:49; 47:29; Josh 2:14) and God (e.g., Gen 32:11; Exod 34:6; Pss 86:15; 138:2) may demonstrate it. Use of the phrase parallel to "fear of the LORD" here suggests the issue is human kindness. Love and fidelity can "cover" a wrong (cf. 10:12)—forgive or overlook it (cf. 17:9; Ps 78:38)—just as "fear of the LORD" steers one away from wickedness (1:7; 4:27; 13:19; 14:16; 16:17).

16:7 Having named behaviors that disgust God and the consequences of those behaviors (cf. 16:5), the sages now celebrate the human capacity to delight God, and God's response. God's pleasure (from the root $r\bar{a}s\hat{a}$) with a person prompts God's peacemaking (from the root $\check{s}\bar{a}lam$) on behalf of him or her. The psalmist makes the same connection: "The LORD takes pleasure (from the root $r\bar{a}s\hat{a}$) in those who fear [God]. . . . [God] grants peace ($\check{s}\bar{a}l\bar{o}m$) within your borders" (Ps 147:11a, 14a). Divine delight is the fount of peace.

16:8 Like 15:16-17, this "better than" proverb challenges any simplistic notion that the reward for wisdom is always wealth and prosperity (e.g., 3:16; 8:18, 21). People can be poor and righteous or, inversely, wicked and rich, but the righteous are always "better off." The proverb may also implicitly caution about wealth acquired dishonestly (e.g., 1:10-19; 10:2; 15:6; 21:6; cf. Sir 5:8).

16:9 Repetition of "heart" or "mind" ($l\bar{e}b$) and "human" ($'\bar{a}d\bar{a}m$) and the motif of planning associate this proverb with 16:1; the two constitute a literary frame, or *inclusio*, around the chapter's opening unit. Whereas mortals have the capacity and responsibility to plan their "way" (cf. 21:29b, and excursus in Proverbs 2), God is proximate—God approves or redirects each step (the conjunction may be translated as "and" or "but"). The proverb may be interpreted as a comforting reminder of God's nearness and sovereignty, a matter-of-fact acknowledgment of human limitations, or, more cynically, as a sigh of resignation (cf. 20:24; Jer 10:23).

The King (16:10-15)

16:10 The portrait of a king begins with a tribute to the quality of his speech (cf. wisdom's self-revelation in Proverbs 8). The term *qesem* (NRSV: "inspired decisions") refers to predictions or decisions made by means of an oracle. Typically such were disparaged or outright condemned (e.g., Deut 18:10; 2 Kgs 17:17; Ezek 13:6, 23), but the second line invites reconsideration: God inspires a *king's* decisions, particularly in matters of justice (cf. Ps 72:1-2). The king is God's regent. The verb in the second line may be read descriptively (NRSV: "does not sin") or prescriptively ("should not sin," e.g., NIV, NEB).

16:11 A hallmark of justice is the practice of fair weights and measures (cf. 11:1; 20:23). Indeed, "all the weights in the bag" are God's business. The Egyptian *Instruction of Amenemope* claims similarly:

> Do not move the scales nor alter the weights,
>   Nor diminish the fractions of the measure. . . .
> Where is a god as great as Thoth,
>   Who invented these things and made them?
> (*AEL* 2:156-157)

Though not explicitly about kingship, the proverb in this context implies a king must keep close watch on everyday transactions in the marketplace. Injustice there is abhorrent to God.

16:12-13 Royal disgust and delight animate this proverb pair. Like personified wisdom and God (6:16-19; 8:7; 15:9), kings deplore wrongdoing by themselves and others. It threatens the stability of their leadership—the justice on which their throne is established (20:8; 25:5; 29:14; cf. Pss 9:7-8 [Heb. vv. 8-9]; 89:14 [Heb. v. 15]; 97:2). Lest rulers forget the foundation of their rule, the Egyptians provide a visual reminder: Pharaoh's throne is often depicted with a base similar to the hieroglyph for ma῾at ("order" "truth," or "justice"). Conversely, kings adore "straight talk" (10:13).

16:14-15 Alliteration and assonance reinforce the association of "wrath of a king" (ḥămat-melek) with death (mal᾿ăkê-māwet, "messengers of death," 16:14a). Though the king's anger is ferocious (e.g., 14:35b; 19:12; 20:2; 24:21-22), a wise person appeases it (cf. 29:8)—as when Abigail's quick thinking convinces David not to exact vengeance on Nabal (1 Sam 25), or Daniel's interpretation of Nebuchadnezzar's dream saves the wise from execution in Babylon (Dan 2).

Royal wrath is counterbalanced by royal favor (16:15). A shining countenance is an effect of wisdom (e.g., Eccl 8:1). To see a bright face inspires joy (cf. 15:30), as do the clouds bearing late spring rains. Whereas early autumn rains prepare the ground for plowing and sowing, late spring rains provide the moisture necessary for the crops to mature. That the rains come, and come on time, is essential. Indeed, Israel interpreted timely arrival of the rains as God's reward for faithfulness (Deut 11:14; Joel 2:23; cf. Jer 3:3). So, too, the king's favor is opportune and sustenance for well-being (cf. 19:12b).

At the Heart of It (16:16-19)

16:16-17 According to the Masorah, the textual apparatus provided by medieval Jewish scribes, 16:17 marks the center of Proverbs. Echoing the father's repeated calls to "acquire wisdom" because its value surpasses that of precious metals (e.g., 3:14; 4:5, 7; 8:10-11, 19), 16:16 anticipates the midpoint by pointing back to Proverbs 1–9—the hermeneutical guide to Proverbs as a whole. The heart of the book, that is, reminds readers what is "at the heart" of the book.

Weaving together language of movement (highway, road, turn [NRSV: "avoid"]) and vigilance (guard, preserve), the sages then urge staying the course (16:17). The term "highway" (*mĕsillâ*) designates major public thoroughfares prepared or constructed by the clearing of obstacles, grading, and smoothing (e.g., Num 20:19; Judg 20:31-32; 1 Sam 6:12; Isa 11:16; 40:3; 49:11; 62:10; cf. Dorsey 1991, 228-33). The "way" of the upright, it seems, is a sort of a superhighway—well maintained, safe, and bustling with travelers. By staying on it, people "turn from evil" (e.g., 8:13) and preserve their lives (see excursus in Proverbs 2).

16:18-19 Humility is necessary to stay the course. These two proverbs are linked by the Hebrew root *gā'â* ("pride," 16:18a; "proud," 16:19b) and the contrast between "elevated of spirit" (16:18b) and "low in spirit" (16:19a; cf. 29:23; Isa 57:15). Verse 18 is one of several "pride precedes a fall" proverbs (e.g., 11:2; 18:12).

Verse 19 values humility in socioeconomic terms:

Better	low in spirit	with	(the) afflicted
than	dividing plunder	with	(the) arrogant

The term "afflicted" (reading the Qere, or oral tradition) refers broadly to persons "bowed" under the strains of socioeconomic oppression, "pushed out of the way" by corrupt neighbors (Amos 2:7; e.g., Isa 32:7); the term may also denote persons humble before God (e.g., 3:34; Zeph 2:3). It is far better to keep their company than to divide *šālāl* ("loot")—a phrase that intensifies the scene: one imagines a violent street gang huddled over bags of "loot" (*šālāl*, cf. 1:13) stolen from unsuspecting passersby (cf. 1:10-19). And finally, just when we expect reference to the "rich," the apt parallel for "afflicted," the proverb identifies the greedy culprits as the "arrogant"—a move that explicitly connects conceit with injustice (e.g., 11:2; 15:33).

Insight and Speech (16:20-24)

16:20 Paying attention is parallel here to trusting God, and both are sources of happiness (e.g., 3:5-6; 28:25; 29:25). That the proverb leaves open exactly to what one pays attention—*dābār* may mean "word" (NASB; cf. "instruction," NEB), "matter"

(NRSV), or "thing" (NAB)—invites a general alertness, a disposition of concern. The correspondence of that concern with reverence reinforces that "trusting God" is not passive, but active and engaged with the world. The root *šakal* ("insight" or "understanding") recurs in 16:22 and 23.

16:21 The second line, which is nearly identical to 16:23b, appears to elaborate on why the "wise of heart" are recognized as such by others: their "sweet lips" (cf. "pleasant words," 16:24a) increase instruction—a goal of the book (cf. 1:5). "Sweet" here refers not to "sugary sweet" as in overly (and perhaps false) words, but to speech that is morally and aesthetically satisfying. As individual proverbs and Proverbs as a whole demonstrate, crafted speech is persuasive. It matters what one says *and* how one says it. So Ecclesiastes "[tried] to find pleasing words, and he wrote words of truth plainly" (Eccl 12:10). R. C. Van Leeuwen compares 16:21b to the contemporary American proverb: "You catch more flies with honey than with vinegar" (1997, 162).

16:22 Wisdom as "a fountain of life" is a particularly potent metaphor given the desert climate of Palestine; wisdom quenches thirst and sustains life as waters from a deep reservoir (cf. 5:18; 10:11; 13:14; 14:27). In contrast, "the discipline (*mûsār*) of fools is folly." Many modern translations construe *mûsār* as "punishment" (NRSV), presumably because folly brings inevitable ruin (e.g., 5:7-14; 10:8, 14). But it may be that the "discipline" of fools—the way they are guided and encourage others to get along—is foolishness and, as such, they stumble off to certain demise. The root *šakal* ("insight" or "understanding") associates this proverb with 16:21 and 23.

16:23 Inverting "heart" and "wise" (cf. 16:21a), this proverb vividly describes the intimate connection between the wise heart or mind and speech (e.g., 10:8, 20; 16:1; 17:20): the heart "causes the mouth to be smart" and increases instruction on the lips. The second line is nearly identical to 16:21b.

16:24 Sweetness lingers with reference to honeycomb and the Hebrew root *mātaq* ("sweet" or "sweetness," 16:24b; cf. 16:21b). The proverb plays with *nepeš*, a term that means variously the self (NRSV), palate, or appetite. For speaker and hearer alike, pleasing words "taste sweet" to the *nepeš*—are morally and aesthetically satisfying—and nourish the bones. "Bones" by synecdoche may represent the whole person (e.g., 3:8; 12:4; 14:30; 17:22). Other proverbs celebrate the healing capacity of wise speech (e.g., 4:20-23; 12:18b; 13:17b; 15:4a).

Ways Ahead (16:25-33)

<u>16:25</u> This proverb is identical to 14:12. Here it anticipates 16:26-32, proverbs that characterize certain types of people and their paths in life—particularly those with bleak "ends" (but cf. 16:31, 32).

<u>16:26</u> First is the laborer (*ʿāmēl*). In Proverbs, as elsewhere, the root *ʿāmal* is largely negative, associated closely with struggle and hardships, such as poverty (31:7), destruction (24:2), grief (Jer 20:18), violence (Ps 7:16 [Heb. v. 17]), and affliction (Deut 26:7). Here, the laborer is driven by appetite (*nepeš*, cf. 16:24). Indeed, as the second line intensifies it, the worker's mouth "presses hard" on him, a verb that occurs elsewhere only in Sirach with enemies who "[press in] on every side" (Sir 46:5). People cannot escape the unrelenting force of their appetites: one labors to eat. Compare Eccl 6:7 (AT): "All the toil of people is for their mouths, and yet the appetite is not satisfied."

<u>16:27</u> The next three proverbs begin with the noun "person" or "man" (*ʾîš*), creating a directory of people whose speech is dangerous. The good-for-nothing "digs" wickedness (NRSV: "concoct") as one would hollow out a pit or grave (e.g., 26:27; Gen 26:25; Jer 18:20, 11). The expression, which occurs only here in the Old Testament, may be an elliptical form of "digs a pit," suggesting the good-for-nothing prepares traps to ensnare others. (The same character is said to "sow wickedness" in 6:14.) The work includes malicious speech—words that singe and burn others and perhaps leave blisters on the good-for-nothing's lips.

<u>16:28</u> The next two characters thrive on instigating conflict. Whereas the "twisted" person unleashes it widely (cf. 2:12; 6:14; 10:31), the malicious gossip works behind the scenes, spreading rumors behind people's backs to alienate the most intimate of friends (e.g., 11:13a; 17:9; 20:19).

16:29 The violent "entice" their friends, presumably to join them. The verb recalls the sinners' invitation to the youth to join them in ambushing innocent passersby (1:10-19)—they "entice" (1:10) participation in violence with the promise of camaraderie and fast, easy money. The second line concurs with the father of Proverbs 1–9: such a path is "not good" (cf. 1:15-19). Other "not good" proverbs are 17:26; 18:5; 19:2; 25:27, and 28:21.

16:30 Outward appearances may reveal malice (cf. 6:12-14). Eyes that "shut" or "blink" (NRSV: "winks") barely shutter the twisted schemes at work behind them (cf. 10:10), whereas "pursed" lips (the same verb used with eyes in 6:13) say nothing but speak volumes about an unwavering determination to see the schemes through to completion.

16:31 Outward appearances may also reveal one's integrity. The road of the righteous winds to old age (e.g., 3:2; 4:10b; 9:11; but cf. Ps 44:22; Isa 57:1), where one finds a splendid "crown" of gray hair. Such (royal) dignity commands respect (Lev 19:32); it is a badge of lifelong persistence and uprightness. The sages frequently describe abstract concepts or qualities as clothing or jewelry (e.g., 1:8-9; 3:3, 21-22; 31:25); other "crowns" include riches (14:24) and grandchildren (17:6).

16:32 Several proverbs urge emotional self-restraint (e.g., 12:16; 14:17, 29; 15:18; 17:27; 19:11). This proverb does so with military imagery: to "rule" oneself, to have self-discipline and self-control, is better than a warrior-hero's defeat of an entire city. Implicit may be that the latter requires the former—one cannot conquer the world without first conquering oneself. The proverb's battle language animates how turbulent the internal struggle can be to restrain one's anger.

16:33 The chapter ends as it began, with an assertion of God's power and presence in the most intimate of occurrences (16:1-7, 9-10). Lots are stones that people cast to obtain a (divinely directed) decision (e.g., 18:18; Lev 16:8-10; Jon 1:7; Matt 27:35; Acts 1:24-26). In this case, the lots are thrown into the ḥêq—one's bosom or lap (NRSV), or a fold in the garment above the belt where a person could conceal hands and property (e.g., Exod 4:6-7; 28:15-30). The term lends an air of intimacy (e.g., 5:20; 6:27), secrecy (e.g., 17:23; 21:14), and acute personal investment to the decision (i.e., "that is in your lap," e.g., Isa 65:6-7; Jer 32:18). Even there, God has the last word.

PROVERBS 17

Literary Analysis

Proverbs 17 lacks apparent structure. There is neither consistency in genre, such as the prevalence of antithetical proverbs in Proverbs 10–15, nor evidence of larger interrelated thematic units, such as those devoted to God and the king in Proverbs 16. Several topics occur repeatedly, including the importance of a good family (17:1b, 2, 6, 13, 17, 21, 25); the value of peace in relationships (17:1, 9, 11, 13, 19); gift or bribe giving (17:8, 23); and condemnation of poor judgment (17:15, 26). Catchwords link several proverbs: "pursue" or "seek" (17:9, 11), "love" (17:9, 17, 19), "rejoice" (17:21-22), and "friend" or "neighbor" (17:17-18). Participles also appear more often, particularly juxtaposed (17:4, 9, 15, 19, and 27). The chapter concludes with a proverb pair about the complex relationship between wisdom, folly, silence, and speech (17:27-28).

Exegetical Analysis

<u>17:1</u> Quantity and quality of food convey the value of peace over conflict (cf. 15:16-17). A quiet meal of *one* crust, a crumb of food basic for survival (e.g., Ruth 2:14; 2 Sam 12:3), that is *dry* presumably because there is neither oil nor vinegar with which to moisten it (19:24; 26:15), is better than a contentious banquet in a house-*full* of food (note the plural "feasts"). That "feast" (*zebah*) connotes a communal sacrificial meal of meat heightens the contrast and underscores its socioeconomic edge: only the affluent could afford such lavish consumption (e.g., Deut 12:7; 18:3; 1 Sam 2:13; 9:12-13; 20:5-6; cf. Prov 7:14). This is supper at a " 'religious,' wealthy household in which public piety is married to internecine conflict" (Van Leeuwen 1997, 166). The Egyptian *Instruction of Amenemope* teaches similarly: "Better is

bread with a happy heart, / Than wealth with vexation" (*AEL* 2:152).

17:2 The theme of a house divided continues (cf. 17:1b). Wisdom or lack thereof can upset even the most time-honored household and communal codes (e.g., 19:10b; 30:21-23; cf. Eccl 10:7). Here a wise slave not only "rules over" a shameful son, but enjoys a portion of the inheritance—a son's privilege (cf. 10:5). Depending on one's perspective, the proverb may offer encouragement (cf. 12:24) or serve as a cautionary tale.

17:3 Crucibles are used to extract precious metals from ore. At high heat, the metal is melted, refined by pouring off its impurities (or dross), and tested for purity. God so "tests" or evaluates the worthiness of the human heart (e.g., Pss 17:3; 26:2; Jer 11:20; cf. God "weighing" the heart in 21:2; 24:12; cf. 16:2). God is depicted as the refiner of individuals and communities (e.g., Job 23:10; Isa 48:10; Jer 6:29; Ezek 22:17-22; Zech 13:9; cf. 1 Pet 1:7). Proverbs 27:21a repeats 17:3a.

17:4 The sages emphasize repeatedly that the company we keep matters (e.g., 14:7; 29:12). One can imagine the wicked person leaning in, captivated by the "malevolent lips" and "destructive tongue" of others, soaking in talk that is harmful to everyone. As a result, the wicked become what they hear—a point the proverb underlines by using the abstract noun "lie" or "deceit" for the wicked in the second line (cf. "lazy" in 12:27).

17:5 This proverb again aligns God with the poor: how we behave toward one, we behave toward the other (14:31; 19:17; 22:2; 29:13; Sir 11:4). That "the poor" is parallel to "calamity," a term that in Proverbs is always a consequence of one's actions (1:26-27; 6:15; 13:15; 24:22; 27:10), suggests the poor suffer by their own doing (e.g., 6:9-11; 13:18; 28:19; but cf. 13:23; 28:3). The proverb cautions against *Schadenfreude*, the enjoyment of another's troubles—even, perhaps especially, when those troubles are self-inflicted. Those who rejoice "will not go unpunished"; the passive verb leaves open exactly how and by whom, thereby heightening the ominous tone (e.g., 10:9).

17:6 The honor of each generation depends on the generations that precede and follow. The proverb emphasizes this by repeating

COMMENTARY

"son" three times and progressing from grandparent to grandson (17:6a) and then the reverse, from sons to their parents (17:16b). The values of longevity and fertility are implicit (Murphy 1998, 129) and the consequences of a wise or shameful child are more profound (e.g., 17:2). As we have seen, other "crowns" in Proverbs are a "woman of substance" (12:4), riches (14:24), and gray hair (16:31).

17:7 This is the first of three "not fitting" proverbs in the book (19:10; 26:1; cf. "not right" or "not good" proverbs, e.g., 17:26; 18:5; 19:2). The term *nā'wâ* (NRSV: "becoming") denotes "proper" or "fitting" (Pss 33:1; 147:1) or "beautiful" or "delightful" (e.g., Song 1:5; 2:14; 4:3; 6:4); appropriateness has an aesthetic dimension. Whereas fine speech does not "fit" the fool, lies by a leader are more loathsome, perhaps because their speech has wider impact (e.g., 8:16; 19:6; cf. 16:10, 13).

17:8 From a briber's perspective, a bribe is a "stone of favor" (an expression found only here in the Old Testament), a magical charm of sorts that guarantees success at every turn (cf. 15:27; 17:23; 18:16; 21:14). But there is an implicit caution: a bribe seems so "in the eyes" of the briber. The phrase is a red flag in Proverbs. The sages warn repeatedly against relying too much on one's perceptions—being "wise in [one's] eyes"—for one may be sorely misguided (e.g., 3:7; 26:5, 12, 16; 28:11; 30:12).

17:9 Those who "cover" an offense, not in the sense of condoning the wrong but forgiving or overlooking it (e.g., 10:12; 16:6; Ps 78:38), "pursue" or "aim for" love. In contrast, those who "repeat a thing" by harping on it (NRSV) and gossiping about it to others, separate close friends (cf. 16:28; Sir 42:1).

17:10 Hyperbole underscores the comparative effects of discipline on the wise and the incorrigible fool (e.g., 9:7-9; 13:1; 15:12): *one* rebuke strikes deeper than *one hundred* blows. The latter number is conspicuously extreme; the law forbade more than forty lashes for any offense lest the punishment be too degrading (Deut 25:1-3; cf. 2 Cor 11:24).

17:11 With single-minded intensity, the wicked "pursue" contention (cf. 17:9); the Hebrew particle *'ak* adds emphasis ("above all" or "certainly") and singularity ("only" NRSV). Ironically,

192

even as the wicked chase after it, a cruel messenger "is sent" against them; the passive verb leaves open by whom, though God is likely implied (cf. 21:12).

17:12 The imperative "Go!" from the presence of the fool (14:7) is elevated to a fever pitch by this comparison of the fool not only to a bear—a creature renowned for its strength and ferocity (e.g., 28:15; 2 Kgs 2:23-24; Isa 59:11; Lam 3:10)—but one enraged by the loss of her cubs (e.g., 2 Sam 17:8; Hos 13:8). A fool consumed by his or her own folly is *more* dangerous.

17:13 Ironically, when one returns wickedness for something good, wickedness, like a stubborn guest, refuses to leave one's "house," a term that refers variously to the physical structure, its inhabitants, and a person's descendants (e.g., 12:4; 18:22; 19:14; 21:9, 19; 25:24; 27:15-16; 31:10-31). The proverb evokes the prophet Nathan's condemnation of David after David ordered Uriah killed on the battlefield and then married Uriah's wife, Bathsheba. Because of David's treachery, Nathan prophesies that "the sword will never depart" from David's house; God will stir up trouble against David from within his household (2 Sam 12:1-15).

17:14 To start a quarrel is to open a dam: once released, water surges forth with incredible force, spraying and flowing in every possible direction. At the prospect of such raw, uncontrollable energy, this proverb urges simply, "Drop it!" (17:14b; cf. *TANAKH*).

17:15 Literary symmetry in the first line ironically describes asymmetric judgment: *maṣdîq rāšā ʿûmaršîa ʿṣaddîq* ("one who declares righteous the wicked and/or one who declares wicked the righteous," cf. 24:24). Both are abhorrent to God (see excursus in Proverbs 3). The proverb speaks to distorted judgment generally (e.g., Job 27:5; Sir 10:29) and, in particular, to abuse of judicial power (e.g., Exod 23:2-3, 6-8; Deut 25:1; Isa 5:23).

17:16 Even if fools have in hand the means to "acquire" wisdom—and instruction may be purchased, evidence for which remains a matter of dispute (e.g., 4:5, 7; Sir 51:25)—they lack the heart to do so. The proverb implicitly pokes fun at the fools' misunderstanding: the fools interpret the command "acquire wisdom" (e.g., 4:4, 7) literally, in its economic sense (e.g., Gen 47:19;

Isa 43:24; Jer 32:9), and altogether miss its figurative connotations (e.g., 4:4-9; 8:22; Isa 55:1-3).

<u>17:17</u> Interpretation of this proverb hinges primarily on two matters. First, the term "brother" (17:17b; NRSV: "kinsfolk") is multivalent. It may refer to blood relations (e.g., Gen 4:8; Hos 12:3 [Heb. v. 4]), companions (e.g., Job 30:29), or members of one's tribe or country (e.g., Gen 31:32; Exod 2:11; Judg 9:18). As such, "brother" may or may not be distinct from "friend" or "neighbor" in 17:17a (cf. 27:10). Second, the *waw* that joins the two lines may be conjunctive ("and") or disjunctive ("but"). The two lines may therefore be: (*a*) synonymous, valuing equally the affection of "the friend" who chooses to be loyal and the "brother" born to be so at critical moments; (*b*) antithetical, valuing kinship over friendship like the modern saying "Blood is thicker than water" (14:20; 19:4, 6-7; Murphy 1998, 131); or (*c*) antithetical, valuing friendship "at all times" over "brothers" who show up only in a crisis (cf. 18:24). A few modern translations preserve the ambiguity by not translating the conjunction (e.g., *TANAKH*).

<u>17:18</u> Not every neighbor is "the friend" (cf. 17:17), however, so the sages discourage again what they consider a risky practice: the granting of surety (6:1-5; 11:15; 20:16; in contrast, see Sir 8:13). The phrase *lipnê rēʿēhû* in 17:18b may be translated "on behalf of one's friend [or neighbor]" (cf. NRSV) and "in front of one's friend [or neighbor]" (NASB, RSV). One should never grant surety—privately or in public.

<u>17:19</u> Ambiguities confound interpretation of this proverb. The first line does not distinguish subject and object; it simply juxtaposes "one who loves transgression" and "one who loves strife" (compare, e.g., NRSV with NIV or NAB). The second line then begins with the puzzling phrase "one who raises high one's opening" (or "doorway"). An elevated opening or doorway may suggest that the contentious "raise the bar" or make it particularly difficult for people to get through conflicts. A high doorway may also be a metaphor for pride (e.g., 16:18) or, alternatively, "opening" may refer to the mouth (e.g., Mic 7:5), so the concern is arrogant speech. Whichever the case, such people seek "destruction"—

of others and, ironically, themselves (e.g., Isa 30:13-14). The NRSV translates loosely: an "opening" or "doorway" is not a threshold, and "bones" is not in the Hebrew.

17:20 The proverb summarily describes the radical disorientation and demise of the wicked. With "crooked hearts," an abomination to God (11:20; Ps 101:4), and tongues that "turn things upside down," the wicked are utterly lost—they "do not find" good and they "fall" into trouble. The second line may also be translated, "One turned upside down *by* his tongue will fall into trouble" (cf. Van Leeuwen 1997, 169); as such, the proverb describes the fate of the wicked and those foolish enough to listen to them.

17:21 Many proverbs speak to how wise and foolish youth affect their parents. Repetition of the topic emphasizes its gravity (e.g., 10:1, 5; 13:1; 15:20; 17:25; 19:13a).

17:22 This proverb would strongly caution the parents of the fool in 17:21. That they do not "rejoice" (*śāmaḥ*, 17:21) imperils their health. A "joyful" (*śāmaḥ*) heart restores well-being (cf. 15:13a). A defeated spirit withers the body. "Bones" by synecdoche represent the whole person (e.g., 3:8; 12:4; 14:30; 15:14, 30).

17:23 The problem is not gift giving (cf. 18:16) but the purpose of the gift: in this case, distortion of justice (e.g., Exod 23:2, 6; Deut 16:19; 27:19). This is a "pocketed bribe," so to speak, a gift from the *ḥêq*—the chest, lap, or fold in the garment above the belt used to conceal one's hands or property (16:33; e.g., Exod 4:6-7). The wicked "takes" (*yiqqāḥ*) it; indeed, sound readily connects the two. The sages acknowledge that some secretive "gifts" may be beneficial (21:14), even as they condemn bribery (17:8; 15:27).

17:24 Physical and spatial language highlight the contrast. Wisdom is right in front of—literally in the "face of" (*pĕnê*)—those who understand (e.g., 8:9; 17:10); it is proximate, and the wise stay focused (cf. Deut 30:11-14). By contrast, the fools' eyes (*'ēnê*) dart across the far horizon. For them, wisdom is nowhere to be found.

17:25 See discussion of 17:21. Proverbs 19:13a is nearly identical to 17:25a.

<u>17:26</u> Several proverbs designate certain behaviors as simply "not good" (e.g., 16:29; 18:5; 19:2; 25:27; 28:21; cf. 17:7). Here the concern is miscarriage of justice (cf. 17:15)—to impose a fine on the innocent (e.g., Deut 22:19; Amos 2:8) and, presumably worse, to flog nobles who, given the parallel "righteous," are most likely honest (cf. 8:16; 17:7; Deut 25:1-3). The last two words of the second line (ʿal yōšer) may be translated (a) "against what is right," and understood as parallel to "not good," or (b) "for their integrity" (NRSV), referring back to the nobles' character.

<u>17:27-28</u> This proverb pair develops more fully the relationship between wisdom, folly, silence, and speech. The first resonates with the many proverbs that urge restrained speech (e.g., 10:19; 12:23; 13:3; 15:28). Reference to a "cool spirit," or calm temperament, calls to mind the markedly opposite "heated man" described in the *Instruction of Amenemope* (*AEL* 2:146-163).

The second proverb complicates matters (17:28). Silence is not a fail-safe indication of wisdom because "even fools" can, presumably with effort, pull it off. The proverb thus cautions against rushing to judgment—deciding someone is wise on the basis of one behavior or attribute. At the same time, it may subtly implore fools to stop babbling just long enough for someone to slip a wise word in edgewise (e.g., 10:8, 14; 12:23; cf. Eccl 10:12-14a).

PROVERBS 18

Literary Analysis

Proverbs 18 lacks apparent structure. The chapter begins with a proverb about the antisocial person (18:1) and concludes with a tribute to the true friend (18:24b; cf. Horne 2003, 223), but within that loose frame the proverbs reveal little arrangement other than occasional catchwords and wordplay. Some topics figure prominently, including speech (18:2, 4, 6-8, 20-21, 23), the importance of listening (18:13, 15, 17), and the nature of and means for resolving disputes (18:16-19). There are two proverb pairs (18:6-7, 10-11).

Exegetical Analysis

<u>18:1</u> This proverb condemns one who is separated from the community, likely by his or her own volition, and seeks (presumably) his or her own desire (the Hebrew lacks a possessive suffix). Bent on self-indulgence, the loner is aloof and unreasonable, quarrelling with any sound judgment. He or she refuses communal wisdom.

<u>18:2</u> Wordplay links this proverb to 18:1: *yitgallā*ʿ ("showing," 18:1b) and *hitgallôt* ("expressing" or "revealing," 18:2b). Fools "reveal" their hearts or minds; the verb in this form occurs elsewhere only in Gen 9:21 when Noah, drunk with wine, lies down "exposed" in his tent. Whereas the wise guard their hearts (e.g., 4:23), fools bare theirs for all to see (e.g., 12:16, 23; 13:16).

<u>18:3</u> Repetition of the Hebrew letter *bêt* (*b*) and the verb "to come" or "enter" (*bô*ʾ) readily associates the wicked with contempt, their traveling companion: *běbôʾ-rāšāʿ bāʾ gam-bûz* (lit. "When comes the wicked, comes also contempt," 18:3a). (NRSV emends unnecessarily to the abstract noun "wickedness.") The contempt may be that of the wicked for others (e.g., 11:9, 12) or that of others for the wicked (e.g., 11:10; 12:8). The second line develops the latter. The wicked suffer unwelcome guests—shame and reproach. The proverb is a variation on "Pride precedes a fall" (e.g., 11:2; 16:18; 18:12a).

<u>18:4</u> Words are deep waters drawn up from the heart (20:5) and poured out of the "mouth" (e.g., 1:23; 10:11; 13:14; 15:2), a term that denotes the organ of speech, the mouth of a river (Isa 19:7), or opening of a well or gorge (Gen 29:2-3, 8, 10; Jer 48:28). Interpretation of the second line depends on how one construes "deep waters." If the metaphor is negative, suggesting that which is unfathomable, even chaotic (e.g., Ps 64:6 [Heb. v. 7]; Eccl 7:24), then 18:4b contrasts such speech with wisdom, which is an accessible, on-the-surface fountain of life (NIV, NAB; e.g., 13:14; 16:22). If the metaphor is positive, "flowing stream" and "fountain of wisdom," which are simply juxtaposed, elaborate on the flow and efficacy of wise speech (cf. *TANAKH*).

<u>18:5</u> This "not good" proverb (16:29; 17:26; 19:2; 25:27; 28:21) uses physical language to condemn injustice: "to raise the face"

(NRSV: "to be partial") of the wicked, a gesture of pardon (Gen 4:7; Job 11:15; cf. 2 Sam 2:22), and "to thrust" or "turn aside" the righteous from a fair judgment (e.g., 17:15, 26; 24:23-24).

18:6-7 The catchword "fool" and the pattern lips/mouth/mouth/lips link these two proverbs about the harm of foolish speech. The first proceeds from verbal to physical injuries invited ("calls out for") and suffered by fools and, presumably, those foolish enough to listen to them (10:13; 13:20; 14:3; 17:21; 19:29; 22:24-25). The second proverb concentrates on the fools: their speech brings "terror" or "ruin" (e.g., 10:14; 13:3; 21:15) and ensnares them, possibly to their death (e.g., 12:13; 13:14).

18:8 Caution about harmful speech continues with this description of gossip as delicious morsels that descend (*yordû*) to the "dark chambers" (*hadrê*) of the body—the deepest, hidden recesses of the self (20:27, 30). Like junk food, gossip is "delicious to taste before it settles inside to do its destructive work" (Van Leeuwen 1997, 173; e.g., 16:28; 26:20). The proverb is identical to 26:22.

18:9 Those who are careless and do not do their work are family (lit. "He is a brother," 18:9b) to those who destroy their own work or that of others (the proverb leaves open both possibilities). "Destroyers" are raiding parties (e.g., 1 Sam 13:17; 14:15); armed fighters who slay their own prophets (Jer 2:30); messengers or angels of destruction (e.g., Exod 12:23; 2 Sam 24:16-17); and brutal men "skillful to destroy" (Ezek 21:31 [Heb. v. 26]; cf. Jer 22:7). The lazy similarly devastate the community and themselves (e.g., 10:4-5, 26; 19:24; 20:4; 21:25; 24:30-34).

18:10-11 Architectural imagery and the catchwords "strong" and "to be high" or "inaccessible" (hence "safe," 18:10b) join these two proverbs. A "strong tower" affords protection and strategic advantage. When Abimelech and his army laid siege to Thebez, for example, its citizens fled to a "strong tower" and shut themselves in; moments later, from high on its roof, an unnamed woman dropped a millstone on Abimelech, mortally wounding him (Judg 9:50-57). The psalmist also uses the metaphor for God, praising God as "my refuge, a strong tower against the enemy" (Ps 61:3 [Heb. v. 4]).

The first line of 18:11 repeats 10:15a—that the wealth of the rich is their "strong city." But the second line destabilizes the claim immediately: money is a "high" wall in their imagination (or, more strongly, delusion; cf. "follies," Ps 73:7). It is a false refuge. The proverb thus bolsters 18:10. God is the only true security and advantage.

18:12 The motif of height (18:10-11) is applied now to a person's heart (NRSV: that is, "haughty") before destruction (cf. "pride precedes a fall" proverbs, 11:2; 16:18; 18:3). The first line of this proverb is similar to 16:18a and the second duplicates 15:33b. The combination functions as a hinge proverb that both cautions against arrogance such as that of the wealthy (18:11) and extols the humility characteristic of those who listen carefully (18:13).

18:13 Highlighting the reciprocal nature of dialogue, the proverb condemns "causing a word to return"—that is, answering—before listening (e.g., 22:20-21; 24:26; Sir 11:8). It is impossible to respond wisely if one has not paid attention. Implicit is critique of the fool who babbles on and on and refuses to listen to anyone (e.g., 10:8; 18:2; Job 35:16; Eccl 6:11; 10:14). Eventually those who interrupt others find they have no one to talk to but themselves.

18:14 The health of the body depends on the health of the *rûaḥ* ("wind," "breath," or "spirit," e.g., 1:23; 15:13; 17:22). As if to emphasize the point, the second line itself breaks immediately after "but a *rûaḥ* broken"—sputtering abruptly, "Who can bear it?" The rhetorical question assumes a negative answer (e.g., 20:6, 9, 24; 24:22). A healthy spirit can uphold a broken body, but a healthy body cannot bear a crushed spirit.

18:15 A variant of 15:14a, the proverb portrays the wise as receptive listeners (18:13). Internally the heart or mind (see excursus in Proverbs 2) acquires knowledge while externally the ears pursue it.

18:16 A gift has power—it "makes room for" and "leads" one before great people. Gift giving was common in ancient Israel, part of everyday sociopolitical, religious, and commercial interactions (e.g., Gen 34:12; Lev 23:38; 2 Chr 21:3; Esth 9:22; Ezek 20:26,

31, 39). Gifts engender goodwill and loyalty, making it easier for people to advance themselves and their interests. But what if any difference is there between this gift giving (19:6; 21:14) and bribery, which the sages condemn (e.g., 15:27; 17:8, 23; Eccl 7:7)? The proverb leaves the question open. It may be construed as a simple and perhaps cynical observation of the way people get ahead, or as encouragement to give generously so that one might.

18:17 Gifts of any sort should never stop one from listening carefully and "examining" or "searching things out," because there are (at least) two views on every matter. The proverb applies in judicial and more general contexts (e.g., 25:2; 28:11; cf. 1 Sam 20:12).

18:18 Much as gifts can wield power beyond their size (18:16), so a "lot"—or a stone cast to get a decision (cf. 16:33)—can settle disputes. Juxtaposition of one "lot" (sg.) with the "powerful" (pl.) highlights its power. One small stone can "separate" (16:28; 17:9) many people of physical, numerical, or sociopolitical strength (e.g., 7:26; Gen 18:18; Exod 1:9; Ps 135:10; Isa 53:12; Dan 8:24; 11:25).

18:19 The Hebrew here is obscure. The sense is that an offense can turn even the most devoted loyalty (that of a "brother," e.g., 6:19; 17:17) into impenetrable resentment ("strong city," cf. 10:15; 18:11). "Bars of a castle" (NRSV) are strong metal bolts that secure a gate or door to a fortified palace from the inside (e.g., Deut 3:5; Judg 16:3; Neh 3:3; Isa 45:2). The catchword "disputes" links this with 18:18.

18:20-21 The word "fruit" frames the next two proverbs; it is the first word of 18:20 and the last of 18:21. Just as gossip is like delicious morsels that descend into the body's innermost parts (18:8), speech—whether positive or negative—is like fruit and harvest ("yield") that fills the bellies of speaker and hearer alike. Proverbs 18:20a is a variation of 12:14a and 13:2a.

The "fruit" one consumes is, for the sages, a matter of life and death (18:21). The proverb portrays the tongue, a feminine noun in Hebrew, as a woman with lovers. Life and death are "in the hand of the tongue" (18:21a); "hand" may refer to a person's power, much as the English expression "The matter is in your hands" means you have control over it (e.g., Deut 32:36; Josh 8:20). The tongue or speech one "loves" determines one's fate, just as the choice between wisdom and folly has life and death consequences (Prov 1–9; see esp. wisdom's "fruit," 8:19; cf. 31:31).

18:22 Repetition in the first line (*māṣāʾ ʾiššāh māṣāʾ ṭôb*) equates finding (*māṣāʾ*) a "wife" (*ʾiššâ*) with finding "good" (*ṭôb*, cf. "to find good" in 16:20; 17:20; 19:8). The proverb is one of several that associate a (good) wife with prosperity (e.g., 12:4; 19:14; 31:10-31). At the same time, it alludes to personified wisdom's assurance that to find her is to obtain favor from God (18:22a is similar to 8:35a; 18:22b repeats 8:35b). The proverb thus extols the value of a good partner *and* wisdom. Both are to be diligently pursued and, when found, are sources of divine blessing.

18:23 Speech often reflects one's socioeconomic circumstances. Whereas the poor have no choice but to plead for favor and ingratiate themselves to others, the wealthy can afford to be rude. They respond to the poor "strongly," an adverb that suggests impudence and harsh defiance (e.g., Deut 28:50; Dan 8:23). The proverb may be construed as an observation or (implicit) condemnation of callousness to the poor (e.g., 14:31; 17:5; 19:17; 22:2; 29:13; Sir 11:4).

18:24 The first line is obscure. Following a few ancient versions, NRSV interprets the first word (*ʾîš*, "person" or "man") as a particle of existence (*yēš*, "there are"; but cf. NIV, NASB). Confusion between the two terms occurs elsewhere (e.g., 2 Sam 14:19; Mic 6:10) and the emendation affords a good parallel with the second line—the first word of which is *yēš*. A second concern is *lĕhitrōʿēaʿ*, which NRSV interprets as from the Hebrew root meaning "to associate with" (*rāʿâ*) but which may be from the root "to be beaten up" or "shattered" (*rāʿaʿ*, Isa 24:19; e.g., NIV, NASB). The proverb apparently distinguishes between *many* (pl.) who appear to be friends—and possibly do harm—and the *one* who, even more than family members, "clings to" a person through thick and thin (e.g., 17:17; 19:4; 25:19; Sir 6:10). The same verb is used for Ruth who "clung to" Naomi (Ruth 1:14).

PROVERBS 19

Literary Analysis

Many of the proverbs in this chapter emphasize the value of instruction (19:2, 8, 13a, 16, 18-20, 25-27, 29), but there is very little indication of arrangement beyond an occasional shared word or theme, such as the metaphor of the "way" coupled with a motif of movement (19:1-3) and the impact of money on relationships (19:4, 6-7). There are four YHWH proverbs (19:3, 14, 17, 21; cf. also "fear of the LORD" in 19:23) and three proverb pairs (19:6-7, 13-14, 28-29). Verses 5 and 9 are nearly identical. The chapter also includes the only direct address of the youth in 10:1–22:16 ("my child," 19:27).

Exegetical Analysis

<u>19:1</u> The "way" and a motif of movement animate the first three proverbs. Juxtaposition of a poor person who "walks with integrity" (e.g., 2:7; 13:6; 20:7) and a fool with "twisted lips" is surprising; we expect the contrasts of poor/rich and walks/ways (28:6). The text makes sense, however, and privileges honesty over deceit—even at the cost of poverty (19:4, 7). "Good" is a catchword with 19:2.

<u>19:2</u> Without knowledge, even well-intentioned desire can result in harm, just as "one who is hasty with feet misses"—presumably the path forged by God and the community (cf. Theological and Ethical Analysis of Proverbs 1). The wise are informed and deliberate. Other "not good" proverbs are 16:29; 17:26; 18:5; 25:27; and 28:21.

<u>19:3</u> Folly is self-destructive; it "twists" and "brings to ruin" a person's path (the verb has both senses, e.g., 13:6; 21:12; 22:12; Exod 23:8). The fool's rage against God may be symptomatic of his or her distorted perspective or an audacious act of finger pointing—it is the fool's folly, but he or she blames God (Sir 15:11-20). The proverb condemns indignant rage that denies any personal responsibility. It does not follow that all rage against God is foolish (e.g., psalms of lament, Pss 13, 44, 60).

19:4 Wealth makes friends, an observation this proverb conveys in stark bottom-line terms: money "adds" (NRSV: "brings") *many* friends, whereas a poor person "is separated" from his or her *one* friend (19:6-7). The passive verb intensifies the poor person's powerlessness and isolation.

19:5 "False witness" (e.g., 6:19; 12:17; 14:5) may refer to dishonesty in general and, in particular, to testimony in court (e.g., Jer 32:10, 12; Ruth 4:9-11). Prohibited by the Ten Commandments (Exod 20:16; Deut 5:20) and condemned by the sages as an "abomination of YHWH" (6:19), perjury is subject to stiff penalties (Deut 19:18-19)—which this proverb and its near equivalent in 19:9 consider unavoidable (21:28).

19:6-7 These two proverbs develop the observations of 19:4. *Many* flatter, literally "caress" or "soften the faces" (e.g., Job 11:19; Ps 45:12 [Heb. v. 13]), of "nobles" (e.g., 8:16; 17:7, 26). *Everyone* is "the friend" (17:7) of a gift giver. The comprehensiveness may implicitly question the quality of such friendships.

In contrast, people stay far away from the poor (19:7). With equally sweeping brushstrokes, the proverb moves from intimate companions ("every brother") who hate the poor to members of the wider community ("friend" or "neighbor") who "distance themselves" from them; the verb suggests aloofness *and* physical avoidance (e.g., 22:5; Deut 14:24; Job 30:10; Ps 103:12; Isa 49:19; Jer 2:5). The third line is unclear ("Whoever pursues words, they are not").

19:8 The proverb nearly bursts with key terms that together emphasize the direct relationship between wisdom or understanding (e.g., 5:1; 8:1) and well-being. "Acquire," "love," "keep," and "find" resonate with injunctions to get wisdom throughout Proverbs (e.g., 15:32; 16:16; 17:16; 18:15; 23:23) and, in particular, with the (grand)father's appeal to "acquire" personified wisdom, the most desirable of brides (4:5-9). To keep her is in one's best interest (to "love oneself") for she offers her companions safety, honor, happiness, and prosperity. They *will* "find good" (NRSV: "to prosper"; cf. 16:20; 17:20; 18:22).

19:9 This proverb is nearly identical to 19:5. The second line escalates the penalty for bearing false witness.

<u>19:10</u> This "not fitting" proverb (cf. 17:7; 26:1) points to signs that the world is out of kilter: fools enjoy comfort and servants exercise royal power—a circumstance under which "the earth trembles" (30:21-22; cf. 17:2). Ecclesiastes similarly describes his topsy-turvy context: "The fool is set on great heights, but the rich sit in a low place. I have seen slaves on horseback and princes walk on foot like slaves" (Eccl 10:6-7).

<u>19:11</u> Several proverbs urge the restraint of anger (e.g., 12:16; 14:17a, 29; 17:27b). Ironically, positive regard of others comes from *dis*regarding ("to cross over" or "bypass") an offense. The proverb leaves ambiguous whether the wrongdoing was done to oneself or to others (10:12; 17:9).

<u>19:12</u> From self-restraint of one's anger (19:11a), the sages turn to an observation about royal self-restraint or lack thereof. Because the conjunction may be "and" or "but," the two lines may be complementary or antithetical. Read as complementary ("and"), the proverb highlights how a king's reactions, like forces of nature, are beyond anyone's control but his own. Read as antithetical (NRSV: "but"), the proverb contrasts a king's *anger*, which is ferocious and life threatening (19:12a // 20:2a; cf. 14:35b; 16:15b; 24:21-22; 28:15), with a king's *favor*, which is predictable, abundant, and life-giving like morning dew (19:12b // 16:5b; e.g., 3:20; Gen 27:28; Exod 16:13). The association of kings (or future kings) and leaders with lions, a common phenomenon in the ancient Near East, is found elsewhere in the Old Testament—literally (e.g., Samson tears a lion apart with his bare hands, Judg 14:5-6; David pursues and slays lions single-handedly, 1 Sam 17:34-36; carved lions are elements of the royal throne, 1 Kgs 10:19-20 // 2 Chr 9:18-19) and metaphorically (e.g., Jer 50:17; Ezek 32:2-3; Zeph 3:3).

<u>19:13-14</u> Morning dew (19:12) gives way here to an irritating leaky roof and to causes of domestic misery seen from a male perspective. The first line, which is a close variant of 17:25a, reiterates how disastrous a foolish child is to a father (e.g., 10:1b; 15:20b; 17:21). The second line then shifts unexpectedly to a "wife's quarreling" (cf. 21:9, 19; 25:24; 27:15-16). Whereas the beginning of a quarrel is like unleashing a dam (17:14), constant

marital conflict is a steady drip that over time makes a home uninhabitable (cf. Eccl 10:18).

A "wise wife," by contrast, is a divine gift—implicitly more valuable than any wealth and house inherited from one's parents (19:14; cf. 12:4; 14:1; 18:22; 31:10-31). Whereas the bequest of property from fathers to sons was a predictable, common practice in ancient Israel (e.g., Gen 25:5-6; cf. Job 42:15), no human effort ensures a prudent companion. For the sages, that is the work of God.

19:15 Laziness causes people to fall into a "deep sleep" (Gen 2:21; 1 Sam 26:12; Job 4:13; cf. the verb of the same Hebrew root in Jon 1:5-6). They turn on their beds like a door on its hinges (26:14), oblivious to the happenings and urgencies of the world around them—including their own need to eat. Other proverbs describe the lazy as unwilling to plow their fields and tend their vineyards (20:4; 21:25; 24:30-32) and even to lift food to their mouths at the dinner table (19:24). Concern about laziness pervades Proverbs (e.g., 6:6-11; 10:26; 13:4; 15:19; 22:13; 26:16; 31:27).

19:16 Repetition in the first line (*šōmēr miṣwâ šōmēr napšô*) equates one who keeps a commandment (*miṣwâ*) with one who keeps "one's life" (*napšô*). In Proverbs, "commandment" typically refers to parental instruction (e.g., 2:1; 3:1; 4:4; 6:20), but ambiguity does not preclude divine teaching and law. The sages, after all, readily associate the two (e.g., 3:11-12). The referent for the third-masculine singular suffix ("*his* ways") in the second line is ambiguous; most likely, it is the "one who despises" (NRSV: "those who are heedless"), but it may be the parent who tries to teach him or her, or it may be God if "commandment" refers to divine law. The sages repeatedly associate instruction with life and folly with death (e.g., 7:2; 9:6, 18; 13:13).

19:17 Generosity pays. The proverb motivates by reversing assumptions. To be gracious toward those without money is to end up with money—literally and figuratively—because God, who assumes their debt, repays it (e.g., 14:21, 31; 17:5; 22:9; 28:8, 27; Matt 25:31-46).

19:18 Discipline is an investment in children and thus in the future (cf. 22:6). The particle *kî* in the first line may be causal (*"because* there is hope") or temporal (*"while* there is hope" NRSV, NASB). Further, because the conjunction may be read as "and" or "but," the two lines may be complementary or antithetical. If complementary ("and"), then 19:18b suggests that the pain of disciplining one's children is negligible compared to the certain death that children without discipline suffer for their wrongdoing (e.g., 13:24; 20:30; 22:15; 23:13-14; 29:15, 17). Not to discipline children is to hasten their death. If the two lines are antithetical ("but"), 19:8b warns against excessive punishment, perhaps in light of legal limits to parental discipline (Deut 21:18-21).

19:19 The Hebrew of this proverb and the relationship between its two lines are uncertain. It begins with an observation that the hothead "carries a fine" (*nōśē' 'ōneš*), or bears the penalty for his or her actions—an implicit encouragement to restrain one's anger (cf. 19:11). It ends with a warning against any attempt to rescue the hothead from those consequences. Not only will the angry not learn and likely repeat their wrongdoing, but their rescuers wind up trapped, consigned to intervene again and again. Juxtaposition of this proverb with 19:18 provides a contrast between the young who learn from parental discipline and hotheads who, in order to learn, must endure the consequences of their actions.

19:20 Reminiscent of the father's exordia in Proverbs 1–9, this is one of many injunctions to pay attention to instruction (e.g., 1:8; 4:1, 10; 23:12). "For the future" is literally "in your end" (5:11), an expression that may mean one's future generally (23:18; 24:14; NRSV); the latter days of one's life (e.g., Job 8:7; 42:12); one's eventual attainment of wisdom (NAB); or one's death (e.g., Num 23:10; 24:20; cf. NEB). Learn now so you may be wise later.

19:21 Picking up the word "advice" or "purpose" (19:20), this proverb distinguishes sharply between humans and God by juxtaposing the plural and the singular ("many plans" or "machinations," "the plan"), the devised and the realized ("in the mind," "established") and, in the second line, by using an independent personal pronoun for emphasis—"The plan of YHWH *it* will be established" (16:1, 3-4, 9; 20:24; 21:30-31).

19:22 The translation of and relationship between the two lines is debated. At issue are two terms in the first line that may be construed positively or negatively: (*a*) *ḥesed*, which means "loyalty" (e.g., 11:17; 20:6; e.g., NRSV) and, more rarely, "disgrace" or "reproach" (cf. 14:34; e.g., *TANAKH*, NAB) and (*b*) *taʾăwâ*, which means "desire" (e.g., NRSV) or "greed" (e.g., *TANAKH*, NAB; cf. 21:26). The second line reiterates the value of honesty over wealth (e.g., 16:8, 19; 19:1).

19:23 "The fear of the LORD—for life!" reads as a shorthand version of 14:27 (cf. 22:4; excursus in Proverbs 1). The second line is dubious but appears to celebrate benefits of a reverent life, namely, contentment and security (e.g., 1:33; 3:24-26).

19:24 The Hebrew particle *gam* ("*even* to the mouth") intensifies the ironic humor of this proverb. With food on the table right in front of them, the lazy starve because they are unwilling or unable (perhaps in their "deep sleep," 19:15) to lift a finger to feed themselves. They do not seize opportunities—even those within easy reach. Proverbs 26:15 is nearly identical.

19:25 The sages again urge receptiveness to discipline, here with the sharp contrast between striking scoffers, which has no effect on them (e.g., 9:7-8a; 15:12) but instructs the naive (e.g., 1:4; 14:15), and reproving the wise—for whom a corrective word is sufficient. Proverbs 21:11 is a variant.

19:26 Contrary to NRSV, the first line of this proverb is impersonal: "one who does violence to *a* father, one who chases away *a* mother." That the behavior is usually that of a criminal (e.g., 24:15; 28:24) makes the first word of the second line alarming— "a son." What appeared initially to be an attack on the household from *outside* that would merit the community's sympathy is instead an assault from *inside* and, as such, more grievous: the household suffers shame and public reproach (e.g., 20:20; 30:11).

19:27 This proverb, the only direct address to the child in 10:1–22:16, is puzzling and prompts many emendations. That it blatantly contradicts numerous exordia and proverbs urging attention—"*Stop*, my child, listening to discipline, *to stray* from words of instruction"—suggests it is probably ironic (e.g., 19:20). As did the Jewish interpreter Rashi (Solomon ben Isaac,

1040–1105 CE), NRSV tries to make sense of the contradiction by inverting the infinitives of the two lines. Other translations read the first line as conditional and the second as its consequence ("Stop listening . . . and you will stray," e.g., NIV, NASB).

19:28-29 The Hebrew three-letter roots *lyṣ* ("to mock") and *špṭ* ("to decide" or "judge") connect these two proverbs. Whereas 19:5 and 19:9 stipulate penalties for lying, 19:28 points to motivations for it. Play with sound associates the "worthless witness" (*ʿēd bĕliyyaʿal*), his speech (*yālîṣ*, "he mocks") and the consumption of iniquity: he "swallows" it (*yĕballaʿ*, cf. 18:8). Liars spit back what they internalize.

Ironically, the very justice the scoffers mock "is ready" for them (19:29). The verb denotes that something is established and certain (e.g., 4:26; Gen 41:32; Deut 13:14 [Heb. v. 15]); its passive form leaves every possibility for justice wide open.

PROVERBS 20

Literary Analysis

The chapter is an assortment of proverbs with, again, few indications of arrangement beyond the occasional shared word or theme. Catchwords or phrases include "person" or "man" (20:5, 6), "made clean" or "pure" (20:9, 11), "both alike" (20:10, 12), and "eye" (20:12, 13), while three proverbs play with alternate meanings of the Hebrew root *ʿārab* (20:16-17, 19). YHWH proverbs (20:10, 12, 22-24, 27) and proverbs about the king figure prominently (20:2, 8, 26, 28).

Exegetical Analysis

20:1 Taking up the term "mock" (19:28-29), the proverb personifies wine and beer—elsewhere signs of prosperity and delight (e.g., 3:10; 9:2, 5)—as troublemakers who thwart wise living (e.g., 23:29-35; 31:4-5). Two of its terms also evoke intoxication of a different sort: sex (Van Leeuwen 1997, 185). The Hebrew root for "brawler" is used to describe the "strange" woman or personified folly (7:11; 9:13; NRSV: "loud"), and the verb "to stagger" or "stray" recalls the father's caution not to "stagger" with the "strange" woman but instead with one's wife (5:19-20, 23). The wise understand that there are legitimate and problematic ways to engage in certain behaviors and they choose the former.

20:2 The first line of this proverb is nearly identical to 19:12a. In the second, the first verb plus its third-masculine singular object suffix can be understood as "bring the king's anger on himself" or "infuriates the king." The concluding phrase (ḥôṭēʾ napšô) may mean to commit a wrong against oneself or forfeit one's life (cf. on the king's anger, 14:35; 16:14; 24:21-22; 28:15).

20:3 Fools are utterly dishonorable. *Every* fool loves to start a fight (e.g., 17:14; 18:6; 22:10), even though honor is reserved for those who "turn away" from one—the verb can mean to avoid (30:30) or to abandon (e.g., 1 Kgs 13:33; Jer 4:28). On the heels of 20:2, one imagines the fool is stupid enough to pick a fight with the king.

20:4 Assonance associates the season (ḥōrep, "winter," e.g., Gen 8:22; Jer 36:22; Zech 14:8) with the work appropriate to it (yaḥărōš, "one ploughs")—that the lazy does not do. There are two primary seasons in Palestine: the wet, cool months (October–April) when crops were typically planted, and the dry, warm season (May–September), the time of harvest (e.g., Jer 8:20; Mic 7:1). Later at harvest time, when the lazybones "seeks," a verb that means variously "to ask," "demand," or "beg," there is nothing to be found (6:6-11; 10:4-5; 21:25; 24:30-34).

20:5 A person's thoughts are "deep waters" (cf. 18:4a) that the wise are able to draw up—in themselves and presumably others—and pour out as speech (e.g., 1:23; 10:11; 13:14; 15:2). "Deep waters" denotes abundance and mystery, even chaos (e.g., Ps 64:6 [Heb. v. 7]; Eccl 7:24), and "drawing up" water is notoriously hard work. Recall Rebekah's exertion to provide water for Abraham's servant and his camels (Gen 24:15-20; cf. Exod 2:15-19) and the Samaritan woman's desire for "living water" so that she would never again need to return to the well to fill her water jar (John 4:7-15).

20:6 Whereas many profess the celebrated virtue of loyalty (19:22), the rhetorical question, "Who can find?" suggests the trustworthy are few and far between (31:10; Eccl 7:24; cf. similar contrasts between many and few, e.g., 18:24; 31:29). The proverb may be a warning, an observation, or a pessimistic commentary on human hypocrisy. Repetition of "person" or "man" (*ʾîš*) in 20:6ab is paralleled in 20:5ab.

20:7 This proverb reiterates how intertwined are the generations (e.g., 10:1; 15:20; 17:6; 17:21, 25; 19:26; cf. 3:33). Those who "walk with integrity" (cf. 19:1) will not only have children, a sign of blessing, but their children will be "happy" (or "blessed"). The preposition "after" may be interpreted chronologically, physically, or metaphorically: the children follow in their parents' footsteps.

20:8 To "winnow" is to throw threshed grain (cf. 20:26) into the air, usually with a wooden shovel or fork, so that the wind may separate its components—grain, straw, chaff—by weight (e.g., Isa 28:27-28). Elsewhere in the Old Testament, the verb is used most frequently for God's scattering of wrongdoers as an act of judgment (e.g., Jer 31:10; Ezek 5:10-12; 20:23) and occurs alongside language of devastation: desolate lands with cities laid waste (e.g., Lev 26:33; Jer 51:2; Ezek 29:12), calamity (Jer 49:32), nations uprooted (1 Kgs 14:15), and people dispersed like "sheep for slaughter" (Ps 44:11 [Heb. v. 12]). The king's gaze thus discerns and expels "all wickedness" in a manner analogous to God's own justice (16:12; 20:28; 25:5; 29:14).

20:9 But the king cannot dispel all wickedness. No one—not the king, members of the royal court, or the royal family—can respond affirmatively to this rhetorical question. The proverb thus relativizes the description of royal power in 20:8 as it invites broader reflection about what it means to be human (16:1-15).

20:10 A balanced first line—"stone and stone, ephah and ephah"—ironically conveys economic *im*balance: the existence of different weights and dry measures. The language recalls the injunction against "stone and stone, great and small . . . ephah and ephah, great and small" (Deut 25:13-15). Proverbs repeatedly condemns false weights and measures as abhorrent to God (11:1; 20:23; cf. 16:11).

20:11 Reputations start early. Sound associates the *na'ar* ("young man" or "adolescent," cf. 1:4; Gen 22:12; Jer 1:6) with the verb *nākar* ("make oneself known"), for which the second line invites two possible readings. If the youth's actions are "pure and right," *nākar* is understood positively—the youth establishes a good name. If the youth's actions are not, the verb takes on its more negative connotation: the youth "acts as a stranger" or "disguises himself" (e.g., Gen 42:7; 1 Kgs 14:5-6). The same Hebrew root (*nākar*) is used to designate the *nokrîyyâ* ("strange" woman, 2:16; 5:20; 6:24; 7:5; cf. 23:27) and the *nokrî* ("strange" man, 5:10; cf. 27:2).

20:12 Active participles ("hearing . . . seeing") emphasize the capacity to perceive as divine gift. Possible implications of the claim include: (*a*) as creations of God, the attentive ear and eye are reliable; (*b*) the eye and ear should be used appropriately, that is, to pursue wisdom (e.g., 15:31; 17:24; Sir 17:6); or (*c*) if God created human perception, how much more God must perceive (e.g., Exod 4:11; Ps 94:9). The phrase "both alike" also concludes 20:10.

20:13 Closed eyes are a problem (20:12). The lazy love sleep (19:15), preferring to turn on their beds like a door on its hinges (26:14) than to plow their fields or tend their vineyards (20:4; 21:25; 24:30-32). As such, they go hungry. That the imperative in the second line breaks an idiom ("Open [your] eyes and see," e.g., Gen 21:19; 2 Kgs 6:17, 20) highlights the connection between get-up-and-go and abundant provision ("Open your eyes and *eat your fill* of bread!"). Concern about laziness pervades Proverbs (e.g., 6:6-11; 10:26; 13:4; 15:19; 19:15, 24; 22:13; 26:13, 15-16; cf. 31:27).

20:14 Quoted speech lends immediacy to this marketplace scene in which a haggler, likely with a shake of the head and wave of the hand, dismisses as "bad, bad" the product he aims to acquire, only later "to boast"—the verb suggests both to others and himself—about the purchase. The proverb may be interpreted as an observation about "trade talk" or as an indictment of self-congratulation, especially for dishonest gain (e.g., 25:14; 27:2).

<u>20:15</u> This proverb, one of many that extol the value of wisdom over precious metals and jewels (e.g., 3:13-15; 8:10-11, 19), provides an ironic contrast to the haggler and his prize (20:14). The proverb heightens its claim by juxtaposing *many* jewels (*pĕnînîm*, cf. 3:15; 8:10; 31:10) with *one* precious *kĕlî* ("vessel," "instrument," or "ornament"), namely, wise lips or speech. The result conveys the surpassing worth and relative rarity of wisdom.

<u>20:16</u> The sages of Proverbs caution repeatedly against the practice of "granting surety" (ʿārab, cf. 20:17, 19). The personal and financial risks are for them always prohibitive (6:1-5; 11:15; 17:18; 22:26-27; but cf. Sir 8:13) and extremely so in the case of surety for strangers who ostensibly have less social pressure to honor their commitments. Should a person be so foolish as to guarantee the loan of a stranger, the creditor might as well seize whatever is pledged, typically a garment (cf. Deut 24:10-13). Proverbs 27:13 is a close variant.

<u>20:17</u> This proverb invokes a second possible meaning of the Hebrew root ʿārab ("to be pleasant" or "sweet," cf. 20:16, 19) in its play with sensory expectations. "Bread of deceit" may refer literally to stolen food and, figuratively, to a steady diet of dishonesty. Reminiscent of the meal offered by personified folly (9:17), the bread is tasty at first, perhaps all the more so because one has "gotten away with it." But its aftertaste and texture are starkly otherwise: like "gravel." A mourner captures the sharpness of the metaphor:

> [God] has filled me with bitterness,
> . . . sated me with wormwood.
> [God has caused] my teeth [to] grind on gravel,
> and made me cower in [the dust]. (Lam 3:15-16)

Compare other proverbs that describe deceptive speech as junk food (18:8; 26:22).

<u>20:18</u> The general claim that wise people seek advice (e.g., 11:14; 13:10b; 15:22; 19:20) is given life-and-death expression in this proverb about waging war. The proverb's progression from establishing plans (20:18a) to conducting battle (20:18b) reinforces

its assertion about the necessity of good planning for (military) success. Compare 24:5-6.

20:19 The first line of this proverb is similar to 11:13a. "Babbler" in the second is one who "opens" lips, a verb that with the meanings "to chatter" and "to be inexpert and foolish" disparages both the quantity and quality of speech—akin to the present-day expression "loose lips." "Do not associate" invokes a third possible meaning for the Hebrew root *ʿārab* ("to get involved with someone," cf. 20:16, 17; 24:21). Slander is emblematic of personal and communal immorality, a mark of those who do not know God (e.g., Lev 19:16; Jer 9:3-6; Ezek 22:9). Compare the Egyptian *Instruction of Amenemope*:

> Broadcast not your words to others,
> Nor join with one who bares his heart.
> Better is one whose speech is in his belly
> Than he who tells it to cause harm. (*AEL* 2:159)

20:20 Cursing one's parents is likewise volatile speech. The law codes stipulate that the offense was punishable by death (Exod 21:17; Lev 20:9; cf. Deut 27:16), a penalty suggested by the metaphor of an extinguished lamp (e.g., 13:9; 24:20; Job 18:5-6; 21:17). That "lamp" may also refer to one's descendants (e.g., 1 Kgs 15:4) lends irony to the fate: those who curse their parents in turn find themselves without children. See 30:11.

20:21 The first word is "ancestral inheritance" (NRSV: "estate"). On the one hand, the proverb indicts those who wrongfully acquire the (family) property of others ("greedily," so the Kethib or written tradition; e.g., Ahab's seizure of Naboth's vineyard, 1 Kgs 21). On the other, it condemns attempts by family members to take control of their inheritance prematurely ("quickly acquired," so Qere or the vocalized tradition), a reading that reinforces the concern for parental respect in 20:20. Proverbs cautions repeatedly about wealth acquired hastily and by unjust means (e.g., 1:10-19; 10:2; 13:11; 15:6; 16:8; 28:8, 20b, 22). Although such gain seems good in the "beginning" (20:21a), "its end" (20:21b) is not.

20:22 This is the second of three "do not say" proverbs in the book (3:28; 24:29; cf. Eccl 5:5; Sir 5:3-4, 6; 15:11-12). The sages quote an unnamed opponent to refute a bad idea, here the instinct for personal retaliation. The proverb urges instead trust in God's justice and thereby a relinquishment of control over the timing ("wait") and nature of judgment.

20:23 This proverb is a variant of 20:10 and 11:1. Following 20:22, it reinforces God's commitment to justice.

20:24 Stark juxtaposition between the first words of each line ("from YHWH . . . but the human") underscores the tension between human choice and responsibility and God's sovereign freedom (e.g., 16:1-7, 9; cf. Ps 37:23-24; Jer 10:23). The second line may be construed variously—as a realistic reminder of human limitations, an expression of exasperation, or a cynical sigh of resignation.

20:25 Think before you act. To declare something "holy" is to consecrate it, to offer personal property to the temple for a specified or indefinite period (Lev 27). To "stammer carelessly" or rashly (cf. Job 6:3) about such matters is to trap oneself. The second line suggests why. Afterward, when it is time to make good on the vow, the gift giver is apparently unable or unwilling to do so; instead, he or she "searches" or "inquires" (contra NRSV: "reflects") for a way out, possibly with a substitute gift or by avoiding payment altogether. (For comparable cautions about the seriousness of a vow, see Judg 11:29-40; Eccl 5:4-6; Matt 14:1-12.)

20:26 Agricultural metaphors give vivid expression to royal justice. The first line is similar to 20:8b. The "wheel" in the second is debated, but refers arguably to the heavy wheel or drum rolled over grain to thresh it, or separate the seeds or grains from the straw (Isa 28:27-28). The Ode to Solomon makes analogous connections between a wheel, agricultural imagery, and royal government (Franzmann 1991). Notably, this proverb reverses the order we expect—in practice, threshing precedes winnowing. Perhaps the inversion serves to emphasize the comprehensive and perpetual effort of the king to eradicate wickedness.

20:27 "Spirit" here is not *rûaḥ* (e.g., 1:23; 15:4, 13; 16:2) but the less common *něšāmâ*—the "breath" breathed by God into the human body to give it life (Gen 2:7; cf. 7:22). The proverb entwines imagery of air and light (20:20) searching out the "inner parts" of the body, coursing through the deepest, hidden recesses of the self (18:8; 20:30). The proverb leaves the subject ambiguous: by means of the life breath, God knows our innermost thoughts (e.g., 15:11; 16:2; 17:3) and we are able to know ourselves (e.g., Job 32:7-8).

20:28 "Loyalty (*hesed*) and faithfulness" (20:28a; cf. 3:3; 14:22; 16:6) stand as royal guards. The word-pair likely refers to God's loyalty and faithfulness, which elsewhere are said to protect the king (e.g., Pss 40:11; 57:3 [Heb. v. 4]; 61:7 [Heb. v. 8]; cf. Pss 26:3; 89:24 [Heb. v. 25]). The second line turns to the king who, by his own practice of *hesed*, helps secure the vitality of his leadership (16:13).

20:29 At various moments in life different qualities garner respect. The term "youths" refers to strong, young adult men, typically those eligible for military service or assigned hard physical tasks (e.g., Isa 40:30; Jer 49:26; 50:30; 51:3; Lam 5:13); they include Saul who "stood head and shoulders above everyone else" (1 Sam 9:2). The second line recalls the description of gray hair as a crown in 16:31. Because the conjunction may be read as "and" or "but," the proverb may be construed as valuing the two moments in life equally (NASB) or as favoring the mark of age and wisdom over youthful vigor (NRSV). Some modern translations leave out the conjunction to preserve the ambiguity (*TANAKH*, NIV).

20:30 The text and translation of this proverb is uncertain but NRSV conveys its apparent sense. That physical discipline was understood to cleanse a person's "inner parts" (20:27) sheds light on the sages' repeated endorsement of corporal punishment (e.g., 13:24; 22:15; 23:13-14).

PROVERBS 21

Literary Analysis

Within a loose frame of YHWH proverbs (21:1-3, 30-31), the chapter offers assorted proverbs on various subjects. There are a few catchwords and phrases—"heart" or "mind" (21:1-2); "doing justice" (21:3, 7, 15); "joy" (21:15, 17); the verb "to instruct" or "observe" (*śākal*, 21:11-12); "desire" (21:25-26; cf. 21:10)—and two proverb pairs (21:5-6 and 30-31). Antithetical proverbs, prevalent in the first half of 10:1–22:16, recur with greater frequency here near its end; they comprise nearly a third of the chapter.

Exegetical Analysis

<u>21:1</u> God's sovereignty is celebrated again by God's rule over the king, the most powerful member of the human community (e.g., 16:1-15; 20:8-9, 28). By God's power ("in the hand of God," e.g., Deut 33:3; Eccl 9:1) and according to God's "desire" or "delight," a king's heart or innermost self turns like "streams of water," a metaphor that suggests channeled energy and a source of nourishment. Waterways and irrigation canals, particularly in a desert climate, are necessary for life to flourish (e.g., Ps 1:3; Isa 32:2; cf. Prov 5:16). God so directs a king's heart.

<u>21:2</u> Linked to 21:1 by the catchword "heart" or "mind," this close variant of 16:2 underscores God's authority over everyone, including the king (e.g., 16:10). The first line is, "Every *path* of a person is right in his [or her] eyes" (contra NRSV).

<u>21:3</u> The proverb stipulates God's preference for doing justice over doing religious rituals, a claim that resonates across the Bible (e.g., Ps 51:16-17 [Heb. vv. 18-19]; Isa 1:10-17; Hos 6:6; Amos 5:21-24; Matt 23:23; Mark 12:28-34). The comparative does not reject the value of sacrifices altogether (3:9; 15:8; 21:27).

<u>21:4</u> The sages sketch the arrogant with haughty eyes (e.g., 6:17; 30:13) and a "broad," or unrestrained, heart (Ps 101:5; cf. "greedy," 28:25). In the second line, *nîr* is "prepared soil or land that is cultivable for the first time" (e.g., 13:23a; Jer 4:3); NRSV follows ancient versions to read *nēr* ("lamp"). "Prepared soil" focuses attention on what the wicked cultivate (cf. 6:14b), while "lamp" connotes their very lives (e.g., 13:9; 20:20). Both "miss the mark" (NRSV: "are sin"; cf. Theological and Ethical Analysis of Proverbs 1).

<u>21:5-6</u> Means and ends occupy these two proverbs. The first contrasts the "plans of the diligent" with "everyone who hurries,"

presumably without a plan. Parallel phrases at the end of each line evaluate the consequences: plans lead "only [or certainly] to advantage" ('ak lĕmôṭār, cf. 14:23) and rushing around "only [or certainly] to lack" ('ak lĕmaḥsôr, cf. 19:2b). It pays to plan.

But deceitful plans and their profits afford no advantage (21:6). Illicit gains are *hebel* ("air," "vapor," or "breath," Ps 62:9 [Heb. v. 10]; Isa 57:13)—that which is ephemeral and unreliable (e.g., 31:30; Job 7:16; Eccl 1:2; Isa 30:7). "Fleeting" intensifies this illusory sense: elsewhere it modifies a fallen leaf (Lev 26:36; Job 13:25), dried-up plants (Isa 19:7), and chaff (Isa 41:2). Deceitful profit is short-lived and even perhaps deadly (e.g., 13:11; 28:20).

21:7 The opening noun *šōd*, which may mean "violence" (NRSV; cf. 24:2) or "destruction" (e.g., 11:3), is used for acts perpetrated against others (e.g., Hos 7:13; Hab 2:17) and the consequences of a person's conduct—often as an expression of God's judgment (e.g., Isa 13:6; Joel 1:15; Amos 5:9). The wicked sow what they reap. Indeed, it "sweeps" or "drags" them away like fish trapped in a fisherman's net (Hab 1:15).

21:8 The proverb is puzzling. The NRSV construes the obscure word *wāzār*, a *hapax legeomenon*, as cognate with an Arabic word meaning "to be burdened with guilt," but the rendering is speculative. Other translations, including some ancient versions (e.g., Vulgate, Syriac), interpret it as the conjunction ("and") plus *zār* ("strange") and read "crooked is the way of a person, and strange, but the pure—[his] work is right." The matter is not settled. But the alliteration and assonance that bind the end of the first line to the beginning of the second in the Hebrew are striking ('îš wāzār wĕzak yāšār).

21:9 Whereas 19:13b compares a wife's quarreling to a leaky roof, this "better than" proverb ushers readers up *onto* the roof, back into a corner, and says it is better to live *there*—alone and exposed to the elements—than down inside the house with such a companion (21:19; 25:24; 27:15-16).

21:10 Wordplay underscores how desire may distort a person's worldview (21:26): the wicked (*rāša'*) so crave evil (*rā'*) that they do not see the need of their neighbor (*rē'eh*).

21:11 The subject of the verb in the second line is ambiguous: "At the instruction of the wise, he gains knowledge." Who is "he"? If "he" is a naive person, as the parallel line suggests, the proverb gives two examples of how to teach him: by punishing the scoffer ("imposing a fine," cf. 17:26; Deut 22:19) and, more positively, by teaching the wise. If "he" refers to the wise person, however, the proverb suggests that education of the gullible requires more extreme measures than education of the wise, who readily embrace it. Compare 19:25.

21:12 Several matters complicate interpretation of this proverb. Most significant is the identity of "a righteous one" in the first line. Is it a human being (so ancient versions, RSV) or God (so NRSV and most modern translations)? The latter is arguably preferable because the sages typically designate God—not righteous people—as the agent of judgment (22:12) or leave the agent ambiguous. Moreover, "righteous" is used as a substantive adjective for God elsewhere (Isa 24:16). The proverb thus associates God's attentiveness to the wicked with God's (immediate) judgment of them. It also picks up the verb śākal ("to keep an eye on") from 21:11 (used there in a causative sense, "to instruct").

21:13 "Do unto others," enjoins this proverb. To "close one's ear" is to "stop it up"—to make oneself deaf (Ps 58:4-5 [Heb. vv. 5-6]; Isa 33:15). The terse opening phrase of the second line (gam-hû, "even that one") keeps the spotlight squarely on the one who chooses to ignore the poor, while lack of an object for "cries out" and the passive verbal form "not answered" invites reading comprehensively: no one, not even God, will respond when "that one" cries out (e.g., 14:31; 17:5; 19:17; 22:22-23; 28:27).

21:14 This proverb observes matter-of-factly the power of a bribe. The illicit gift subdues anger; it proves stronger than "strong wrath" (17:8, 23; 18:16; 19:6; but cf. 6:35).

21:15 The NRSV reads the opening phrase as a passive circumstantial clause ("when justice is done"), but it is rendered better as the active subject: "doing justice" (21:3, 7) is joy to the righteous, but it is "terror" or "ruin" (e.g., 13:3; 14:28; Isa 54:14; Jer 17:17) for those who "do iniquity"—that is, precisely the opposite.

21:16 Getting off track has grave consequences. Mention of the *rĕpā'îm*, spirits of the dead that inhabit the underworld, recalls descriptions of the "strange" woman's fatal path (e.g., 2:18; 9:18; cf. 7:25-27). Like many ancients, the Israelites believed Sheol was a gated, dark, silent, and dusty place to which the deceased descended after death (e.g., Job 17:13-16; Ps 31:17; Isa 38:10-11). Imprisoned there, the deceased or shades pass their days in a sort of reclined stupor, stirred occasionally by new arrivals (e.g., Isa 14:9-11) including, apparently, those who stray from wisdom's path.

21:17 Not every joy (NRSV: "pleasure") should be pursued with abandon. "One who loves joy" is identified in the second line more narrowly as "one who loves wine and oil"—liquids that, particularly together, suggest prosperity and indulgence, feasting and anointing the body (e.g., 9:1-6; Eccl 9:7-8; Song 1:2-3; Amos 6:6). When what are ordinarily benefits of hard work (e.g., 3:10; 31:16) become the goals of one's affection and effort, poverty soon follows.

21:18 This proverb echoes the notion of justice found in 11:8—when the righteous are in trouble (perhaps caused by the wicked), the wicked "switch places" with them. A *kōper* may be a "bribe" (e.g., 6:35; 1 Sam 12:3; Amos 5:12), which implies the righteous are innocent, or a "ransom to avoid punishment" (e.g., Exod 21:30; Isa 43:3), which connotes guilt. Isaiah 43:3-4 is suggestive; addressing Israel in exile, God interweaves assurances of divine love, protection, and redemption for God's people:

> I give Egypt as your ransom,
> Ethiopia and Seba in exchange for you.
> . . . .
> I give people in [exchange] for you,
> nations in exchange for your life.

21:19 The sages propose putting greater distance between oneself and a contentious wife, moving readers from the corner of a rooftop (21:9) into a "desert land," a place of comparative if not complete solitude (e.g., Job 38:26; Jer 9:2 [Heb. v. 1]) and fierce wildness (e.g., Judg 8:7; Job 24:5; Lam 4:3) that is preferable, even at its most dangerous, to the misery of a quarreling spouse.

21:20 Imbalance between the Hebrew of the first line (five words) and comparatively brief second line (three words) reinforces the proverb's claim about the material disparity between the wise and foolish. The term *'ôṣār* may mean "treasure" (e.g., Jer 15:13; 17:3) or "supplies," such as grain and wine (e.g., 21:6; Neh 13:12); similarly, "oil" may be a luxury (e.g., 21:17; Amos 6:6) or a household staple (e.g., 1 Kgs 17:12; 2 Kgs 4:2). The wise enjoy abundant and ready resources (e.g., 3:9-10; 8:21; 24:3-4)—they gather and save over time—while fools "swallow" theirs and are quickly left with nothing.

21:21 The NRSV reads the second line with LXX; the Hebrew of the line includes "righteousness," suggesting that those who pursue righteousness and kindness find what they seek and, along the way, also accrue welcome benefits—life and honor (e.g., 3:1-4, 16; 8:17-21, 35; Matt 6:33).

21:22 This brief narrative celebrates wisdom over brute strength (20:18; 24:5-6) by juxtaposing one wise person (sg.) with a city of warriors (pl.) and describing the wise person's success in military terms: "to go up" can refer to an army's advance (e.g., 1 Sam 7:7; 1 Kgs 20:22; Isa 7:1) and "to bring down" to the conquest or destruction of enemies (e.g., Ps 59:11 [Heb. v. 12]; Amos 3:11). Compare Eccl 9:13-18.

21:23 A variation of 13:3a and 18:21a, this proverb practices what it preaches. Advocating careful speech, it uses balanced lines (three words each), assonance (long o recurs six times), repetition (the imperative "Guard!" is the first word of both lines), and wordplay: to safeguard the mouth and tongue (organs of speech) is to protect the *nepeš*, namely, the "throat" or "neck"—the windpipe through which one breathes—and, by metonymy, the "life" or "self."

21:24 Framed by the adjective "presumptuous" (21:24a) and the noun "presumptuousness" from the same root (21:24b), this proverb inundates readers with terms that describe and indeed define (24:8) the scoffer—a figure of considerable concern in Proverbs (e.g., 1:22; 9:7-8; 13:1; 14:6; 15:12).

21:25 The sluggard is his own victim. The proverb illustrates this by ascribing agency to the sluggard's desire (presumably to be lazy), which "kills" him, and to his hands, which "refuse" to work (e.g., 6:6-11; 10:4, 26; 12:24, 27; 19:15).

21:26 The motif of "desire" continues (21:10, 25) with this contrast between those who focus on their desires "all day long" and the righteous who, with equivalent single-mindedness ("do not hold back"), give to others. Read alongside 21:25, the proverb accentuates the inactivity of the lazy and (re)frames their desire as selfish.

21:27 The first line is nearly identical to 15:8a, but lack of "to YHWH" (cf. 15:8a) suggests the sacrifices of the wicked are repugnant generally—to God and human alike ("abomination to all," 24:9). The second line intensifies the censure depending on one's motives; *zimmâ* ("plan") is nearly always negative (NRSV: "*evil* intent," e.g., 10:23; 24:9 [where it is parallel to scoffing]; but cf. Job 17:11). The proverb leaves open what the wicked intend— whether to ridicule religious rituals and those who participate in them, to make a public display of piety to distract from on-going misdeeds, to curry divine and human favor, or some other possibility.

21:28 The first line retells the grim fate of the false witness (esp. 19:5, 9; cf. 6:19; 12:17; 14:5; 19:28). Focus on the listener's *speech* in the second line implies the liar's testimony also perishes; the liar does not have the last word. Rather, those who listen speak credibly and convincingly. Their words endure (e.g., Job 23:7).

21:29 The "hardened face" of the wicked, like that of the "strange" woman (7:13), signals bold defiance. The wicked are obstinate about going their way, regardless of how misguided it may be. In contrast, the upright "establish" (so the Kethib or written tradition) and "understand" or "discern" their ways (so the Qere or vocalized tradition). The first reading suggests the upright maintain a steady course; the second, that they consider it carefully (e.g., 4:25-27; 14:15; 16:9; but cf. 20:24).

21:30-31 The chapter concludes with a proverb pair that reasserts the limits of human wisdom before God. Repetition of

ʾ*ên* ("there is no . . . there is no . . . there is no," 21:30) serves as a sort of threefold exclamation mark, reminding readers that, like the waters circumscribed by God in creation (8:29), wisdom is an enterprise bounded by divine sovereignty and mystery (e.g., 3:5; 16:1-9; 19:21).

The second proverb (21:31) gives a concrete example. Even with the finest of resources and planning, no one but God can guarantee success (Pss 33:13-17; 76:6 [Heb. v. 7]). Horses in ancient Israel symbolized power and wealth. Not native to the region, they were imported, making them costly to purchase and maintain. As such, few people beyond kings, nobles, and armies rode them (e.g., Deut 17:16; 1 Kgs 10:26-29; Esth 6:8-9; Eccl 10:7). Other texts caution against trusting too much in one's horses—in one's military might—instead of trusting in God (e.g., Ps 20:6-8 [Heb. vv. 7-9]; Isa 31:1, 3; Hos 14:3 [Heb. v. 4]; Hag 2:22).

PROVERBS 22:1-16

Literary Analysis

The first sixteen verses of the chapter, which close the first Solomonic section of the book (see Introduction to Proverbs 10:1–22:16), reflect the mix of themes and literary forms typical of the last few chapters. Whereas the early chapters of 10:1–22:16 were intent on distinctions between righteous and wicked, wise and foolish, the prevalent topic here is wealth and poverty (22:1-2, 4, 7, 9, and 16). Further, the sages admonish readers directly to discipline children (22:6; cf. 22:15), as compared to earlier observations about the effects of wise and foolish children on their parents (e.g., 10:1, 5; 13:1, 24; 14:26; 15:20; cf. 19:18). The proverbs are of assorted genres, including a "better than" proverb (22:1), YHWH proverbs (22:2, 4, 12, 14), imperatives (e.g., 22:8, 10), synthetic proverbs (e.g., 22:5, 7, 9), and antithetical proverbs (22:3, 12).

Exegetical Analysis

22:1 A name (following most ancient versions, NRSV adds "good") in life and after death is far more valuable than riches, which are comparatively fleeting—even when they are *rab*, an adjective that refers to quality (NRSV: "great") and/or quantity ("many" or "much"; cf. 10:7; Eccl 7:1). Ben Sira claims similarly: "Have regard for your name, since it will outlive you / longer than a thousand hoards of gold; / The days of a good life are numbered / but a good name lasts forever" (Sir 41:12-13; cf. Isa 56:5). The Egyptian *Instruction of Amenemope* concurs: "Better is praise with the love of men / than wealth in the storehouse" (*AEL* 2:156).

22:2 The verb in the first line—"encounter one another" (e.g., 22:13; Ps 85:10 [Heb. v. 11]; NRSV: "have this in common")—suggests a chance meeting of the rich and the poor who, despite their vastly different socioeconomic circumstances, share a Creator and thus a common humanity ("YHWH is the maker of *all of them*," cf. 29:13). The sages appeal to this notion frequently to urge generosity to the poor (e.g., 14:31; 17:5; 19:17).

22:3 Two people went out for a walk one day. The clever person saw (*rā'â*) wickedness (*rā'â*) and hid, but the naive person continued on and "paid for it," a verb that connotes payment of a fine or similar punishment (e.g., 17:26; 21:11). The ability to look ahead and anticipate trouble is a mark of wisdom (27:12 is nearly identical to this proverb; e.g., 12:16, 23; 13:16; 14:8, 15, 18).

22:4 "Reward" is related to the Hebrew word for "heel" or "hind quarters" and, like the English expression "on the heels of," it refers to the ends or consequences of something (e.g., Pss 19:11 [Heb. v. 12]; 119:33, 112). The simple juxtaposition of "humility" and "fear of the LORD" in the first line affords two possible interpretations: (*a*) "fear of the LORD," like the benefits listed in the second line, is a consequence of humility (e.g., *TANAKH* and several ancient versions), or (*b*) "fear of the LORD" and humility together lead to prosperity and honor (NRSV). Given the close association of reverence and humility elsewhere (e.g., 15:33), the second reading is more likely. The proverb urges humility and reverence—*not* prosperity—as aspirations (21:21; e.g., 3:1-4, 16; 8:17-19, 35; 11:27; 18:22; 24:14); it should not be "absolutized (as in a prosperity gospel, which says, 'God wants you to be rich')," as R. C. Van Leeuwen rightly cautions (1997, 198).

<u>22:5</u> Although the wicked cannot avoid the thorns and trapping nets in their way (e.g., 1:17-19; 5:22; 11:6), those who guard their lives (NRSV: "the cautious") keep their distance from "them"; the antecedent for "them" is most likely "thorns and snares" but may be the "crooked." The cautious pay attention to the road, taking deliberate steps to avoid trouble—and those who provoke it.

<u>22:6</u> The catchword "way" associates this proverb with 22:5, but the sages turn now to urge training of the young (e.g., 19:18; 29:17). The verb "to train up" (NRSV) elsewhere in the Old Testament always means "to dedicate," whether the temple or a house (Deut 20:5; 1 Kgs 8:63; 2 Chr 7:5); the noun derived from the same root (ḥănukkâ, "dedication") is used most frequently with religious objects, such as the temple (Ps 30:1; cf. the city walls, Neh 12:27) and altars (e.g., Num 7:10-11, 84, 88; 2 Chr 7:9). Recall that the Feast of Hanukkah commemorates the rededication of the temple in 165/164 BCE after its desecration by Antiochus Epiphanes IV (cf. 1 Macc 4:36-61; 2 Macc 2:19; 10:1-8; John 10:22). The verb thus conveys some sort of dedication, perhaps formally and perhaps with religious connotations. That the person so dedicated is a na ʿar suggests to T. Hildebrandt the issue is social position (i.e., a "squire" to someone of high rank; 1988a, esp. 10-14). But na ʿar commonly refers to a "youth" whose age may vary from childhood to adolescence—in Proverbs, a gullible yet teachable young person (e.g., 1:4; 7:7; 22:15; 23:13; 29:15). The parent is to dedicate the youth "in the right way" (NRSV), literally "according to *his* way"; the possessive suffix indicates the "way" is specific to the youth, not a uniform or universal path. The sense is that parents must orient and commit (perhaps publicly) the youth on the way that best ensures his or her maturity into wise adulthood and, eventually, "old age," a blessing of wisdom (e.g., 17:6; 20:29). "*Even* when old" (22:6b), the youth will not stray from it.

The proverb reiterates the sages' conviction that parents are responsible for vigorous instruction of the young. It sees a straight path from early discipline to long life and well-being. At the same time, the sages recognize that the young must choose again and again to stay on that path (e.g., 3:21-26; 4:10-27; 9:1-6, 13-18;

10:5). So we must be careful: not every "wicked" adult is so because parents shirked their responsibility.

22:7 Despite the common humanity of rich and poor (22:2), the sages recognize that economic disparities fuel disparities in power and social position (cf. 6:1-5). Parallelism equates borrowers with the poor (cf. 19:17).

22:8 On the heels of 22:7 comes a caution against the abuse of power. The metaphor "sow and reap" is used commonly to describe the relationship of acts and consequences (e.g., 1:31; 11:18b; Job 4:8; cf. Hos 8:7; Gal 6:7-10). The Hebrew of the second line is somewhat obscure. The "rod of his fury [or excess]" (cf. 21:24; NRSV omits the possessive suffix) may refer literally or metaphorically to (a) a scepter of authority (e.g., Isa 14:5-6); (b) a weapon (e.g., 2 Sam 18:14; 23:21); or, continuing the agricultural imagery of the first line, (c) a stick used for threshing grain (e.g., Isa 28:27). That on which the unjust rely to sow harm will inevitably fail.

22:9 "Generous" is "good of eye," an expression that suggests a gracious expression and attentive, kind regard for others. Its opposite, "evil of eye" (i.e., stinginess, cf. Deut 15:9), occurs in 23:6 and 28:22. The passive verb "are blessed" leaves open the agent of the blessing, presumably God or the poor for whom the generous provide (cf. 10:6; 11: 26; 14:21; 19:17; 31:20).

22:10 This proverb evokes a gang of thugs led by the scoffer (cf. pride and shame as traveling companions, 11:2). If one drives away the ringleader, the others respond variously: strife wanders off, quarreling and abuse take a break. The notion that getting rid of a troublemaker restores communal well-being prompts Sarah, for example, to demand that Abraham "drive out" Hagar and Ishmael (Gen 21:10) and Gilead's sons to "drive away" Jephthah (Judg 11:2).

22:11 The problematic Hebrew of this proverb prompts many conjectural emendations. Further, the relationship between the three phrases is ambiguous—"one who loves a pure heart," "gracious are his lips," and "his friend is the king." Does love of a pure heart lead to gracious speech and royal friendship? Or do a pure heart and gracious speech garner the king's favor (NRSV)?

Both interpretations are possible and highlight the (ideal) correlation of integrity and access to power (cf. 16:13). Parallelism reinforces again the intimate connection between the "heart" and "lips" (e.g., 10:8; 16:21; 24:2; cf. Job 33:3).

<u>22:12</u> Parallelism closely associates knowledge and a vital means of its expression: words (cf. 5:2). God has purview and power over both, safeguarding the former and subverting the latter when distorted and dangerous (cf. 15:3; 21:12).

<u>22:13</u> No excuse is too absurd for the lazy. One pictures the sluggard curled up inside (e.g., 19:15, 24; 26:14-15) and pointing outside, stammering about an imaginary lion wandering the streets (cf. 26:13). Wordplay links the "lion" (ʾărî) to the sluggard's alleged fate, "I will be killed!" (ʾērāṣēaḥ), while the exclamation intimates that the attack on the sluggard is an injustice to everyone—the verb rāṣaḥ ("to kill") is typically used for a homicide that particularly offends the community, such as the killing of an innocent citizen (e.g., Num 35:16-21, 31; Deut 22:26; Job 24:14). The sluggard's unprecedented use of the verb to describe an animal attack and, implicitly, to characterize himself as innocent lends further ridiculousness to the claim.

<u>22:14</u> An old acquaintance, the "strange" woman, appears here for the first time since Proverbs 1–9—and in the plural, suggesting a significant threat (unlike the sluggard's lion, 22:13). The pressing issue again is her mouth or speech (e.g., 2:16-19; 5:3-4; 7:5, 21). The "deep pit" is likely a hunter's trap dug into the ground (Jer 18:20, 22; cf. Ps 35:7), an image that evokes the "strange" woman as a huntress (e.g., 7:12, 21-27; cf. 6:26); the noun "pit" is also derived from the verb used to describe her path—it "sinks down" to death, namely, to *the* Pit (2:18). Whereas the "wife of one's youth" is a well of water (5:15-20), the mouth of the "strange" woman is a snare that God uses as an instrument of divine wrath. Proverbs 23:27, the only other proverb outside of Proverbs 1–9 to mention the "strange" woman, pushes the claim further: *she* is the pit (cf. similar metaphors in the Babylonian *Dialogue of Pessimism*, "Woman is a pitfall—a pitfall, a hole, a ditch," *BWL* 147).

<u>22:15</u> Folly is characterized as innate in children, so "bound up in" their hearts that at times it must be driven out by physical

discipline (e.g., 13:24; 23:13-14; 29:15). With the same verb ("to bind"), the father of Proverbs 1–9 commends fetters of a different sort: parental instruction (6:21; cf. 3:3; 7:3).

22:16 The proverb observes a quandary for anyone trying to get ahead. There are, it suggests, two options: (a) oppress the poor, take everything you can from the needy; or (b) give to the rich (perhaps a bribe, e.g., 15:27; 17:8, 23; 21:14), the very people who do not need it, and end up with nothing. Presumably, the rich accept the gift, but with an abundance of money already, need not change their behavior or bestow favor because of it. Given the options, one understands why in practice those who strive to gain an advantage typically do so at the expense of the poor—an observation that lends urgency to the sages' frequent assertions that God is aligned with and protective of the poor (e.g., 14:31; 17:5; 22:22).

PROVERBS 22:17–24:22:
"WORDS OF THE WISE"

Introduction and Literary Analysis

The 1923 publication of the Egyptian *Instruction of Amenemope* sparked new energy for the study of Proverbs and Old Testament Wisdom literature more generally. Dated to the late second millennium BCE and written as thirty instructions of Amenemope to his youngest son, the *Instruction* promotes the "ideal man," who is self-controlled, quiet, honest, kind, and humble, over against his irascible counterpart, the "heated man" (*AEL* 2:146-163). Striking resemblances between *Amenemope* and 22:17–24:22 (particularly 22:17–23:11) stirred considerable and ongoing debate as to whether and how the two might be related. Although scholars have made various proposals, including that the Egyptian text is dependent on 22:17–24:22 or that both derive from a prior Hebrew or Egyptian original, the majority today consider this section of Proverbs an artful adaptation of *Amenemope*.

If this is so, then readers move from wisdom identified explicitly as Israelite ("the proverbs of Solomon," cf. 1:1; 10:1) to internationally inspired instructions, a trajectory that becomes explicit at the end of the book with two sections that are or are made to appear foreign: Agur (30:1-33) and King Lemuel's mother (31:1-9). That the transition occurs rather seamlessly in MT—"Incline your ear and hear the words of the wise"—suggests movement between Israelite and foreign wisdom is rather ordinary (22:17a; NRSV reads "the words of the wise" as a superscription, presumably on the basis of 24:23a). The sages assume their work entails a sort of "intellectual ecumenism," a honing of thought on the wisdom of the ages and the cultures that precede and surround them (Fontaine 2002, 16). At the same time, because the sages rework *Amenemope* by, for example, drawing freely from its disparate sections; replacing less familiar Egyptian elements with Hebrew analogies (e.g., "casket of the belly" becomes "belly" in 22:18); adding Hebrew expressions without Egyptian parallels (e.g., "redeemer" in 23:11); inserting an unparalleled theological objective ("so that you may trust in the LORD," 22:19); and including an abundance of self-reference ("my words," "my teaching"), they teach that the borrowing of traditions and texts is not done mechanically but critically, mindful of one's context and purposes.

Although MT lacks a superscription, readers experience a shift to direct and personal address at 22:17 after a paucity of the same in 10:1–22:16 (only 14:7; 16:3; 19:18, 19b, 27; 20:20; 22:10). Moreover, use of repeated exordia (e.g., 22:17; 23:19, 22, 26), the address "my son" (five times in 23:15–24:22), and heightened attention to family and household (e.g., 23:15-16, 22-25; 24:3), sparks a sense of déjà vu: this revised "foreign" wisdom reads much like Proverbs 1–9. It is taught as "mother-wit," knowledge passed from parent to child. The implied reader, however, no longer sits in quite the same place as the youth of Proverbs 1–9 (see Theological and Ethical Overview).

The literary and linguistic landscape also continues to change. All but gone are antithetical proverbs (23:17; 24:16). Front and center are positive and negative admonitions, many of which extend the almost exclusive use of two-line proverbs to include three-line proverbs and longer units (23:29-35; 24:30-34).

Further, rhetorical questions (e.g., 22:27b; 24:12, 22) and conditional statements (e.g., 22:27a; 23:13b, 15; 24:10-12a, 14b) occur more frequently. One even finds a riddle (23:29-30). The "words of the wise" thus contribute to the reader's repertoire of and facility with wisdom genres and pedagogy, whereas its similarities to Proverbs 1-9 and heavy use of direct address resummon readers, regardless of location in life, to listen—to renew the attentive, receptive posture most conducive for becoming wise (e.g., 2:1-5).

Theological and Ethical Overview

Whereas 10:1–22:16 spoke of assorted social roles, the shift to direct address in 22:17–24:34 puts the implied reader in more of them. Addressed variously as a youth in the family home (e.g., 23:15-16, 19-21, 22-25, 26-28; 24:13-14), an adult responsible for building and tending a household (23:13-14; 24:3-4, 27; cf. 24:30-34), a neighbor and citizen (22:22-23, 28-29; 23:10; 24:28), a commoner (e.g., 22:26-27), a present or potential member of the royal court (22:29; 23:1-5), and a military leader (24:6), readers move "between" social roles (Brown 2004, 169). Even the teacher-parent aims to prepare them for a "between" position, that of a messenger (22:21; cf. 25:13; 26:6)—an important responsibility in the ancient world. This sense of being "between," of moving back and forth from one role to another, suggests a time of social transition, a time when the reader is poised to assume new opportunities and responsibilities.

Threshold or liminal seasons in life are notably precarious, as our own experiences may testify, whether of puberty, leaving home, marriage, a new job, divorce, death, and so on. When we are betwixt and between, there is greater potential to either embrace or reject personal and communal values. The teacher of 22:17–24:34 employs several strategies to keep readers on "the way" to a good future (23:18; 24:14; cf. 24:20). First, the teacher speaks authoritatively and personally—as one of the wise who is savvy in the ways of the world (e.g., 23:1-9; 29-34; 24:5-7, 23b-26) and a parent whose commitment is intimate and unwavering (22:17-21; 23:15-16, 19, 22-28; 24:13-14, 21-22). Wearing both mantles, the teacher conveys consistency between "what your parents taught you" and the wisdom of the "real world" (cf. Introduction to Proverbs 1:8–9:18). Second, the teacher cautions repeatedly about getting involved with the wrong crowd. Prevalent are the admonishments "make no friends with" (22:24), "do not be among" (22:26; 23:20; cf. 24:15), and "do not envy" (23:17; 24:1, 19; cf. 3:31). Shifting loyalties often accompany periods of transition and can all too easily go wrong. Finally, the teacher offers specific advice about how to navigate new situations wisely. For the first time in Proverbs, we learn how to eat at a ruler's table (23:1-5) and recognize a reluctant host (23:6-9). There are also extended warnings about excessive drinking, eating, and overwork (23:4-5, 20-21, 29-35). Throughout, the teacher endeavors to keep the reader's attention, motivate avoidance of anyone engaged in mayhem and violence, inspire self-restraint and hard work, and promise that wisdom will lead (nearly inevitably, 24:16) to a happy, prosperous future (22:29; 24:4, 13-14). Even in the seemingly most mundane of matters, choices today dramatically shape tomorrow.

The "words of the wise" are not only about personal well-being and advancement, however. Interwoven are poignant appeals for moral courage. The teacher subtly shifts theological weight from God's sovereignty as the mysterious boundary of human wisdom—a dominant theme of 16:1–22:16—to God's sovereignty as motivation for justice and compassion, particularly on behalf of those in peril: the poor and afflicted for whom God pleads (22:22-23), the orphans for whom God is the redeemer (23:10-11), and those unjustly "taken away to slaughter" for whom God looks for rescuers (24:10-12; cf. Brown 2004, 166). The teacher confronts those who strive to get ahead with the reality of injustice and suffering. Readers cannot avoid it, minimize it, or deny knowing about it—tendencies of we who live in the modern West (Taylor 1989, 12-14). Moreover, the teacher sets that suffering within an expansive cosmic, historical, and global frame: God, "your ancestors" (22:28; 23:10; cf. 15:25), "peoples" and "nations" (24:24) are on the side of the wronged. How we respond to or fail in the face of injustice is thus known and judged by God, our forebears, and the world.

Exegetical Analysis

22:17-21 An extended exordium reminiscent of those in Proverbs 1–9 (e.g., 1:8-9; 3:1-2; 5:1-2) signals the beginning of a new section. What the NRSV sets apart as a superscription—"the words of the wise" (cf. 24:23a)—is in the Hebrew part of the opening phrase: "Incline your ear and hear the words of the wise" (22:17a). The tone is personal and urgent, presumably to capture attention. The teacher addresses the reader directly (e.g., "yes, to *you!*" 22:19), emphasizes the timeliness of the instruction ("today," 22:19), and extols his or her efforts already on the student's behalf ("I have made known to you. . . . Have I not written for you?" 22:19-20). Body language also figures prominently. The student is to keep the instruction heard by "your ear" deep "in your belly" from where it may be drawn up as speech "ready on your lips" (e.g., 2:2-3; 5:1-2; 18:4; 20:5; excursus in Proverbs 2). Compare the opening lines of the first chapter of *Amenemope*:

> Give your ears, hear the sayings,
> Give your heart to understand them;
> It profits to put them in your heart,
> Woe to him who neglects them!
> Let them rest in the casket of your belly,
> May they be bolted in your heart. (*AEL* 2:149)

At the heart of the exordia is the goal of the teaching—"so that you may trust YHWH" (22:19; *Amenemope* includes no equivalent reference to the divine). Yet a much-debated word in 22:20 obscures details about the teaching's composition. The Kethib, or written tradition, suggests "three days ago" or "previously" (*šilšôm*), while the Qere, or vocalized tradition, reads rather nonsensically, "officers" or "soldiers" (*šālîšîm*). The ancient versions struggled, proposing variously "in three ways" or "three times over" (LXX, Vulgate) or "three times" (Targum, Syriac). And since the discovery of *Amenemope*, many modern interpreters and translations—including NRSV—read "thirty" (*šělōšîm*) in light of the injunction "look to these thirty chapters" near the conclusion of that work (*AEL* 2:162). The proposal is intriguing but contentious.

Debate continues as to whether thirty distinct "chapters" or teachings may be identified in this section of Proverbs.

However one resolves the dilemma, the teacher intends the instruction to model honesty ("to show you") so that the student may respond reliably to those who send him or her—that is, be a trustworthy messenger (e.g., 13:17; 25:13; 26:6). The prologue of *Amenemope* similarly stipulates as a purpose: "Knowing how to answer one who speaks, / To reply to one who sends a message" (*AEL* 2:148). Trustworthy messengers were particularly important in the ancient world where, without the conveniences of a postal service, phones, or e-mail, people had to depend on others not only to represent and communicate clearly for them, but to persevere through the many hardships associated with travel (e.g., difficult terrain, limited water and shelter, bad weather, impassable roads, wild animals, and bandits). A reliable messenger was vital and valuable; an unreliable one—trouble.

22:22-23 The teacher gives two reasons not to steal from the poor or crush the afflicted at the "gate," the center of communal justice and power (e.g., 1:21; 8:1-3; 24:7; Deut 21:19). The first, "because they are poor," simply observes that the poor do not have much and are vulnerable; one should not take advantage of them (22:16). The second is theological: because God "pleads their plea" (*yārîb rîbām*) even as God "robs those who rob them" (*qāba' 'et-qōbĕ'ēhem*). Repetition of the Hebrew roots stresses God's evenhanded justice. God defends the defenseless (e.g., 14:31; 17:5) and does to oppressors what they do to the poor (a principle of equivalent retaliation known as *lex talionis*, e.g., Gen 9:6; Exod 21:23-25; Deut 19:21). The second chapter of *Amenemope* begins likewise—"Beware of robbing a wretch, / Of attacking a cripple" (*AEL* 2:150).

22:24-25 The teacher cautions again about the company one keeps (e.g., 1:10-19; 13:20; 16:29). Unable to restrain their anger, hotheads explode with little warning, igniting conflict and bringing adverse consequences on themselves (e.g., 12:16; 14:17; 19:19; 29:22)—much like the "heated man" in *Amenemope* (e.g., "Do not befriend the heated man nor approach him for conversation," *AEL* 2:154). The second proverb (22:25) gives the rationale:

you will learn their ways and, as a result, imperil your "life." The final word leaves no doubt about what is at stake (cf. Theological and Ethical Analysis of Proverbs 1).

22:26-27 One ought to also avoid those who "strike hands"— who, with a handshake, pledge their property to guarantee another's debt (6:1-5; 11:15; 17:18; 20:16; 27:13; but cf. Sir 8:13; 29:14-20). Whereas biblical law stipulates that the cloaks of debtors must be returned to them at night (presumably because they sleep on the floor with a cloak as covering, e.g., Exod 22:25-26; Deut 24:12-13), there is no comparable provision for guarantors. The teacher's question emphasizes the risk: if guarantors cannot pay, they stand to lose their beds, a relative luxury (e.g., 7:17; 1 Kgs 1:47; Isa 57:2), and will have to sleep on the floor— where debtors do.

22:28 Whereas 15:25 heralds God's protection of the widow's boundaries (cf. 23:10-11), this proverb argues for their inviolability on the basis of history. The property marker is "ancient," one that "your ancestors" set up to designate allotments of the land given by God to Israel (Deut 19:14). The Old Testament soundly condemns violating another's property rights, particularly those of the marginalized (e.g, Deut 27:17; Job 24:2; Isa 5:8; Hos 5:10). *Amenemope* cautions:

> Do not move the markers on the borders of the fields,
>   Nor shift the position of the measuring cord.
> Do not be greedy for a cubit of land,
>   Nor encroach on the boundaries of the widow.
> The trodden furrow worn down by time. (*AEL* 2.151)

22:29 With, "Do you see?" (e.g., 26:12; 29:20) the teacher invites readers to observe for themselves that one skilled in "his work" (*mĕlā'ktô*) ends up in the presence of "kings" (*mĕlākîm*). The pun reinforces their association. The "skilled" are able and experienced at what they do, such as proficient writers and interpreters (e.g., Ezra 7:6; Ps 45:2) and, in the case of the Davidic king, seek justice (Isa 16:5). They "stand before" (NRSV: "serve") kings, an idiom that connotes presenting oneself in the court of the powerful, as Moses does before Pharaoh (Exod 9:13; cf. Josh 24:1). *Amenemope*'s closing observation is similar: "The scribe who is skilled in his office, / He is found worthy to be a courtier" (*AEL* 2:162).

23:1-3 If you find yourself in a ruler's presence (22:29), watch your manners. The teacher urges paying attention to *everything* by using the injunction "Observe carefully!" (*bîn tābîn*, not simply "look") followed by the relative *ʾăšer*, which can mean "what" or "who." Then, with wordplay, the teacher commends utter self-restraint—a knife "to your throat" (*bělō ʿekā*) for the "(owner of) an appetite/throat" (*ba ʿal nepeš*). The food is not what it seems. The delicious morsels (e.g., 23:6; Gen 27:4, 7, 9) are deceptive, served by the ruler to learn more about the guests at the table. Ironically, to navigate the meal successfully, the diner must outwit the ruler by not revealing the extent of his or her appetite. Table manners figure similarly in *Amenemope*:

> Do not eat in the presence of an official
> > And then set your mouth before him;
> If you are sated pretend to chew,
> > Content yourself with your saliva.
> Look at the bowl that is before you,
> > And let it serve your needs. (*AEL* 2:160; cf. *Instruction of Ptahhotep* [*AEL* 1:65]; Sir 31:12–32:13)

23:4-5 Self-restraint is necessary with regard to another appetite: the pursuit of money. "Cease from your understanding" may mean (*a*) stop because you understand (NRSV: "Be wise enough to desist"), or (*b*) stop relying on your insight in this regard (cf. "your insight" as a negative, 3:5, 7). Your eyes "fly" (*ʿûp*) to riches but riches are fleeting—they sprout wings and "fly" (*ʿûp*) like an eagle, a bird celebrated for its strength and speed (e.g., Job 9:25-26; 39:27-30; Isa 40:30-31). The imbalance of 23:5a plays up just how fleeting: "Will your eyes fly to it?" (three words)—"It is gone!" (one word). Compare Eccl 4:7-8; 5:10-17 (Heb. vv. 9-16); Matt 6:19-21; 1 Tim 6:6-10. *Amenemope* cautions likewise about (stolen) wealth:

Do not strain to seek increase,
  What you have, let it suffice you.
If riches come to you by theft,
  They will not stay the night with you.
Comes day they are not in your house,
  Their place is seen but they're not there. . . .
They made themselves wings like geese,
  And flew away to the sky. (*AEL* 2:152)

23:6-8 The topic returns to table manners (23:1-3; note 23:3a //
23:6b), but the host this time is not a ruler but one who is "evil of
eye," that is, stingy and begrudging (cf. "good of eye," 22:9;
28:22). The guest is arguably uninvited and unwanted, which puts
the host in an awkward, duplicitous position of saying one thing
while his "heart" thinks another (cf. Römheld 1989, 7). The
Instruction of Anii has a compelling parallel:

Do not intrude on a man in his house,
  Enter when you have been called;
He may say "Welcome" with his mouth,
  Yet deride you in his thoughts. (*AEL* 2:142)

The translation of 23:7a is uncertain; the metaphor of a "hair in
the throat" is analogous, however, to *Amenemope*'s caution about
coveting a poor person's belongings ("A poor man's goods are a
block in the throat, / It makes the gullet vomit," *AEL* 2:154-155).
Though the guest expects an enjoyable, satisfying feast, things
turn sour quickly. The guest vomits the food, and any "pleasant
words" or compliments he or she utters are wasted on a host who
neither asked for nor appreciates them.

23:9 Words are also wasted on fools (but cf. 26:4-5). To speak
"in the ears of" suggests the words are direct (e.g., 2:2; 22:17;
Judg 9:3; Ezek 3:10), important (e.g., Gen 20:8; Exod 11:2; Deut
5:1), and perhaps confidential (e.g., Gen 44:18; 1 Sam 18:23).
Alliteration emphasizes that such counsel is squandered "in the
ears of a fool" (*bĕ'oznê kĕsîl*), for the fool "will despise wisdom"
(*yābûz lĕśēkel*).

23:10-11 The first line is identical to 22:28a. The second intensifies the warning with, "Do not enter!" and focuses on orphans who, like widows and foreigners, are particularly vulnerable to exploitation (e.g., Deut 14:28-29; Job 22:9; Jer 7:6). One responsibility of a "redeemer" or "next of kin" is to buy back alienated lands of family members (e.g., Lev 25:25; Ruth 4:3-4). For those without a human redeemer, as presumably is the orphan, God acts as redeemer (15:25; 22:22-23; e.g., Isa 41:14; Jer 50:34). *Amenemope* shares similar concern about property rights (*AEL* 2:151-152). The general parallels with *Amenemope* end with 23:11.

23:12 A renewed call for a receptive ear and heart (e.g., 2:2; 15:31; 18:15; 19:27; 22:17) suggests the beginning of a new literary unit. The proverb may be read independently or, given repetition of "discipline" (*mûsār*; NRSV: "instruction") in 23:12a and 23:13a, as coupled with what follows: openness to discipline (23:12) engenders motivation to discipline one's children (23:13-14).

23:13-14 Taking up "discipline" (*mûsār*, 23:12), this proverb pair insists on it, particularly the physical chastisement of one's children (e.g., 13:24; 20:30; 22:15). Alliteration and assonance lend emphasis to its opening command (*ʾal-timnaʿ minnaʿar mûsār*, "Do not withhold from a youth discipline"). The assumption is that the pain of physical discipline for parent and child alike is negligible compared to the child's inevitable death without it (19:18b). To discipline is thus to "rescue" one's children from Sheol. The Aramaic *Proverbs of Ahiqar* likewise implores: "Do not withhold your son from [the] rod. If not, you will not be able to save him" (*TAD* 3.1.1.176).

23:15-16 The teacher-parent appeals again to parental joy as motivation for the youth to embrace wisdom. Use of body language and a concentric literary structure (ABB'A') accentuate the connection between the generations: "if your heart (A) . . . then my heart" (B) and "my kidneys (B', NRSV: 'soul') . . . when your lips" (A'). The kidneys, along with the heart, are the innermost parts of a person and are associated particularly with emotions (e.g., Pss 73:21; 139:13; Job 16:13).

23:17-18 Cautions against envy recur in Proverbs (e.g., 3:31; 24:1, 19-20; cf. Pss 37:1; 73). Envy is self-destructive; it overwhelms (27:4) and makes the body rot (14:30). The second proverb, which motivates the first, leaves open for whom continual "fear of the LORD" (see excursus in Proverbs 1) affords hope and a good "end" (e.g., 5:4, 11; 14:12; 19:20; 23:21), but it is presumably the listener, his or her community, and future generations.

23:19-21 With, "Listen, my child, yes, you!" the teacher renews the call to attention and invokes the parent-child relationship before warning about relationships of a different sort ("Don't be among," 22:26a). Drunkards and gluttons thoughtlessly and selfishly overindulge (the glutton *"for himself,"* 23:20b) and thereby squander their resources. Reference to the pair recalls the parental public charge against a stubborn son: "He is a glutton and a drunkard!" (Deut 21:20); perhaps the language is standard for rebellious behavior (e.g., 28:7). Although the penalty for the delinquent son is stoning, the sentence here is drowsiness and, as a result, poverty (as with the lazy, e.g., 6:9-11; 20:4; 24:30-34). The parent personifies drowsiness clothing in rags—literally "ripped things" (1 Kgs 11:30-31; 2 Kgs 2:12)—the drunkards and gluttons.

23:22-25 The string of proverbs continues to appeal to parental joy as motivation for the youth to embrace wisdom (e.g., 23:15-16). Threefold repetition of the verb "to bear" (23:22, 24, 25) and mention of "when your mother is old" (23:22) establish the parents' lifelong commitment to the youth, while the imperative "Acquire!" calls to mind the grandfather's repeated command to "acquire" wisdom (4:5, 7; e.g., 16:16; 17:16; 18:15; 19:8). The appeal spans generations. And the parent leaves no doubt about the happiness the youth will inspire: the pattern "greatly rejoice / rejoice / rejoice / rejoice" (using two different verbs) frames 23:24-25 (cf. 10:1; 17:21, 25; 27:11; 28:7; 29:3a).

23:26-28 This proverb captures in brief the parent's struggle in Proverbs 1–9 to garner the youth's loyalty while dissuading him from other dangerous but compelling companions, represented here again by the prostitute (6:26; 29:3) and parallel "strange" woman (7:10). The intimacy of the parent's appeal—*"my* son," "Give your heart to *me*," "May your eyes observe (or 'delight in') *my* ways"—is matched by the hostility with which he describes the "strange" woman. The parent shows little restraint, recalling the metaphor of a "deep pit" (22:14), twisting a positive metaphor into a negative (i.e., the wife as a well, 5:15), and reiterating that the woman "lies in wait" to ambush the unsuspecting (7:12, 21-27). The result is a stark contrast between the parent's promise of companionship and well-being, and the "strange" woman's entrapment of the youth in shadowy isolation and imminent harm. Does the youth really want to be one more person she adds to the "faithless" (11:3)?

23:29-35 The parent turns from the "deep pit" of the "strange" woman (23:26-28) to another potential trap—wine. The poem has five movements: (*a*) a riddle comprised of six questions ("Who has?") that highlight certain emotional, physical, and communal consequences of excessive drinking (23:29); (*b*) the riddle's answer (23:30; cf. "mixed wine" in 9:2); (*c*) the resulting command— given the appealing taste and "eye" (NRSV: "sparkle") of wine, do not even look at it! (23:31); (*d*) justification for the command that details the deadly "bite" of wine and, shifting to direct address ("you") for immediacy, describes its hallucinatory, seasick-like effects (23:32-34); and, finally, (*e*) the hung-over boast of a drunkard that reveals how utterly unaware he or she is of the precarious situation ("I am not hurt"; "I do not know"). Indeed, the drunkard intends to drink again (23:35; the Hebrew lacks "you will say"; e.g., Isa 5:11; Sir 31:25-31).

24:1-2 The wicked take the stage again with this caution (23:17-18 and 24:19-20; cf. 3:31-32; Pss 37:1-2; 73:3). Such proverbs urge perseverance in the ways of wisdom, particularly when those of the wicked appear more prosperous (Ps 73:3-12). The verb *hāga* (24:2; NRSV: "devise"), which typically means "to mutter" or "speak" (e.g., 8:7; 15:28; Job 27:4), highlights the heart or mind as the source of speech: the heart "utters," the mouth speaks.

24:3-4 Indefinite nouns ("a house," "rooms") and passive verbs ("is built," "is established," "are filled") render this proverb pair strikingly comprehensive: wisdom is necessary for *anyone* to build *any* "house," a term that refers variously to a dwelling place, its inhabitants, one's property, and descendants. Indeed, God "established" the cosmos with wisdom (3:19-20; 8:22-31), and personified wisdom "builds" her house (9:1-6; cf. 14:1; 31:10-31). That even the "inner chambers" of a household—the most remote of its spaces (e.g., 7:27; 18:8; 20:27; Eccl 10:20; Song 1:4; 3:4)—teem with riches conveys the abundant prosperity wisdom affords (e.g., 3:14, 16; 8:18-19, 21).

24:5-6 The first proverb in the Hebrew—"A wise person, in strength; and one with knowledge grows in power"—associates wisdom with vitality (e.g., 31:17, 25; cf. 24:10). The second (24:6), with its focus on military strategy, invites rereading the first in the manner reflected in NRSV (which follows LXX): wisdom triumphs over brute strength (20:18; 21:22). Many proverbs emphasize the importance of good counsel (e.g., 11:14; 13:10; 15:22).

24:7 The sages turn from advantages of wisdom (24:3-6) to disadvantages of folly (24:7-9). In light of the first line—that wisdom is inaccessible for fools—the second may be interpreted variously. First, it may caution that the fool "must not open his mouth" (the modal sense of the verb) at the gate, the center of communal power and justice (e.g., 1:21; 8:3; Deut 21:19; 25:7; Ruth 4:1-12); this reading resonates with the need for good counsel in 24:6. Second, 24:7b may evaluate the fool's speech. Elsewhere in Proverbs, only kings (31:8-9) and the woman of substance (31:26) "open [the] mouth," suggesting the phrase denotes speech worthy of communal attention (Job 32:20-22). Thus fools may talk at the gate (they are not known, after all, for their restraint, e.g., 17:28b; 18:6), but anything they say is dismissed outright (cf. "He has nothing to say," so NIV, NEB). Finally, 24:7b may poke fun at the fool. C. H. Toy notes the irony that "elsewhere . . . the fool is only too ready to open his mouth, and the one moment in his life when he may be called wise is when he closes his lips" (1899, 443).

24:8-9 Public contempt for folly and wickedness continues (24:7) with these two proverbs linked by the Hebrew root meaning "to plan" or "scheme" (zāmam). The root, which appears as a noun ("master of schemes," 24:8) and a verb ("devising," 24:9), refers to discretion, private thoughts, and plans devised in secret—the capacity to think and plan freely, creatively, and even cunningly, to get things done. Practiced with wisdom, such scheming can be positive and desirable (e.g., 1:4; 2:11; 3:21; 5:2; 8:12). Practiced for harm, it sparks communal disdain (e.g., 12:2; 14:17; 21:27).

24:10-12 The abrupt shift to second person singular address ("If *you* . . .") grabs attention and lends immediacy to this condemnation of failure to act in the face of injustice. A pun on "adversity" (*ṣārâ*) and "meager" or "small" (*ṣar*) relates the crisis and feeble response (24:10), while the imperative "Deliver!" demands action (24:11; NRSV reads it conditionally). The portrait of injustice that follows is graphic. *Many* (pl.) are taken to death, *many* (pl.) stagger to slaughter (24:11). In the face of the horror, any protest of ignorance—here in the first common plural, which obscures individual responsibility ("*We* did not know this," 24:12a)—is inexcusable. The sages let no one off the hook. They retort sharply in the second-person singular ("*your* soul," 24:12b) and, with rhetorical questions packed with active participles and repetition of the third-person masculine singular pronoun, underscore God's knowledge: "Does not the one who weighs hearts—*he* [God] understands? The one who guards your life—*he* [God] knows? And will not the one repay a human according to his [or her] work?"

24:13-14 Wordplay enhances this celebration of wisdom. Just as honey is good for the "palate" (NRSV: "taste"), wisdom satisfies the *nepeš*—that is, the "throat" or "neck" and, by metonymy, the "appetite," "life," or "self" (16:24; Pss 119:103; Ezek 3:3; cf. 5:3). A steady diet of it makes for a good "end," meaning the outcome or waning days of a person's life (e.g., 5:4, 11; 19:20; 24:14; Job 8:7). Personified wisdom echoes the comparison: "For the memory of me is sweeter than honey, / and the possession of me sweeter than the honeycomb" (Sir 24:20). Proverbs 24:14bc is nearly identical to 23:18.

24:15-16 Caution not to "lie in wait" recalls descriptions of the street gang and "strange" woman in Proverbs 1–9 (1:18; 7:12, 21-27; cf. 23:28). "Home" and "resting place" suggest the concern is attacks on the property of the righteous; the latter refers to the resting place of livestock (Isa 65:10; Jer 50:6; cf. Isa 35:7). The second proverb explains why the ambushes are doomed to failure.

Seven times, a number that signifies completeness, the righteous will fall and get up again (Ps 20:7-8). (The proverb assumes that the righteous know hardship.) By contrast, the wicked, who by "lying in wait" assume they have an upper hand, are tripped up by their own wickedness. Lack of a parallel "arise" or similar verb of recovery in 24:16b underscores the finality of their fate. They do not get up again.

24:17-18 Picking up the verbs "to fall" and "to stumble" (24:16), the first proverb prohibits expressions of *Schadenfreude*, or enjoyment of another's suffering, at the downfall of one's enemies (who, on the heels of 24:15-16, may be associated with the wicked). Although some texts acknowledge and even encourage *Schadenfreude* by people and God—particularly when the wicked stumble (e.g., 11:10; Job 22:19-20; Pss 37:10-13; 52:5-7; 58:10-11; Isa 14:3-21; Rev 18:20)—others like this proverb pair condemn it (e.g., Job 31:29; Ps 35:11-16, 19). No occasion warrants self-righteous smugness. Ambiguity in the second proverb raises questions. Does God so disdain *Schadenfreude* that, when one expresses it, God withdraws God's anger from one's enemies? Does God then turn God's wrath to the one who rejoiced? The possibilities underscore the gravity of the offense (25:21-22).

24:19-20 A reprise of the fate of the wicked draws the section to a close (23:17-18; 24:1-2; cf. 3:31; Ps 37:1). Unlike the wise who find a good "end" (e.g., 23:18; 24:14; cf. 19:20) the wicked have "no end." For the lamp metaphor, see 13:9.

24:21-22 Although Proverbs frequently associates God and the king (e.g., 16:10; 21:1), the imperative "fear" is used exclusively with reference to God until here (3:7; 14:2). Well-being requires respect for those who wield considerable power. The Hebrew of 24:21b is difficult. The NRSV follows LXX, while many other translations follow MT (i.e., "Do not associate with those who change") and interpret "those who change" as rebels (e.g., NIV, *TANAKH*). The second proverb motivates the first by describing disasters wrought by God and king as utterly unpredictable—with regard to timing ("suddenly") and scope ("Who knows?" cf. Eccl 2:19; 3:21; 6:12; 8:1).

APPENDIX
PROVERBS 24:23-34: "THESE ALSO ARE OF THE WISE"

Literary Analysis

The superscription "these also are of the wise" (24:23a) indicates these twelve verses, which may or may not have circulated originally as an independent unit, were appended to 22:17–24:22 at some point in the book's development, perhaps on the basis of the verses' purported setting ("the wise") or to reinforce the themes of justice and hard work (e.g., 22:22-23, 28, 29; 23:10-11; 24:10-12). (In LXX, by contrast, 24:24, which has five additional lines, is followed immediately by MT 30:1-14 and then MT 24:23-34.) The unit addresses two principal concerns—law and work. Whereas discourses typical of different contexts (i.e., court and household) may and often do overlap (e.g., the appeal for honesty in 24:26 may be read generally or as the conclusion to 24:23b-25), the unit unfolds, as A. Meinhold observes (1991, 2:410), in two parallel groups of three teachings. This outline of the unit is an adaptation of his:

Impartiality in Judging (24:23b-25)	False Testimony (24:28)
Honesty and Its Help (24:26)	Vengeance and Its Harm (24:29)
Work (24:27)	Laziness (24:30-34)

Exegetical Analysis

24:23b-25 Following the superscription (24:23a), the proverb condemns "paying regard to the face," or partiality in the administration of justice, as "not good" (18:5; 28:21a is nearly identical to 24:23b). The face is a primary way a person is recognized (e.g., 7:13; 15:13; Isa 29:22). For judges to render judgment on the basis of recognition or impression, whether positive or negative, is a distortion of justice similar to taking a bribe. So Moses charges the first tribal leaders: "[Hear out] the members of your community . . . , and judge rightly between one person and another, whether citizen or resident alien. You must not be partial in judging: hear out the small and the great alike" (Deut 1:16-17; cf. Deut 16:19). The *Instruction of Amenemope* urges similar judicial behavior: "Do not incline to the well-dressed man, / And rebuff the one in rags" (*AEL* 2:158). Just as God's justice is impartial (e.g., Job 34:19), so human judges must not allow anything to intimidate or persuade them (Deut 1:17). The sages acknowledge, however, that such evenhandedness is not easy (28:21).

Safeguarding honesty and justice is a matter of concern for those immediately involved and for the world. People who distort the truth, who declare the wicked just, receive the curse and censure of "peoples and . . . nations," a phrase that denotes everyone (e.g., Pss 47:3 [Heb. v. 4]; 67:4-5; Hab 2:13-14). In a courtroom or elsewhere, dishonest speech elicits universal condemnation. In contrast, those who reprove the wicked receive "a good blessing," presumably from others and God (e.g., 28:23).

<u>24:26</u> This description of "straightforward words" (8:9) as a kiss on the lips makes palpable how intimate and treasured is honesty. Although this is the only explicit reference to "kissing lips" in the Old Testament, where it is implied (e.g., Song 4:11; 5:13), the gesture signals mutual devotion, respect, and loyalty.

<u>24:27</u> Working the land and building a house typically go hand in hand (e.g., Jer 25:9, 28; 35:9; cf. Isa 65:21; Ezek 28:26), but this proverb insists it matters in what order one does the work. The imperative "prepare" recalls the ant that "prepares" food in the summer harvest (6:8; 30:25; cf. 21:29), and "work in the field" is likely tilling the soil (1 Chr 27:26). People must make sure the ground will sustain them before building. The *Instruction of Anii* teaches likewise:

> Learn about the way of a man
>   Who undertakes to found his household.
> Make a garden, enclose a patch,
>   In addition to your plowland;
> Set out trees within it,
>   As shelter about your house. (*AEL* 2:139)

The proverb highlights the importance of priorities—of doing the groundwork necessary so that a project might succeed.

24:28 Proverbs condemns false witnesses, those who testify against their neighbor "without cause" and "entice" with their speech; the father in Proverbs 1–9 uses both terms to describe and denounce the gang's plans to ambush the innocent for quick gain (1:10-11, 17; e.g., 6:19; 12:17; 14:5, 25; 21:28; 25:18).

24:29 Even if there is cause to retaliate against a neighbor, this injunction forbids taking vengeance into one's own hands (*"I will do. . . . I will return"*). The second line echoes 24:12d, with the striking difference that the latter explicitly assigns to God the role of repaying people according to their deeds. Retribution is God's purview (20:22; e.g., Pss 3, 35, 55, 109).

24:30-34 The appendix ends with what may be described as a textbook example of wise discernment. Told as a firsthand account, the story has three stages. The storyteller (*a*) *observes* the overgrown fields and crumbling stone wall of the sluggard (24:30-31; cf. 20:4), (*b*) *takes responsibility to reflect* on what she sees (*"I looked; I inclined my heart; I saw; I received discipline [mûsār]*," 24:32; cf. 1:2), and (*c*) *comes to a conclusion*—in this case that her observations affirm an already known proverb (24:33-34; cf. 6:10-11). The storyteller pays attention (even to what she merely "passes by"), assumes she can learn something, and—without prompting from parent, sage, or teacher—draws on communal wisdom to interpret and convey her experience.

PROVERBS 25–29: "THESE ALSO ARE PROVERBS OF SOLOMON, WHICH THE OFFICIALS OF KING HEZEKIAH OF JUDAH TRANSMITTED"

Introduction to Proverbs 25–29

A superscription introduces a new section (25:1). As in 24:23, "these also" indicates the section was appended to another—perhaps all or part of the first Solomonic collection (10:1–22:16). We are further told by whom: "the men of Hezekiah of Judah."

Hezekiah, king of Judah from ca. 715 to 687 BCE, is renowned for his obedience to God, instituting religious and political reforms following the destruction of the northern kingdom in 722 BCE, and fortifying Jerusalem to defend against the Assyrian advance (2 Kgs 18:1–20:21; 2 Chr 29:1–32:33; Isa 36:1–39:8; Sir 48:17-23). His "men" are likely court scribes who "transmitted" proverbs, presumably by collecting, copying, and editing (the verb *ʿātaq* in the causative sense "to move on further" is awkward here; cf. Gen 12:8; 26:22; Job 9:5; 32:15). The attribution of these proverbs to Solomon, the quintessential sage of Israel, signals their authority and significance (1:1; 10:1; cf. 1 Kgs 3–11).

Like the prior Solomonic section of Proverbs (10:1–22:16), this section has two main subunits distinguishable primarily on the basis of genre: 25:1–27:27 and 28:1–29:27. The first subunit is replete with vivid similes and metaphors. It also includes admonitions, many of which include motive clauses (e.g., 25:6-7b, 9-10, 21-22; 27:10). The second subunit has notably fewer images; its frequent use of antithetical proverbs and focus on the opposition of the righteous and wicked more closely resembles 10:1–15:33 (see Literary Analyses).

PROVERBS 25–27

Literary Analysis

Vibrant metaphors drawn primarily from nature (e.g., clouds and wind, muddied waters, moths, birds, and dogs) and human handiwork (e.g., jewelry, pottery, metalwork, weaponry, digging pits, and crushing grain) animate the first subunit of chapters 25–29. Proverbs 25 employs the imagery to teach about hierarchy and social standing, the power of good and bad speech, and navigating conflict. Following the superscription (25:1), the chapter has two main units. The first (25:2-7b) considers God, the king, subjects, and the royal court (cf. "king[s]" in 25:1-3, 5-6). The second (25:7c-27) focuses variously on speech and strife. Close verbal links between 25:2b (*kĕbōd . . . ḥăqōr dābār*, "honor . . . to search out a matter") and 25:27b (*ḥēqer kĕbōdām kābôd*, "and searching out of their honor is [not] honor") frame the chapter in terms of inquiry and honor. There is also a rather rhythmic back and forth between proverbs (25:2-5, 11-15, 18-20, 23-27) and admonitions (25:6-10, 16-17, 21-22; cf. Van Leeuwen 1988, 57-70).

Proverbs 26 unfolds like a character study in three acts. The fool takes center stage in 26:1-12 (cf. "fool[s]" in each proverb except 26:2). The sluggard then steps forward (26:13-16), followed by a series of people who stir up conflict, mostly by deceitful and malicious speech (26:17-28). Whereas the bulk of the chapter is content to describe the characters, it ends climatically on a note of recompense: wrongdoing does not go unpunished (26:26-28).

Proverbs 27:1-22 is an assortment of proverbs that highlight, in particular, the contours of true friendship and neighborliness. The chapter is dotted with the terms "neighbor" or "friend" (rēaʿ, 27:9, 10, 14, 17), "friend of your parent" (rēaʿ ʾābîkā, 27:10), and "neighbor" (šākēn, 27:10), and addresses such topics as praise (27:1-2, 21), envy (27:4), and the need for reproof from friends (27:5-6, 17, 19, 21). It concludes with a poem about stewardship of one's resources (cf. other poems that conclude units of the book, e.g., 23:29-35; 24:30-34; and 31:10-31).

Theological and Ethical Overview

How do we wisely negotiate social and professional circles? What qualities and practices best position us for an invitation to "come up here" (25:7)—to take on greater responsibilities? Some interpreters posit these chapters were crafted to educate aspiring courtiers for positions in the royal court (cf. 25:6b-7). Although the audience need not be so limited (e.g., "king" is referred to only in 25:1-7, cf. "ruler" in 25:15), many of the proverbs do address how to navigate astutely in a complex moral arena of kings, nobles, bosses, friends, neighbors, enemies, fools, gossips, sluggards, and liars. With the parental home increasingly distant (cf. "my child" only in 27:11), the implied reader continues to discern whether and how to "put [oneself] forward" (25:6) in a world marked by a well-defined social hierarchy, honor, and shame (see Theological and Ethical Overview of Proverbs 22:17–24:34). At every turn, the sages insist on honesty and humility. They warn against trying to get ahead too quickly, and against the use of deception, manipulation, and self-promotion—the pursuit of glory for glory's sake (25:27). They caution against self-praise (25:6-7; 27:2), gossip (e.g., 25:18, 23; 26:22), taking credit for something one did not do (25:14), meddling in other people's business (26:17), revenge (25:21-22), and frivolous lawsuits (25:7c-8). Instead they advocate self-restraint (e.g., 25:16, 27-28; 27:20), patience (25:15), attention to one's superiors and resources (27:18, 23-27), and eloquence (25:11; cf. 26:9)—which the sages model with evocative metaphors. All of this may strike readers as too protective of the status quo and optimistic (i.e., diligence is always rewarded). But the sages stress the ethical significance of here and now for those of us who focus more on there and then. It matters for personal and communal well-being *how* we get ahead.

Prompting much of this guidance is the valuing of friendship and neighborliness over personal gain. Aristotle similarly extols friendship as a crowning virtue in his *Nicomachean Ethics*: "Without friends no one would choose to live, though he [or she] had all other goods" (bk. 8.1). The nearly interchangeable use of "friend" and "neighbor" in these chapters—indeed, the Hebrew term *rēa‘* may mean both (25:8, 9, 17-18; 26:19; 27:9-10, 14, 17)—reminds us that friendship has to do with intimate companions and, more broadly, reliance and affection between members of a community (e.g., 1 Cor 12:12-30). According to the sages, friends and neighbors are reliable, at times more than family (25:19; 27:10). They are honest (e.g., 26:18-19), keep each other's confidences (25:9), work out differences directly and discreetly (25:7c-10), honor grief (25:20), reprove one another (e.g., 27:5-6; cf. 25:12), and do not overstay their welcome (25:17; cf. 27:14). This description of friendship defines its good not principally in terms of pleasure or profit (reasons we may have some friendships) but for its own sake: as something trustworthy and illuminating—as iron sharpens iron (27:17; cf. 27:9) and water reflects the human face (27:19). People are wiser because of it (Rom 12:3-8; 1 Cor 12:12-30; cf. Booth 1988, 173).

Coupled with attention to friendship is emphasis on honor and shame and what is "fitting" (see Theological and Ethical Analysis of Proverbs 5). A person's choices are not wildly free, as we may like to think, but bounded by communal structures and expectations. We are particular *and* accountable (e.g., 25:7c-10, 27; 26:1, 8, 26). Conversely, we learn a lot about what a community values by who it esteems. Who weathers the heat of public scrutiny (27:21)? Who withers in it? Who do we reward and how? And what do our answers reveal about our values? The sages admonish us to be careful. It is treacherous to honor the fool (26:1, 8).

Finally, tucked in the middle of these chapters, is a theological exclamation mark on radical hospitality. Although divine activity may be implied in Proverbs 25–27 occasionally (e.g., 26:26-27), God is named only twice (25:2, 22). The first mention extols God's inscrutability (25:2); the second, God's provision for those who prepare a table for their enemies, pour water, and break bread rather than escalating conflict (25:22; cf. Rom 12:17-21). As readers navigate and negotiate, therefore, the sages are clear: God rewards those who respond with good in the face of hatred.

Exegetical Analysis

25:1 See Introduction to Proverbs 25–29 for discussion of this superscription.

God, King, and Court (25:2-7b)

25:2-3 Repetition of "king" and "to search out" links these two proverbs. Symmetry in the first—"*glory of* God (*'ĕlōhîm*) to conceal *a thing, glory* of kings (*mĕlākîm*) to investigate *a thing*"—associates God and kings closely (e.g., 16:10; 21:1), while the dissimilar verbs highlight their distinct roles. God is praised for mystery, for divine inscrutability (implicit may be hope, even confidence, that God reveals God's ways, e.g., 2:5-6). And kings are praised for the capacity to search things out—to deliberate and comprehend (cf. the same verb in 18:17; 28:11; Job 5:27; 32:11;

cf. Deut 29:29). Kings have an air of mystery about them nonetheless, described here in cosmic dimensions; indeed, "unsearchable" is used elsewhere in the Old Testament solely for creation and God (Job 5:9; 9:10; Ps 145:3; Isa 40:28). Close verbal links between 25:2b and 25:27b frame the chapter in terms of inquiry and honor (see Literary Analysis).

25:4-5 Dross is separated from metal by smelting—heating the metal to high temperatures so that it becomes liquid and its impurities may be poured off when they rise to the surface. The liquid metal is then poured into a mold and hardened to make a *kelî* ("vessel," "equipment," or "weapon") or, as in Judg 17:4, an idol. Repetition of the opening imperative ("Take away!") connects this craft with the handiwork required to establish or "make firm" the royal throne: removal of the wicked (16:12; 20:28; 29:14). The proverb leaves open who participates in that work, arguably the king (20:8), God the great Refiner (e.g., Job 23:10; Isa 1:25; 48:10; Ezek 22:17-22; cf. 1 Pet 1:7), and others loyal to the throne. Jeremiah describes the wicked as "rejected silver" that cannot be refined (Jer 6:29-30).

25:6-7b With the "king's presence" still of concern (25:5), the sages caution against self-promotion (cf. 23:1-3). In 25:6, the negative commands ("do not put yourself," "do not stand") frame "the presence of the king" and "the place of the great ones." The proverb thereby puts "them" on the inside and "you" on the outside—precisely where you should remain, the sages contend, unless you are invited "up" (22:29). Otherwise, you risk "being put down in the presence of a noble"; the line intensifies the (potential) humiliation by moving the phrase "presence of" to the end and making "noble," the last word, singular. It only takes one noble to shame you and there is no way around him. Compare Sir 13:9-10 and Luke 14:7-11.

Good Speech, Bad Speech, and Navigating Conflict (25:7c-28)

25:7c-8 The next two proverb pairs are associated by vocabulary ("dispute" or "case," 25:8a, 9a; "neighbor," 25:8b, 9a; "lest," 25:8b, 10a), the admonitions "do not bring" (25:8) and "do not disclose" (28:9b), and grave personal consequences for mishandling disputes. The pairs may be read in conjunction or independently. The first (25:7c-8) cautions against impetuous lawsuits—rushing to court based solely on what you have seen. Appearances are notoriously deceiving. The rhetorical question, "What will you do at its end?" situates readers in the helplessness that awaits them when, inevitably, the litigation fails (Isa 10:3; Jer 5:31; Hos 9:5). Haste to expose others exposes oneself as dishonorable (20:3; 24:28).

25:9-10 Sight (25:7) gives way to hearing with this admonition to work out any legitimate dispute with your neighbor and maintain every confidentiality lest someone—whether a passerby, one whose confidence you betrayed, an arbiter or judge (e.g., 15:31; 21:28; cf. Deut 1:16-17; 2 Sam 14:16)—overhear and reproach you. Such a "report" about you (NRSV: "ill repute"; cf. Gen 37:2; Ezra 36:3) is not shaken easily: you are a gossip (e.g., 10:8b; 11:13; 20:19). The Aramaic *Proverbs of Ahiqar* similarly warns, "Your secrets do not reveal before your friends; let your name not be light before them" (*TAD* 3.1.1.141; cf. Matt 5:22; 18:15).

25:11-12 The motif of hearing (25:10) continues with these comparisons of good speech to finely crafted gold ornaments and jewelry. Given the topic, it is ironic that the Hebrew of 25:11 is obscure. A "setting" can be an image (e.g., Num 33:52; Ezek 8:12) or sculpture (Lev 26:1), and "fitly" (*ʿal-ʾopnāyw*), a phrase that occurs only here in the Old Testament, may mean appropriate to the circumstances or the time (15:23). The sages often describe words as fruit (e.g., 10:31; 12:14; 13:2).

Wordplay enhances the depiction of a wise rebuke as an exquisitely crafted gold "earring" (*nezem*) on a listening "ear" (*ʾōzen*, 25:12). The two are a match: the rebuke is made for the ear and the ear that receives it is made beautiful (11:22).

25:13 A clash of seasons and wordplay convey the relief afforded by a good "messenger" (*ṣîr*)—cold snow in the heat of "harvest" (*qāṣîr*). In ancient Israel, laborers carried compacted snow down from the high mountains to be stored and used to cool the drinks of the wealthy (Lang 1981, 219-32). A good messenger, like the runner, brings refreshment to the *nepeš*, namely, the "throat" and, by metonymy, the "life" or "self" (e.g., 13:17; 25:25; 26:1).

25:14 Weather imagery continues (cf. 25:13) and use of suspense in the first line—"Clouds, and wind, and rain . . . not!"—highlights how the self-congratulating giver is all talk and no action.

25:15 This proverb generates intensity with its movement from patient persuasion of the powerful (e.g., 20:18; 21:22; 24:5-6) to the startling, indeed violent, paradox of the "soft" or "gentle" tongue as a weapon that *shatters* bone, one of the hardest substances in the human body (15:1). Indeed, the violent imagery of the second line invites rereading the verb *pātâ* (NRSV: "to be persuaded") in the first more sharply: the verb can also mean "to seduce" or "entice" (e.g., 1:10; 9:13; 16:29) and may connote sexual seduction and rape (e.g., Exod 22:16 [Heb. v. 15]; Sir 42:10; cf. Deut 11:16). Hence the ruler may not know he has been swayed by the patient counselor or, more pointedly, "been screwed" (cf. Brown 2004, 150-51). The Aramaic *Proverbs of Ahiqar* uses similar imagery: "Soft is the tongue of a king, but the ribs of a dragon it will break like death which is not seen" (*TAD* 3.1.1.89-90).

25:16-17 Both of these proverbs caution against "having enough" (*śāba ʿ*, 25:16b, 17b) of a good thing. Recognition of limits is necessary for personal and communal well-being: eat only "what you require," and "make your foot precious" in the home of others (25:27; Sir 37:27-31).

25:18 A cache of lethal blunt and piercing weapons conveys just how violent and deadly is a false witness (6:19; 12:17; 14:5, 25; 19:5, 9). Gritty and unrelenting ("a *sharp* arrow"), the proverb debunks any notion that "sticks and stones . . . but words can never hurt me" (cf. 5:4; 30:14).

25:19 The metaphors convey the sharp pain and disabling effects of misplaced trust in difficult times. Because we often take our teeth and feet for granted, when they break down—a decaying tooth, an unsteady (NRSV: "lame") foot—we realize just how much we rely on them for everyday functioning and how debilitated we are without them.

25:20 The NRSV reads with LXX. The Hebrew text is shorter: "One who takes off a garment on a cold day, one who pours vinegar on a wound, is one who sings songs to a heavy heart." The metaphors denote insensitivity and poor judgment in circumstances of discomfort and pain, as is singing (presumably joyful) songs to the heartbroken (e.g., Ps 137). The remedy affords no relief and may worsen the pain (e.g., 10:26).

25:21-22 This proverb pair is well known, in part because Paul quotes the LXX version of it in Rom 12:17-21. The first proverb urges one to be aware of and to provide for the basic needs of one's enemy. Indeed, offering food and water may ease or even resolve the conflict (e.g., 10:12; 24:29). The second proverb (25:22) motivates the first, but the expression "heaping coals on the head" is obscure. Given the sages' repeated injunctions against seeking revenge (17:13; 20:22; 24:17-18), "heaping coals" is not likely a form of punishment. As Augustine and Jerome proposed, it may signify burning pangs of guilt and the blush of shame inflamed on the enemy's face in the wake of one's kindness. The proverbs thus resonate with other biblical texts that instruct "loving" one's enemies (e.g., Exod 23:4; Lev 19:17-18, 34; Matt 5:43-48). A few ancient Near Eastern wisdom texts teach likewise. The *Instruction of Amenemope*, for example, exhorts:

> We do not act like [the wicked's] kind;
> Lift him up, give him your hand,
> Leave him in the hands of the god;
> Fill his belly with bread of your own,
> That he be sated and weep. (*AEL* 2:150)

And the Babylonian *Counsels of Wisdom* advises:

> Do not return evil to the man who disputes with you;
> Requite with kindness your evil-doer,
> Maintain justice to your enemy,
> Smile on your adversary. (*BWL* 101)

25:23 The sages again compare wind and speech (25:14). In Palestine, however, the west wind, not the north, brings the rain (cf. Luke 12:54). Either the term is meant broadly (i.e., it includes northwesterly winds) or, more likely, "north" (ṣāpôn) is a word-play with the Hebrew root meaning "hidden" or "concealed" (ṣāpan). "North" or "hidden" winds unleash a downpour as "hidden" or "secret" words generate downcast expressions.

<u>25:24</u> The weather imagery of 25:23 lends concreteness to the precariousness of the roof's corner in this proverb, which is a nearly verbatim repetition of 21:9 (cf. also 21:19). There, poised on the edge, one is utterly exposed to the elements.

<u>25:25</u> A reliable messenger (25:13) and a good message provide relief. The metaphor of water to drink—much less *cold* water—is particularly compelling in the desert climate of Palestine. Similarly, that the good news was carried "from a distant land" heightens its significance and thereby the delight it inspires.

<u>25:26</u> Water imagery associates this proverb with 25:25 (cf. 25:13). At issue is how to interpret the verb māṭ ("shakes" or "staggers"; NRSV: "give way") in the second line. Do the righteous have weak moments when, for whatever reason, they compromise or "muddy" their commitments and values? Or do the wicked occasionally triumph over the righteous, stirring up trouble and disrupting their welfare by devious plots and plans (12:6; 16:27)? The proverb affords both options; the latter in particular challenges confident assertions that the righteous are never "shaken" (māṭ; 10:30; 12:3; e.g., Pss 16:8; 30:7). The sages acknowledge that things do not always work out the way wisdom and we would prefer.

<u>25:27</u> The first line recalls 25:16. The Hebrew of the second is corrupt—either, "and searching out of their honor is honor" or, if the negative in the first line does double duty, "is [not] glory." Close verbal links with 25:2b suggest the line is part of an *inclusio*, or frame to the chapter (see Literary Analysis). The point may be that a relentless pursuit of honor, like eating too much honey, is "not good" (16:29; 17:26; 18:5; 19:2; 28:21).

<u>25:28</u> Boundaries are also imperative with respect to one's rûaḥ, that is, spirit or temperament (e.g., 1:23; 14:29; 16:19, 32). Absent limits, without walls, one is defenseless—exposed to everything and vulnerable to attack.

The Fool (26:1-12)

<u>26:1</u> There are two primary seasons in Palestine: the wet, cool months (October–April) and the dry, warm season (May–September), during which harvest typically takes place (e.g., Jer 8:20; Mic 7:1). Aberrant weather is bewildering any time of the year; so too an honored fool simply does not "fit" (26:8; cf. "not fitting" proverbs, e.g., 17:7; 19:10). Both subvert expectations and disrupt the rhythm and work of the season. The expression of social upheaval in cosmic terms is found elsewhere (e.g., 30:21-23; 1 Sam 12:16-18; Amos 7:10). Such claims legitimize the social order as grounded in creation—thereby "quashing" revolutionary thoughts (cf. Van Leeuwen 1996a, 610).

<u>26:2</u> A curse "for naught" (*ḥinnām*, cf. 1:11, 17; 3:30)—like "aimless" or "homeless" (NRSV: "flitting") birds in flight—has no destination. It does not "land." An unjust curse is ineffective, perhaps because God renders it so (e.g., Num 23:8; Deut 23:5). The Aramaic *Proverbs of Ahiqar* similarly compares speech to birds: "For a bird is a word and he who sends it forth is a person of no heart" (*TAD* 3.1.1.82).

<u>26:3</u> Just as there are tools appropriate to motivate and direct stubborn, large animals, so the rod is how the sages contend one disciplines a fool. A fool, like such an animal, responds only to brute force (e.g., 10:13; 17:10; 19:25; 22:15).

<u>26:4-5</u> Shared vocabulary tightly couples these two proverbs; apart from the opening "not" of 26:4, the first four words of each are identical. Direct address further makes the quandary of how to deal with fools personal for readers—"Do not answer!" "Answer!" So which do you do? On the one hand (26:4), if you respond to fools, you risk being ignored, hated, harmed, and becoming "like [them]—*yes, you!*" (e.g., 13:19b-20; 14:7-8; 15:5; 17:12; 23:9). On the other hand, you dare not let fools have the last word lest they (and others) arrogantly mistake their folly for wisdom ("wise in [one's] eyes"; e.g., 3:7; 26:12; 28:11). Caught in the juxtaposition, the ambiguity and limits of human wisdom are palpable. The proverb pair says nothing about which circumstances require one or the other behavior—only that each is at times fitting and necessary. Readers must discern the difference.

This proverb pair is arguably the best-known example of the contradictions inherent to Proverbs (see Introduction to Proverbs 10:1–22:16). Indeed, the Talmud reports that 26:4-5 threatened the book's inclusion in the canon (*b. Sabb.* 30b). The rabbis ultimately settled the matter by proposing a "conditional variability" behind the two proverbs, namely, that despite their absolute language, one should only correct the fool in cases involving the Torah. More recent interpreters posit various ways to read the juxtaposition, including that life experience tempers their absolutism, or that, within the literary context of 26:1-12, the pair gives "condensed expression to profound ambivalence" about how the sages should best fulfill their didactic responsibilities (Hoglund 1987, 175).

26:6 Graphic imagery conveys how self-destructive it can be to send a foolish messenger. It is to "chop off" one's feet, because the message will surely not reach its intended recipient, and to "drink violence" (4:17)—to bring on oneself the harm that results (13:17; 25:13, 25).

26:7 Fools cannot "move" a proverb; they do not know when and how to use it. So it just hangs there, limp and ineffective, like the legs of a person who is lame (cf. 26:9).

26:8 Whereas the second line, a variant of 26:1b, makes clear the concern is how ill fitting honor is for a fool, the metaphor in the first line is obscure. The first word can mean "to bind" (NRSV), a "small stone" or "pebble" (2 Sam 17:13; Amos 9:9), or a "little bag" (e.g., 7:20a; Gen 42:35); and the third word, a *hapax legomenon*, or word found only here in the Old Testament, may mean "slingshot" or a "pile of stones." The NRSV translation follows LXX. To bind a stone in a sling is counterproductive and even dangerous to the one who wields it.

26:9 The second line repeats 26:7a. What exactly the drunkard holds is debated, however. The term *hôah* most often means "thorn(bush)" (so NRSV), suggesting that as "a thorn(bush) 'goes up' in(to) the hand of a drunkard" so a proverb pierces the mouth of a fool—even if the fool, like a drunkard, is oblivious to the injury. *Hôah* may also refer to a hooked tool such as that put through the gills of a fish to transport it (Job 41:2 [Heb. 40:26]) or to bind prisoners (2 Chr 33:11). When the word is read this way, fools are unable to "hook" their targets. Both interpretations highlight the fools' willy-nilly use of proverbs and the immediate harm this poses to themselves and others.

26:10 The NRSV offers a reasonable translation of this textually corrupt proverb that widens the circle of those harmed by the hiring of fools or drunkards (a link to 26:9) from the employer (26:6) to everyone.

26:11 This proverb also compares fools to animals (26:3), but its rhetoric is more biting. In the ancient Near East, dogs (and pigs) were largely despised; they were regarded as disgusting scavengers, dirty and unsuitable for sacrifice (e.g., 26:17; Exod 22:31 [Heb. v 30]; 1 Kgs 21:19, 23-24; Eccl 9:4; Jer 15:3). The proverb plays up the repulsion with mention of the dog's vomit. Fools go back time and again to what ails them in the first place: their folly.

26:12 The proverb uses sight ("Do you see?") to caution against putting too much confidence in one's sight—in one's perceptions of self and the world ("wise in [one's] eyes"; cf. 3:7; 26:5, 16; 28:11). Arrogance is a form of blindness. As R. C. Van Leeuwen observes: "Even as 'you' look down upon the fool whose self-perception is awry, you yourself may be 'wise in your own eyes' " (1988, 105). The second line asserts that being "wise in [one's] eyes" is *more* foolish than the folly of fools. Humility is integral to wisdom (e.g., 3:7, 34; 15:33; 18:12; 22:4).

The Sluggard (26:13-16)

26:13 The next four proverbs focus on the sluggard (26:13-16). The first line is nearly identical to 22:13a. The second reinforces the sluggard's absurd protest but with completely different vocabulary ("A *lion* in the squares!"); the lion is everywhere yet nowhere ("on the way," "in the squares"; cf. 1:20-21; 8:1-3). Assumed is the sluggard's earlier protest: "I shall be killed!" (22:13b).

26:14 The image is vivid: a lazy person fastened to the bed as a door to its hinges. When the sluggard turns, the range of movement is small and the movement itself monotonous, as alliteration conveys (ʿal . . . wĕ ʿāṣēl ʿal, "on . . . so a lazybones on . . . ," cf. 19:15).

26:15 With some variations in language and syntax, this proverb repeats 19:24. Following 26:14, it underlines the immovability of sluggards—even when their survival is at stake.

26:16 In light of 26:13-15, the sluggard's inflated self-regard ("wise in [one's] eyes," cf. 3:7; 26:5, 12; 28:11) is all the more laughable. The proverb heightens the absurdity with the comparison to *more* than "seven"—a number that suggests plenty and completeness (e.g., 9:1; 26:25)—who answer "with sense" (NRSV: "discreetly"). The seven may allude to a tradition of "seven sages." Artaxerxes, for example, employed seven advisers (Ezra 7:14) and there were seven antediluvian sages (cf. Clifford 1999, 24-26, 233).

A Cast of Troublemakers (26:17-28)

26:17 This warning about getting involved in other people's quarrels plays again on the widespread disdain for dogs in the ancient Near East (26:11). To grab the ears of such a scavenger "passing by" is to expose oneself needlessly to its filth, fangs, and ferocity.

26:18-19 Deception is portrayed again as a deadly weapon (cf. 25:18), and the injury is made all the more grievous by the perpetrator's question, "Am I not playing?" (NRSV: "I am only joking!"). The question exposes the perpetrator's utterly confused notions of good and bad behavior, lack of empathy, and callousness to the consequences—qualities which, for the sages, indicate a sort of madness.

26:20-22 As wood fuels fire, gossips inflame strife with slander, half-truths, and innuendo (16:28; 18:8; Deut 1:27). Without them, conflicts burn out. The second proverb (26:21) reverses the imagery, stoking the ashes with another metaphor (charcoal to embers) and a pun that links "fire" (ʾēš) and the "person" (ʾîš) who quarrels. The third proverb (26:22) repeats 18:8; in this context, the gossip's tasty words evoke hot, spicy food—stinging the lips, burning the throat, inflaming the belly, and generating discomfort for everyone.

26:23-25 These three proverbs contrast external appearances with internal intent. Because "silver dross" is the scum poured off from liquid silver during the smelting process, the finish on the earthenware is substandard. It is not the silver it appears to be. (NRSV: "like the glaze" is an emendation based on a putative Ugaritic cognate.) The parallel "burning" lips (NRSV emends to "smooth" unnecessarily) continues the motif of speech as fire (26:18-21; cf. 16:27) and suggests the high heat necessary for smelting and firing clay. The next two proverbs (26:24-25) reinforce, and even intensify, the first. "Seven abominations" denotes utter wickedness (cf. 26:16).

26:26 What is hidden is revealed, however (cf. 26:23-25). Disguised "hatred" (*śin'â*) is exposed for all to see, though the proverb does not specify how (for "assembly," e.g., 5:14). The referent for the third-person masculine singular suffix on "wickedness" is ambiguous; in this context, it arguably refers back to the "one who hates" (*śōnē'*; NRSV: "enemy") in 26:24 (cf. 26:25), but it could be anyone.

26:27 The first line likely refers to hunters who dig and then camouflage pits to trap their prey, and the second to persons who quarry and build with stones. The proverb may be read as (*a*) a simple observation of the risks inherent in everyday work (e.g., Eccl 10:8), or (*b*) a statement of retribution—the just consequences that come to those who strive to entrap or harm others (e.g., 1:10-19; Pss 7:15 [Heb. v. 16]; 9:15-16; 35:7-8; 57:6 [Heb. v. 7]; Jer 18:22). The latter interpretation continues the theme of recompense (26:26; cf. 26:28).

26:28 The Hebrew of this proverb is difficult. "Its victims" are "those it crushes," and "flattering" is "smooth" or "slippery," a description used previously for the mouth or speech of the "strange" woman (5:3; 7:21). The sense is that lying harms others and the liar (continuing the theme of recompense, cf. 26:26-27).

On Friendship (27:1-22)

27:1-2 The verb "to praise" associates these two proverbs. The first urges realism about what one knows and, in turn, may boast about—a sentiment shared by the Egyptian *Instruction of Ptahhotep*

("One plans the morrow but knows not what will be," *AEL* 1:69), the *Instruction of Amenemope* ("Indeed you do not know the plans of god, / And should not weep for tomorrow," *AEL* 2:159; cf. *AEL* 2:157), and in the New Testament by James 4:13-17. The second (27:2) cautions against self-congratulation. That one should wait for praise from "another" and a "stranger," terms used to this point only negatively to describe those outside the community, is noteworthy (2:5; 5:10; 6:24; 7:5; 20:16; 23:27). Praise is particularly significant when it comes from people who do not know you (27:21).

27:3-4 Syntax and logic in these proverbs move from lesser to greater and literal to metaphorical. The pattern occurs elsewhere, as in the *Proverbs of Ahiqar*: "I have carried sand and loaded salt and there is not anything which is heavier than a stranger; I have carried straw and lifted bran and there is not anything which is lighter than a resident" (*TAD* 3.1.1.159-160). The first proverb likens the anger of fools to an extremely heavy load (cf. Sir 22:14-15). The second depicts envy as a force more powerful than a "flood of anger" (NRSV: "anger overwhelms"), which, if one survives it, eventually abates. The rhetorical question heightens the effect: no one can stand before envy. For the sages, it is always destructive (6:34-35; 14:30; Job 5:2; Eccl 4:4).

27:5-6 How does one distinguish between true and false "love" (a noun in 27:5, a participle in 27:6)? One indication is whether the affection is revealed or concealed. A rebuke, while uncomfortable for everyone involved, demonstrates devotion and commitment (e.g., 1:23; 3:11-12; 6:23; 25:12). Someone cares enough to speak honestly, to say what may be hard to hear. Unexpressed love is comparatively worthless.

The second proverb (27:6) intensifies the distinction. Instead of the simple relative ("better than"), the comparison is made in terms of "true" (NRSV: "well meant") versus "excessive" (or "deceitful" or "dangerous"—the translation is disputed). Moreover, the proverb invokes strong physical language: "wounds," which always refer to bodily injury (20:30; 23:29; Gen 4:23; cf. Job 9:17), and kisses.

27:7 Play with the term *nepeš* ("throat," "appetite," or "self") recurs in this proverb about how satiation and hunger affect judgment. One who is satisfied "treads down" (NRSV: "spurns") a honeycomb—that is, tramples over it (e.g., Ps 44:5 [Heb. v. 6]; Isa 14:25; 63:6)—whereas one who is hungry does not taste accurately. When we have had enough of something and it is readily available, we tend to lose our "taste" for it. Conversely, when we are starved for something, it tastes unusually delicious (on honey, e.g., 16:24; 24:13; 25:16, 27). The Aramaic *Proverbs of Ahiqar* teaches likewise: "Hunger will sweeten bitterness" (*TAD* 3.1.1.123).

27:8 The image is of a bird that takes flight unwillingly from a nest that is no longer safe; the bird may or may not know where it is going (cf. Ps 55:6-7 [Heb. vv. 7-8]; Isa 16:2; Jer 4:25; 9:10 [Heb. v. 9]; Hos 9:17). Those who are forced by circumstances (e.g., disaster, disease, poverty, conflict) to flee from their "place" (NRSV: "home") share similar distress. The proverb assumes everyone has a "place" which, like the bird's nest, affords relative safety.

27:9 The first line observes the power of aesthetic pleasures to make a person happy (e.g., 21:17; Ps 133:2; Song 1:2-3; 4:10). The second continues the motif of sensory delight, but the Hebrew is difficult—"sweetness of a friend from counsel of a soul" (NRSV follows LXX). The point is likely that the sweetness of a friend comes from his or her counsel. Other proverbs refer to "sweet lips" (16:21) and wisdom as "sweet" like honey (24:13-14).

27:10 "Friend" links this proverb with 27:9b. The third line, with its contrast of the near neighbor and far brother, likely motivates the first two. In a time of crisis, one needs to be able to turn to friends—described here as family friends and next-door neighbors—because family members may be too distant (17:17; 18:24).

27:11 The parent interrupts with a direct appeal for the youth to be wise ("my child"; cf. 24:21) so that the *parent* might be happy and ready with "a word" for anyone who taunts him or her. The assumption is that good children are sure defense against misery and public humiliation, whatever the cause (e.g., 10:1; 17:21, 25; 19:26; 23:24-25; 28:7; 29:3).

27:12 This proverb repeats 22:3 almost exactly. In this context, its description of the naive may anticipate those foolish enough to provide surety for strangers in 27:13.

27:13 This proverb is nearly identical to 20:16, except the second line refers to a "strange" woman rather than to "strangers." The difference may elevate the gravity of the situation: the guarantor has not only granted surety to a stranger but to a "strange" *woman*—a person who, at best, likely has fewer opportunities to repay than her male counterparts and, at worst, resembles personified folly in Proverbs 1–9 (cf. 6:1-5; 11:15; 17:18; 22:26-27; but Sir 8:13).

27:14 Humor helps convey the importance of timing and tone in communication. When overplayed ("in a loud voice"), ill timed ("early in the morning"), and too insistent (cf. "to do early" in Jer 7:13; 25:3; 35:14), what is ordinarily a welcome greeting ("blesses") is reckoned a curse instead.

27:15-16 These two proverbs say more about the contentious wife (19:13b; 21:9, 19; 25:24). The first takes up the comparison with dripping rain (19:13b) and adds "on a rainy day," intensifying the bleakness. The second proverb (27:16), connected to the first by storm imagery and a third-person feminine singular suffix ("her"), then turns to wind and oil. Any attempt to "hide" her, that is, "to shelter" (Ps 27:5; 31:21) and "to keep [her] close" (e.g., 2:1; 7:1; 10:14; Job 23:12), fails because one cannot restrain the wind. A storm is loose in the house. "His right hand meets oil" is obscure (27:16b). Perhaps the husband reaches to restrain her but, like oil (and wind), she slips through his grasp (cf. the association of oil with the "strange" woman in 5:3).

27:17 The sages play here with *pānîm* ("face"; NRSV: "wits"). Because the term can refer to the sharp edge of a sword or tool (e.g., Eccl 10:10; Ezek 21:21), it invites rereading the first line ("Iron sharpens iron") with fresh detail. One imagines blades clashing and sparks flying as metal strikes metal to improve an instrument's quality. So, too, interaction with others "sharpens" the human "face," a metonymy for a person's disposition and character. One does not become or remain wise in isolation.

27:18 Those who are loyal enjoy the "fruit" of their commitment. One who "keeps watch" (NRSV: "tends") and "guards" (NRSV: "takes care"), a fixed pair in Proverbs (e.g., 2:8; 13:3; 16:17), offers protection, perhaps by shooing away birds intent on eating the fruit of the fig tree or, similarly, fending off threats to a superior—that is, defending social arrangements and boundaries. The fig tree suggests the longevity of such service (the fruit ripens in two or three months) and, in turn, the superior's beneficence: fig trees are symbolic of prosperity and peace (e.g., Mic 4:4). Use of the passive "will be honored" implies the esteem one enjoys will be widespread.

27:19 Just as water may serve as a mirror and permit a person to examine his or her outward appearance, "thus a human heart to a human." On the one hand, the line suggests a person's heart, like water, self-reflects, enabling self-awareness and introspection. On the other, it reveals something more about friendship—how, as iron sharpens iron (27:17; cf. 27:9), the reflections of a friend teach us about ourselves (NRSV). The ambiguity leaves open both as means by which one gains self-knowledge.

27:20 Biblical writers draw on depictions in Canaanite mythology of deified Death as an insatiable monster—one lip touching the underworld, the other the heavens, the tongue the stars—to describe Sheol and Abaddon (two names for the underworld) as ravenous for human lives. Agur observes that the belly of death never says "Enough!" (30:15-16), and Isaiah depicts Sheol "opening its mouth beyond measure" to swallow many nobles (Isa 5:14). The same imagery is also, at times, appropriated to describe human insatiability. Although here the claim is general (i.e., all human eyes), elsewhere the imagery is used specifically for the greedy (cf. 1:12), wealthy, arrogant, and oppressive who "set their mouths against heaven, and their tongues range over the earth" (Ps 73:9), who widen their gullets like Sheol (Hab 2:5) and are never satisfied (cf. Seow 1997, 227). Implicit are the dangers of self-destruction (e.g., 1:17-19; Eccl 4:7-8; 5:8-12 [Heb. vv. 7-11]) and the destruction of anyone who gets in the way.

27:21 The first line repeats 17:3a exactly but, unlike the earlier proverb, the second line indicates a person is "tested" by his or her reputation (as by God in 17:3b). Like a crucible, which separates liquid metal from dross at high heat, public opinion can "extract" and "purify" the honorable from those who are not (e.g., 12:8). But caution is warranted: the public can be fickle (e.g.,

19:4, 6). For the sages, the esteem of one's community is a high value (e.g., 3:3-4; 5:3-14; 27:18; cf. Theological and Ethical Analysis of Proverbs 5).

27:22 The severe pounding of milling grain with a mortar and pestle—the sheer effort required to pulverize the grain to separate it from its husk—highlights the fool's intractability ("fool" here is 'ĕwîl, or one known for moral distortion and stubborn refusal of discipline, e.g., 1:7b). No discipline, no matter how extreme, can part such a person from his or her folly (e.g., 17:10, 16; 26:11).

27:23-27 This five-verse concluding poem (compare 24:30-34) elaborates on why it is important to "know the needs" of one's animals (12:10). Whereas "treasure" or "stocks" (ḥōsen) must be replenished and may be easily squandered or stolen (e.g., Jer 20:5; Ezek 22:25), and a crown does not last forever, flocks and herds are self-renewing resources. Their continued existence depends not on fortresses, deadbolts, or dynasties but on good stewardship of the resources provided by creation: time and again, the earth sustains the grass, which sustains the animals, which sustain one's household with "enough" food, clothing, and money. Mention of a "crown" (27:28) may also evoke the metaphor of the king as a "shepherd," one charged to know and provide for the community's well-being (e.g., Ezek 34); if so, the poem anticipates the sages' emphasis on just government in Proverbs 28–29.

PROVERBS 28–29

Literary Analysis

Interpreters commonly divide the second Solomonic collection (chapters 25–29) into two units, 25:1–27:27 and 28:1–29:27 (see Introduction to Proverbs 25:1–29:27). The opening and closing proverbs of the latter (28:1; 29:27) signal much about its content: both are antithetical proverbs, the unit's most prevalent genre, and both feature the opposition of the righteous and the wicked—the unit's thematic backbone. To this extent, the chapters resemble 10:1–15:33. Notably different, however, is a persistent concern for just government. The scribes refer repeatedly to rulers (28:2,

15, 16; 29:4, 12, 14, 26) and to the exercise or abuse of authority (28:3, 12, 28; 29:2, 7, 14, 16). Indeed, the refrain of the two chapters, which juxtaposes the righteous and wicked, describes the impact both have on the community when in power (28:12, 28; 29:2, 16). Some interpreters thus contend that chapters 28–29 (prefaced by the poem in 27:23-27) were composed as a manual for future rulers (e.g., Malchow 1985; Meinhold 1991, 2:464-65). Although circumscribing the audience so narrowly is dubious given the chapters' diverse content and the considerable difficulty of establishing the original context of a proverb (or biblical text), it is clear that the sages press readers to think critically about power and government.

A second theme is tôrâ (28:4 [2x], 7, 9; 29:18), a term that in Proverbs typically refers to the "instruction" of the wise (e.g., 1:8; 3:1; 4:2) but may also evoke God's instruction or law (broadly or more narrowly as in Mosaic law)—particularly when, as here, the term occurs without a possessive (e.g., "the tôrâ of your mother," 1:8; "my tôrâ," 3:1; 4:2; 7:2). The sages reflect variously on "transgressions" or "crimes" (pešaʿ, 28:2, 13, 24; 29:6, 16, 22) as they urge obedience to tôrâ for wisdom, well-being, and the struggle against injustice. Lastly, a number of the proverbs take up the recurrent theme of wealth and poverty (e.g., 28:6, 8, 15, 19-20, 22, 27; 29:7, 13).

Theological and Ethical Overview

Headlines almost daily confront us with disturbing if not tragic accounts of corrupt leaders. From ethical blunders to brutal, bloody crimes against humanity, we are keenly aware that those who govern are fallible and may wield their power to considerable harm. It is an awareness the sages had too. Whereas the portrait of the king to this point in Proverbs is rather idealistic (see the Theological and Ethical Overview of Proverbs 16:1–22:16 and 25:2-7), the sages shift in chapters 28–29 from wholesale admiration to caution about the reality of wicked rulers—who, like roaring lions or charging bears, trample the poor (28:15), callously and ignorantly extort from their people (28:16; 29:4b), and let transgressions go unchecked (29:16). The rulers' damage is far- reaching: the king who entertains lies emboldens wicked officials (29:12), and whole communities cry out or go into hiding (28:28; 29:2; cf. 28:2). For many readers, the sages' warning is a much-needed corrective to their earlier veneration of government; it wrests apart the king and God—who were previously conjoined (e.g., 16:10, 15; 19:12; 21:1; 24:21-22). Moreover, the sages highlight the political, indeed national, dimensions that the struggle between the righteous and wicked may assume (e.g., 28:4, 12, 28; 29:2) and the bitter loathing each has for the other (29:10, 27). The result is a markedly nuanced portrait of government: the sages insist rulers must be wise and practice justice, and caution that we err if we place too much confidence in them to do so (29:26).

The hallmark of corrupt leadership in chapters 28–29 is economic injustice. Government is good and endures when it protects and provides for the poor (29:4, 14)—a standard very much alive and debated in national conversations today. The claim is indicative of the sages' increasingly critical reflection about wealth and poverty. Although they still associate poverty with laziness and folly (e.g., 28:19; see, e.g., 6:9-11; 10:4), the sages consider poverty preferable to crooked money (28:6; e.g., 16:8, 19; 17:1; see Theological and Ethical Overview of Proverbs 16:1–22:16), and say more about injustice and oppression, whether by the government (28:15), greedy creditors (28:8), or even other poor people (28:3; cf. 13:23). The result is a more sympathetic portrait of the poor as vulnerable and with legal rights that the righteous know and defend (29:7; cf. 28:27)—a conviction King Lemuel's mother takes up earnestly with her son in 31:1-9. Wealth is likewise complex. The righteous and wise do not always prosper (28:6; e.g., 16:8, 19; 17:1; 19:1, 22), and people too readily pursue money for its own sake (likely at ethical expense, 28:20b) or hoard it to their demise (28:22). Caution that money also inspires arrogance (28:11) anticipates Agur's rationale for praying only for his daily bread: any more than that endangers his faithfulness to God (30:7-9).

A priority for justice and protection of the poor is mandated, as elsewhere in Proverbs, by God's priority for the same. Proverbs 28–29 emphasize that God is the creator of everyone (poor and oppressor alike, 29:13); God is just (28:5; 29:26); and God provides for those who trust in God (28:25; 29:25)—even (implicitly) when it appears the wicked are successful (e.g., 28:8, 20, 27). The worldview again is one of moral polarities, of conflict between good and evil in which the good are aligned with God (see Theological and Ethical Analyses of Proverbs 1:1-7 and Proverbs 3, and Theological and Ethical Overview of Proverbs 10:1–15:33). Readers may well be troubled by such thinking, particularly when we know persons and groups who fanatically maintain and promote their beliefs; who use coercion and violence, often in the name of God, to force those beliefs on others. A bifurcated worldview, we worry, lends too readily to absolutes and dogmatism. At the same time, however, the sages' notion of the world in struggle cautions us not to rest too long on the laurels of our tolerance—to "elevate moral ambiguity . . . to the point of relativism"—lest we slide into moral indifference and remain still and silent in the face of evil (Van Leeuwen 1997, 247; cf. 24:10-12 and Theological and Ethical Overview of Proverbs 22:17–24:34). Tolerance is not always a virtue. The challenge is to know when it is not.

Exegetical Analysis

28:1 Found only here and in Lev 26:17, "flee though none pursue" occurs in God's description of penalties for disobedience: "I will set my face against you, and you shall be struck down by your enemies; your foes shall rule over you, and *you shall flee though no one pursues you.*" The phrase suggests that the wicked are afraid; their guilty consciences compel them to run as though hunted (but cf. Pss 17:8-12; 58:3-6 [Heb. vv. 4-7]). By contrast, the righteous are "secure" or "confident" (NRSV: "bold") like lions—majestic creatures celebrated for their fearless instincts and skillful pursuit of prey (e.g., 22:13; 26:13; 30:29-30; Isa 5:29; 31:4; Ezek 19:3).

28:2 The Hebrew of this proverb is difficult. The transgression of a "land"—that is, of its inhabitants (e.g., 29:4; 30:21)—results in many rulers, whether concurrently as a large bureaucracy (e.g., 1 Sam 8:10-18; 1 Kgs 4:1-28) or successively, as at times in the unstable northern kingdom (e.g., 1 Kgs 16:8-28; 2 Kgs 15:8-26). Implied is that none of the many leaders can restore order. By contrast, one intelligent person "prolongs" (likely elliptical for "prolongs days," Exod 20:12; Eccl 7:15; 8:12) his or her reign and/or life.

28:3 Perhaps in light of 28:2 and because the Bible tends not to talk about the poor as oppressors, the NRSV emends "poor" man to "ruler." But the Hebrew makes sense and calls attention to the capacity of the downtrodden to take advantage of one another. Although rain is ordinarily welcome (16:15; 25:14; 26:1), when torrential and unrelenting it washes away everything, including any hope for harvest.

28:4 "Commandment" (*tôrâ*) in Proverbs typically refers to parental instruction (e.g., 2:1; 3:1; 4:4; 6:20) but may evoke Mosaic law. One's behavior toward instruction has an inverse effect on the wicked—to abandon *tôrâ* is to praise the wicked, to observe *tôrâ* is to strive against the wicked. The equivalencies emphasize that obedience or lack thereof has direct and significant implications for the community: one either empowers or opposes the wicked.

28:5 That the wicked "do not understand" justice conveys the severity of their disorientation; they do not know the good so they do not recognize right from wrong, much less practice fairness. Seekers of the LORD, however, understand "all," an ambiguous claim that likely refers back to justice. The proverb couples faith-seeking with knowledge and moral clarity (e.g., 1 Cor 2:15). Implicit is a call to action: those who know the good do it. Seekers of God practice justice. There is no true knowledge of God without it (e.g., Jer 22:15-17; Hos 4:1; 6:6).

28:6 The first line of this proverb is identical to 19:1a (cf. 15:16; 16:8). "Ways" in the second line is dual ("two ways," cf. 28:18), suggesting duplicity (i.e., "double heart," Ps 12:2), double-dealing, or a mixed mind about which "way," good or evil, one should take (28:5; e.g., 1 Kgs 18:21; Sir 2:12).

28:7 Proverbs that feature the relationship between parents and children are frequent in Proverbs (e.g., 10:1, 5; 17:25; 19:26; 27:11; 29:3). Here the contrast is between the child who observes "instruction" (*tôrâ*, cf. 28:4) and the one who hangs out with "gluttons" who are thoughtless about what they consume, who squander and overindulge (e.g., 23:20-21). The latter submit their parents to public ridicule. The juxtaposition recalls the parents' public charge against a rebellious child: "This son of ours is stubborn and rebellious. He will not obey us. He is a glutton and a drunkard" (Deut 21:20).

<u>28:8</u> Biblical law forbids charging interest on loans to Israelites (but not foreigners, Exod 22:25 [Heb. v. 24]; Deut 23:19-20). Profits so acquired somehow—the proverb leaves open the possibilities (e.g., divine intervention, legal action, poetic justice)—end up in the hands of the gracious who, in turn, redistribute them to the poor (e.g., 13:22b; 14:31; 19:17). What is taken unjustly is ultimately returned.

<u>28:9</u> On the heels of 28:8, this proverb sounds the more general warning: how one treats *tôrâ* ("instruction" or "law"; cf. 28:4, 7) is how one will be treated. Those who refuse to listen to it will, in turn, not be heard (e.g., 15:8, 29; see excursus in Proverbs 2).

<u>28:10</u> The proverb recaps the fates of the righteous and wicked (for other triplets, e.g., 27:10, 14). The first line introduces one who "misleads" the upright, who "causes [them] to stagger" (*šāgâ*, cf. 5:19, 20, 23; 19:27; 20:1) down a wicked path. (Note the sages assume the upright may be misled.) The second line tersely describes that person's fate, emphasizing with a possessive suffix (*"his* pit") and an independent personal pronoun before the verb (*"he,* he will fall") that it is the person's own doing (e.g., 26:27). The third line then heralds the good fortune of the "blameless" (2:21).

<u>28:11</u> Yet good fortune (28:10c), in this case wealth, cannot be equated with being wise (28:6). Wealth easily distorts judgment, inflating one's confidence to the point that one is "wise in [one's] eyes," a hallmark of fools (e.g., 3:7; 14:12; 26:5, 12; 28:26). Such was the case with Nabal, the rich fool (1 Sam 25). A discerning poor person "searches out" the ruse (18:17b; 25:2b). Given wisdom's surpassing value, the poor person is ironically the more rich (e.g., 3:13-15; 8:18-21).

<u>28:12</u> The fate of a community hinges on who is successful. When the righteous "rejoice," there is much glory. People bask in

it. But when the wicked "arise," a verb that connotes standing up (as in court, e.g., Ps 27:12), rising to power, or waging war (e.g., 2 Sam 18:31; Isa 31:2), people hide. Success by the righteous inspires pride and communal solidarity; triumph by the wicked prompts shame and personal isolation (28:28; 29:2, 16).

28:13 Whereas a mark of love is "concealing" the offense of another (17:9), that is, forgiving (Ps 78:38) or overlooking it, the sages do not condone covering up one's own transgression. Rather, this proverb urges revealing the offense publicly ("confess and forsake"), assured of mercy from God and likely others (e.g., Pss 32; 103:13; Isa 49:15; Jer 6:23).

28:14 "Fear" here is *pāḥad* ("trembles," cf. Isa 51:13) not *yārē*ʾ (as in "fear of the LORD"). The phrase "fear constantly" occurs only one other time, in Isa 51:13, where it refers to fear of an oppressor. In contrast, those who "harden the heart" are obstinate (e.g., Exod 7:3; Ps 95:8; Ezek 3:7; cf. "hardened neck" in 29:1). The sense is that some fears promote well-being (28:1; 29:25) whereas stubbornness leads to calamity.

28:15-16 Unjust rulers take center stage in these two proverbs. The comparison of kings to lions, common in Proverbs and elsewhere (e.g., 19:12; 20:2; cf. 30:29-31 [the Hebrew term is different]), is made ominous here by: (*a*) pairing the lion with a bear, another predatory animal (1 Sam 17:34, 37; Amos 5:19); (*b*) the active participles "growl" (Isa 5:29) and "charging," which signal imminent attack; (*c*) the preposition "over"; and (*d*) description of the people as "poor" or "powerless" (*dāl*, e.g., 10:15; 14:31; 28:3, 8, 11; 29:7, 14). A wicked king is a ferocious predator of his people.

The second proverb (28:16), the Hebrew of which is difficult, associates a leader's ignorance with escalating extortion. By contrast, those who despise "unjust gain" (1:19; 15:27) prolong their days—as leaders and in life (e.g., 3:2, 16; 4:10; 8:35; 9:11).

28:17 The proverb describes the power of a guilty conscience. A person "burdened" by having taken the life of another, whether accidentally or deliberately, "flees" (28:1) for his or her own life and there is no safe haven, not even in cities of refuge designated to protect murderers from blood vengeance by relatives of the victim (Exod 21:13; Deut 19:9-10; Josh 20). The last line may be interpreted: (*a*) "do not help him" (NRSV, e.g., Isa 41:10); or (*b*) "do not take hold of (i.e., stop) him" (NJB; e.g., 3:18; 4:4; 11:16; 31:19).

28:18 Whereas the "blameless" are helped in times of trouble, presumably by God and others (e.g., 10:9; 20:22; Deut 22:27), a double-dealing crook ("a twisted one of two ways," cf. 28:6) falls "in (or by) one" (so MT), that is, into a deception of his or her own making (26:27).

28:19 This proverb is a variant of 12:11. Here it offers specific examples of the figures described in 28:18. The second line also anticipates 28:20b; the pursuit of "empty nothings" (28:19b) or quick money (28:20b) leads to ruin.

28:20 Juxtaposition of "the faithful person" with "one who hurries to get rich" implies that haste somehow involves dishonesty. The sages caution against being in a rush (e.g., 19:2)—particularly to make money (e.g., 13:11; 20:21; 23:4-5; cf. 1 Tim 6:9-10).

28:21 Although one should never show partiality ("to recognize a face," cf. 24:23; Deut 1:17; 16:19), the sages concede a mere pittance can motivate someone to do so (e.g., 17:23; 18:5, 16). That the bribe is a single crust of bread, a scrap of food basic for survival (e.g., 17:1; Ruth 2:14; 2 Sam 12:3), highlights how tenuous justice can be. Other "not good" proverbs are 16:29; 17:26; 18:5; 19:2; and 25:27.

28:22 The issue is not haste but anxiety. The stingy ("evil of eye," 23:6; cf. "good of eye," 22:9) is "out of [his or her] senses" (*bāhal*) about money; in the niphal conjugation, the verb means "to be anxious" or "dismayed" (NAB: "be perturbed about"; e.g., Exod 15:15; Eccl 8:3; Isa 13:8). Misers consumed by anxiety do not know that poverty comes for them—presumably as a result of their stinginess. Money slips between tightfisted fingers.

28:23 Literary imbalance in the Hebrew bolsters the claim. The five-word first line extols those who rebuke others, noting "afterward" they "find favor," presumably from everyone and God (3:4). Their words sting at first, but people come to recognize and respect their value (e.g., 9:8; 19:25; 25:12; 27:5-6). The two-word second line—"more-than-one-who-makes-smooth—a tongue" (e.g., 2:16; 5:3; 7:5; 29:5)—denies the flatterer a predicate, an "afterward." People quickly write off a smooth talker.

28:24 Lack of detail with regard to the theft leaves open possible scenarios, including the claiming of one's inheritance prematurely and piecemeal. To steal from one's parents and then to rationalize it ("that is no crime") is an egregious violation. Moreover, it breaks the family apart: the thief forsakes the company of two parents to partner with an unnamed "destroyer" (18:9b; e.g., 19:26; 20:20; 30:11, 17; Mark 7:10-13).

28:25-26 The catchword "trust" associates these two proverbs. "Open wide [one's] throat" (NRSV: "greedy") elsewhere describes Sheol, the underworld, with its insatiable appetite for human life (Isa 5:14; Hab 2:5). Greed, like hatred and anger, stirs up conflict (10:12; 15:18; 29:22). In contrast, trust in God satisfies the appetite. It "makes one fat" (11:25; 13:4).

The second proverb (28:26) develops the theme of trust by contrasting two different figures. Independent pronouns add emphasis. The proverb first points to one who "trusts in his heart," a phrase similar to "wise in one's eyes" (e.g., 3:7; 14:12; 26:12; 28:11), and dismisses him outright: "*He* is a fool." It then points to one who walks with wisdom, who fears the LORD, and declares: "*He* comes through safely."

28:27 Ironically, whereas poverty comes to the miser (28:22), it does not to those who are generous to the poor (e.g., 14:31; 17:5; 21:13; 22:2; 29:13). "Lift up the eye" (NRSV: "turns a blind eye") is an idiom for arrogance (6:17; Ps 101:5; Isa 5:15) and evokes the tendency of many of us to glance away in an awkward and obvious attempt to avoid eye contact with the poor as we hurry by.

28:28 With a first line nearly identical to 28:12b, the proverb returns to the impact of wicked people on the community. Wordplay accentuates human mortality—"people" (*'ādām*) and "they perish" (*'obdām*)—offering implicit assurance that the wicked will not prevail forever (29:2, 16).

29:1 The opening phrase "person of reproof" may refer to one who reproves or one who receives reproof. The remainder of the proverb clarifies the latter is of concern—a person who refuses to listen to correction, who "stiffens the neck" as the Israelites did time and again (e.g., Deut 10:16; 2 Kgs 17:4; Jer 7:26). The consequence of such stubbornness is both sudden ("in an instant") and graphic: "it [or he] is broken"—the subject may be the neck or the obstinate person—and there is no healing (29:1b // 6:15b). To refuse wisdom is to irreparably break one's neck (e.g., 12:1; 15:10).

29:2 The sounds of a community suggest the quality of its leadership. Juxtaposition of the righteous (pl.) with one wicked ruler (sg.) lends gravity to the claim—it takes only one corrupt leader to provoke an outcry. The proverb also plays with the infinitive rĕbôt ("to be numerous" or "to be powerful"). The first line may be read initially as about the public joy that accompanies "many" (rĕbôt) righteous; the parallel "ruling" in the second line then invites rereading it as about public sentiment when the righteous "are powerful" (rĕbôt, NRSV; cf. 28:12, 28; 29:16).

29:3 The "child" (NRSV) is grown up here (lit. "a person" or "man"), but the parental joy he inspires by loving wisdom is not diminished (e.g., 10:1; 15:20; 17:21). The proverb's contrast between loving wisdom and companioning "prostitutes" (zônôt) evokes the youth's choice in Proverbs 1–9 between wisdom/one's wife and folly/the "strange" woman (with "clothing of 'a prostitute,' " zônâ, 7:10; cf. 6:26). There, as here, those who choose the latter give up everything (e.g., 5:8-14).

29:4 The proverb contrasts a king, who by means of justice creates stability (e.g., 16:10-13; 20:28), with one who is eager for "contributions," a term that nearly always refers to what is given voluntarily (i.e., "offering" or "donation," e.g., Num 15:17-21; Deut 12:6, 11). The former works hard so the land may "stand"; the latter exacts so much from the hard work and generosity of others that the kingdom falls.

29:5 References to traps associate the next two proverbs. A flatterer is one who "makes smooth," likely an elliptical form of "makes smooth the tongue" (e.g., 2:16; 5:3; 7:5; 28:23). One pictures the flatterer speaking earnestly to a friend—weaving together a mesh of disingenuous and overdone praise, and casting it as a net around "his feet" like a bird or animal trap (e.g., Ps

140:5 [Heb. v. 6]; Lam 1:13; Ezek 19:8); the ambiguous suffix "his" may refer to the friend and, ironically, the flatterer. The scene recalls the sinners who set out to ambush the innocent only to ensnare themselves (1:10-19), and the "strange" woman whose "smooth words" captivate and capture the youth who is without sense (7:21-23).

29:6 The proverb ensnares (cf. the net in 29:5) the wicked in their offense (12:13) while the righteous move freely, "shouting for joy" (*rānan*) and singing—confident in their security and well-being. Elsewhere in Proverbs, personified wisdom "cries out loudly" (*rānan*, 1:20; 8:3) in the heart of the city; the righteous, like her, are bold and forthright while the wicked are devious and scheming (e.g., 12:2; 24:8-9).

29:7 Alliteration and assonance in the first line align the righteous and the poor (*yōdēaʿ ṣaddîq dîn dallîm*). The righteous know the "judgments" (NRSV: "rights") of the poor—namely, legal causes and claims on their behalf (e.g., 31:5, 8; Deut 17:8; Isa 10:2; Jer 5:28)—and presumably act on that knowledge to protect and advocate for the less fortunate (12:10 and 27:23 ascribe to the righteous similar concern for creatures). They know what is good and do it (cf. 28:5). That the wicked do not understand "knowledge" likely refers back to the rights of the poor (NRSV) but may also be construed generally: they are fools. Their callous disregard for the poor reveals their ignorance.

29:8 The phrase translated "scoffers" is found otherwise only in Isa 28:14, where it refers to corrupt rulers who fill the city of Jerusalem with lies and make a "covenant with death." Arrogant and contentious, cynical and insolent, scoffers inflame anger and conflict in the community (e.g., 9:7-8a; 21:24; 22:10), whereas the wise turn anger away (e.g., 15:1).

29:9 The proverb conveys the futility of arguing with a fool (26:4). The verb in the first line, "to dispute" or "enter into judgment" (e.g., 1 Sam 12:7; Jer 2:35; Ezek 17:20), suggests a legal context. Although lack of an explicit subject in the second line makes it possible to attribute the agitation and laughter (NRSV: "ridicule") to either party, it most likely depicts the fool's trembling rage and derisive reaction—behavior that affords no "rest" or "repose" (Eccl 9:17). The wise person pursues appropriate means to settle the dispute; the insolence of the fool precludes it.

29:10 From hatred to murder, the proverb conveys how fiercely the bloodthirsty loathe the upright. The idiom "seek the life" of someone nearly always indicates malicious intent (e.g., Exod 4:19; 1 Sam 20:1; Ps 35:4), and the construction—"as for the upright (pl.), [the bloodthirsty] seek each life (sg.)"—suggests they are relentless and thorough.

29:11 As if unleashing the wind, fools vent *all* of their *rûaḥ*, a term that encompasses a person's frame of mind, thoughts, and temperament (e.g., 1:23; 11:13; 14:29; 16:19, 32; 18:14); this includes, but is not limited to, their anger (NRSV). In contrast, the wise "hold it back." Self-restraint is a celebrated virtue in Proverbs (e.g., 12:16; 14:17, 29; 15:2).

29:12 This proverb draws a direct line between a ruler's abdication of the responsibility to ensure integrity and justice (e.g., 14:35; 16:10, 12-13; 25:5; 29:4) and the corruption of his court: if a ruler listens attentively to lies, then all of his officials become wicked—leading eventually to the kingdom's demise (cf. Sir 10:1-3). That the corruption is comprehensive ("*all* of his officials") adds intensity to the warning and underscores the necessity of good counsel (e.g., 11:14; 13:10; 15:22).

29:13 A variant of 22:2, the scene is a chance encounter (NRSV: "have this in common" is loose) between a poor person and an "oppressor," a description that refers generally to oppressors (e.g., Jer 9:5) and, in particular, to those who cheat in business affairs (e.g., Ps 55:11 [Heb. v. 12]). Perhaps debtor and creditor meet. The proverb again appeals to a common Creator to promote a common humanity—"light [in] the eyes" is an idiom for life (e.g., 15:30; Job 3:16; Ps 13:4).

29:14 The king must act on that common humanity (29:13) and ensure justice for everyone (but cf. 29:26). The proverb lends concreteness to the righteousness by which the king's throne is established (16:12; 20:28): the stability of his rule and kingdom hinges on fairness to the poor (e.g., Isa 11:4; Jer 22:6). The king who endures and is worthy of praise, the psalmist elaborates,

delivers the needy when they call,
the poor and those who have no helper.
He has pity on the weak and the needy,
and saves the lives of the needy.
From oppression and violence he redeems their life;
and precious is their blood in his sight.
Long may he live! (Ps 72:12-15a)

29:15 The sages condemn lenient parenting. Given the means to teach wisdom—the rod (physical) and reproof (verbal)—there is no excuse for a youth "let loose," a verb that means variously "to send," "chase away," or "abandon" (e.g., Isa 16:2; 27:10; Dan 10:11; Obad 1). A child's lack of discipline is a parent's shame (e.g., 13:24; 19:18; 23:14-15; Sir 22:3-6; 30:1-13). See 29:17.

29:16 Repetition of the Hebrew root *rābâ* in the first line readily associates the status of the wicked and the extent of transgressions: when the wicked are "numerous" and/or "powerful" (*rĕbôt,* cf. 29:2), offenses "increase" (*yirbeh*). The proverb glimpses eventual victory for the righteous nonetheless—the "downfall" of the wicked, a term used for God's utter destruction of cities and kings (e.g., Ezek 26:15; 27:27; 31:16; 32:10).

29:17 Should the threat of public embarrassment not be sufficient (29:15), this proverb appeals to self-interest to motivate parental discipline (e.g., 10:1; 15:20; 23:15-16). The second line affords a more literal translation: "[the child] will give you 'delicacies' (Gen 49:20; Lam 4:5) for your 'throat' or 'appetite' (*nepeš*)." The disciplined child provides for the parent one day, and the provision is lavish.

29:18 Interpretation of this proverb hinges on how one understands *tôrâ* ("instruction" or "law," cf. Literary Analysis of Proverbs 28-29) and "vision" (*ḥāzôn;* NRSV: "prophecy"), a noun that, found only here in Proverbs, refers to revelation typically by means of a dream or hearing (e.g., Dan 1:17; 8:2; 9:21-23; in book titles, e.g., Isa 1:1; Nah 1:1). We find similar terms in Proverbs (i.e. "inspired decisions," 16:10; "oracle," 30:1; 31:1), and the verb related to "vision" (*ḥāzâ,* "to see") is used three times to describe or prompt an observation that gives wisdom (22:29;

24:32; 29:20; e.g., Job 15:17: 19:26-27; 27:12). In Job, the sage Eliphaz recounts a "vision" (*ḥāzôn*) that came to him in the night (Job 4:13). "Vision," like *tôrâ*, may thus refer broadly to revelation that conveys knowledge. Understood as such, 29:18a is reminiscent of 11:14a. Without wisdom, a people or nation "runs wild"—they are out of control, even riotous (e.g., Exod 32:25; the same verb elsewhere in Proverbs means "to neglect" or "leave unattended," 1:25; 4:15; 8:33; 13:18; 15:32). By contrast, just one person who follows *tôrâ* ("instruction") is happy.

Whereas it is right to interpret the terms first within Proverbs and the wisdom tradition, it is likely, particularly given the concern for just government predominant in Proverbs 28–29 (see Theological and Ethical Overview), readers will think of the prophets and Mosaic law—vital sources of guidance, inspiration, and correction for king and community (e.g., Deut 17:18-20; 18:15-22). Indeed, in the one other place where "vision" and *tôrâ* are parallel, Israel has lost its way with regard to both and teems with arrogance, violence, and lawlessness (Ezek 7:26; cf. Lam 2:9).

<u>29:19</u> The implication is that servants are willful; they understand reproof but "there is no response." Another means of discipline is necessary (cf. 29:15, 21). Compare *Papyrus Insinger*: "If the stick is far from his master, the servant does not listen to him" (*AEL* 3:196).

<u>29:20</u> This proverb is nearly identical to 26:12 but replaces "who is wise in [one's] own eyes" with "who is hasty in speech." The sages warn against being in a rush generally (e.g., 19:2; 21:5), and unrestrained and ill-considered speech particularly (e.g., 10:19; 17:27a). "Do you see?" occurs also in 22:29.

<u>29:21</u> Taking up the topic of disciplining one's servants (29:19), the proverb cautions against indulging them. The subject of the first line, contrary to NRSV, is one who "pampers," a *hapax legomenon*, which in cognate languages means to permit someone to live in ease and affluence. The master fails to train the servant early. Interpretation of the second line is confounded by an ambiguous suffix (the antecedent of "his end" may be the master or servant) and an uncertain last word (NRSV: "bad"). The sense

is that the master's failure results in hardship for everyone—the servant is unskilled and unruly and the master is miserable. These and other master-servant proverbs reinforce the perception that the book is intended primarily for young men of the upper class (e.g., 19:10; 29:19; 30:10, 21-23; cf. 1:8-19).

29:22 The first line is nearly identical to 15:18a (cf. 28:25). The second elaborates, leaving open whether the many offenses (29:16) are perpetrated by the wrathful and those they provoke. The sages warn that to associate with hotheads is to set a trap for oneself (22:24).

29:23 Play with high and low animates this proverb. "Pride" is from the Hebrew root "to be high." Those who presume for themselves such status find it "brings [them] low" (the verb šāpal), while those who are "low" (šāpal) in spirit, namely humble, take high standing in the eyes of others (e.g., 15:33; 16:18-19; 18:12).

29:24 "To partner" with a thief suggests sharing in the crime and its spoils (1:10-19; e.g., Josh 22:8, which is a form of self-destruction. The second line explains and compounds the grief. Its language evokes Lev 5:1, which stipulates that if a person "hears" a public "curse" or adjuration to testify—that is, the victim's charge of the crime—and knows something, that person must "testify" (NRSV: "disclose") or be subject to punishment (cf. Judg 17:2-3). The thief's partner does not. So in the aftermath of one crime, the accomplice commits another.

29:25 "Fear" here is ḥărādâ, a trembling, panicky fear (e.g., 1 Sam 14:15; Isa 21:4; Jer 30:5). "Fear of a human" may be read as: (a) a subjective genitive, that is, any human terror, or (b) an objective genitive, fear of another person. Both are paralyzing and potentially deadly: a snare. But one who trusts in God, a "fearer of the LORD," is protected, literally made "high" or "inaccessible"—well beyond the reach of traps.

29:26 With only one exception (1 Kgs 10:24 // 2 Chr 9:23), the idiom "to seek the face" is used for seeking God's presence and favor (e.g., 2 Sam 21:1; Ps 24:6; Hos 5:15). To "seek the face" of a ruler instead is to misplace one's reverence and trust. The inverted word order of the second line adds emphasis—"but *from* YHWH is justice." Rulers must practice and protect justice (e.g.,

16:12; 20:28; 29:14), but its definitive source, inspiration, and guarantee is God.

<u>29:27</u> The chapter and larger section (chs. 25–29) ends with this statement about the revulsion with which the righteous and wicked regard each other. In Proverbs, the term "abomination" is used primarily for what God finds abhorrent (e.g., 11:1, 20; 15:8, 26; 17:15; see excursus in Proverbs 3). A few proverbs, like this one, indicate the righteous share God's aversions (e.g., 16:12; 24:9). The wicked do not (e.g., 13:19b; 21:27).

PROVERBS 30: "THE WORDS OF AGUR"

Literary Analysis

This chapter, particularly 30:1-9, is arguably the most difficult of the book; it presents many exegetical dilemmas and, consequently, inspires many interpretations. Readers debate how to understand the character of Agur. Is he a skeptic? An agnostic? Or, as this reading contends, a devout "fearer of the LORD"? Further, how much of the chapter do we attribute to him? Some, for example, see a dialogue between a skeptical Agur (30:1-4) and a pious Jew (30:5-6, 7-9; e.g., Scott 1965, 176; Crenshaw 1989). Others argue Agur's opening lament (30:1-3) is met by a sharp rebuke by God or someone on God's behalf (30:4; e.g., Brown 2004, 176). But lack of a new superscription or obvious shift in speaker coupled with the largely discontinuous texture of Proverbs 10–31 suggests the chapter as a whole is Agur's "oracle," or inspired word from God (30:1). As the "Gatherer" (the interpretation of his name in Aramaic), Agur pulls together a collection of proverbs that heralds God's power and wisdom, the wonder of God's creation, and, in light of it all, the limits of human knowledge and resolve. (The purported compiler of Ecclesiastes is identified similarly as *Qohelet*, namely, "Gatherer" or "Collector"; cf. Eccl 1:1.)

The chapter may be divided into two main units (30:1-9, 10-33). (The division and placement of the chapter in LXX— 22:17–24:22; 30:1-14; 24:23-34; 30:15-33—is a secondary development.) The first unit (30:1-9) resembles the weary psalmist's movement from lament over his or her ignorance to affirmation of God's presence (esp. Ps 73): an exhausted Agur laments his ignorance (30:1b-3), remembers God's incomprehensible power over the cosmos (30:4), insists God's word alone as trustworthy (30:5-6), and prays for his "daily bread" (30:7-9). Two rhetorical questions that require the response "(only) God" balance the unit (30:4, 9). Notably, in his distress, Agur turns to Scripture, including Num 24:3, 15 (cf. 2 Sam 22:31), Ps 73:22, 2 Sam 22:31bc (// Ps 18:30 [Heb. v. 31]), Deut 4:2, and rhetorical "who" questions like those found in Job 38–41 and Isa 40. Agur finds voice, in part, in the language and forms of tradition.

Verse 10 is a hinge verse. It resembles 30:6 syntactically and, with the catchword "curse," is linked to 30:11-14, a list of wretched persons that, although not strictly a numerical proverb, sets the stage for them. The remainder of the second unit (30:15-33) is comprised largely of numerical proverbs, in which two numbers typically occur in parallel (x, x + 1) and the second governs the content (30:15-16, 18-19, 21-23, 24-28, 29-31; cf. 6:16-19). Numerical proverbs are found elsewhere in biblical wisdom (e.g., Job 5:19-22; Sir 25:7-11) and in other ancient Near Eastern wisdom texts (e.g., *Proverbs of Ahiqar* 6.92-93). Agur's extensive use of them here, alongside a variety of other genres (e.g., petition or prayer, 30:7-9; rhetorical questions, 30:4) and literary devices such as anaphora (repetition of a word or phrase at the beginning of each line, e.g., 31:11-14, 21-23), further develops the reader's repertoire of wise speech.

Exegetical Analysis

From Despair to Prayer (30:1-9)

<u>30:1</u> The opening verse is riddled with interpretive challenges. The personal names Agur and Yaqeh are otherwise unknown in the Old Testament, and Agur is not a typical Hebrew name. Second, the "words of Agur" are identified as *hammaśśā'* (*"the* oracle," contrary to NRSV)—an utterance, which, like some prophecy, is inspired by God (e.g., Isa 13:1; Hab 1:1; Mal 1:1). The very next word (*nĕ'um*, "oracle") reinforces the claim. For

some interpreters, however, the redundancy suggests the first word should be emended slightly to read "the Massaite" or "from Massa," that is, as the ethnic designation of a north Arabian tribe, descendants of Ishmael's son Massa (31:1; Gen 25:14; 1 Chr 1:30). Agur may thus be non-Israelite. Lastly, the remainder of 30:1b is puzzling. It may designate Agur's audience ("to Ithiel, to Ithiel, and Ukal"), but only the name Ithiel is found elsewhere (Neh 11:7), repetition of one name but not the other is odd, and Ukal is not attested as a proper name in any Semitic language. Accordingly, some translators emend the line variously, including "I am weary, O God, I am weary, O God. How can I prevail?" (NRSV; cf. Jer 20:9) or, less compellingly, "I am not God; I am not God, that I should prevail" (NAB). There is no consensus.

The phrase "oracle of the man" is found also in introductions to the last words of David (2 Sam 23:1) and oracles of Balaam in Numbers (Num 24:3, 15). The former may suggest Agur is near the end of his life. As for the latter, notably, Balaam claims to have the very knowledge that eludes Agur:

> the oracle of the man whose eye is [open]
> . . . who hears the words of God,
>   and [who] knows the knowledge of the Most High.
> (Num 24:15-16a)

But Balaam's confident assertion may well be ironic. Balaam is an ambiguous prophet (e.g., Num 31:8, 16; Deut 23:4b-5 [Heb. vv. 5b-6]; Josh 24:9-10; Mic 6:5) and the son of bĕ'ôr ("cattle" or "animal")—that is, as a pun, the "son of Stupid" (Van Leeuwen 1997, 251-52). The same Hebrew root appears in 30:2 ("stupid").

30:2-3 Agur's self-abasement elevates and extols wisdom. His self-identification as "stupid" or "brutish" (ba'ar, cf. 12:1)—animal-like in his ignorance—recalls the psalmist's hyperbolic use of the same noun: "I was stupid (ba'ar) and ignorant; / I was like [an animal] toward you" (Ps 73:22) and, "How great are your works, O LORD! / . . . / The [stupid] (ba'ar) cannot know" (Ps 92:5-6 [Heb. vv. 6-7]; cf. 49:11). The psalmist claims similarly: "I am a worm and not a man" (Ps 22:6 [Heb. v. 7]; cf. Job 25:4-6). Agur defines being "human" as having learned wisdom or, as the parallel indicates, da ʿat qĕdōšîm (NRSV: "knowledge of the holy ones"). The same phrase is parallel to "fear of the LORD" in 9:10, as is da ʿat ʾĕlōhîm ("knowledge of God") in 2:5. The sages of Proverbs thus appear to use qĕdōšîm and ʾĕlōhîm interchangeably; qĕdōšîm is likely an epithet for God (cf. Hos 12:1) rather than a reference to heavenly beings ("holy ones"). Agur's confession conveys poignantly the limits of human understanding and the elusiveness of wisdom (e.g., Job 28). Many things remain a mystery. (Compare Khonshotep's protest in the epilogue of the Egyptian *Instruction of Anii* that his father's teachings are too difficult for him to learn, *AEL* 2:144-145.)

<u>30:4</u> Eyes now on God (30:4), Agur builds a case in cosmic terms that God alone is the source of wisdom (e.g., Job 28; Bar 3:29-37). As with similar rhetorical questions in Job 38–41 and Isa 40:12-14, Agur's four "who" questions, the answers to which are "only God," herald God's power and, by implication, human incapacity. Agur encompasses creation by moving vertically (heaven to earth) and horizontally ("the ends of the earth") and by including all four elements: fire (heaven), air, water, and earth (e.g., Eccl 1:5-7). He begins with God alone as the one who can journey between heaven and earth (e.g., Gen 11:7; Deut 30:11-12; Bar 3:29; cf. Van Leeuwen 1997b), and then extols God's capacity to bound and shape the natural world ("gather . . . wrap up . . . establish")—particularly the wild forces of the wind and sea (e.g., 8:27-29; Job 26:8; Ps 104:6-9). One after another Agur's questions recall God's activity, stir amazement, and compel humility: only God.

Agur's query culminates with two "what" questions. The four "who" questions anticipate "God" as the answer to the first (Exod 3:13; cf. Amos 9:5-6). The answer to the second ("What is the name of the person's *son*?") is less clear. Some interpret "son" as the community of Israel, but the tradition of Israel as the "son of God" (e.g., Exod 4:22; Deut 14:1; 32:5-6; Isa 43:6; Hos 11:1) is foreign to Proverbs. Others emend slightly and read the plural "sons" as a reference to the heavenly beings (cf. Job 38:7). It makes better sense, however, to read "son" here as we have throughout the book—as the student of wisdom: in this context, Agur (e.g., 1:8, 10; 2:1; cf. 3:12 in which God is likened to a parent). The last line ("Surely you know!"), which forms an *inclusio* with 30:2 ("I do not know"), is Agur's final stroke (cf. Job 38:5). Like the psalmist (e.g., Pss 22, 73), Agur moves from despair and fatigue to renewed conviction by recalling what he *does* know: God's incomprehensible power. Moreover, as "son," Agur understands his weary wrestling to be part and parcel of wisdom.

30:5-6 Given God alone as the source of wisdom (30:4), Agur urges reliance upon the divine word. He repeats with minor variation the claim of 2 Sam 22:31bc (// Ps 18:30 [Heb. v. 31]) that God's word is trustworthy (30:5). God's word is as "pure" as precious metal refined by smelting (e.g., 25:4; 26:25; cf. Ps 12:6 [Heb. v. 7]), and God is a shield—strong protection for those who seek refuge (e.g., Gen 15:1; Pss 3:3 [Heb. v. 4]; 28:7). God's word is sufficient. (Agur does not state what exactly he means by "God's word," whether written revelation or otherwise.) Anyone who attempts to "add" to it, which can mean to develop and/or surpass it, is a liar (Deut 4:2; 12:32 [Heb. 13:1]). Agur's claim calls back the excesses of wisdom. He indicts any pretense that one knows more (e.g., Job 13:1-12).

30:7-9 Finally, Agur prays. The symmetry of this prayer, the only one in Proverbs, mirrors the "balanced," moderate life Agur requests. Following the introduction (30:7), he opens with two negative petitions, placing the nouns at the beginning of each line for emphasis: no lying and "deceit" (e.g., Ezek 21:29 [Heb. v. 34]), no poverty and riches. At the crux of the prayer Agur restates his hope positively—God's provision of the "bread of my portion" (*ḥōq*), or what is sufficient. The request calls to mind God's provision of manna in the wilderness, an omer of which per person was ample (Exod 16); it also anticipates the "portions" (*ḥōq*) offered by the "woman of substance" (31:15) and the "daily bread" of the Lord's Prayer (Matt 6:11; Luke 11:3). Agur concludes with the twofold rationale that life at either socioeconomic extreme leads to faithlessness. On the one hand, abundant wealth encourages arrogant self-sufficiency, a lost appreciation of one's dependence on God and denial of God's requirements (e.g., Deut 8:17-18). It is Pharaoh, after all, who asks, "Who is the LORD?" (Exod 5:2). On the other, poverty all too easily drives one to steal from others and "lay hold of" or "seize" (NRSV: "profane") God's name, an odd phrase that likely means to hold God accountable for one's situation and hence for one's crime (cf. Ezek 36:20).

Numerical Proverbs (30:10-33)

30:10 The verb "to slander," which is derived from the noun "tongue," is found here and in Ps 101:5, where it refers to accusations made secretly against a neighbor. To disparage a "servant"—the term may refer to any subordinate—to his or her master implicitly challenges the master's awareness of matters and endangers the servant, whose only recourse may be to "curse" you (cf. Eccl 7:21; 10:20). The meddler assumes the upper hand given the servant's status. But things do not go as planned. He or she is instead "held guilty" and punished; the proverb leaves open by whom (e.g., Num 5:6-7; Isa 24:6; other proverbs about slander include 16:28; 18:8; 25:23; and 26:20, 28).

30:11-14 Picking up the verb "to curse" (30:10), Agur commences a list of wretched persons (cf. 6:16-19) that is held together by anaphora, or repetition of a word or phrase at the beginning of each line—in this case *dôr*, "generation," "circle," or "class" (NRSV: "there are those"). The list probably depicts one and the same "generation," a significant number of the population who engage variously in these behaviors. First are those who curse their parents (e.g., 20:20; 30:17), a capital offense according to biblical law (Exod 21:17; Deut 27:16); they disdain their elders and, as such, the wisdom of prior generations. Second are the self-righteous who are "pure in [their] eyes" (e.g., 16:2; 20:9; 26:12) yet are dirty with their own "excrement" (2 Kgs 18:27; Isa 4:4; 36:12). Third are the arrogant who—Agur exclaims with amazement ("How!")—look down at the world through lofty eyes (e.g., 6:17; 16:5; 21:4). And fourth are those who devour the poor and needy (Ps 57:4 [Heb. v. 5]; cf. Mic 3:1-3).

30:15-16 The theme of voracious consumption continues (cf. 30:14). The "leech" has anterior and posterior suckers ("two daughters") with which it attaches, clings fiercely, and draws blood until it is bloated, possibly up to five times its body size.

"Give, Give" may be the names of the suckers or what they cry—an ambiguity that only reinforces the leeches' insatiability. The line may be read independently (30:15a) or as an apt introduction for the numerical proverb that follows, each item of which cannot be satisfied (30:15b-16). Sheol has an insatiable appetite to end human life (27:20; Isa 5:14; Hab 2:5) whereas a barren womb yearns to create it, as the stories of Sarah, Rachel, and Hannah suggest (e.g., Gen 16:2; 30:1; 1 Sam 1). Similarly, the earth thirsts for water to nourish life, whereas fire, consuming everything in its path, destroys it. The proverb thus teaches about insatiability *and* the inexorable clash of hungers in the world (Waltke 2005, 2:488).

30:17 Eyes can speak volumes (cf. 30:13). Continuing the concern of 30:11, Agur condemns any contemptible glance at one's parents. Indeed, the behavior is so abhorrent that the natural world swoops in to carry out the punishment. Mention of two unclean birds—one that "plucks out" the eye and the other whose young "eat it"—intensifies the horror (cf. Lev 11:13-19; Deut 14:11-18). The spiteful child is as a corpse on which carrion birds feed (1 Sam 17:44, 46; 1 Kgs 14:11; 21:24).

30:18-19 The form of this list compares to onomastica, or noun lists that the ancients compiled to study and explain natural phenomena (e.g., Eccl 3:1-15). Here, Agur ponders four wonders of nature in terms of their "way" (see excursus in Proverbs 2). With the first three, he points to realms of creation—heavens, earth, and the "heart of the sea"—and celebrates the mystifying, beautiful movement of creatures in those habitats. The "eagle," the same bird referred to in 30:17, soars through the sky (cf. 23:5); the snake moves without feet over the rock; and the ship somehow makes its way through deep waters and rolling waves (cf. 23:34; Exod 15:8). The culminating wonder is the human sexual relationship, the "way" of a young man "with" or "in" (the preposition may mean either) a "young woman" (contra NRSV the term is used for young married women and women of marriageable age, e.g., Gen 24:43; Exod 2:8; Song 1:3; 6:8; Isa 7:14). Mysterious is the course of such a relationship and the act of intimacy itself.

30:20 The catchword "way" and theme of sexual intimacy links this to 30:19, but mention of the adulteress shifts the mood abruptly (e.g., 6:20-35; 7:1-27). Agur's matter-of-fact description—"she eats, she wipes her mouth, she says"—accentuates her casualness and sets up her claim of no remorse (cf. 26:19; 28:24), while his repeated use of the labials *m* and *p*, sounds made by the lips, makes her feasting audible. Sex for her is a quick meal, something she wipes away like crumbs from her face. She is apparently oblivious to or callous with regard to the consequences.

30:21-23 Portrayals of the world "upside down" are common in the ancient Near East (e.g., 19:10; 1 Sam 2:1-10; Eccl 10:5-7; the Egyptian *Prophecies of Neferti* [*AEL* 1:139-145] and *The Admonitions of Ipuwer* [*AEL* 1:149-163]; cf. Luke 1:46-55). This example, which is woven together by anaphora ("under . . . when"), contends the earth cannot hold up "under" the weight of social upheaval—when men and women of relatively low social standing assume positions of power without adequate preparation. (Implicit may also be a lack of humility.) The servant or subordinate (30:10) as king suggests anarchy (Eccl 10:5-7; but cf. 17:2; Gen 41:37-41). The fool "glutted with food" savors a blessing of hard work (e.g., 12:11; 28:19) though he or she neither worked for it nor recognizes it as such (e.g., Deut 32:6; Ps 14:1). The "hated" woman who marries is likely analogous to the contentious wife (19:13b; 21:9, 19; 25:24), but may be a woman who moves from less favored to favored status in a polygamous household (Gen 29:31; Deut 21:15-17). And the maidservant who dispossesses her "mistress" (*gĕbîrâ*) upsets the domestic order (e.g., Sarah and Hagar in Gen 16:1-16; 21:1-21; Rachel and Bilhah in Gen 30:1-23); the term may also mean "queen mother" (e.g., 2 Kgs 10:13; Jer 13:18; 29:2), which creates a good parallel to the servant and king of 30:22a. The proverb, whether serious (albeit hyperbolic) social critique or humorous commentary, legitimizes the social order as grounded in creation—thereby "quashing" revolutionary thoughts (cf. 26:1; Van Leeuwen 1996a, 610).

30:24-28 Breaking the pattern three/four (cf. 30:15-16, 18-19, 21-23), this proverb depicts four creatures as "peoples" who, though small and without characteristics commonly thought necessary to be effective (e.g., strength, power, and leadership), demonstrate wisdom by their resourcefulness. The ant is mentioned in the Old Testament only in Proverbs—here and 6:6-8, which similarly highlights its instinctive gathering of food in the summer in order to have plenty through the winter. The rock badger, a small, rabbit-sized creature with pads on its feet that help it climb rocks, nests high in cliffs out of reach of predators (Ps 104:18). Locusts, without a leader, move quickly as vast swarms and wreak unspeakable devastation (e.g., Exod 10; Judg 6:5); Joel informs Agur's description of them going forth as to battle "divided into groups" (NRSV: "in rank"):

> Like warriors they charge,
> like soldiers they scale the wall.
> Each keeps to its own course,
> they do not swerve from their paths.
> They do not jostle one another,
> each keeps to its own track. (Joel 2:7-8a)

Finally, the "lizard," probably a type of gecko, may be caught with two hands but moves easily through holes and cracks. Some lizards also blend easily into their surroundings, making them even more unobtrusive in the halls of power.

30:29-31 Agur turns from vulnerable yet wise creatures (30:24-28) to those whose strength and dignity is evident in their gait—who "make good" their steps (e.g., 4:12; 16:9). The description of the lion as a "hero" among animals (a *gibbôr* is a vigorous man, typically a warrior or champion, e.g., 1 Sam 17:51; 2 Kgs 24:16) and one who "does not turn back" from anything (e.g., Job 39:22) informs how to interpret the remaining two creatures and the king in 30:31, the Hebrew of which is obscure. These are magisterial, fearless creatures. The king, who is frequently compared to a lion (e.g., 19:12; 20:2; 28:15), stands out as the last of the list and the only human; at the same time, the comparison makes clear he is but one of many regal creatures.

30:32-33 Agur's parting words urge self-restraint—literally putting "a hand to the mouth" to curb self-promotion or the pursuit of devious plans. The second proverb motivates the first.

Threefold repetition of "to press . . . produces" impresses on readers the predictability of the consequences if one does not, while wordplay animates the analogies: "curds" (*ḥemʾâ*) resembles a common word for anger (*ḥēm â*) and "nose" (*ʾap*) may also mean "anger," as it does in the last line (*ʾappayim*, "two nostrils").

Theological and Ethical Analysis

Many readers empathize with Agur's weariness—whether because we too tire in our efforts to understand, or are simply worn out by those who profess more certainty about the way the world works than we think humanly possible. His weariness does not mean he has lost faith or rejects the pursuit of knowledge, however. Rather, Agur expresses poignantly what many proverbs in the book claim about the life of a wisdom seeker. Agur "knows" (30:4) God is mysterious and powerful. Agur describes the scope of God's knowledge and activity in spatially vast terms (e.g., "ends of the earth," heaven), and invokes different epithets for God (i.e., El, *qĕdōšîm*, Eloah) before settling on the divine name YHWH, used prevalently throughout the book (30:9). That is, Agur grasps to name the elusive he holds as reliable—God and God's word (30:5). At the same time, Agur is adamant that he "does *not* know" (30:3, 18). He describes his understanding as lacking or limited ("brutish"), indicates there are many things that for all their wonder he cannot do or comprehend (30:4, 18-19), and warns that any attempt to "add" to God's word makes one a liar (30:5). Certain of God's greatness and his own ignorance, Agur knows no other way to be than humble: he trusts in God and God's word, prays, and observes the world for instruction—characteristics of a "fearer of the LORD" (e.g., 11:2; 15:33; 22:4; 26:12; 28:11, 26). As such, Agur stands firmly within the wisdom tradition and cautions, as the sages do throughout Proverbs (and in Eccl and Job), against pretense, against any overconfidence in human ingenuity (being "wise in your own eyes," e.g., 3:7; 26:12; 28:26). Here, at nearly the end of the book, just as we may believe we have "found" wisdom and understand the sages, one of them warns us to be careful. Given what comes next, perhaps the warning is needed: Proverbs 31 envisions the implied reader as a king (31:1-9) and a mature adult living in wisdom's household (31:10-31).

Agur insists our moral purview is the whole creation. He moves back and forth between proverbs about human characters and creatures (e.g., 30:11-14, 15-16, 17). More strikingly, though, he blurs distinctions between humans and creation. He compares himself and the king to animals (30:2, 31); ascribes humanlike qualities to creatures (e.g., 30:15, 24-28, 30); animates earth and fire (30:16); tells of birds punishing humans who transgress social boundaries (30:17); and describes the earth shaking as a result of social upheaval (30:21-23). By doing so he underscores how deeply connected we are with the natural world, how creaturely we are, and how vital is the lesson "Go to the ant!" (6:6-8)—that nature promotes our moral understanding. Like the parent of Proverbs 1–9, Agur urges us to consider familiar creatures in a new way, to see their existence as imbued with dignity and purposes that disclose something about the God who, by wisdom, created them and us (e.g., Matt 6:25-34). Even the smallest and least powerful creatures can show us how to be wise creatures of God.

So, as one sage in the world, for what does Agur pray? Honesty and daily bread (30:7-9). Agur's conviction that "enough" is his best hope for staying faithful should give serious pause to those of us in a culture of "never enough," grossly distorted notions of what constitutes "my portion" (30:8), and an ever-widening gap between the rich and poor. Agur draws a straight line from one's socioeconomic circumstances to one's belief and testimony about God, and cautions that the expectation of anything more or less than daily bread imperils not only faith but the very fabric of community.

PROVERBS 31: "THE WORDS OF LEMUEL, KING OF MASSA, WHICH HIS MOTHER TAUGHT HIM," AND THE WOMAN OF SUBSTANCE

Literary Analysis

Two units comprise the final chapter of Proverbs: the instruction of King Lemuel's mother (31:1-9) and an alphabetic acrostic celebrating a "woman of substance" (31:10-31). That LXX separates the two (31:1-9 precedes 25:1–29:27) may suggest they were considered independent compositions. Presented consecutively, however, certain commonalities are evident, such as key words and phrases (e.g., *ḥāyil*; NRSV: "strength" or "capacity" 31:3, 20, 29; "open your/her mouth," 31:8-9, 26), specific attention to women, and concern for the poor and needy (31:5-9, 20). The juxtaposition of caution about some women with veneration of a wise woman also recalls a similar dynamic in Proverbs 1–9.

The instruction of King Lemuel's mother (31:1-9) is analogous to ancient Near Eastern instructions of kings to their sons, such as the Babylonian *Advice to a Prince* (*BWL* 110-115), the Egyptian *Instruction Addressed to King Merikare* (*AEL* 1:97-109), and *Instruction of King Amenemhet I for His Son Sesostris I* (*AEL* 1:135-139). There is no known parallel advice attributed to a king's mother, however. Following the superscription (31:1), she opens with an exhortation (31:2) followed by two admonitions for self-restraint—with women (31:3) and alcohol (31:4-5). She turns from abuse of the latter to its possible use with a (cynical) injunction about alcohol (31:6). She then closes with two positive commands, each of which begins, "Speak out!" (*pĕṭaḥ pîkā*, literally "Open your mouth!" 31:8-9) and includes the noun "claim(s)" (*dîn*; NRSV: "rights"). A smattering of foreign loanwords (e.g., Aramaic *bar* ["son," 31:2] and *mĕlākîn* ["kings," 31:3])—a couple for which the mother also uses the Hebrew equivalent (*bĕnê* ["sons of," 31:5, 8]; *mĕlākîm* ["kings," 31:4])—adds to the sense established by the superscription that the unit is non-Israelite in origin. It may be. It may also be the work of an Israelite who wanted the instruction to appear foreign.

The companion and concluding unit of the book is a hymn of praise for a "woman of substance" (31:10-31). Its frame, a sequential and complete alphabetic acrostic (each line begins with the next letter of the twenty-two-letter Hebrew alphabet, e.g., Ps 119), suggests these are the "*A* to *Z*s" of such a woman. The poem features her many activities and attributes; indeed, the Hebrew root meaning "to do" or "make" (*ʿāśâ*) leaps out—occurring as a verb or noun five times (31:13, 22, 24, 29, 31). There is no apparent order apart from an introduction (31:10-12), an enumeration of her qualities and deeds (31:13-27), and concluding praise (31:28-31). Rather, the poem reads like an impressionistic painting. Viewed up close, the individual brushstrokes seem scattered and haphazard but, from a step or two away, dots and splatters merge to become the cumulative image of a wise and valiant woman.

Numerous lexical and thematic parallels suggest the "woman of substance" is to be identified with personified wisdom in Proverbs 1–9. The two women who frame the book essentially coalesce as one. Note, for example, that both are difficult to "find" (31:10; cf. 1:28; 8:17) and are more precious than "jewels" (31:10; cf. 3:15; 8:11). Both have a house (31:15, 21, 27; cf. 9:1) and a staff of "servant-girls" (31:15; cf. 9:3). Both provide "food" (31:14; cf. 9:5) and a life of security (31:11; cf. 1:33). Their "fruit" is valuable (31:16, 31; cf. 8:19); indeed, the noun "merchant profit" is found in Proverbs only in 31:18 and 3:14. Both are known at the city gates (31:23, 31; cf. 1:21; 8:3) and bestow honor on their companions (31:25; cf. 3:16; 4:8). Both are strong (31:17, 25; cf. 8:14) and loathe wickedness (31:12; cf. 8:13). Both stretch out their "hands" to the needy (31:20; cf. 1:24). They laugh (31:25; cf. 1:26; 8:30). And both teach (31:26; cf. 1:23, 25; 8:6-9, 14, 32-34); their identities and instructions are associated with "the fear of the LORD" (31:30; cf. 1:29-30; 8:13). The nature and extent of these parallels indicate readers encounter personified wisdom here one last time—and glimpse life abundant in her household.

Exegetical Analysis

A Mother's Instruction (31:1-9)

<u>31:1</u> Lemuel the king, whose name means "belonging to God" (cf. "son of my vows," 31:2), is not mentioned otherwise in the Old Testament. The term *maśśā'* (cf. 30:1) may be construed as "oracle" (NRSV) or as an ethnic designation (i.e., likely a north Arabian tribe, descendants of Ishmael's son Massa, Gen 25:14 and 1 Chr 1:30). These are the instructions of his mother (1:8; 6:20).

31:2 Lemuel's mother appeals to the parent-child relationship to motivate him to embrace her instruction (e.g., 4:1-4). The threefold repetition lends urgency, while her descriptions of the king ("my son . . . son of my womb . . . son of my vows") emphasize their intimate connection and her long-standing care of him. The precise meaning of *mah/meh* (usually the interrogative "what," "why," or "how") is debated. NRSV translates, "No!" presumably based on the occasional use of *mah* to convey a negative (e.g., Exod 15:24; 1 Kgs 12:16; Job 31:1; Song 8:4; cf. Arabic *mā*). Other interpreters consider it an Arabic loanword for "listen" or "take heed." But it is more likely simply elliptical for "What (is it with you)?" (cf. Gen 21:17; Isa 3:15; Clifford 1999, 269), indicating a tone of rebuke. "Son of my vows" evokes Hannah's dedication of Samuel (1 Sam 1:11, 28).

31:3 The mother's warning focuses on sex and alcohol. She first cautions Lemuel not to hand over his *ḥāyil* to women (cf. 31:10); the term refers variously to strength (so NRSV; e.g., 1 Sam 2:4; Eccl 10:10); wealth, property, or profits (e.g., 13:22; Job 20:18; Isa 30:6; Jer 15:13); ability (e.g., Gen 47:6; Exod 18:21); and bravery (e.g., Judg 11:1; 1 Chr 5:24). That is, the king must not be so preoccupied with women, whether those of the harem or others, that he forsakes his demeanor, capacity, and prosperity— his "ways" as the parallel suggests. The caution calls to mind David, who learned the "sword shall never depart" from his house following his pursuit of Bathsheba and the orchestrated murder of her husband, Uriah (2 Sam 11:1–12:15). It also evokes Solomon, whose downfall is attributed in part to his many marriages to foreign women (1 Kgs 11:1-13).

31:4-5 Lemuel must not hand over his good judgment to alcohol either (e.g., 20:1; 23:29-35; Isa 28:7-8). Other narratives portray inebriated rulers as immature, indulgent, incapable, and unjust (e.g., Esth 1:7-12; Eccl 10:16-17; Isa 5:11-12, 22-23). The mother focuses particularly on the latter, warning that a drunken king will "forget what is decreed" generally and, even worse, "change a judgment" (a judicial idiom) for every oppressed person, namely, fail to protect—if not outright reverse—laws that protect the vulnerable.

31:6-7 Whereas Lemuel should avoid getting drunk *lest* he forget, his mother suggests those who are suffering may do well to get drunk so they *can*. Although this advice may be interpreted straightforwardly, as prescribing prudent use of alcohol to numb the pain of the poor and needy, it seems more likely a cynical comment that anticipates 31:8-9. (Use of the indefinite plural imperative ["Give!"] distinguishes it from the mother's direct, second-person imperatives in 31:3, 4, and 8.) One imagines the mother scolding Lemuel ("No!" or, "What is with you?" 31:2), seizing a bottle from him ("It is *not* for kings, O Lemuel," 31:4), and waving it toward the masses whose plight she depicts without mincing words: "one who is perishing," "those who are bitter," "poverty," and "misery." Her aim is not to anesthetize *them* but to snap *the king* out of his stupor so that he might get to the work she turns to next.

31:8-9 With the imperatives "Open your mouth!" (twice; cf. 31:20) and "Judge righteously," the mother implores Lemuel to do his job, to enact and protect just laws and judgments and to advocate for the poor, whose lack of voice and powerlessness she captures with the expressions "mute" and "those passing away." When people cannot speak—*especially* when they cannot—the king must speak for them. They depend on it, as does the longevity of his kingdom (e.g., 16:10, 12; 25:5; 29:4a, 14).

The Woman of Substance (31:10-31)

31:10 Picking up the term *ḥayil* (31:3), attention turns now to the *'ēšet–ḥayil* (NRSV: "capable wife"). At issue is what it means for a woman, here a wife (31:11-12, 23, 28), to have *ḥayil*, a term that refers variously to physical strength (e.g., 1 Sam 2:4; Eccl 10:10), wealth and property (e.g., 13:22; Isa 30:6; Jer 15:13), capacity (e.g., Gen 47:6; Exod 18:21), and bravery (e.g., Judg 11:1; 1 Chr 5:24). Men with *ḥayil* tend to be well regarded and affluent; they may be kings (as Lemuel), landowners, or those who serve with courage and loyalty, often in the military (e.g., Exod 18:25; Ruth 2:1; 2 Sam 23:20; 2 Kgs 15:20). They are persons of "substance"—strength and capacity, wealth and skill—like the woman to whom this poem pays tribute.

The opening question, "Who can find?" suggests such a woman is uncommon. Indeed, although there are many men with *ḥayil* in the Old Testament, there are only two other references to women with *ḥayil*: in 12:4, where one is described as "the crown of her husband," and in Ruth 3:11, where Boaz assures Ruth the community knows her to be a "woman of substance." (Notably, in the Hebrew Bible, the book of Ruth follows Proverbs and thus this tribute). Both texts imply the women are extraordinary. The parallel line (31:10b) intensifies the claim, and evokes an alternative sense of the verb "to find" (*māṣa'*). Not only is a "woman of substance" difficult to find (*māṣa'*), it seems, she is expensive "to attain" (*māṣa'*, e.g., Gen 26:12; Lev 12:8; Job 31:25; Hos 12:8 [Heb. v. 9]). Her "price" (*meker*)—perhaps an allusion to the value of her dowry (her financial "worth") or to a bride-price paid by the groom to the bride's family or agent—is more than "corals" (personified wisdom is valued similarly in 8:11). A woman of great value, she is a very desirable bride (cf. Yoder 2001, 49-58, 77-79).

31:11-12 The poet turns from general praise (31:10) to specific celebration of the woman's value to her husband (cf. the inverse pattern in the concluding frame of the poem, 31:28-31). He trusts her because he never lacks for "loot" (*šālāl*). The term, which is surprising in this context, is found elsewhere in Proverbs in the father's description of the sinners' get-rich-quick scheme (1:13; cf. 16:19); whereas the sinners' ill-gotten gain is to be avoided at all costs, that acquired by marriage to the "woman of substance" is most desirable. Her provision of "loot" further suggests her warrior-like status, a motif that recurs in the poem (31:15, 17, 29). Strong, resourceful, and tenacious "all the days of her life," she guarantees for her husband certain and perpetual resources.

31:13 Enumeration of the woman's qualities and deeds begins with the work of her hands. (Compare the celebration of a woman's physical beauty in the Song of Songs, e.g., 4:1-15). Spinning and weaving of textiles was symbolic of women's skill throughout the ancient Near East. Even queens and wealthy women are described or depicted holding a spindle (e.g. Judg 16:14; *ANEP* 43, pl. 144). The "woman of substance" gathers her raw materials of wool and flax (which was imported from Egypt) and gets to work. The translation "willing hands" (NRSV) is based on the meaning "delight" for ḥēpeṣ (e.g., 1 Sam 15:22); the noun may also denote a "matter" or "business" (Eccl 3:1, 17; 5:7; 8:6; cf. Sir 10:26), suggesting this is, as other lines of the poem indicate, the "work" or "business" of her hands (31:19, 22, 24).

31:14 Reference to "merchant ships" calls to mind the Phoenician maritime merchants who traded throughout the Mediterranean. Nehemiah tells of them selling their wares in the Jerusalem marketplace (Neh 13:16), and Ezra reports they imported Lebanon cedar to Joppa to rebuild the temple (Ezra 3:7). That the "woman of substance," like merchant ships, "brings her food from afar" may be construed two ways: she buys food at a location far away from home or, alternatively, the food she purchases is imported "from afar," which implies expensive delicacies. Either way, her family does not live the hand-to-mouth existence of a subsistence agrarian culture. They consume what she buys or barters for in the marketplace.

31:15 She rises early, doubtless to gain every advantage (e.g., Judg 9:34; 16:3; 2 Sam 17:1). The "young women" or "girls" (nĕʿārôt; cf. 9:3) may be female freeborn servants or slaves who do primarily domestic labor. To have one, much less several, is a mark of privilege; women with nĕʿārôt are typically royalty or from well-to-do families, such as the daughter of Pharaoh (Exod 2:5), Esther (Esth 4:4, 16), and Abigail (1 Sam 25:42). At the same time, the nĕʿārôt may be young female workers, like the contingent of female harvesters in the fields of Boaz (Ruth 2:8, 22-23; 3:2; cf. 2:5). The "woman of substance" might thus have a female work group, possibly weavers or other laborers who assist in her textile production. The woman feeds her household and, to those in her service, she provides "allotted portions" (cf. 30:18; contra NRSV: "tasks").

31:16 Savvy about property, she "ponders" a field (the verb suggests she has a plan in mind, e.g., Jer 4:28; 51:12), acquires it, and then draws from her earnings, arguably from her production of textiles, to plant a vineyard (cf. personified wisdom's provision of mixed wine, 9:2). Isaiah describes the work as arduous—

digging up the field, clearing it of stones, planting, building a watchtower and a wall, hewing out a wine vat, pruning, and hoeing (Isa 5:1-6). Her physical labor and investment ensures further provisions for her household and additional income if she sells her grapes or wine in the marketplace (e.g., Neh 13:15).

31:17 The woman "girds up her loins with strength," meaning she tucks up the skirts of her garment in preparation for prolonged and difficult activity (e.g., Exod 12:11; 2 Kgs 4:29; 9:1)—perhaps her spinning and weaving or work in the vineyard. That those who "gird up" are often warriors implicitly underscores her vitality (e.g., Deut 1:41; 1 Sam 25:13).

31:18 Her profits are "good" and she knows it. The parallel line suggests she has ample supplies of oil to burn her lamp all night (a sign of affluence) and that her success is at least in part because of her tireless efforts. The image also evokes the long-burning lamps of the righteous (e.g., 13:9). She "burns the midnight oil" to make certain all is well.

31:19-20 A chiastic pattern—stretches out her hands / her hands / her hand / stretches out her hands—associates these two proverbs and, as such, the woman's industriousness with her generosity (cf. Deut 15:7). The hands she extends to weave skillfully she extends also to others. The link of her business with her charity also suggests she has plenty to spare (31:16, 31).

31:21 "Fear" frames the second half of the poem: she "does not fear" stormy weather (31:21), she is "fear of YHWH" (31:30). She is fearless, in part, because her family is prepared. Crimson, an expensive dye, is a color of wealth, luxury, and royalty (2 Sam 1:24; Jer 4:30; Matt 27:28; Rev 18:12, 16). It was used on clothing of quality—not on cheap, thin fabrics that offered little protection from the cold.

31:22 The list of fineries continues. The term "coverings," which refers to the bed covers of a king in an Ugaritic inventory (KTU 4.270.11), is found in the Old Testament only here and in 7:16—the "woman of substance" makes them, the "strange" woman drapes them across her bed in anticipation of sex. What is a symbol of one woman's virtue is, for the other, a mark of her vice. The "woman of substance" also makes for herself clothing of high quality, namely, imported Egyptian linen and clothing dyed in Phoenician red-purple, an expensive, fast-color, nonfading dye extracted from marine snails. Linen is associated with wealth and royalty (e.g., 1 Chr 15:27; Ezek 16:10, 13) and listed among the accoutrements of affluent women (Isa 3:23). Similarly, red-purple is the color of royal garments (Judg 8:26; Esth 8:15; Mark 15:17, 20; Luke 16:19).

31:23 Some interpreters ascribe the husband's position among the elders at the city gates, the center of the jurisprudence and power (1:21; 8:3; cf. Deut 21:19; 25:7; Ruth 4:1-12), to *his* affluence. But this disrupts the content and rhetorical force of the poem. First, although there is no mention of the husband's wealth, the poem clearly and repeatedly establishes hers (e.g., 31:16, 18, 20-22, 24). Second, his prominence is not distinguished from what is otherwise a catalogue of her activities; his rank is but one of her many works. Third, the woman herself is well known at the city gates (31:31), challenging the notion that her husband makes a name for himself while she tends quietly behind the scenes to his domestic worries. She makes a name for him.

31:24 She produces and sells *sādîn* (NRSV: "linen garments"), likely a fine fabric or a garment made of such fabric (Judg 14:12-13; Isa 3:23). She also sells to the traders "belts," a noun from the same Hebrew root as the verb "to gird" in 31:17.

31:25 Even in the abstract, the woman wears garments of dignity and power (e.g., Job 40:10; Ps 104:1; Isa 52:1). Fearless, she laughs at the future, undaunted by whatever it may bring.

31:26 As King Lemuel's mother implores him ("Open your mouth!" 31:8-9), so the woman "opens her mouth" with wisdom; her speech, like that of personified wisdom, is disciplined, informed, and trustworthy (8:6-10). The expression "teaching of kindness" (*tôrat-ḥesed*) is ambiguous. It may be an attributive genitive (i.e., kind teaching), indicating the quality of her words, or an objective genitive (i.e., teaching about kindness). *Ḥesed* is a virtue of the wise (e.g., 11:17; 20:26).

31:27 She is vigilant, overseeing the ways ("goings") of her household and, unlike the sluggard, refusing to eat "bread of idleness," or food not earned by her own work.

31:28-31 Inverting the order of the introduction (31:10-13), the closing lines complete the frame of her portrait by moving from praise by her family (31:28-29) to that by the community (31:30-31); the verb "to praise" (*hālal*, familiar in English as "Hallelujah" or "Alleluia") appears three times (31:28, 30-31). Her children "rise up," a gesture that signals the importance of their declaration (e.g., Jer 1:17; Mic 6:1). And her husband extols her worth to her, comparing her favorably to other "daughters who have achieved *hayil*"—a group the poet has already identified as extraordinary (31:10). "Daughters" is synonymous occasionally with "women" (so NRSV; e.g., Gen 30:13; Song 6:9) and here, parallel to "sons" (31:28), may implicitly celebrate the woman's evident embrace of her own parents' instruction. The phrase "to do *hayil*" elsewhere refers to obtaining wealth (e.g., Deut 8:17-18; Ezek 28:4) and/or military victory (e.g., Num 24:18; 1 Sam 14:48).

Shifting to a call for public praise, the poet lauds her over "favor," which is untrustworthy, and beauty, which is ephemeral and unreliable (*hebel*, e.g., 21:6; cf. 11:16, 22). Neither compares to this woman who, in the Hebrew, is identified as "fear of the LORD" (the phrase is substantive, not adjectival as the NRSV translation suggests). She is fear*less* because she is "fear of YHWH." No wonder the poet's parting appeal is that everyone, including and perhaps especially those at the city gates (31:23), "give her" (e.g., Pss 28:4; 68:34 [Heb. v. 35]) credit and recognition for her labors. She is the epitome of wisdom.

Theological and Ethical Analysis

The last chapter of the book addresses the implied reader—once an amenable, silent son on the brink of adulthood (Prov 1–9)—as a king (31:1-9) and invites imagining life as the respected spouse of a "woman of substance" or wisdom (31:19). The "you" is an adult (31:3). The attentive, dependent child has become ruler and patriarch. Yet the end of Proverbs is not *the end* because details remind us the quest for wisdom is perpetual: the palace is now home and the parent continues to instruct her son (we may say the mother's voice balances the father's of Proverbs 1–9), even as the next generation of "sons" in wisdom's household embrace her teaching and stand to praise her (31:26). Old and young, royal and common, the quest for wisdom endures. The *Instruction of Ptahhotep* describes well the persistent, cyclical nature of the quest for wisdom:

> It goes well with [a son] when he has heard.
> When he is old, has reached veneration,
> He will speak likewise to his children,
> Renewing the teaching of his father.
> Every man teaches as he acts.
> He will speak to the children,
> So that they will speak to their children. (*AEL* 1:75)

What do we consider vital for good leadership? Lemuel's mother stresses: (*a*) self-restraint (the problem is neither women nor alcohol but the king's indulgence in both); (*b*) openness to correction and advice (e.g., 11:14; 13:10; 15:22); and (*c*) defense of justice, which she identifies specifically with protecting and advocating for the poor and needy. Her instruction assumes a gulf between those with *hayil* and those "passing away," and recognizes the latter are effectively mute, unable to stand up for their interests—indeed, their very survival. With urgent intensity, she looks straight into the eyes of the most powerful and privileged and puts responsibility there: "Speak up!" "Speak up!"

The poet of 31:10-31 depicts leadership as about hard work, resourcefulness, and generosity. The woman devotes her energy and efforts to the betterment of the earth (31:16), her family, and the wider community (31:20, 23), and establishes to the extent possible a self-sufficient household. Though much of her work takes place away from public scrutiny, even by a lamp in the predawn darkness, she neither compromises nor cuts corners, preferring instead the quality and assurance that comes from digging her hands into the soil and spinning the wheel yet again. In both units, Proverbs depicts wise leadership as being about service, power as duty-bound to the powerless.

For many, the tribute to a "woman of substance" (31:10-31), which is typically read in churches only on Mother's Day or during a woman's funeral, is a mixed blessing. On the one hand, coupled with Proverbs 1–9 and its praise of personified wisdom, 31:10-31 is the frame of Proverbs: celebration of women's (extra)ordinary, everyday enterprises—"women's work"—envelop a book about living wisely in the everyday. What is more, because a "woman of substance" is identified with wisdom and "fear of the LORD," "women's work" is set apart and named as the beginning, indeed the standard, of faithfulness (e.g., 1:7). Whether bartering in the marketplaces, weaving, trading, feeding and clothing others, planting vineyards, mixing wine, or burning the midnight oil, the labor of women is here elevated, theologically legitimated, and claimed as a preferable means for moral and theological instruction of the faith community. It is "God-talk." Indeed, with climatic poetic flourish, the parent identifies this wisdom as the preeminent companion of God and the delight of all creation (8:22-31). Ben Sira, for whom personified wisdom was Torah, would make similar claims (cf. Sir 24). This reverence for "women's work," particularly for the everyday management of hearth and home, is sorely needed in a culture that today too often devalues it.

At the same time, the tribute is troubling. It reinforces the values and customs of a context that is patriarchal in structure and androcentric in bias. Like the parent of Proverbs 1–9, the poet of 31:10-31 objectifies the woman being praised, describing her as merchandise to be found and purchased. She has a "price" higher than that of other expensive items (31:10b; cf. 3:14-15; 4:5, 7; 8:11). She is desirable for the "loot"—the imported delicacies, garments, real estate, money, and status—she brings her husband. Moreover, she embodies not *one* woman but the desired aspects of *many* (Yoder 2001, 109); the idealized portrait assumes, among other things, that such a woman is heterosexual, married, and a mother. It is no wonder, then, that while some say they know a "woman of substance," far more consider her a "superwoman"—yet another utterly unrealistic and dehumanizing depiction of women crafted to entice and promote the values of men. At a time when young girls are increasingly "oversexualized," when thin and stupid are marketed regularly as attractive and the "dumb blonde" is iconic, when "successful" women are those who "do it all," when good mothering is linked to highly scheduled children, and so on, 31:10-31 raises the question of how a present-day alphabetic acrostic would describe a most desirable woman.

Thus Proverbs leaves us with a profoundly captivating and disconcerting portrait of wisdom—one that was repainted and renamed by sages for generations to come (e.g., Sir 24; Bar 3:9–4:4; Wis 7:7–9:18; 1 Enoch 42:1-2).

SELECT BIBLIOGRAPHY

WORKS CITED AND CONSULTED

Alter, Robert. 1985. *The Art of Biblical Poetry*. New York: Basic Books.

Barré, Michael L. 1981. "'Fear of God' and the World View of Wisdom." *BTB* 11:41–43.

Blenkinsopp, Joseph. 1991. "The Social Context of the 'Outsider Woman' in Proverbs 1–9." *Bib* 72:457–73.

Booth, Wayne C. 1988. *The Company We Keep: An Ethics of Fiction*. Berkeley: University of California Press.

Boström, Lennart. 1990. *The God of the Sages: The Portrayal of God in the Book of Proverbs*. ConBOT 29. Stockholm: Almqvist & Wiksell.

Brenner, Athalya. 1993. "Proverbs 1–9: An F Voice?" In *On Gendering Texts*. Edited by A. Brenner and F. van Dijk-Hemmes. Leiden: E. J. Brill. 113–30.

Brown, William P. 1996. *Character in Crisis: A Fresh Approach to the Wisdom Literature of the Old Testament*. Grand Rapids, Mich.: Eerdmans.

———. 2002. "The Pedagogy of Proverbs 10:1–31:9." In *Character and Scripture: Moral Formation, Community, and Biblical Interpretation*. Edited by W. P. Brown. Grand Rapids, Mich.: Eerdmans. 150–82.

———. 2004. "The Didactic Power of Metaphor in the Aphoristic Sayings of Proverbs." *JSOT* 29:133–54.

Brueggemann, Walter. 1989. "Praise to God is the End of Wisdom— What is the Beginning?" *Journal for Preachers* 12:30–40.

Bryce, Glendon E. 1972. "Another Wisdom-'Book' in Proverbs." *JBL* 91:145–57.

Byargeon, R. W. 1997. "The Structure and Significance of Prov 9:7-12." *JETS* 40:367–75.

Camp, Claudia V. 1985. *Wisdom and the Feminine in the Book of Proverbs*. Bible and Literature Series 11. Sheffield: JSOT/Almond.

——. 1987. "Woman Wisdom as Root Metaphor: A Theological Consideration." In *The Listening Heart: Essays in Wisdom and the Psalms in Honor of Roland E. Murphy, O. Carm.* Edited by K. G. Hoglund, E. F. Huwiler, J. T. Glass, and R. W. Lee. JSOTSup 58. Sheffield: JSOT. 45–76.

——. 1991. "What's So Strange about the Strange Woman?" In *The Bible and the Politics of Exegesis: Essays in Honor of Norman K. Gottwald on his Sixty-Fifth Birthday*. Edited by D. Jobling, P. Day, and G. Sheppard. Cleveland: Pilgrim Press. 17–31, 301–4.

——. 1995. "Wise and Strange: An Interpretation of the Female Imagery in Proverbs in Light of Trickster Mythology." In *A Feminist Companion to Wisdom Literature*. Edited by A. Brenner. The Feminist Companion to the Bible 9. Sheffield: Sheffield Academic Press. 131–56.

Carasik, Michael. 1994. "Who Were the 'Men of Hezekiah' (Prov 25:1)?" *VT* 44:289–300.

Carr, David M. 2005. *Writing on the Tablet of the Heart: Origins of Scripture and Literature*. New York: Oxford University Press.

Clifford, Richard J. 1993. "Woman Wisdom in the Book of Proverbs." In *Biblische Theologie und gesellschaftlicher Wandel für Norbert Lohfink, S. J.* Edited by G. Braulik, W. Groß, and S. McEvenue. Freiburg: Herder. 61–72.

——. 2004. "Your Attention Please! Heeding the Proverbs." *JSOT* 29:155–63.

Crenshaw, James L. 1981. "Wisdom and Authority: Sapiential Rhetoric and Its Warrants." In *Congress Volume: Vienna 1980*. Edited by J. A. Emerton. VTSup 32. Leiden: E. J. Brill. 10–29.

——. 1984. "A Mother's Instruction to Her Son (Proverbs 31:1-9)." In *Perspectives on the Hebrew Bible: Essays in Honor of Walter J. Harrelson*. Edited by J. L. Crenshaw. Macon, Ga.: Mercer University Press. 9–22.

——. 1989. "Clanging Symbols." In *Justice and the Holy: Essays in Honor of Walter Harrelson*. Edited by D. A. Knight and P. J. Paris. Atlanta: Scholars Press. 51–64.

——. 1998. *Education in Ancient Israel: Across the Deadening Silence*. ABRL. New York: Doubleday.

Dell, Katherine J. 2006. *The Book of Proverbs in Social and Theological Context*. Cambridge: Cambridge University Press.

Dietrich, Manfried, O. Loretz, and J. Sanmartín, eds. 1995. *The Cuneiform Alphabetic Texts from Ugarit, Ras Ibn Hani and Other Places*. 2d. ed. ALASP 8. Münster, Germany: Ugarit-Verlag.

Dorsey, D. A. 1991. *The Roads and Highways of Ancient Israel*. Baltimore: Johns Hopkins University Press.

Estes, Daniel J. 1997. *Hear, My Son: Teaching and Learning in Proverbs 1–9*. New Studies in Biblical Theology 4. Grand Rapids, Mich.: Eerdmans.

Fontaine, Carole R. 1985. "Proverb Performance in the Hebrew Bible." *JSOT* 32:87–103.

———. 1992. *Traditional Sayings in the Old Testament*. Sheffield: Almond.

———. 2002. *Smooth Words: Women, Proverbs and Performance in Biblical Wisdom*. JSOTSup 356. Sheffield: Sheffield Academic Press.

Forti, Tova. 1996. "Animal Images in the Didactic Rhetoric of the Book of Proverbs." *Bib* 77:48–63.

Fox, Michael V. 1994. "The Pedagogy of Proverbs 2." *JBL* 113:233–43.

———. 1995. "World Order and Maʿat: A Crooked Parallel." *JANES* 23:37–48.

———. 1996a. "ʾAmon Again." *JBL* 115:699–702.

———. 1996b. "The Social Location of the Book of Proverbs." In *Texts, Temples, and Traditions: A Tribute to Menahem Haran*. Edited by M. V. Fox, V. A. Hurowitz, A. Hurvita, M. L. Klein, B. J. Schwartz, and N. Shupak. Winona Lake, Ind.: Eisenbrauns. 227–39.

———. 1997a. "Ideas of Wisdom in Proverbs 1-9." *JBL* 116:613–33.

———. 1997b. "Who Can Learn? A Dispute in Ancient Pedagogy." In *Wisdom, You Are My Sister: Studies in Honor of Roland E. Murphy, O. Carm., on the Occasion of his Eightieth Birthday*. Edited by M. L. Barré. CBQMS 29. Washington, D.C.: Catholic Biblical Association. 62–77.

———. 2004. "The Rhetoric of Disjointed Proverbs." *JSOT* 29:165–77.

Franklyn, Paul. 1983. "The Sayings of Agur in Proverbs 30: Piety or Scepticism?" *ZAW* 95:238–52.

Franzmann, Majella. 1991. "The Wheel in Proverbs 20:26 and Ode of Solomon 23:11-16." *VT* 41:121–32.

Gilbert, Elizabeth. 2006. *Eat, Pray, Love: One Woman's Search for Everything Across Italy, India, and Indonesia*. New York: Penguin.

Goldingay, J. E. 1994. "The Arrangement of Sayings in Proverbs 10–15." *JSOT* 61:75–83.

Grube, G. M. A., trans. 1974. *Plato's Republic*. Indianapolis: Hackett.

Harris, Scott L. 1995. *Proverbs 1-9: A Study of Inner-Biblical Interpretation*. SBLDS 150. Atlanta: Scholars Press.

Heim, Knut M. 2001. *Like Grapes of Gold Set in Silver: An Interpretation of Proverbial Clusters in Proverbs 10:1–22:16.* BZAW 273. Berlin/New York: Walter DeGruyter.

Hildebrandt, Ted. 1988a. "Proverbs 22:6a: Train Up a Child?" *Grace Theological Journal* 9:3–19.

——. 1988b. "Proverbial Pairs: Compositional Units in Proverbs 10–29." *JBL* 107:207–24.

Hoglund, Kenneth G. 1987. "The Fool and the Wise in Dialogue." In *The Listening Heart: Essays in Wisdom and the Psalms in Honor of Roland M. Murphy, O. Carm.* Edited by K. G. Hoglund, E. F. Huwiler, J. T. Glass, and R. W. Lee. JSOTSup 58. Sheffield: Sheffield Academic Press. 161–80.

Hurowitz, Victor A. 2001. "The Seventh Pillar—Reconsidering the Literary Structure and Unity of Proverbs 31." *ZAW* 113:209–18.

Kaminsky, Joel S. 1995. *Corporate Responsibility in the Hebrew Bible.* The Library of Hebrew Bible/Old Testament Studies. Sheffield: Sheffield Academic Press.

Kant, Immanuel. 1980. *Lectures on Ethics.* Trans. by L. Infield. Indianapolis: Hackett.

Kovacs, Brian W. 1974. "Is There a Class-Ethic in Proverbs?" In *Essays in Old Testament Ethics (J. Philip Hyatt, In Memoriam).* Edited by J. L. Crenshaw and J. Willis. New York: KTAV. 173–89.

Lambert, W. G. 1960. *Babylonian Wisdom Literature.* Oxford: Clarendon.

Lang, Bernhard. 1981. "Vorläufer von Speiseeis in Bibel und Orient. Eine Untersuchung von Spr 25, 13." In *Mélanges bibliques et orientaux en l'honneur de M. Henri Cazelles.* Edited by A. Caquot and M. Delcor. AOAT 212. Neukirchen-Vluyn: Neukirchener. 219–32.

Lenzi, Alan. 2006. "Proverbs 8:22–31: Three Perspectives on Its Composition." *JBL* 125:687–714.

Lichtenstein, Murray H. 1982. "Chiasm and Symmetry in Proverbs 31." *CBQ* 44:202–11.

Lichtheim, Miriam. 1973–1980. *Ancient Egyptian Literature.* 3 vols. Berkeley: University of California Press.

MacIntyre, Alasdair. 1981. *After Virtue: A Study in Moral Theory.* Notre Dame, Ind.: University of Notre Dame Press.

——. 1988. *Whose Justice? Which Rationality?* Notre Dame, Ind.: University of Notre Dame Press.

Malchow, Bruce V. 1985. "A Manual for Future Monarchs." *CBQ* 47:238–45.

McCreesh, Thomas P. 1985. "Wisdom as Wife: Proverbs 31:10-31." *RB* 92:25–46.

———. 1991. *Biblical Sound and Sense: Poetic Sound Patterns in Proverbs 10–29*. JSOTSup 128. Sheffield: JSOT.

Meider, Wolfgang, and Alan Dundes, eds. 1981. *The Wisdom of Many: Essays on the Proverb*. New York: Garland.

Melchert, Charles F. 1998. *Wise Teaching: Biblical Wisdom and Educational Ministry*. Harrisburg, Pa.: Trinity.

Murphy, Roland E. 1981. "The Faces of Wisdom in the Book of Proverbs." In *Mélanges bibliques et orientaux en l'honneur de M. Henri Cazelles*. Edited by A. Caquot and M. Delcor. AOAT 212. Neukirchener-Vluyn: Neukirchener. 337–45.

———. 1985. "Wisdom and Creation." *JBL* 104:3–11.

———. 1986. "Wisdom's Song: Proverbs 1:20-33." *CBQ* 48:456–60.

———. 1988. "Wisdom and Eros in Proverbs 1-9." *CBQ* 50:600–603.

Nel, Philip J. 1982. *The Structure and Ethos of the Wisdom Admonitions in Proverbs*. BZAW 158. Berlin/New York: Walter DeGruyter.

———. 2002. "The Rhetorics of Wisdom's Ethics." *OTE* 15:435–52.

Newsom, Carol A. 1989. "Woman and the Discourse of Patriarchal Wisdom: A Study of Proverbs 1-9." In *Gender and Difference in Ancient Israel*. Edited by P. L. Day. Philadelphia: Fortress Press. 142–60.

———. 2003. *The Book of Job: A Contest of Moral Imaginations*. New York: Oxford University Press.

Nussbaum, Martha C. 2001. *Upheavals of Thought: The Intelligence of Emotions*. Cambridge: Cambridge University Press.

Overland, Paul. 2000. "Did the Sage Draw from the Shema? A Study of Proverbs 3:1-12." *CBQ* 62:424–40.

Packer, J. I., and S. K. Soderlund, eds. 2000. *The Way of Wisdom: Essays in Honor of Bruce K. Waltke*. Grand Rapids, Mich.: Zondervan.

Perdue, Leo G. 1981. "Liminality as a Social Setting for Wisdom Instructions." *ZAW* 93:114–26.

———. 1994. *Wisdom and Creation: The Theology of Wisdom Literature*. Nashville: Abingdon Press.

———. 1997. "Wisdom Theology and Social History in Proverbs 1-9." In *Wisdom, You Are My Sister: Studies in Honor of Roland E. Murphy, O. Carm., on the Occasion of his Eightieth Birthday*. Edited by M. L. Barré. CBQMS 29. Washington, D.C.: Catholic Biblical Association of America. 78–101.

Pritchard, James B., ed. 1969a. *The Ancient Near East in Pictures Relating to the Old Testament.* 2d ed. with supplement. Princeton, NJ: Princeton University Press.

——, ed. 1969b. *Ancient Near Eastern Texts Relating to the Old Testament.* 3d ed. with supplement. Princeton, N.J.: Princeton University Press.

Römheld, Diethard. 1989. *Wege der Weisheit: Die Lehren Amenemopes und Proverbien 22:17–24:22.* BZAW 184. Berlin/New York: Walter DeGruyter.

Ross, W. D., trans. 1942. *The Student's Oxford Aristotle.* London/New York: Oxford University Press.

Sandoval, Timothy J. 2006. *The Discourse of Wealth and Poverty in the Book of Proverbs.* Leiden: E. J. Brill.

Scherer, Andreas. 1997. "Is the Selfish Man Wise? Considerations of Context in Proverbs 10.1–22.16 with Special Regard to Surety, Bribery and Friendship." *JSOT* 76:59–70.

Segert, Stanislav. 1987. " 'Live Coals Heaped on the Head.' " In *Love and Death in the Ancient Near East.* Edited by J. H. Marks. Guilford, Conn.: Four Quarters. 159–64.

Seow, C. L. 1996. "The Socioeconomic Context of 'The Preacher's' Hermeneutic." *PSB* 17:168–95.

——. 1997. *Ecclesiastes.* AB 18c. New York: Doubleday.

Shupak, Nili. 1985. "Some Idioms Connected with the Concept of 'Heart' in Egypt and the Bible." In *Pharaonic Egypt: The Bible and Christianity.* Edited by S. Israelit-Groll. Jerusalem: Magnes. 202–12.

——. 2005. "The Instruction of Amenemope and Proverbs 22:17–24:22." In *Seeking Out the Wisdom of the Ancients: Essays Offered to Honor Michael V. Fox on the Occasion of His Sixty-Fifth Birthday.* Edited by R. L. Troxel, K. G. Friebel, and D. R. Magary. Winona Lake, Ind.: Eisenbrauns. 203–17.

Simpson, J. A., and E. S. C. Weiner, eds. 1989. *Oxford English Dictionary.* 2d ed. Oxford: Clarendon.

Skehan, Patrick W. 1948. "A Single Editor for the Whole Book of Proverbs." *CBQ* 10:115–30. Revised in *Studies in Israelite Poetry and Wisdom.* CBQMS 1. Washington, D.C.: Catholic Biblical Association, 1971. 15–26.

Sneed, Mark. 1996. "The Class Culture of Proverbs: Eliminating Stereotypes." *JSOT* 10:296–308.

Snell, Daniel S. 1993. *Twice-Told Proverbs and the Composition of the Book of Proverbs*. Winona Lake, Ind.: Eisenbrauns.

Sternberg, Meir. 1985. *The Poetics of Biblical Narrative: Ideological Literature and the Drama of Reading*. Bloomington: University of Indiana Press.

Suileman, Susan Rubin. 1993. *Authoritarian Fictions: The Ideological Novel as a Literary Genre*. 2d. ed. New York: Columbia University Press.

Taylor, Charles. 1989. *Sources of the Self: The Making of the Modern Identity*. Cambridge, Mass.: Harvard University Press.

Trible, Phyllis. 1975. "Wisdom Builds a Poem: The Architecture of Proverbs 1:20-33." *JBL* 94:509–18.

Van Leeuwen, Raymond C. 1986a. "Proverbs 30:21-23 and the Biblical World Upside Down." *JBL* 105:599–610.

———. 1986b. "Proverbs XXV 27 Once Again." *VT* 36:105–14.

———. 1988. *Context and Meaning in Proverbs 25–27*. SBLDS 96. Atlanta: Scholars Press.

———. 1990. "Liminality and Worldview in Proverbs 1–9." *Semeia* 50:111–44.

———. 1992. "Wealth and Poverty: System and Contradiction in Proverbs." *HS* 33:25–36.

———. 1997. "The Background to Proverbs 30:4aα." In *Wisdom, You Are My Sister: Studies in Honor of Roland E. Murphy, O. Carm., on the Occasion of his Eightieth Birthday*. Edited by M. L. Barré. CBQMS 29. Washington, D.C.: Catholic Biblical Association of America. 102–21.

Von Rad, Gerhard. 1972. *Wisdom in Israel*. Trans. by J. D. Martin. London: SCM.

Waltke, Bruce K. 1979. "The Book of Proverbs and Old Testament Theology." *BSac* 136:302–17.

Walzer, Michael. 1994. *Thick and Thin: Moral Argument at Home and Abroad*. Notre Dame, Ind.: University of Notre Dame Press.

Washington, Harold C. 1994a. *Wealth and Poverty in the Instruction of Amenemope and the Book of Proverbs*. SBLDS 142. Atlanta: Scholars Press.

———. 1994b. "The Strange Woman (*'iššâ zārâ/nokriyyâ*) of Proverbs 1–9 and Post-Exilic Judaean Society." In *Second Temple Studies 2: Temple and Community in the Persian Period*. Edited by T. C. Eskenazi and K. H. Richards. JSOTSup 175. Sheffield: JSOT. 217–42.

Weeks, Stuart. 2006. "The Context and Meaning of Proverbs 8:30a." *JBL* 125:433–42.

White, James Boyd. 1984. *When Words Lose Their Meaning: Constitutions and Reconstitutions of Language, Character, and Community.* Chicago: University of Chicago Press.

Whybray, R. N. 1990. *Wealth and Poverty in the Book of Proverbs.* JSOTSup 99. Sheffield: Sheffield Academic Press.

———. 1994a. *The Composition of the Book of Proverbs.* JSOTSup 168. Sheffield: Sheffield Academic Press.

———. 1994b. "The Structure and Composition of Proverbs 22:17–24:22." In *Crossing Boundaries: Essays in Biblical Interpretation in Honour of Michael D. Goulder.* Edited by S. E. Porter, P. Joyce, and D. E. Orton. Leiden: E. J. Brill. 83–96.

———. 1995. *The Book of Proverbs: A Survey of Modern Study.* History of Biblical Interpretation Series 1. Leiden: E. J. Brill.

———. 1996. "City Life in Proverbs 1–9." In *"Jedes Ding hat seine Zeit . . .": Studien zur israelitischen und altorientalischen Weisheit Deithelm Michel zum 65 Geburtstag.* Edited by A. A. Diesel, R. G. Lehmann, E. Otto, and A. Wagner. BZAW 241. Berlin/New York: Walter DeGruyter. 243–50.

Williams, James G. 1980. "The Power of Form: A Study of Biblical Proverbs." *Semeia* 17:35–58.

———. 1981. *Those Who Ponder Proverbs: Aphoristic Thinking and Biblical Literature.* Bible and Literature Series 2. Sheffield: Almond.

Wolters, Al. 1988. "Proverbs 31:10-31 as Heroic Hymn: A Form-Critical Analysis." *VT* 38:446–57.

Yee, Gale A. 1982. "An Analysis of Prov. 8:22-31 According to Style and Structure." *ZAW* 94:58–66.

———. 1989. " 'I Have Perfumed My Bed with Myrrh': The Foreign Woman (*'iššâ zārâ*) in Proverbs 1–9." *JSOT* 43:53–68.

———. 1992. "The Theology of Creation in Proverbs 8:22-31." In *Creation in the Biblical Traditions.* Edited by R. J. Clifford and J. J. Collins. CBQMS 24. Washington, D.C.: Catholic Biblical Association. 85–96.

Yoder, Christine Roy. 2001. *Wisdom as a Woman of Substance: A Socioeconomic Reading of Proverbs 1–9 and 31:10-31.* BZAW 304. Berlin/New York: Walter DeGruyter.

———. 2005a. "Forming 'Fearers of the LORD': Repetition and Contradiction as Pedagogy in Proverbs." In *Seeking Out the Wisdom of the Ancients: Essays Offered to Honor Michael V. Fox on the Occasion of His Sixty-Fifth Birthday.* Edited by R. L. Troxel, K. G.

Friebel, and D. R. Magary. Winona Lake, Ind.: Eisenbrauns. 167–83.
———. 2005b. "The Objects of Our Affections: Emotions and the Moral Life in Proverbs 1–9." In *Shaking Heaven and Earth: Essays in Honor of Walter Brueggemann and Charles Cousar.* Edited by C. Roy Yoder, K. M. O'Connor, E. E. Johnson, and S. P. Saunders. Louisville: Westminster John Knox Press. 73–88.

COMMENTARIES ON PROVERBS

Clifford, Richard J. 1999. *Proverbs.* OTL. Louisville: Westminster John Knox Press.
Davis, Ellen F. 2000. *Proverbs, Ecclesiastes, and the Song of Songs.* Westminster Bible Companion. Louisville: Westminster John Knox Press.
Farmer, Kathleen A. 1991. *Who Knows What is Good? A Commentary on the Books of Proverbs and Ecclesiastes.* ITC. Grand Rapids, Mich.: Eerdmans.
Fox, Michael V. 2000. *Proverbs 1–9.* AB 18A. New York: Doubleday.
Horne, Milton P. 2003. *Proverbs–Ecclesiastes.* Smith & Helwys Bible Commentary 12. Macon, Ga.: Smith & Helwys.
Longman III, Tremper. 2006. *Proverbs.* Baker Commentary on the Old Testament Wisdom and Psalms. Grand Rapids, Mich.: Baker Academic.
McKane, William. 1970. *Proverbs: A New Approach.* OTL. London: SCM Press.
Meinhold, Arndt. 1991. *Die Sprüche.* Zürcher Bibelkommentare 16. 2 Vols. Zurich: Theologischer.
Murphy, Roland E. 1998. *Proverbs.* WBC 22. Nashville: Thomas Nelson.
Perdue, Leo G. 1989. *Proverbs.* Interpretation. Louisville: John Knox Press.
Scott, R. B. Y. 1965. *Proverbs and Ecclesiastes.* AB 18. Garden City, N.Y.: Doubleday.
Toy, Crawford H. 1899. *A Critical and Exegetical Commentary on Proverbs.* ICC. Edinburgh: T & T Clark.
Van Leeuwen, Raymond C. 1997a. "Proverbs." In *The New Interpreter's Bible.* 5:17–264. Nashville: Abingdon Press.
Waltke, Bruce K. 2005. *The Book of Proverbs.* 2 Vols. NICOT. Grand Rapids, Mich.: Eerdmans.
Whybray, R. N. 1994. *Proverbs.* NCB. Grand Rapids, Mich.: Eerdmans.

INDEX

Abomination, 221, 258, 278. *See also under* God

Act-consequence worldview, xxxi, 19, 48–51, 107, 115–16, 137, 161, 165–66, 225, 258

Adornments, 14, 38, 42, 53, 142, 162, 164, 176, 189, 192, 250, 263

Adultery, 30–31, 65–68, 70, 77–80

Agur, 9, 228, 262, 265, 278–88

Alcohol. *See* Food and Drink

Anger, 145, 162, 165, 171, 185, 189, 204, 206, 209, 218, 232, 259, 273, 274, 287

Ant, 73–75, 81, 285–86, 288

Anxiety, 148, 270

Arrogance, 34, 76, 92, 131, 152, 158, 178, 186, 194, 199, 256, 265, 271, 277, 283

Authority, 3–4, 21, 52, 59, 91, 155, 216, 264

Authorship of Proverbs, xxi–xxv

Beauty, 78, 136, 138, 293, 297

Blessing, 46, 50–51, 121, 126, 134, 151, 225, 243. *See also* Curse

Body imagery, xxx, 38, 39, 57–58, 75–76, 115, 116, 123, 148, 175, 195, 199, 200, 215, 231, 236, 251

Bribe, 152, 192, 195, 200, 218, 219, 227, 242, 270

Capable wife. *See* Woman of substance

Choice, 12, 13, 24, 99, 106, 108–9, 115, 214, 248

City, 9, 10, 18, 44, 89–90, 124, 134, 189, 199, 220, 296, 297

Cleverness, 4, 5, 90, 92, 154, 160, 161–62, 168, 223

Community
as formative, 20–21, 155–56, 159–60, 175, 191, 232–33
well-being of, 134, 268–69, 271, 272, 275–76
See also Friend (Neighbor); Honor; Shame

Conflict, 10–11, 75, 77, 111–12, 124, 152–53, 171, 177, 188, 190–91, 194, 204–5, 232, 250, 252, 257, 271, 273

Contradiction, 111–12, 207–8, 254–55

Cosmogony. *See* God, as Creator; Wisdom, personified

Crown. *See* Adornments

Curse, 47, 50–51, 213, 243, 254, 261, 277, 283. *See also* Blessing

Dating of Proverbs, xxii–xxiv

Desire, 22, 47, 53–54, 68–69, 78, 87, 101, 115, 127, 132, 138, 144, 151, 153, 155, 197, 202, 207, 216, 217, 221

Despair, 170, 252

Diligence, 73–74, 120, 144, 148, 149, 151, 216–17. *See also* Laziness

Discipline, 3–5, 29, 41–42, 55, 91, 115, 125, 141–42, 150, 155, 156–57, 168, 169, 175, 187, 192, 205–6, 207–8, 215, 224–25, 236, 244, 254, 263, 275

Discretion, 5, 45, 58, 239–40

Emotion, 7, 18, 22–23, 25, 115, 119, 127, 141–42, 150, 165, 170, 171, 172, 189, 236. *See also* names of specific emotions

Enemy, 252, 258. *See also* Hate
Envy, 47, 236–37, 259
Exogamy, 33, 63–64
Family. *See* Household
Fear of the LORD. *See under* God
Folly, personified ("Strange" Woman),
    xxxii, 30–32, 60–64, 68, 78–80,
    81–89, 99–102, 107–8, 158
Food and Drink, 105–6, 108, 171, 190–91,
    207, 234, 235, 252, 259–60, 270,
    294
    as euphemism for sex, 88, 285
    as metaphor for human condition, 56,
    157, 212, 296
    warning about excessive consumption
    of alcohol, 208–9, 219, 238, 291. *See
    also* Speech
Fool
    danger of, 193, 209, 254, 273–74
    fate of, 19, 48–49, 116, 126, 140, 160,
    162, 187, 198, 220
    misplaced affections of, 18, 127, 155,
    172, 202
    refusal of wisdom by, 18, 90, 124, 145,
    166, 168, 192–95, 235, 263
    speech of, 122, 124, 147–48, 158, 169,
    192, 197, 199, 239, 255–56
Friend (Neighbor), 46, 155–56, 162–63,
    194, 203, 230, 246, 247–48, 260, 262

Generosity, 116, 139, 163, 205, 225, 271,
    295
Gift, 195, 199–200, 203, 218. *See also* Bribe
God, xxxi–xxxii, 116, 178–79, 230, 248,
    265–66, 287–88
    abomination of, 48, 76–77, 130–31,
    137–38, 147, 169, 174, 183, 193
    as aligned with the poor and widow,
    165, 173, 191, 205, 218, 232, 236
    as Creator, 44–45, 94–98, 163, 223, 281
    as judge of the human heart, 25, 182,
    191, 240
    as source of wisdom, 26–27, 34, 39,
    211, 281–82
    delight of, 97–98, 142, 169, 183
    discipline of, 41–42
    fear of, 6–8, 26, 92, 107, 128, 158, 164,
    171, 175, 183, 223, 297
    justice of, 80–81, 182, 184, 214, 216,
    232, 244
    knowledge of, 6, 26
    sovereignty of, 120–21, 169–70, 172,
    181, 182, 189, 206, 214, 216,
    221–22

trust in, 38–39, 271, 277
    watchfulness of, 68, 168
    way of, 95–96, 128
Gossip, 134–35, 146, 188, 192, 198, 250,
    257

Hate, 63, 106–7, 141–42, 151, 153–54,
    156–57, 158, 162–63, 168, 169,
    171, 175, 203, 258, 285. *See also*
    God, abomination of
Heart (Mind), 24, 25–26, 27, 38, 58, 84,
    114, 126, 148, 169–70, 191, 197,
    262, 267, 269
Hezekiah, xxii–xxiii, 9, 39, 94, 244–45
Honor, 38, 43, 47–48, 53, 60, 63, 69, 136,
    143–44, 155, 165, 175, 191, 209,
    223, 248, 253, 254, 255, 261–62.
    See also Reputation; Shame
Hope, 128, 132–33, 153, 205–6, 237
Hospitality. *See* Food and Drink
Household
    as a moral unit, 47, 50, 114, 119, 140,
    143, 160–61, 172, 175–76, 191–92,
    195, 207, 210, 213, 236–37, 238–39,
    260, 267–68
    as primary setting for education,
    xxv–xxvi, 10–12, 52–53, 156–57,
    205–6, 224–25, 236, 275
    and importance of a good spouse, 158,
    201, 204–5, 217, 219–20, 253, 261
    of personified folly, 32, 87–89, 107–8
    of personified wisdom, 99, 104–6
    See also Woman of substance
Humility, 39, 131, 175, 186, 223, 247, 256,
    277. *See also* Arrogance

Injustice, 193, 196, 197–98, 225, 240,
    242–43, 268
Instruction of Amenemope, xxix, 227–28,
    231–36

Jewelry. *See* Adornments
Joy, 119, 127, 128, 134, 146–47, 160, 161,
    170, 172–73, 175, 195, 218, 219,
    236, 272, 273
Justice, 4, 26, 50–51, 93, 177, 184, 216,
    218, 242–43, 267, 270. *See also*
    God, justice of; King, justice of;
    Righteous; Righteousness

King, 164–65, 176–77, 264–65
    anger and/or favor of, 166–67, 185,
    204, 209, 241
    as discerning, 248–49

King—continued
  as lion, 204, 286
  as representative of God, 180, 216
  justice of, 184–85, 210, 214, 215, 249,
    274–75, 292
  speech of, 184
  caution about, 269, 272, 274
  See also Ruler

Land, 32–33, 35, 129, 144, 216, 233, 236,
  243, 266–67
Laziness, 74, 120, 128, 148, 149, 151, 171,
  205, 207, 209, 211, 221, 226,
  256–57
Lemuel, 9, 228, 265, 288–92, 298
Lion, 204, 226, 256, 266, 269, 286
Lots, 15, 189–90
Love, 68–69, 124, 192, 194, 201, 219, 259
  parental, 41, 156–57, 172
  of wisdom, 42, 53–54, 83–84, 93–94,
    98–99, 203
Loyalty, 261–62. *See also* Adultery
Lying. *See* Speech, true and/or false

Ma'at, 4, 100, 182, 185
Messenger, 154–55, 193, 229, 232, 250,
  253, 255
Mind. *See* Heart
Moral polarities, 12, 15, 29, 32, 82, 111,
  266
Moral terms, thick and thin meanings,
  8–10

Nature, as instructive, 73, 81, 284, 288
Neighbor. *See* Friend (Neighbor)

Oracle, 184, 275, 278, 279–80, 290

Parent. *See* Household
Path (Way), xxx, 28–30, 51–52, 55–57, 68,
  125, 131, 138, 158, 161, 169, 173,
  188, 189, 202, 216, 224–25, 268
Personification, 17, 77–78, 156, 208–9,
  237. *See also* Wisdom, personified;
  Folly, personified
Poor, 116, 120, 124, 152, 156, 162–63,
  165, 170, 191, 201, 202, 203, 218,
  223, 225, 227, 232, 267, 268, 269,
  271, 274, 292
Poverty, 15, 74, 111–12, 116–17, 120, 124,
  155, 162–63, 178, 202, 219, 237,
  265, 270, 271, 282–83, 292. *See
  also* Wealth
Pride. *See* Arrogance

Proverb, xxi–xxvii, 2, 110–11, 113
  genres of, 36, 70, 111, 167, 222,
    228–29, 245, 263, 279
Prudence. *See* Discretion

Repetition as pedagogy, 112–14
Reputation, 80, 121, 155, 211, 262–63. *See
  also* Honor; Shame
Retribution, doctrine of. *See* Act-consequence worldview
Righteous, 125, 128, 133, 138, 143, 144,
  151, 218, 219
  advocate for poor, 273
  fate of, 115–16, 121–22, 127, 132, 138,
    141, 143, 147, 156, 157, 162,
    168–69, 189, 266, 268, 273
  source of communal joy, 134, 221,
    268–69, 272, 275
  speech of, 123–24, 126, 129, 140–41,
    143, 158
  stability of, 129, 142, 152, 160–61,
    240–41
  See also Justice; Righteousness
Righteousness 4, 26, 120, 151–52, 166,
  220. *See also* Justice; Righteous
Ritual, 39–40, 50, 86–87, 174, 216, 221
Ruler, 92–93, 234, 251, 264–65, 266–67,
  269, 272, 274, 277–78. *See also*
  King

Schadenfreude, 134, 191, 241
Scoffer, 18–19, 47, 106–7, 150, 159, 170,
  207, 208, 218, 220, 225, 273
Servant, 104–5, 140, 144, 166–67, 204,
  276–77, 283, 285, 294
Sex and Sexuality, 64–67
Shame, 69, 79, 131, 151, 155, 191, 197,
  249
Sheol, 16, 32, 108, 154, 170, 219, 262,
  271, 284
Simple (Naive), 4, 17–19, 85, 90, 106,
  107–8, 161–62, 218, 223
Sin, 21–22, 99, 125, 151–52, 163, 166,
  184, 216
Sinners, 15–17, 21–22, 141, 156, 163, 293
Solomon, 1, 2, 6, 9, 10–11, 27, 43, 73,
  92–93, 110, 117, 244–45, 291
Speech
  as fruit, 145, 150, 200, 250
  as water, 123–24, 197, 209
  and education, xxv, 10–11
  erotic, 67
  flattery, 272–73
  gentle, 167, 168

Speech—continued
heart as source of, 126, 169, 187, 238
limits of, 160
pleasing, 187, 220, 250
restraint of, 58, 125–26, 133–35, 150–51, 196, 199, 213, 276
true and/or false, 145, 146, 159, 164, 168, 192, 203, 208, 212, 221, 243, 244, 251, 258
See also Fool; Gossip; King; Righteous; Wicked; Wise
"Strange" Woman, 226, 237–38, 261. *See also* Folly, personified
Surety. *See* Wealth

Tradition, 21, 28, 52, 59–60, 113, 228, 279
Tree of life, 43–44, 140–41, 153, 168

Water, 96, 139, 193, 262, 284
as metaphor for the "wife of one's youth", 64–66, 108
as metaphor for "fear of the LORD," 164
as metaphor for speech, 123–24, 154, 197, 253
as metaphor for thoughts, 209, 216
as metaphor for wisdom, 187
See also Food and Drink
Way. *See* Path
Wealth, 14–15, 131–32, 265
acquired dishonestly, 15–16, 120, 131–32, 136, 153, 174, 213
as distorting of judgment, 268, 282–83
as relative good, 116–17, 131–32, 140, 152, 199, 207, 234–35, 268
as reward for wisdom and diligence, 40–41, 43, 55, 60, 93–94, 120, 126–27, 153, 156, 164, 171, 183
and friends, 162–63, 203
granting surety, 71–72, 135–36, 194, 212, 261
protection afforded by, 124
Weights and measures, 48, 76, 130–31, 184, 210–11
Wicked, 29–33, 35, 56–57, 76–77, 125, 137, 138, 143, 144–45, 151, 182, 191, 197, 216, 221, 267, 273
as impermanent, 127, 142, 152, 160–61

fate of, 32–33, 47, 48–49, 57, 120–22, 127, 128, 129, 132–33, 138, 141, 144–45, 147, 154, 157, 165–66, 168–69, 195, 217, 224, 240–41, 266, 268
harm to community of, 106–7, 134, 192–93, 217, 239, 268–69, 271, 272, 275
speech of, 29, 121, 124, 129, 143, 145, 174, 238
"Wife of one's youth," 64–68
Wisdom
as divine gift, 26–27, 34, 39, 281–82
as language 3, 13–14
benefits of, 19, 27–28, 40–41, 43–44, 48–49, 53–54, 60, 93–94, 128, 169, 171, 183, 187, 203, 220, 240
and creation, 44–45, 48–49, 94–98, 102–3
definition of, xxxii
limits of, 161, 221–22, 253, 287–88
pursuit of, 3, 5, 24–25, 34, 98–99, 170, 297–98
value of, 43, 91, 212
See also Proverb; Wisdom, personified; Wise
Wisdom, personified, xxxii, 10–11, 17–20, 42–44, 51, 53–55, 83–84, 89–103, 104–6, 158, 290, 299–300. *See also* Woman of substance
Wise
as receptive to instruction, 4–5, 12, 122, 124, 145, 150, 152–53, 170, 192, 199, 207, 212–13, 218
source of familial and communal joy, 119, 143, 172, 236, 237
speech of, 124, 125–26, 146, 147, 154, 158, 164, 168, 169, 187, 196, 250
See also Wisdom
Woman of substance, xxviii, 142, 289–90, 292–300
World "upside-down," 204, 285

Vengeance, 80, 178, 244, 269–70
Violence, 16, 21–22, 56, 121, 136, 150, 189, 207, 217, 255

LaVergne, TN USA
09 November 2010

204052LV00004B/22/P